ENDORSEMENTS

The Donald Williams II Journey To Authentic Service

Perhaps one of the most dedicated and committed social servants in the history of the United States was the late Reverend Dr. Martin Luther King, Jr. His service and sacrifice to this nation is matched by few in modern times. In a sermon, Dr. King was inspired by the biblical scripture, "Not so with you. Instead, whoever wants to be great among you must be your servant," (Mark 10:43). His words served as a message to all those who seek to be effective in the lives of others by doing good and great things through service."

I grew up in the period of Reverend Dr. Martin L. King Jr. who became the most visible leader of the Civil Rights Movement that emphasized the message to all leaders the importance of "service" to others with this quote:

"You don't have to have a college degree to serve."

"You don't have to make your subject and your verb agree to serve."

"You don't have to know about Plato and Aristotle to serve."

"You don't have to know about the second theory of thermodynamics in physics to serve."

"You don't have to know Einstein's theory of relativity to serve."

"You only need a heart full of grace, a soul generated by love."

"And you can be that servant."

This book captures one man's desire to serve with a single-minded focus to be effective in the life of a child. In fact, the author's goal was through his Christian spirit to galvanize the support of friends and family to embrace this mission on behalf of every child in need of support, care, direction, mentoring, and unconditional love. Donald Williams used his deep spiritual commitment to be effective in the lives of as many children that crossed his path.

This book captures Donald's journey of service. He served his country for 20 years in the United States Army, rising to the rank as a Lieutenant Colonel. I was one of those individuals that joined his social service army through the efforts of the Unity Christian Fellowship (UCF) Youth Development Organization. I first met the author while serving as the principal of Magruder High School in Rockville, Maryland. I was able to witness firsthand his dedicated work on behalf of students enrolled in my school. He enlisted my help in inspiring countless students to perform at the highest level of their cognitive abilities. I am very grateful for the work he has done and the many gifts given to so many young individuals through his organization. This book allows the reader to share in the many social deeds and heartwarming miracles he provided through the organization he created on his journey to serve.

—Dr. Lee Evans
Principal, Colonel Zadok Magruder High School

A *GAME CHANGER'S* PURSUIT

EDUCATING, EQUIPPING, AND ENCOURAGING OUR YOUTH FOR SUCCESS

AN AUTOBIOGRAPHY

BY

DONALD WILLIAMS II

First Edition 2024 Copyright © 2024 Donald Williams II
All rights reserved. No portion of this book may be reproduced mechanically, electronically, or by any other means, including photocopying, without permission of the publisher or author except in the case of brief quotations embodied in critical articles and reviews. It is illegal to copy this book, post it to a website, or distribute it by any other means without permission from the publisher or author.

This book is strictly for informational and educational purposes only, unless otherwise indicated, all Scripture quotations are taken from the Holy Bible.

Publishing Services are provided by Paper Raven Books LLC.
Printed in the United States of America
Editor: John Harris III
Editing Consultants: Sarah Brower, Sylvia Anderson, Jack Smith, Larry Kroll, Gail Taylor and Tim Alston
Cover Design By: Dr. Jessica L. Perkins
Photographers: Felix Bryant Photography, LLC., and Michael Johnson

First Printing, 2024
Hardcopy ISBN 979-8-9889749-0-1
Paperback ISBN 979-8-89298-708-0
Publisher Name: Donald Williams II

TABLE OF CONTENTS

FOREWORD .... **VII**
PREFACE .... **IX**

PART 1: SEEDS
— Foundation: Faith-based Fundamentals

Introduction 1
Chapter 1: Parents: Service Mindset 9
Chapter 2: Early Education 31
Chapter 3: Early Entrepreneurship 37

PART 2: SEEDLINGS TO SAPLING
— Creation of a Service Mindset Development: Food and Fertilization of Early Adulthood

Chapter 4: Secondary Education—Youth Development Shaping – Education Top Priority 51
Chapter 5: Mona: My Nubian Queen 75
Chapter 6: Military Service and Career—In My Father's Footsteps 83
Chapter 7: Order My Steps in the Lord 119
Chapter 8: My Basketball Story 137
Chapter 9: Fraternal Brotherhood 169

PART 3: TREES
— Branches and Fruits of a Dynamic Mentorship Program
ELSP Overview - Saving Our Youth One at a Time

Chapter 10: UCF Aim High Educational
 Life Skills Program 207
Chapter 11: Dream Chaser College Tour Program 267
Chapter 12: SAT/ACT Boot Camps 281
Chapter 13: Basketball Ministry 289
Chapter 14: Leadership and STEM Enrichment Programs 311
Chapter 15: What Leaders Do in a Crisis? 339
Chapter 16: The Game Changer Conference
 for Young Males 353

PART 4: IMPACT
— QUINTESSENTIAL SERVANT LEADERSHIP

Chapter 17: Leadership Philosophy 397
Chapter 18: How to Start a Mentoring Program......... 445
Chapter 19: Community Partnership Collaborations Model &
 Divine Connection 467

CLOSING MESSAGE............................499
ADDITIONAL REFERENCE SOURCES 505

FOREWORD

Retired military officer, finance, and logistics professional, coach, teacher, church leader and coordinator, well respected in the community, and partner in raising his own blessed children, Donald Williams II was ready.

A whole new energy came to campus at Montgomery College (MC), in Rockville, Maryland. A force of endless possibilities, a sense of vision, and the discipline to see things through permeated the essence of Coach Williams. In 1999, he stepped into my office with a warm smile and a hearty handshake and began to let his light shine as he shared his vision for students who were extending themselves to be athletes in his basketball program at MC.

As a counseling faculty with an extended commitment to student-athletes, I was immediately on board. I joined the team as the "academic coach." With a heart for student success, the heart of a champion, and a mind and spirit of faith and know-how, Coach Williams began forging his mark. His energy and fortitude would attract or ferret out the right participants and players. Then, we heard and responded to the call. Complementing his efforts, assistant coach Tarlough Gasque and former players would stay engaged on the court and in the classroom long after graduation or transfer.

Donald's commitment to helping his student-athletes succeed was so contagious that the students could buy into the possibilities, perhaps tapping into a faith and a belief not previously recognized. Putting in extra hours necessary to reach players on pretty much a soul level led to amazing results on a regular basis on the court, in the classroom, and most importantly, in their personal lives. Coach Williams' transformative leadership in nine years left a huge impact at

Montgomery College, and the six years as head coach of the Women's Basketball program the campus was better for his presence!

Donald and his wife and life partner Mona would capture that same spirit with Unity Christian Fellowship, Inc. (UCF). Sitting at my wife Michele's and my kitchen table, Donald and Mona would begin to talk about a family in need. They would share a personal story, followed by a conversation regarding Esther in the Old Testament, who came to understand that she was uniquely placed to save a people, her people in the midst of the most dire of circumstances.

Mona and Donald would then share a vision as to how we could set mechanisms in place to be that bridge over troubled waters for youth facing turbulent, sometimes deeply troubling issues. They quickly went from vision to the decision that gave birth to UCF Inc. "... for such a time as this!"

As in all things with the Williams, God was and is at the center of it, faith in action at every turn.

Faith-filled works continue to flow from that moment at the table, touching the lives of thousands of youth through a variety of initiatives and programs.

Continuing the vision, you are invited to accompany Donald Williams, along his journey so that your vision, stimulated by the eyes you have to see, the skills your journey has prepared in you, "for a time such as this."

— **CLIFTON A. MCKNIGHT**

M. ED. ACADEMIC ADVISOR/COUNSELOR, MONTGOMERY COLLEGE (RETIRED)

PREFACE

This book will change your life, the life of your family, and the lives of those in your neighborhoods and communities. I wrote for everyone with a heart and willingness to serve humanity. I will share real-life examples to encourage you to be creative and use innovative approaches to mentorship that will set the framework for sustaining a meaningful, purposeful, and impactful program.

This book will cause you to act and increase your commitment to making a positive difference in the lives of our young people. There is no better investment than our young people; mentoring makes a difference in their lives. Mentoring was my calling; it has been an exciting and fulfilling journey. A journey I have embraced fully and without reservation.

The book cover art picture reflects everyone I know who found themselves in a puddle of water, despite standing in the water, you must find a way to move forward live beyond your life circumstances to accomplish your goals. The book cover also reflects the old sentiments; it's not how or where you start, but where you finish.

Many of us have been at a crossroads on our life journey. Standing in a puddle of water, contemplating, I want to be successful in life, to take care of myself and my family. How do I go about it? Which direction and path should I pursue? Do I step forward or move backward, or stand longer without taking any action? All of us have been there, standing, and self-reflecting on life circumstances.

UCF models to our young people that it is about how you live in the moment on the way to achieving greatness. It is about the choices you make on your life journey and not about the destination. We want young people in this unforgiving world to stay out of trouble, change their mental mindset and attitude, pursue excellence, stay on track, graduate from high school, and acquire new skills that position them for success on their life journey. The journey is about the people you meet, the places you have been, the special moments, and the memories you make along the way! How are you moving forward on your journey to greatness?

I wrote this book for the following reasons: to motivate and encourage you to become a mentor today! Our communities are in crisis! The pandemic has heightened the need for the younger generation to step up and become mentors for the generation behind them. Our communities need mentors and seed planters for the young people crying out. If we do not mentor youth now, then who will and when?

You should know "no one" makes it alone and "no one" accomplishes anything significant alone! As a mentor, you must help uplift, inspire, challenge, and encourage young people behind you to get set for the journey. I want to motivate you, as an individual, to do more and to inspire others to become mentors. You may also be encouraged to join an organization that works directly with mentoring youth in your community. Prayerfully your heart will be touched to start a youth organization in your neighborhood or team with reputable youth organizations that work directly with young people.

Another reason for the book is to encourage elected officials, public school districts, community decision-makers, local churches, policymakers, government officials, youth mentoring organizations, and stakeholders to work together for a more significant impact. I highly encourage them to become "force multipliers" and reimagine using mentoring as a force multiplier. The "force multiplier" concept creates highly motivated groups of people, a wave passionate about making hope matter for our young people. What a difference it can make using the power of ten to reach others to become mentors in every community – now that a Game Changer! As a decision-maker, you can earmark resources to youth organizations that are effective in youth development and mentoring programs. Trust mentors to be wise stewards over mentoring work to help young people improve and be the best person so that they can positively contribute to the community.

Again, there is no better investment than our young people. Identify youth mentoring organizations that promote positive youth development, and incorporate them in your school, churches, and organizations to work together to impact and change lives. Our young people face many challenges in the post-pandemic era while navigating adolescence, and as the world continues to shift, young people are crying out!

Many organizations in your community, like Unity Christian Fellowship (UCF), Inc., operate on a limited budget while providing outstanding service to youth. Reimagine teaming with them and making the youth organization a part of your mission, working together to affect change. It is time to support mentoring organizations that add value to the community's mission.

For example, as we work together to put the COVID-19 pandemic in the rearview mirror, school administrators should establish a resource budget line annually for implementing in-school mentoring programs. We should also provide social-emotional support for this new generation impacted by isolation and learning loss caused by the pandemic. Pay them a stipend just like coaches receive stipends for impacting student athletics. Our young people are crying out!

We have either seen on TV or read a report reflecting every measurable category on the status of African Americans and minority males of color. Although my youth organization—Unity Christian Fellowship (UCF), Inc. – currently serves children, the launching of UCF centered on at-promise young male students who were misguided, labeled with behavioral challenges, unfocused on goal achievement, and devoid of positive experiences.

A new community strategic model must be implemented to meet the demands of the 21st century that engages the business community and educational districts. We must reimagine how to connect students to endless possibilities for workforce career readiness development and college preparation. Our children are bright, intelligent, and they have great potential if provided access and opportunities with a new strategic model. The reality is that the world continues to change rapidly and transforms right in front of us drastically. Part of the solution is collaboration, working together to strengthen the community effectively.

Therefore, I would like to see equal resources earmarked to nonprofit organizations that are tirelessly spending time, effort, and energy with mentoring. Nonprofit organizations fill the gaps that communities and schools cannot. Nonprofits are not funded equitably or equally while serving the community, providing direction and guidance for young people to be overcomers. I'd like to see resources go to local mentoring organizations on the front lines with proven performance records that positively impact students. I'd like to see funders be transparent with sharing their common frameworks and language to define and measure success to ease funding delivery to mentoring organizations.

I'd also like to see local businesses provide mentoring support to assist workforce career readiness by offering apprenticeships and internships. For example, local companies and government agencies can award employees credit hours for providing mentoring services to their community. This is an example of an innovative and bold approach to impacting and bridging the gap in workforce development and mentoring. Under a flexible work schedule, the business community may grant employees opportunities to earn credit hours for mentoring at school and youth organizations. Local companies may allow employees to earn credit hours only by working within the flexible time bands established by the agency or union agreement.

There are organizations in the community that are committed to positive youth development with mentoring, coaching, nurturing, and creating new pathways for youth. I have attended countless meetings with local officials, councilpersons, and others involving community dialogue hosted by school districts to roundtable discussions with churches. I have participated in the National My Brother's Keeper meetings to address the persistent gaps young people face, especially young males and men of color. They shared studies that documented that there aren't enough non-profits led by men or employ men of color; therefore, it is harder for non-profit staff to reach and support young males effectively. UCF learned early on that measuring intangibles such as youth satisfaction and "happiness" levels, with all that is going on in the world and in their homes, is challenging work. This mentoring movement, inspired by the tragic death of Trayvon Martin in Florida, encourages communities to work together to solve problems for young men. The Game Changer Conference was launched approximately three weeks after the horrific 2012 murder.

No matter your circumstances and situations, you can focus forward and be more than a conqueror; be an authentic mentor with loving assurance and guidance for mentees. The Bible says greatness is when you serve others. True greatness is when you help others succeed and shine on their life journey. Let's celebrate each other's successes and be caring people that push others toward their destiny. UCF focused on working together to improve our families and community over the years.

UCF has intentionally stepped out on faith; to reverse the trend regarding the alarming and unfavorable disparities of black males in education, employment, health, and economics; and provide them with the necessary social-emotional support for goal achievement. Our objective is to help encourage our young people, especially young males, to work to reach their full potential as a person, students, and athletes and to achieve greatness in their lives. The expected outcome for all participants in the Aim High In Life Educational Program is as follows:

1. To take education seriously
2. Practice citizenship and good behavior
3. Practice leadership acquiring positions such as athletic team captain, organizational president, etc.
4. Practice scholarships, extol high GPAs, encourage Advanced Placement Courses, Dual College programs, and early planning for college
5. Abstain from drugs, gangs, and peer pressure

GOD gives us boys, not men! He provides us with the responsibility to shape and mold these young males into young men—seedlings who will grow, mature, and enrich their lives to help them learn how to contribute to their homes, churches, and communities in a positive way. You and I are responsible for motivating, supporting, and bringing people together collectively and purposefully to achieve this mission to accomplish a greater good for our communities to prosper.

The faith-based foundation was established for me early on in life, and the growth further developed in early adulthood prepared me for this mission enough to know that mentoring is not about fame or fortune; it's not about self-serving, self-promotion or just setting specific dates when results should somehow magically happen. Instead, it is a commitment for a lifetime! And it is you who must decide your commitment and engagement level working to help increase young people's physical and mental wellness and academic confidence!

As I inspire and encourage others to be post-pandemic mentors, we must focus forward to help students by providing social and emotional support. UCF has been effective by meeting youth and their families where they are. Although we have taken some losses, the wins have been many and exceeded the losses. It does not matter where you start but how you finish. The UCF team approach has helped youth regain their confidence and use their youthful energy to refocus on their life's goals to achieve positive outcomes.

Stakeholders must recognize the shared responsibility and commitment to connect, inspire, equip, and engage in making hope happen collaboratively. Our shared commitment must be a top priority to develop youth of promise, to encourage every student with a desire to improve their quality of life and position them for the future. It takes all of us working together to make a difference truly. In the words of Dr. Lee Evans, Principal of Magruder High School, UCF helps "close the windows" of vulnerabilities, providing a focus-forward pathway for success to encourage students to win in life after high school!

Part 1 - SEEDS

Foundations of Faith-based Fundamentals

- Introduction

- Chapter 1: Parents: Service Mindset

- Chapter 2: Early Education

- Chapter 3: Early Entrepreneurship

INTRODUCTION

The bottom line is this: How we view things determines how we do things! The makings of my mentorship and the layout of this book —**Seeds to Trees**—stem from the evolution of the progression and experiences from my upbringing, through development and influential stages during my young adult years, and then maturity into full adulthood—all played a part of my road to lifetime mentorship.

As I see it, the road to a successful mentorship takes careful **"planting"** of the right seeds and the proper **"germination"** and **"pruning"** of those seedlings and saplings to **"produce"** the tree's supportive solid branches to hold the ripe and wholesome **"fruits"** of your labor. It must be planted from the right mindset, to begin with, not that is predicated on wealth, popularity, or fame, but from a caring heart and sincere desire to have influence in the lives of others, our communities, and the world at large.

I recall a mentor who shared his "why" for being a mentor who has made a difference in others' lives. He grew up living in a project housing community. In the early segregated period of the civil rights movement, Blacks were housed in these planned communities. It wasn't easy to see beyond the current conditions where children lived and played daily.

Those who lived in the "projects" had difficulties seeing their way out, let alone thinking about goal achievements. This mentor recalls the day his life changed when a community center was built, and a servant leader at the center implemented a youth program that included field trips for neighborhood children. This was a "game changer" because the field trips allowed him and his friends to change their perspectives due to their exposure to new experiences. It allowed them to see something beyond their current circumstances. The mentor was a "seed planter" and helped them see endless possibilities beyond their living conditions. I connected with this story because my mother shared that in her childhood, she lived in the Jervay public housing projects in Wilmington, North Carolina, and eventually moved to 9th Street across from the projects.

This book is my journey-- beginning with the healthy seeds of humble, faith-based fundamentals (from my parents, early education, and early entrepreneurship efforts). Next, the careful germination of those seedlings, with the essential food and fertilization (comprising my marriage, secondary education, fraternal, and military influences), formed healthy, upright "saplings" for my mentorship experience.

Part two is the impact spiritual journey with God's continual guidance and pruning, these "saplings" developed into mature and mighty trees that bore healthy branches of collaborative and community partnership connections and "fruits"—those mentoring programs and activities that have been produced thus far include: an 11-year annual scholarship program; a decade of Christian Youth Basketball Ministry that brought churches together across the District of Columbia, Maryland and Virginia (DMV) to help keep our children off the streets and involved in a Christian and fitness-based activity during the summer; an 11-year annual "Game Changer" conference for young males; a 10-year annual "Dream Chaser" college tour of Predominantly White Institutions (PWI) and Historically Black Colleges and Universities (HBCU) with related activities to help students think more broadly and expose them to early stages of college planning; membership in the USTEM/NSBE (Science Technology Engineering and Mathematics and National Society of Black Engineers) in its eighth year; monthly youth leadership enrichment workshops; SAT/ACT boot camps held in the Spring, Summer, and Fall since 2010. Other academic and athletic enrichment programs include a combined summer reading program and lacrosse instructional program in its eighth year.

And in the final phase, I share from personal experience an insight into my leadership philosophy. Again, I wrote this book to encourage and inspire you and others to join in this important, meaningful, and impactful mentoring work that touches the hearts and minds of young people. You will be inspired to stand up, step up and lend your gifts, talents, and leadership to establish your mentoring program or team with another youth organization. And lastly, the importance of establishing community collaboration relationships. Do not minimize and underestimate your level of influence. I remember an African Proverb: "If you want to go fast, go alone. If you want to go far, go together."

CONNECTING THE PAST TO THE PRESENT

To help you understand the question that others have asked me many, many times, "Why did you dedicate your life to servant leadership." I have wondered about this myself many times. Taking this journey into the winding road helped me learn about my family tree roots and provided a perspective of my mentoring story over the many years. In addition, I encourage you to discover your family history and learn your "why" for yourself.

I discovered that it's in my DNA; by accident, a group of co-workers in a season of ancestors.com came and sorted family information together. So, I was encouraged to trace my ancestors' roots as far back as I could, resulting in taking a DNA test in June 2017. I believed our family was related to the North Carolina Cherokee Indians due to our dark skin tone, hair, and hue. Due to DNA results, I discovered that my dad and I are 92% African, and my beloved mother was 94%; our roots are traced back to the motherland from the western region of Africa.

My family tree from the DNA test was linked to the following countries and regions: Nigeria, 38%; Cameroon, Congo & Western Bantu Peoples, 17%; Mali, 14%; and Ivory Coast, 9%. My ancestors in the 1700s probably came from the same place or cultural group.

Ancestors.com shares the historical perspective that the majority of Black Americans can trace their ancestry back to West Africa in the present day. Unfortunately, not many specifics were known about this community before 1850 because record-keeping for us before the Civil War was extremely limited.

For more than 200 years, many were enslaved and brought to the South (including my native North Carolina) to work on plantations, and my DNA was traced to these two regions. During the mid-1800s, many were enslaved; some had gained or purchased their freedom. Some continued to live as indentured laborers, and slavery wasn't always a lifelong sentence. The real story is that this great country that we live in and enjoy many liberties today was built from this period where white Americans exploited their unpaid labor to grow lucrative crops, like cotton, tobacco, and rice, but fed our ancestors the scraps off their tables.

Despite the prevailing circumstances, some Black people escaped and lived in a free, independent community on the dismal swampy coastline; tangled vegetation and muddy terrain made life unpleasant, but its isolated location ensured they would not be discovered. My family's descendants from South Carolina and North Carolina lived in the coastal areas, and enslaved workers' nautical skills contributed vastly to the cities' economic success. The free Black Americans also lived primarily in port towns, where job opportunities were more plentiful.

My father's family roots can be traced to Wilmington, North Carolina. My mother and her mother worked as "housemaids," working in white homeowner's houses, taking care of children as nannies, cooking, cleaning, etc. My mother made $10 a week for cleaning houses and bring home left over meals. If you saw the movie "The Help," which focused on two black maids from the civil rights movement in 1963 with Emma Stone and Viola Davis, tells my family's story as I grew up in my youth. My grandmother would come home in the evening, especially Sunday evening, with a greasy brown paper bag. As young children, we knew it would be good eating and a good time for Sunday dinner.

In addition, my dad shared stories of family members that cleared land for farming purposes. His remarkable statement was that everything the family needed was grown on the family land, it was our Food Lion grocery store and our CVS store from what we ate and used for medicine for sickness. They hunted and fished for the family and community to survive their living conditions. My father shared many stories from his youth on how the Cape Fear River was used to navigate and transport goods between port cities. I learned during the early morning high tides, men and women would load up the wooden log raft and place farm produce and animals to be sold at the markets on Front Street. And in the evening during low tides the reverse would occur, using the river to return to their homes in their coastal homes. This impacted me as I heard this story repeated throughout my youth and as an adult. Whether in a city or on a farm, enslaved Black Americans struggled with little hope for freedom. However, dreams for a better life, not for them but for future generations, would come true.

This was how the early Black Americans lived during my dad's grandfather's time. My great-grandfather raised my father from infancy to adulthood to be an honorable, respected, and serious-minded person who used his intellect to improve things.

As I digress, I'd like to share an account with a close friend. During his fifties, he shared this story about visiting the South and seeing a cotton field for the first time. He shared that he learned about the cotton fields during Black History Month from school. He saw movies and heard stories, but this was his first time seeing an actual cotton field. He drove down the dirt road to the house and knocked on the door. The homeowner answered the door and asked, "can I help you?" My friend Jerome Doye asked the homeowner if he could pick some cotton. The homeowner, looking puzzled, stated, "we don't do that here anymore." Jerome smiled and explained that this was the first time he had seen natural cotton and asked if he could take some home as a souvenir.

While I never asked him exactly why he did it, Jerome felt free enough to pick crops we were once made to pick as free laborers.

QUOTE:
"Whatever you've done so far is not enough."
— President Barack Obama

This is a quote from the former president, who warned Democrats against becoming complacent about the presidential election. This applies to mentoring as the world rapidly changes due to the globe pandemic.

SCRIPTURE:
"And do not forget to do good and to share with others, for with such sacrifices, God is pleased."
Hebrews 13:16

CHAPTER 1

Creation of a Service Mindset:
Seeds Sown to Inspire and Save Our Youth

"Faith allows things to happen. It is the power that comes from your list apart, and when a fearless heart believes, then miracles happen."
—Source Unknown

I am grateful to be the son of Lula and Donald Williams from Wilmington, North Carolina, and proud to be my father's namesake. I dedicated this book to my parents. Today, I honor my parents whose legacy is far-reaching and the foundation of life lessons they taught me and my siblings to live by. You have probably heard the mantra that my mom instilled, "Good, better, best. Never let it rest until your good is better and your better is best." My parents taught us to be proud and do our best in every undertaking. To be the best in whatever role you are assigned. Our parents taught us always to place God first and trust Him because He has a greater purpose for your life. Your name is the first gift your parents give you. Your name connects you to culture, ethnicity, and faith background. There is a story and history connected to your name. We were taught that your family name is special, and it means everything. You must protect your name and your reputation is extremely important. There is something special about your name!

While completing this book, my mother, born on May 9, 1935, was called home to be with the Lord on Tuesday, June 7, 2022, at approximately 5:45 p.m. She was born to the late Willie Robinson and Ruth Robinson Earst. My mother was a praying woman, a "seed planter" who poured positivity into my life. She shared wisdom and knowledge and believed in me that I could achieve greatness first conceived in her mind. She believed in exercising her faith to put God's works into action. She taught me a strong work ethic to be twice as good just to be equal to whites. She taught me the foresight to always wear clean undergarments in case I had an accident. She taught me that there can only be one fool in the room, and don't let it be you. She taught me the awareness that empty wagons make a lot of noise, and add no value. She taught me to value relationships, love, and treat everyone with respect. My mother taught me how to pray in the morning, at noon, and at night before I closed my eyes. Much of my life is based on her faith and love that she poured in me into action every day, living one day at a time.

My parents grew up as teenagers in the segregated South. As a young couple, they grew up influenced by the following historical events: The Great Depression, World War II, Korean War, Vietnam War, and the Civil Rights Movement. Notable Supreme Court cases in my parents' youth included Brown vs. Board of Education, a landmark decision in which the Court ruled that "separate but equal" was unconstitutional for public schools and educational facilities even if the segregated schools were otherwise equal quality. The courts essentially overruled its 1896 decision Plessy vs. Ferguson. It paved the way for integration and was a significant victory of the civil rights movement. The second was the Civil Rights Act of 1964, signed into law by President Lyndon B. Johnson after the assassination of President John F. Kennedy on November 22, 1963.

The U.S. Supreme Court prohibited tactics from limiting voting, guaranteed racial and religious equal access to public accommodation, and outlawed job discrimination based on race, color, religion, sex or national origin. My parents experienced race riots during the era

of the nonviolent civil rights protesters, blacks and whites standing up for justice and fighting for equality guaranteeing human rights for the underserved.

During their youth, my parents lived through three assassinations that resulted in national mourning: the 35th President of the United States, John F. Kennedy's assassination on November 22, 1963, Reverend Dr. Martin Luther King Jr. on April 4, 1968, and Robert Kennedy, a Democratic presidential candidate was assassinated on June 6, 1968. I am sure those of you from my generation can remember the "famous picture" of the three in a picture frame that hung prominently in your parents' family room.

My parents started from humble beginnings in Wilmington. They learned how to navigate their experiences, which allowed them to provide for their young family of five, both parents and three children: Sylvia, my oldest sister who is five years older than me, and my younger sister Andra who was born in Germany.

My parents trusted God and put Him first. Their guidepost was a family prayer we recited before every meal consumed, "God is great, and God is good, let us thank Him for our food. By his hands we are fed, give us Lord our daily bread." We have passed this on to our grandchildren.

The following are principles my parents established for our family to live by:

1. **God: <u>Always</u>** put and keep him in your life, no matter what! They taught us, "He is the Truth, the Light, and the Way!" So, in my life, God is the Alpha, Omega, and everything in between.
2. **Character:** Be a person of good character; treat everyone with respect and love—even when it may be a struggle. When you're important to another person, that person will always find a way to make time for you.
3. **Integrity:** It's the core quality of a successful and happy life. Commit to being honest and truthful. My parents would say, "your word is your bond." Honor your word!
4. **Education:** My parents' message was clear throughout my upbringing. Education was a **top** priority. Performing your best work—no matter the assignment(s) —is the standard of excellence, as education transforms a person's life to provide a higher standard of living for your family.
5. **Preparation:** "Be Prepared!" Do not wait for the night of the championship game to get in shape. Preparation is important! So, practice the "5 P's"—Proper Planning Prevents Poor Performance.
6. **Service:** Be a "Helping Hand" by lifting up those most in need, as well as those traveling in the wrong direction because they have lost their way!
7. **Protect:** Protect and honor your name given by your parents. I remember hearing, growing up, "don't embarrass our family name. It's the only thing you have."
8. **Friendship:** Surround yourself with positive friends. I

remember hearing the statement, "show me your friends, and I will show you your future!"
9. **Excellence:** Aim high and always strive for excellence. Be the best at whatever you are assigned to do—big or small!
10. **Purpose:** Be purpose-driven! Value something greater than yourself. Be a Doer!

ARTHUR DUNCAN MCDONALD

I must introduce you to my dad's grandfather to understand my story. He raised my father from infant to adulthood to be an honorable, respected, and serious-minded person who used his intelligence to make things better. I am a descendant of Arthur Duncan McDonald, a dark-skinned, short-statured man born in the late 19th Century. He was born on April 14, 1884, and died on August 31, 1978. His parents Henry and Julia Ann McDonald were born into slavery. Julia lived to be 90 years old, (1850-1940), while Henry was born in 1840 and died on July 27, 1915, at 75. They had eleven children together and Arthur Duncan was one of the eleven children.

On June 19, 1907, in Hanover, North Carolina, my dad's grandfather Arthur Duncan McDonald was married at 23 to Mary Rose McGhee (age 22) with her father, George McGhee, and mother, Lucy McGhee looking on. Together they laid the foundation and formed the tree trunk of our family's humble beginnings. My dad's grandmother Mary Rose McGhee was born March 22, 1885, and died April 19, 1935, six months before my dad was born on September 28, 1935.

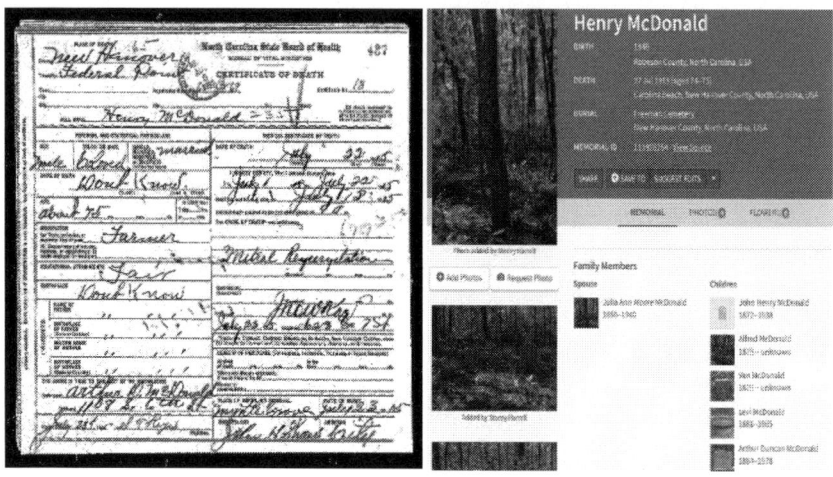

On June 19, 1907, in Hanover, North Carolina, my dad's grandfather Arthur Duncan McDonald was married at 23 to Mary Rose McGhee (age 22) with her father, George McGhee, and mother, Lucy McGhee looking on. Together they laid the foundation and formed the tree trunk of our family's humble beginnings. My dad's grandmother Mary Rose McGhee was born March 22, 1885, and died April 19, 1935, six months before my dad was born on September 28, 1935.

Although slavery ended in 1865, the institutional practice continued long afterward. We will never know slavery's full story; suffice it to say that my dad's grandfather was exposed to it and experienced it first-hand in his youth. Historical records revealed that he was a butler, and his wife was a maid. I discovered that my dad's grandfather worked for three prominent families in Wilmington, the Fronts family, Bellamy Mansion, and the Cameron family, that owned many properties.

Like many families, I don't ever recall any of my family members speaking openly about the harsh painful conditions of slavery. The message for today's generations is that every American lived a life touched by slavery, and enslaved Blacks provided other Americans with a higher standard of living through cheap consumer goods and infrastructure that stands today.

I was so moved and emotionally overcome to discover my ancestors' history. As I learned about my family history, the common thread from my great grandfather, Arthur Duncan possessed the characteristic of a servant leader.

He was a selfless servant who cared for others, he was serious-minded, a problem solver, trustworthy, and put others first. He was a respected community leader who provided sound advice to others.

From a historical perspective, my great-grandparents, Arthur Duncan, and Mary Rose, lived during the same period as the great

American social reformer and Maryland native Frederick Douglass. Douglass was born on February 1818 and died on February 20, 1895, and became a leader of the abolitionist movement, which sought to end the practice of slavery before and during the Civil War. He was known as a great orator and statesman who coined the phrase, "no struggle, no progress." My dad's grandfather was approximately 13 years old when Douglass died and he was certainly influenced by him.

In 1978, my great-grandfather died at the age of 94. I had just turned 20 years old, a sophomore at Rider College when he passed away. This was my first homegoing service experience with a family loved one. I knew my great-grandfather in a real way, how he communicated and operated with a sense of purpose, discipline, respect, fairness, and accountability. My father shared that he was very stern and serious-minded in all his interactions and very religious. His top priority was taking care of the family. He raised my dad and uncle with a firm hand of love and modeled the highest standards for them to emulate in their life journey. He was known in the community as a man of faith, and well-versed in the bible. He was a member and served on the Trustee Board for several years at St. Luke African Methodist Episcopal Church. He was a quiet and devoted member of the Church he loved so well. There was never a day too long or night so dark that he would not commit his time and effort for what he believed to be right. He was a dedicated father and grandfather.

In addition, several people that grew up in the Wilmington neighborhood shared stories about my Great-Grand Father, Arthur Duncan McDonald. I learned he was a gifted arborist. Arborists care for trees and plants, pruning. He was known in the community to be a specialist in the cultivation and care of trees, shrubs, and transplant flowers, including diagnosis, treatment, and prevention of diseases. Three friends, Brenda Williams, Reggie Payton, and George Hall, called him the planted doctor and were witnesses and recipients of my Dad's Grandfather's arborist gifts, wisdom, and knowledge. At their home estate, he gifted them with his handy work of beautiful flowers, shrubs, and trees planted that still existed by Arthur Duncan McDonald when he was alive. He mastered fusing and grafting limbs of branches together to create beautiful color combinations. The planted shrubbery and oak trees exist alive today.

My dad recalls several life lessons from his grandfather passed to him, and he has passed to his family. Especially the life lesson that differentiates between "your needs vs. your wants." My great-grandfather imparted the knowledge that you must manage your limited resources and money thoughtfully to make ends meet. It's essential to understand the responsibility for addressing your needs, such as paying the rent, buying food, and saving money for emergencies. He passed on the use of proper manners and effective communication using "yes sir/ no sir" and "yes ma'am/ no ma'am," along with "thank you, and no thank you." Each generation needs to use effective communication. Other lessons included speaking to others upon entering a room or passing someone on the street, being responsible for oneself, and doing better because you know better.

His circle of friends knew him as a "man's man. My mother said he always showed respect to women by tilting his hat as they passed by. He was a take-charge and proper man in how he ran his household. For example, Sunday was a day of reverence to the Lord. He taught that you should give reverence to your behavior as well as your attitude. As a child, I remember there was no running or playing in or outside the house. He expressed his gratitude by keeping God's commandments and keeping the seventh day, a day of honor, reading the bible, and praying. My siblings and I saw this in my youth as we watched him interact with the community with dignity and respect.

My dad described his grandfather as a loving, wise man who was fair in helping others. He was a shining beacon in the family who used his intelligence to make things better in the community. He did a lot of reading despite only having an eighth-grade education. My father is incredibly proud of the family legacy of overcomers and achievers. The family DNA from Henry McDonald (father) born into slavery, to (son) Arthur Duncan McDonald who died as a free man, has served the Williams family exceptionally well in terms of generations achieving high school diplomas and obtaining undergraduate and advanced degrees in higher education.

Henry McDonald and Arthur Duncan McDonald became trusted servants of the plantation owners who, in turn, passed on significant pieces of (more than 1,000 acres) property on River Road in Wilmington. This property was the land that my ancestors lived off, farmed, raised livestock, fished, and sold goods on Front Street known as the marketplace. My father called his grandfather a bright star in the community where he lived and worked. For today's youth, we refer to these ways as "Black Excellence" and "Black Intelligence." We encourage young people to use the intelligence and energy of their youth to plan strategically for their entire family. The 21st-century family plan should include, as a parent, identifying which child will be a professional athlete, medical doctor, attorney, tradesperson, engineer, artist, scientist, an artificial intelligence analyst, etc.

My Dad shared that with all the racial injustice and tensions, from 1935 until 1954, he grew up in an integrated neighborhood on 1108

South 6th Street on the south side of town. He played with white friends from his community while attending separate segregated schools. I found that to be an amazing childhood story. And while serving in the military during the height of the civil rights movement, he was out of the country for approximately 12 years either in Germany or Vietnam.

As a historical footnote, my great-grandfather, at the time of his life, lived during the presidency of Ulysses P. Grant, the 18th President of the United States. During the historical events that occurred during my great grandfather's life, the United States population totaled 39 million, the Transcontinental Railroad was completed, Negroes were given the right to vote by the 15th Amendment, the telephone was perfected by Alexander Graham Bell, Colorado became a state, and The Reconstruction period ended (1865-1877).

There were two notable Supreme Court cases in my great-grandfather's lifetime. President Eisenhower signed the Civil Rights Act of 1957 into law on September 9, 1957. This was the first major civil rights legislation since Reconstruction. Interestingly, these laws created a commission to investigate voter fraud, allowing federal prosecution of anyone who tried to prevent someone from voting. Sound familiar? This is exactly occurring in our lifetime of underlying racial and cultural divisions!

The second case was the Plessy vs. Ferguson case, which gave us the phrase "separate but equal." The Supreme Court decision ruled that racial segregation laws did not violate the U.S. Constitution if the facilities for each race were equal in quality. The decision legitimized the many state laws reestablishing racial segregation that had been passed after the end of the Reconstruction Era (1875-1877).

1108 South 6th Street, Wilmington, NC

Very few people of color were homeowners during Arthur Duncan McDonald's lifespan, but they nonetheless triumphed over adversity and built lives for themselves and their communities.

His house was one of the first in the neighborhood to have indoor plumbing and electricity.

Although his parents were born as slaves, my Dad's grandfather died as a free man and rose to be a well-respected community leader. He was a respected worker for the prominent Cameron family in Wilmington. He was given employment authority to select workers for the Cameron's family properties. My great-grandfather did the payroll for many years and was counted on to provide a labor force to maintain their various properties and farms. The people in the community would say they liked working for Mr. Duncan because he was a fair but stern man who fed and paid you for an honest day's work. He was a trusted advisor to the community; many sought him out for business decisions.

The Cameron family depended on him to run their operations in Wilmington. I learned in 2021 that the New Hanover Regional Medical Center built an additional wing for the Women's and Children's Hospital and was named after Betty H. Cameron.

God made a way out of no way for Arthur Duncan and Mary McGhee McDonald and their three children (two daughters and one son). They were the "tree trunk and roots" for the Williams family tree. Arthur and Mary had two daughters, Annie Ruth McDonald and Hazel McDonald-Williams, and one son, who died in infancy. Hazel was born on September 18, 1913; my grandmother died on November 13, 1993, at 80, in Southport, NC. Hazel was the wife of Bennettsville, SC native Monroe Williams, who died at just 32 in 1935. He lived in New Hanover, NC, and passed away in 1935 from heat stroke while working installing a fence around gas fuel tankers on Front Street in Wilmington.

My granddad Monroe Williams left my grandmother Hazel with two sons. My great-grandfather brought his daughter Hazel and the two boys into his home. As a result, my father was raised by his single mother and my great-grandfather. He was the father figure and helped raise both boys into adolescence and adulthood. They were both shaped and groomed to be gentlemen with high standards and expectations of law-abiding, respectful citizens.

My father, Donald was born on September 28, 1935. My uncle Duncan was born one year earlier, on August 7, 1934. He died on October 7, 1983, at the age of 49. As young boys, they never knew their father because he died when they were babies. In a recent conversation, my dad shared that his father's funeral occurred in the family house. Someone in attendance took the only picture he had of his father and was never recovered.

My parents Lula and Donald were high school sweethearts who graduated from Williston High School in Wilmington. They were high school graduates and proud members of the Williston High School Classes of 1953 and 1954, respectively.

They had extremely humble beginnings building a life together during some of our country's history's most difficult racial periods. My mother shared that they took a bus over the bridge to the Conway courthouse to sign marriage papers on December 22, 1954.

After graduating from high school, my dad hoped to attend college and play football, as he was a standout in high school. In a conversation, as I was viewing his team picture, I noticed his jersey number, emblazoned with the number 41. I asked him if he played offense or defensive and what position he played? He responded with "I played them all." I thought he was joking in his response. He shared that the football we enjoy watching today on television was in the developmental stages when he played. As a player you literally played every position. Dad said that we "played football to win the game."

He waited for a football scholarship, and when none came, he wound up leaving Wilmington to enlist in the U.S. Army in 1954. He would complete boot camp at Fort Jackson, SC. Two weeks after he joined the Army, he received a congratulatory letter from Xavier University in New Orleans, Louisiana, to play football. Our lives could have been different if he had not enlisted, stayed in Wilmington upon graduation, and played football.

My parents left Wilmington as a young family in 1957 with my older sister Sylvia, born August 2, 1953. After completing boot camp at Fort Jackson, he completed the Military Occupational Specialty (MOS) school at Fort Gordon, Georgia. At the time, military pay for a PFC was $79, that he lived off monthly.

After graduation from the MOS school, he received orders for his first duty station in Stuttgart, Germany. He spent two years and three months away from Wilmington. While in Germany he lived off $25 from his monthly paycheck and sent the remaining amount to his wife to put in the bank for the family. He didn't like the long separation from his young family. So, when he returned from Germany to Wilmington, his mind was made up to leave the Army, and he wound up leaving the Army for a short time. He found that working for his grandfather was backbreaking labor, doing yard work and other work in town didn't pay either.

It lasted three months before he and my mother decided that it was best for him to return to the military and make it a 20-year career. He was welcomed back into the Army and could retain his rank of Sergeant (E-5), immediately received medical benefits, an increase in pay and a higher standard of living for his family. Upon reenlisting in Wilmington, my father received a Permanent Change of Station (PCS). He was sent off to his second duty station, the home of the Signal Corp at Fort Huachuca, an Army installation located in Arizona, the place of my birth.

My parents remembered good times in Arizona as a young couple living in a trailer and buying their first car, which in today's parlance would be called a "hooptie." I recalled my mother talking about how their first trailer was without a bathroom and their first car always had mechanical problems throughout the tour.

They were so proud of being on their own for the first time in their lives and fondly remembered their first military duty assignment together at Fort Huachuca. Of course, the excitement for them was the birth of their second child, a boy named Donald II, named after my dad.

Shortly after my birth, my father received PCS orders to Germany for the second time in his short military career. My sister Sylvia was five when we left Arizona and returned to Wilmington, waiting for Dad to secure military housing in Germany. The family was approved for housing and stayed in Germany for approximately three years, during my toddler years. My parents were in their early 20's, making real life decisions for their young family. As mentioned earlier, my parents' journey started from humble beginnings, but they were eventually blessed by making consistently good choices.

My youngest sister, Andra was born in Kitzingen, Germany on September 21, 1960. This was around Greensboro, North Carolina, sit-ins, led by college students from North Carolina A&T State University. The non-violent sit-in protests occurred in Woolworth Department stores. They led to the chain ending its policy of racial segregation in its stores in the southern United States on July 25, 1960.

1954 ERLANGEN, GERMANY

The above picture is my Dad's beginnings in establishing a stable foundation for his family.

In a recent conversation with my 87-year-old Dad, I asked him about his most significant accomplishments. He didn't hesitate to share how proud he was to be a father and grandfather who provided for his family. (Also, he is incredibly proud to build and live on the land that was passed down from his great-grandfather Arthur Duncan McDonald).

The second answer? He enlisted in the Army at a young age. I asked why he gave that answer. He shared that he found that serving in the military was a structure that allowed him to excel, gain experience, and advance to the next enlisted rank in the promotion system. In the '60s, a black man had limited opportunities to provide for his family in America. He said all he desired was to make a better life for his young family than what he experienced growing up. My Dad didn't realize he would create a family legacy of military service by serving in the Army. He served honorably for nearly 21 years as a Non-Commissioned Officer in the rank (E-7). My two uncles served in the military; my father brother Duncan Monroe Williams served in the U.S. Marines from 1953 to 1956. My mother's brother Edward Robinson served in the U.S. Coast Guard during approximately the same time. My younger sister's husband Greg Reevey completed 20 years in the U.S. Army and his daughter Mahaila is currently serving as a 2LT in the Army National Guard.

In a moment of reflection, I am proud to be a product of a military family. I am proud to follow in my father's footsteps where he taught me through example how to operate as one team, treat everyone with respect and balance family responsibilities.

My father received military PCS orders during my childhood, rotating between Germany (three times), Fort Gordon, in Augusta, Georgia, and Fort Monmouth in New Jersey. He spent short one-year assignments at Fort Hood, Texas, and twice in South Korea, (Taegu and Pusan). He served two tours during the Vietnam War. Between military assignments, we would stay with my grandparents in Wilmington, waiting for Dad to get housing quarters in the new community.

Every time the family returned to Wilmington, visiting our relatives and friends was routine.

In the south, it was customary for homeowners to have rocking chairs on their front porch. Every time we arrived at the door of family members; cousins, grandparents, uncles, and aunts, for a visit, we would be greeted with words, "come on in and sit a spell."

It was their way of telling us to make ourselves at home and be comfortable, stay a while, and share in some "catching up" conversations. It enabled visitors to tell the family what was happening in their lives, and their goals and plans.

My great-grandfather's front porch contained the customary rocking chairs which allowed visitors to relax and talk. Serious conversations occurred on the front porch. If we get to know someone and make a difference in their life, we need to find opportunities to extend an invitation to "come on in and sit a spell."

Today's life can get busy. In our action-oriented world, it's hard to get to know people. It is a challenge to find time to connect with someone and ask someone to "sit a spell" with us. We live in a time with social media, smartphones, iPads, a time when we believe more things can be accomplished by using technology. Whether your method is texting, FaceTime, or using virtual Zoom platforms, stay connected and engaged with this generation of youth.

I have learned that mentoring at all levels is about building trusted relationships that require commitment from both people. This involves consistency in being there in all situations and spending time with a young person. At this age, you can text to check up on a mentee, you can call and say, "Hey, how are you doing," or drop by and visit.

My older sister, Sylvia is five years older than me, Donald II, seven years older than our sister Andra and 20 years older than our adopted sister, Bintu. From our young years of growing up as a military family, it was instilled in me by our mother and father to function as one team and to look out for each other. My father often served away in places we could not go, especially when he was stationed in Korea or Vietnam.

My father served two tours in the Vietnam War (1967 and 1970) and the complexities were politically challenging militarily and ultimately claimed millions of lives, (all gave some and some gave all for this country). As a young man, my father also served two tours in Korea.

While he served the country during wartime, we lived in Augusta, Georgia, during my youth.

THE WILLIAMS FAMILY

My father served two tours in the Vietnam War (1967 and 1970) and the complexities were politically challenging militarily and ultimately claimed millions of lives, (all gave some and some gave all for this country). As a young man, my father also served two tours in Korea. While he served the country during wartime, we lived in Augusta, Georgia, during my youth.

My passion and purpose for mentoring nowadays can be traced to this season in my life. I experience the feelings and thoughts resulting from when my dad was out of the home. In my youth, my mentoring experience formed because of men in the neighborhood watching out for my family. The men impacted my life by stepping up to spend time mentoring and showing me what men do and how they solve everyday problems.

My parents built a life together during the upheaval of the most challenging period in our country's history with "Jim Crow" practices that relegated Black Americans to second-class citizens in the mid-1960s.

The Vietnam War lasted from 1964-1975 – the longest war in American history until the recent war in the Middle East. Black Americans have been involved in United States Military service since its inception despite official racial segregation and discrimination policies. We owe a debt of gratitude to all veterans who lost their lives in service to our country in all wars. To the Vietnam veterans who returned from the unpopular war, we express our gratitude for military personnel who served and survived unspeakable horrors, as coming home offered its kind of trauma from the civil rights movement. For those veterans who have been shunned, mistreated, and ostracized for their participation in The Vietnam War, we also say, "**Welcome Home!**"

We were exposed to and lived in many communities because of the military lifestyle of frequent moves. We lived in several new housing developments with primarily military families. I vividly recall our family gatherings in the family room to hear my dad's voice over a cassette tape recorder he had mailed from Vietnam. He always gave each family member instructions. However, my instructions seemed specific from my perspective from the age of 10 to 12. He would say, "Donnie, take care of your mother and sisters."

The influence of my father's no-nonsense, no-excuse-making philosophy resulted in my pursuit of excellence — doing your best every day, first, taking care of your family, and maintaining a positive attitude was the blueprint I followed in my life.

My siblings and I grew up with my father's favorite sayings. As a military brat, one of the most memorable of them was "roll with the punches." This means in life there will be speed bumps. Please find a way to go over, around, or go through them. I imparted the saying to our two daughters while coaching them in basketball: "Practice makes perfect and perfect practice makes perfect." Find a way to strive for excellence in every area of your life, and don't wait for the night of a championship contest to work hard for success.

Part II of this book contains specific details and the significant impact of my military career. However, the fundamentals established by my parents as their guidepost for my siblings' upbringing — God, character, integrity, educational excellence, preparation, service, and purpose — laid the foundation for a successful fulfilling life. These fundamentals, combined with the strict disciplines already required by the military, further enhanced, and solidified the growth and development I would need to make the military a 20-year career where I would flourish and succeed.

As a military family member in my youth, and then later as an army officer in my adult life. I was blessed to have these fundamentals as a solid base as I traveled worldwide, living, working, playing, engaging, and being exposed to many nationalities and ethnic communities.

This was something that enriched my life with a proper knowledge of what diversity means and what it is all about — regardless of race, color, creed, religion, or origin — which is to have HUMANITY, RESPECT, DIGNITY, as well as being equally FAIR and JUST with all people. This is firmly ingrained in me, and it keeps me grounded every day throughout my life, and in mentoring and saving our youth of all nationalities and ethnic communities.

My prayer for mentors and those who work directly with young people is for them to make time to spend with a young person for an honest conversation to encourage, inspire, challenge, and provide uplift.

QUOTE:

"The purpose of life is not to be happy. It is to be useful, to be honorable, to be compassionate, to have it make some difference that you have lived and lived well."

— Ralph Waldo Emerson

SCRIPTURE:

"Very truly I tell you, whoever believes in me will do the works I have been doing, and they will do even greater things than these, because I am going to the Father."

JOHN 14:12

CHAPTER 2

Early Education

3rd Grade – Augusta, GA -
W.S. Hornsby Elementary - (1966 -1967)
Mrs. Willie M. Howard, Mrs. Little – Math

I was born as a military brat, a child of service members who serve in the United States Armed Forces. Being a military brat is a unique experience that creates many opportunities for exposure they would otherwise not have experienced living in one community. Because of the military lifestyle, I grew up in many communities and attended eight schools from kindergarten through high school. Approximately every two years during the time my father was serving in the military, I was always the new kid in the neighborhood.

As a military family member, you grow up with a sense of community, as your neighbors who live in apartment complexes across the hall look out for each other. You pick up food items from the commissary for each other. As a child, you follow instructions, and do as you are told when you are told to do it. For example, back then, when told to take out the trash, you would immediately complete the chore that very second. Not tomorrow, and not when you finished playing with your iPad game. You did just that when told to be in the house before the telephone pole lit up.

As a military brat educated in the Department of Defense Dependents Schools (DoDDS), you join a unique community for life where you learn core values, and that character counts for all people. You learned to get along with others and make new friends while keeping the old friends. Being able to do this resulted in building meaningful relationships. This experience taught me to strive to do better so I can do more during my life's journey.

I started my academic journey in kindergarten in Wilmington. I completed the first and second grades in Hanua, Germany, near Frankfurt. I spent the third and fourth grades in Augusta, Georgia while Dad was assigned at Fort Gordon. In the fifth grade I was in Eatontown, New Jersey when he was assigned to Fort Monmouth.

When he was reassigned back to Augusta, I completed sixth and seventh grades at Sand Bar Ferry. My dad was reassigned back to New Jersey where I completed my secondary education, which consisted of Memorial Middle School (eighth grade), Monmouth High School (first year) and Neptune Township High School.

My dad retired from the Army at Fort Monmouth at the end of my first year and subsequently purchased a new home in Neptune Township, where I grew up as a youth. In my youth, I learned to embrace being the new kid and adjusting to a new community every two to three years. However, through it all I learned to blossom wherever planted. Blossom meant embracing the community and the new friends you meet. As an adult I learned to develop exceptional interpersonal people skills, believe in myself, and live up to my opportunities in every community we lived in.

As I reflect over my life, for a significant time during my youth—I experienced my father being absent from the home because of serving overseas. When my dad was stationed at Fort Gordon, our family lived in Augusta. In my youth, they described me as a rather shy and quiet person who loved animals. While my dad was serving the country during war time, I was trying to figure out who and what I was to become in the event of my dad becoming a casualty in the Vietnam War. While my dad was away, several men who lived in my neighborhood stepped up and filled the gap by mentoring me. This was my first look at what mentoring looked and felt like to a little boy. Looking back, I saw God's "helping hand" through these men; and I believed that God gave them the responsibility to help shape and mold young boys into young males that would grow into young men to contribute to our community and society in a positive way.

Mr. Samuel Herring who worked at the community hospital, made time for me every Saturday by teaching the game of tennis. Saturday morning, early before the "quack" of day, I would hear his horn and he would drive us to the community park where I would hit more balls over the fence (and across the street) instead of across the net! Mr. Herring, although patient, was probably thinking to himself, "that young man needs a lot of work to become more athletic, let alone a tennis player!" Ironically, tennis became one of my favorite sports I enjoyed playing as an adult.

When I was about nine-years old in the fourth grade, William Holmes was the first and only Black male educator, mentor, and coach who taught me the game of baseball at the Sand Bar Ferry Middle School field. Looking back, he was the role model for many young boys in the community. Coach Holmes stood about 6-foot-5 inches tall and had such a powerful presence with his whistle and deep voice barking out instructions, "get to class, turn in your homework, listen to your mother."

Other mentors also surrounded me. Neighborhood men also taught me how to take care of our yard while helping them take care of it. At Thankful Baptist Church in Augusta, my siblings and I actively participated in many youth activities such as Vacation Bible School, Sunday School, Worship Services, and special youth programs.

While living in Augusta, my mother modeled an example of a community leader, doing good to others, in all the places she could, never growing tired of doing good is what I witnessed.

My mother not only served as a substitute teacher but also as an Avon Representative with many customers.

She wanted me to understand that always doing my best is all right. My parents taught me to have pride, to strive to be the best in everything I do, to be the best whatever my role may be, and that God have a more excellent vision for my life. She ensured that my siblings participated in youth activities. My mother even started a Girl Scout Brownie Troop because there was no troop in our area for younger-aged girls that my younger sister could attend.

Because of her, I joined the Boy Scouts, a youth swimming team, and took karate lessons at the local YMCA. I even participated in science fairs and book clubs at the community library. My mother was committed to literacy and ensured that her children read above-grade level. I loved to learn new things by reading, I was curious about learning, and reading books allowed me to read about plans I never dreamed possible.

Mother joined a library book club year-round, and we visited routinely. That is where my love of reading became ingrained at an early age, and why the book club continues to be one of UCF's primary learning units. "Leaders are Readers, and Readers Lead" is the UCF Summer Book Club slogan. As you can see, literacy promotion came from my upbringing as a youth.

Two factors became clear as I probed my 87-year-old mother's memory during the winter of 2022. No one accomplishes anything significant alone and sibling friendships are essential. Our family operated as one unit, one team, and it was strengthened because we worked together as one team. It also dawned on me that my older sister Sylvia and I went everywhere together!

Perhaps, I was following my father's instructions to keep her out of trouble, and she had to take me with her when leaving the house. My mother was "Wonder Woman" in my eyes. She ran the household, made significant decisions, and held the family together in a loving environment while Dad was in Vietnam. She showed me and my siblings the community engagement model by keeping us involved in many community activities. I will never tire of the community engagement and mentoring work that makes a difference in the lives of young people and families. Why? Because I saw my mother in action, she loved people and never tried of serving them.

QUOTE:

"Good – Better – Best. Never let it rest until your good becomes better and your better becomes best! Strive for excellence!"

— Source Unknown

SCRIPTURE:

"Be anxious for nothing, but in everything by prayer and supplication, with thanksgiving, let your request be made known to God; and the peace of God, which surpasses all understanding, will guard your hearts and minds through Christ Jesus."

Philippians 4: 6

CHAPTER 3

Early Entrepreneurship

The makings of my mentorship and the layout of this book stem from the evolution of the progression and experiences from my upbringing, through development and influential stages during my young adult years, and maturity into full adulthood—all these stages, as mentioned above, played a part of my road to lifetime mentorship. As you can see, the emphasis on the Aim High Education Life Skill Program originated from my experience as a youth entrepreneur.

My big sister Sylvia recalled when we lived in Augusta and Dad served the country in the Vietnam War. During that time, I witnessed Sylvia as an active big sister. When she was not at band practice, she enjoyed making additional money by passing out flyers to neighbors in our development to cut grass and babysit. We only had one car and she wasn't driving yet.

So, I had a weekend paper route when I was a young boy, perhaps eight years old. My sister would get up with me on Sunday mornings and help put rubber bands on the newspapers. She would walk my paper route with me to deliver the newspapers.

Afterward, we would go home, get dressed, and walk blocks to Sunday School and Church at Thankful Baptist Church. If Mom and my sister Andra came to church, we would have a ride back home. Otherwise, we would walk.

Another reflection is when we lived in New Jersey at the Fort Monmouth Post Quarters, where I played Little League baseball. My big sister was the one who would walk me to baseball practice. My sister was proud of my accomplishments and continued to support me when I received a wrestling scholarship from Rider College in Lawrenceville, New Jersey. My sister and brother-in-law would travel from York, Pennsylvania, to support me when my team would compete against Princeton University. She was there to support me but could not watch me trying to get out of those gruesome wrestling holds and positions. She hid her face or left the gym to keep from fearing for my safety. It appeared that I was being hurt to her, and it hurt her to watch.

I was also blessed when my sister supported me when I applied for a master's in the business program at Golden Gate University, editing my essay for acceptance. I also fondly remember her attendance at my induction to the Neptune High Athletic Hall of Fame.

These were some anecdotes of my childhood reflections from my big sister, Sylvia.

When I was 12 years old, my entrepreneurial spirit was cultivated when I started a lawn care service. I had watched Sylvia make money cutting grass during my younger years and wanted to do the same. My big sister was raised to be very independent and kind-hearted. Along with these admirable attributes, she also possessed an entrepreneurial spirit. She always thought of ways to make money in the neighborhood from a lemonade stand at an early age. By the time she was a teenager, she had worked various odd jobs, cutting grass, babysitting, and even cleaning a house for a teacher, where she learned numerous life lessons still etched in her mind. She said the teacher's house was very unkempt, and the kids were not taught how to clean up their rooms, but she taught them. She not only cleaned this teacher's house, but she also baby sat for their two kids. In this capacity, she would make them clean up after themselves before they went to bed. As time progressed, the kids' room looked a lot better than when she first began cleaning for the family. Eventually, the teacher asked how she got the kids to improve their cleaning habits. Sylvia said she explained to them that it was their responsibility to keep their room clean and, at first, had them work with her. After a while, the kids caught on to her message and began to improve their housekeeping skills. From that point on, when my sister would go to clean or babysit, she would always praise them for how well they kept their rooms.

As a Lucy Craft Laney High School student in Augusta, Sylvia was also busy with school. She played clarinet in the school's marching and concert bands, which were competitive bands requiring lots of practice and often performed in various competitions. The marching band was called the "Marching 100," a precision-style band. Sylvia had to create a schedule to reflect the available times for the babysitting job, band practice, and grass cutting. She made fliers to market services to the community and passed them out in the neighborhood to advertise. She went door to door to cut grass by observing houses where the grass was unkempt, passing the marketing strategy to me. Of course, it worked.

That's how my entrepreneurial skills were cultivated as I grew a lawn care service from just a few customers to more than 50 that paid three dollars per yard. Additionally, between the ages of 12 and 14, I established a TV Guide and newspaper route, selling the TV Guide weekly and the newspaper daily to more than 125 community customers. I perfected what I saw my sister do!

Learning self-reliance, trusting your creativity, and developing courage are great gifts. Many young people find the world of work, alone, daunting and don't know what profession to pursue. But whether performing office work such as filing papers, stuffing envelopes, cutting grass, or shoveling snow from the driveways, they quickly understand the value of hard work if thrown smack dab into the middle of it.

The UCF Business Plan Presentation

One of UCF's youth initiatives originated from my entrepreneurial spirit developed at an early age. My key message to mentors developing a mentoring program is to look at your upbringing as a youth and intentionally shape your program to equip students with a skill set that can be used for the rest of their lives.

From the beginning, UCF searched for ways to educate and expose our young people to entrepreneurship opportunities. UCF's first youth initiative outside of the monthly meetings consisted of teaching students how to develop a business plan. A circle of adults with experience in business came together to empower, educate, and equip students in business plan development. We assigned coaches (Certified Public Accountants) to meet with the students every Sunday for six to eight weeks. This initiative was exciting because it included great competition between girls and boys.

In UCF's first four years (2006-2010), the organization provided "seed planting." We desire to provide exposure experience and teach our young people skills for real-life experience for them to carry into adulthood.

Equally important, it allowed our young entrepreneurs to interact with community leaders who heard their oral presentations and provided feedback. We entered the team into competitions and had them present in the Montgomery County, Maryland alumnae chapter of Alpha Kappa Alpha Sorority Incorporated's Entrepreneurial Competition, where they won first prize.

Since the first experience, UCF has invited speakers and business owners to present workshops at monthly youth meetings. In addition, students learned and gained first-hand knowledge on concession stand operations during summers and weekends at the Christian Youth Basketball Ministry games hosted at John F. Kennedy and Bethesda-Chevy Chase High Schools in Montgomery County. They also plied their talents in the fall operating Club Friday, a teen club hosted by the Upper County Community Center in Gaithersburg.

Although the UCF's top priority focuses on preparing students to attend colleges and universities to earn degrees in meaningful career fields, it is equally important to encourage our students to develop practical skills to pursue entrepreneurial pathways such as starting new businesses, creating revenue streams, and employing others to work in your created business. The critical message for mentors; is to become a "Community Multiplier" by teaching young people at an early age about entrepreneurship by guiding them through the processes for new business development and new pathways to help improve the quality of lives in our community. In the military, we used the term "Force Multiplier," and now we need to become Community Multipliers to develop new pathways for personal and economic growth for the youth. Imagine one person reaching ten other people and repeating the impact of influencing ten others to be committed to making a difference – now that is a Game Changer!

Have them understand that entrepreneurship is not so much a profession as it is a way of thinking; and that some of the essential elements of this entrepreneurial mindset (as I learned early in life) come from curiosity, perseverance, expression, and experimentation. And some of the benefits to go with this?

- **A stronger appreciation for money:** becoming more self-reliant, while gaining more vital **respect** for money.
- **Creative thinking:** exploring better ways to fix problems to keep businesses moving in the right direction.
- **Improved people skills:** forcing us to interact with unfamiliar folks daily —especially with small businesses—to foster people skills to turn our youth into better salespeople down the road.

- **Better goal setting:** setting and achieving goals; rather than starting and stopping, or just giving up and running away when something doesn't look as appealing.

A STORY WITH A KEY MESSAGE: Father's Matter

I am a product of a military family, my father served in the U.S. Army, and I followed in his footsteps after his retirement. When I was young, my father received military orders assigned to Germany at least three times. Between assignments, we would stay with our grandparents in Wilmington, NC, waiting for Dad to get housing in Germany.

As we traveled by car to North Carolina, Georgia, New Jersey, and Arizona, we would ask this question along the way to our destination, "are we there yet?" Every 25 miles, my sister asked, "Are we there yet?"

These days, we are not there yet as far as closing the gap for fathers not living in the home. I need you to understand that the role of fathers in their children's lives is invaluable. In a perfect world, I wish fathers to be engaged in their children's lives through adulthood so that it would put mentoring organizations out of business! However, in the meantime, mentoring must be front and center in communities across the country. Please do not underestimate the value of the father's role in their children's growth and development into adulthood.

My prayer for mentors and those who work directly with young people is for them to make time to spend with a young person for just a plain conversation, encouragement, challenge, uplift, etc.

We want our young people, especially our young males, to live up to the highest possibility of their potential. I tell them that I want to be clear that their responsibilities are the following:
- To get better every day
- To improve yourself
- Learn a new skill
- Make smart choices
- Help another person to get better

1ST YOUTH DEVELOPMENT INITIATIVE

In 2008, The Montgomery County Alumnae Chapter of Delta Sigma Theta Sorority, Incorporated partnered with Unity Christian Fellowship to sponsor a "Young Entrepreneurs Program." The program, "Entrepreneurship Owning Your Future," was designed to teach young people how to write business plans and learn marketing concepts, business budgeting, business communications, etc. Program participants included young males from the Education Life Skills Program (ELS) and the members of the Growing and Empowering Myself Successfully (GEMS) Program. In addition to the GEMS program, this partnership was a stepping-stone for the sorority's new initiative, Empowering Males to Build Opportunities for Developing Independence (EMBODI). This initiative featured my wife Mona Williams' leadership in establishing a creative innovative pathway that engaged and taught students practical business skills to shift their thinking by introducing entrepreneurial skills.

This youth initiative led to unforeseen opportunities for young people to showcase their newfound skills in a summer basketball ministry and the Upper County Teen Center "Club Friday" gatherings. This initiative taught students about customer service skills, math aptitude practice, marketing, etc. In four years, our student enrollment exploded, resulting in the program's outgrowth of meeting space, classrooms, and banquet halls.

Community Leaders Evaluated the Business Plan and Presentation

UCF assembled a distinguished panel of judges to review and critique the students' presentations. The community leaders provided a wonderful experience for the students (who spent six weeks in preparation at the Bohrer Park facility in Gaithersburg where the boys met in the basement and the girls met in the kitchen during the friendly contest). Our community leaders provided the students with a realistic environment to give them a presentation experience. UCF appreciates LTC Jackie Melton (U.S. Marines Retired), Mr. John Tucker, Vice President Peers, Inc., Mr. Sol Graham, CEO/Owner Quality Biological, Inc., and Mr. Terrance Parker, Chick-fil-A Restaurant, Silver Spring, Maryland. Our panel evaluation was based on four key areas:

1. Students' Business Plan (Written)
2. Students' Business Plan (Oral)
3. Commercial Presentation (Focusing on good eye contact and communication)
4. Professional Manner and Appearance

According to a recent CNN report, over 55% of people are unhappy with their jobs. And, according to financial advisor Charles Schwab, recessions provide a natural time for people to go out on their own - not just because a layoff might jump-start their entrepreneurial plans! Labor tends to be plentiful and less expensive during recessions, and potential competitors are likely to pull back. Nearly 40% of small-business owners say the current recession creates opportunities for their companies. Experts say now is the best time to start a business, but most people don't know how.

The key message UCF believes we can "win the future" by working together to be a bridge for future generations. There is no better investment than our young people. I challenge you to be bold in your obedience, stay encouraged, and stay in faith. Each person can make a difference in the lives of our young people.

You only need a heart to serve, mentor, uplift, and nurture our children. Our community can no longer remain silent. We can longer afford to sit on our blessings; instead, let's build on them to win the future.

It is so important to have a team of caring and supportive adults in your circle to provide social, emotional and wellness support. We encourage students to do better than they have ever done before.

Every day is an opportunity to put forth the effort to improve. A good friend, police officer Eric Burnett always shared that "you have two choices; to stay the same or put in the work to get better." UCF believes "you decide to put forth the effort" for anyone working directly with young people and students.

The best way to honor God is to continue leading by example and use my gifts to bring people together to work on solutions-driven outcomes. My obedience to the Lord is why you see a higher commitment and engagement with like-minded community leaders, stakeholders, parents, and students who desire to work together to make a difference.

To students with the desire to work to improve and become successful, you must also be coachable. I am reminded of the poem by Marianne Williamson, "Our Deepest Fear." My favorite lines follow: "You playing small does not serve the world; we are all meant to shine, and as we let our light shine, we unconsciously permit others to do the same. Together we can create good in the community to inspire and reach many people in different places."

As you can see, this is where the community collaboration experience took root. The seed of building relationships and a sense of community was planted, nurtured, and grew. I am clear that God was setting the direction and trajectory for shaping my heart as a servant leader. My heart, mind, and soul were being cultivated in a purpose-driven life to serve and realize that service to the community is a greater action than myself.

QUOTE:

"We expect so much from others and so little from ourselves. And because we constantly seek outside of us, for all the things that we think are missing from within ourselves, we fail to realize that we are powerful beyond measure, and that we can do so much more for ourselves than the whole world can do for us."

— Unknown

SCRIPTURE:

"Trust in the Lord with all your heart and lean not on your own understanding; in all your ways submit to him, and he will make your paths straight."

Proverbs 3: 5-6

Part 2 – SEEDLINGS TO SAPLING

Creation of a Service Mindset Development: Food and Fertilization of Early Adulthood

- Chapter 4: Secondary Education — Youth Development Shaping - Education Top Priority

- Chapter 5: Mona: My Nubian Queen

- Chapter 6: Military Service and Career—In My Father's Footsteps

- Chapter 7: Order My Steps in the Lord (My Heart, Mind and Soul)

- Chapter 8: My Basketball Story

- Chapter 9: Fraternal Brotherhood

CHAPTER 4

Secondary Education – Top Priority

Faith is taking the first step, even when you don't see the full staircase.
—Reverend Dr. Martin Luther King, Jr.

Education throughout my upbringing was more holistic in terms of not being confined to the classroom experience. The most significant benefit of my educational journey was intellectual development, encompassing psychological, social, and emotional growth. This resulted in confidence building about learning and working to create the most excellent version of myself. I was excited to challenge myself, which increased my academic confidence, critical thinking, and social-emotional development.

As a result of my father's overseas assignments during his military career (where my family could accompany him), we benefited from the exposure to living in Germany three different times. This experience provided unique opportunities to learn about the world, such as different cultures, languages, and interactions with the German people. We visited the famous castles and sites that the country had to offer.

My development journey started being shaped in the fourth grade. I recalled my teacher's statement early in the school year "this year the class will be taking a trip around the world, so get ready to travel." I took her word to heart and was excited when I came home. I told my mother to pack my suitcase because the teacher said we would travel around the world this academic year. I soon learned to understand her meaning of traveling around the world due to doing monthly book reports on different countries. At the end of the academic year, we went around the globe via pen and paper: Germany, France, South Africa, Italy, Greece, etc.

I shared this experience because when my father received orders for his final overseas assignment, I was able to appreciate the assignment. As a new student entering a new community every two to three years, I learned exceptional interpersonal skills, how to get along with others, and making new friends while keeping old friends, which resulted in building meaningful relationships.

"Military brats" educated in the Department of Defense Dependents Schools (DoDDS) join a unique community for life where core values for all people are emphasized: including respect, trustworthiness, responsibility, caring, fairness, and citizenship. Every military community has support activities and programs, such as Family and Morale Welfare and Recreation (MWR), designed to enhance the quality of life supporting family members and soldiers. MWR includes youth centers and summer programs for leadership skills, citizenship, academic support, creative arts, and sports. These activities fostered and developed children's physical fitness and intellectual and social-emotional needs.

As my family traveled and lived in different communities, I learned that we have more similarities, bringing us together whether we lived overseas or stateside. There was a sense of pride that came with being an American overseas. In my youth, we worked together as a team to represent the best of being an American. Humanity has more in common than the differences that separate us.

All my secondary education (junior and high school) experience occurred in New Jersey.

My parents made acquiring a quality education a top priority. My parents knew education would be paramount in raising a family in the 1960's. They knew that education would be a great equalizer and a stairway to a higher standard of living for me and my sisters. Many of us grew up with the NAACP quote: "A Mind is a Terrible Thing to Waste" and for the recent generations – "A Great Thing to Invest In!"

I recall a defining conversation with my dad at the age of 15. He asked what I wanted to become when I attended college. You see, there was never any doubt about me attending college. I shared that my goal was to become a successful businessman like Earl Graves, founder of Black Enterprise magazine. His positive image was one of the few that consistently showed Black men in various magazines with a well-dressed suit and tie look, complete with a briefcase in hand creating business opportunities. My dad's advice was direct. He told me that I needed to continue to achieve good grades in school to earn a scholarship because my older sister had exhausted the family college fund. My reply was, "What? No college funds?"

My dad was a loving, thoughtful person who worked two or three jobs to provide for the family. He was a no-nonsense old soldier due to the experiences in the Army. I learned from him early on when expectations were set; he expected me to pursue them with all my effort, heart, and mind. In 1975 my dad retired from Fort Monmouth, which led to our move to our second home in Neptune Township.

This was bittersweet because I had to transfer from Monmouth Regional High School where I was enjoying my freshman year. During that year, I played the trombone in the marching band where we marched in parades, performed at halftime at a Penn State University football game, traveled to Canada to march in a parade, and performed at numerous football and soccer games. I also found wrestling, a sport I enjoyed and excelled in throughout college.

I was truly blessed to enjoy learning, which led to me excelling in school. As a result of being in a military family, I developed practical interpersonal skills where I made friends easily. Several military families lived in Neptune Township that our family connected with. The Washington's were a military family where we spent time engaging in family activities. Their family structure was like ours (two girls and one boy) and shaped my mentoring journey. They continue to be lifelong friends even to this day.

Mrs. Girdie Washington is an ordained preacher who has always been engaged with program development to improve the local community. Mr. George Washington (deceased) was a retired Army nurse and entrepreneur who owned a shoe repair shop in Neptune. He was a person who shared and sowed seeds of knowledge, wisdom, and history while providing thought-provoking conversations about what future possibilities might look like from a teenage perspective. As a mentor, his influence for sharing wisdom and knowledge continues to be a part of my approach to inspiring and motivating young people to reach their full potential. He used to say emphatically that "life as a Black man (or woman) is a thinking man's game." He emphasized while planning your future to develop a "Plan A, B, and C" while making sure "Plan D" was actionable, meaningful, achievable, and well thought out! The Great Depression shaped Mr. Washington as a young person when he endured harsh economic experiences. He passed what he learned - to use your mind, hands, and creative abilities to provide for your family.

Mr. Washington emphasized that young people must develop a "kinesthetic learning style," using their hands to learn a trade to be marketable. UCF realized early on that only some students will succeed in college and that learning a trade is a viable pathway to living independently and raising a family.

UCF students are encouraged to learn vocational skills that used to be called industrial art curricula, such as home repair, auto mechanics, carpentry, metal shop, electric, cosmetology, barber hair grooming, etc. As the world transforms with the emergence of robotics and artificial intelligence, UCF rolled out our latest initiative in the Spring of 2019, the Home Improvement and Repair program. Deacon Michael Smith led this latest initiative as a professional craftsman with 40 years of experience in the construction profession. A Popular Grove Baptist Church member in Gaithersburg, he was committed to growing and expanding the program. UCF was excited to teach students skills that would help them become successful in learning a trade.

Our youth needs to prepare for the 21st-century workforce transformation that emphasizes working with your hands and mind. I always enjoy sharing the story that Michael Jordan and I had a similar experience in high school as I tried out for basketball and was cut from the team at Monmouth Regional High. The two of us experienced different outcomes in life.

COACH BOB TIEDEMANN (CENTER) AND HIS WRESTLERS

After also trying out for the football and gymnastics teams as a freshman, I became interested in wrestling. The message to students and parents encourages your students to be involved in extracurricular activities, clubs, and sports to help with social emotional growth and development.

I attribute my success as a student-athlete to being the new school kid. To be accepted in this new community, I worked extremely hard to become a standout athlete. Along the way, I gained teammates whom I call my lifelong brothers. I excelled as a student-athlete on a successful Neptune Scarlet Fliers wrestling team that pushed me to greater heights. I was grateful as a teenager to mature as a person, student, and athlete through my senior year in 1976. My character traits were shaped, developed, and nurtured as a standout wrestler under the legendary head coach Bob Tiedemann (deceased) and assistant coach Oscar Brown.

As I look back over my life, Coach Tiedemann's impact on young male lives reminded my teammates and me of the sitcom "The White Shadow," which ran from 1978 to 1981. The television show was about a former professional basketball player who took a job coaching basketball at an urban high school with a racially mixed basketball team in Los Angeles, California. To many, Coach Tiedemann had our backs and cared for every student-athlete (black or white) during a time of mending racial challenges on the Jersey Shore. He saw this as his purpose to return home and give back to his community, where he excelled as a standout wrestler at Monmouth University. He was a bridge builder bringing people together through sports. Although these were challenging times in the 1970 after the race riots, Coach was one of the few who built a wrestling program with white and black students. I was unaware of this until a conversation with a teammate. My first thought was a caring person like Coach Tiedemann step out of his comfort zone to make hope happen in the community. Don't underestimate the power of one pulling others together working for a greater outcome. Coach Tiedemann focused on performance merit and looking beyond color during the racial challenges of the time. He wasn't alone in helping to develop talent to create a pathway to attend college and succeed in life. Coach Tiedemann and Coach Brown were our first examples of modeling excellence by working together to impact young male lives. I asked Coach Brown to describe my wrestling abilities, and I thought he would say I was athletic with outstanding balance. Instead, he shared that I was a gifted cerebral wrestler who process information quickly during competition.

Our racially diverse wrestling team dominated the Jersey Shore wrestling scene for over a decade. I am sure Coach Tiedemann, a proud man, wasn't looked upon favorably among the area coaches! I can see Coach Tiedemann in the coaches meeting with his swagger and communication skills, ensuring his wrestlers were ranked properly for seeding purposes.

We had a great team, and our domination started with the Class of 1975 wrestlers. Our squad was led by a strong, lightweight group of wrestlers named after the movie "Three the Hard Way" (1974), starring Jim Kelly, Jim Brown, and Fred Williamson.

BACK ROW: Coach Bob Tiedemann, Greg Coates, Bart Cook, Rich Mebane, Allen Johnson, Derick Oates. MIDDLE ROW: Kim Fellenz, Rich Siskind, Tim Hall. FRONT ROW: Leroy Wallace, Jeff Bills, Louis Chapman, Donald Williams.

Neptune wrestling team's version of Three the Hard Way was led by the 115-pound state champion Lou Chapman, myself, a 122-pound Region 6 and District 24 champion, and 129-pound standout Kim Fellenz. The team consisted of Bart Cook and heavyweight Derick Oates, who placed fourth in the state in the 170-pound class. That year, I won the 122-pound region crown as a junior, the first non-senior to win a region title at Neptune High.

This team was inducted into the Athletic Hall of Fame on October 29, 2010, at a ceremony hosted by the Neptune High Red and Black Booster Club. What an honor and a joyous experience for all my teammates to receive recognition during halftime of a Neptune football game. We also shared and rekindled old friendships, as our respective families reunited for the first time in over three decades! This was a reminder that your life is not about where you come from, it's about your pursuit to achieve higher standards by investing in yourself.

In my senior year, I was selected as team captain, as I led by example in the classroom and on the mat. As a returning district and region champion in 1975, the Asbury Park Press newspaper picked me in the preseason to repeat as champion to win back-to-back titles. An experience that shaped my life in my senior year was the journey to repeat as a regional champion. My first painful emotional setback came in the Championships regional title match finals, falling to a wrestler I had previously beaten. Although losing the championship match was painful, my disappointment was letting down my coaches (Tiedemann and assistant coach Oscar Brown) and teammates. It took a long time to heal from the heartbreaking loss.

Experience New Dimension for Hopeful Wrestling Squad

by Todd Cornelisse

Varsity wrestling is taking on a new outlook in the sport. It's called "experience". "This is the first year sophomores will have had good experience in wrestling", insists Coach Tiedeman. The 74-75 season is the first year that the wrestling program, started three years ago in the younger grades, will be felt by the Varsity in the sophomore ranks.

Coach Tiedeman believes he has the makings of a good squad with young players as well as experienced juniors and seniors.

Among returning players is Tim Hall who was undefeated in duel meets last year. He placed third in the Wall Tournament and third in the Districts. Bart Cook and Derek Oates are returning to the squad with a lot of credentials. Bart was last year's Christmas Tournament Champ. He was also second in the Districts and fourth in region. Derek Oates was the J.V. Red Bank champ.

Lou Chapman, Don Williams and Kim Fellenz, known to fans as "3 the Hard Way", will be back this year also. Lou Chapman is the District Champ at 115 and 5th in the State. Williams was County J.V. Champ with a 12-1 record. Kim Fellenz, who was 13-1 last year, defeated former A-T. Freestyle Champ in the summer tournament.

The rest of the squad includes Leroy Wallace (Jr.), who was third in the J.V. Tournament, Jeff Bills (Jr.), Rich Siskind, Joe Delpizzo, Allen Johnson, Al Flynn and Rich Mebane.

DAVISON RUGS
CARPETS • LINOLEUM
39 PILGRIM PATHWAY
OCEAN GROVE, N.J.
07756

Coach Tiedemann (affectionately called "Coach T") and his wrestlers (all called "Baby T's" by our classmates) he wasn't only our legendary coach, he was a friend, mentor as well as a hall of fame wrestling coach. His sincere interest in each athlete shaped and impacted all student-athletes who crossed his path. He was a teacher of men and a teacher of character from the early 1970s until the early 1990s. He was truly the leader of our Brotherhood!

I am reminded by the many experiences and conversations with my teammates that the sport of wrestling shaped our lives in so many positive ways. It taught us character traits that have served each one of us on our life journey!

The sport taught each one how to balance academics and athletics and maintain mental tenacity and physical toughness. It reinforced how to be a great teammate who's accountable and responsible for themselves and each other. My teammates learned that I could be counted on to prepare correctly without taking short cuts. Other character traits from this demanding sport were a strong work ethic, resiliency, determination, self-control, honesty, loyalty, grit, social intelligence, and leadership. Piercing through the lens of yesterday, my teammate Bart Cook said that "something extraordinary occurred in the wrestling room while doing the many conditioning drills, running on the wall, neck bridges, round robins that shaped us as young males into men of high character."

We have numerous teammates that lead highly successful careers in challenging professions. Everyone became productive citizens and involved in their community. Several of our teammates were called to serve in all forms: spiritual leaders in their church, entrepreneurs, attorneys, military officers, and business owners among other noble positions.

My dedication to this rigorous sport and the experiences gained by competing overseas and across the country shaped my character as a leader, student, and athlete. My coaches and teammates were there when I was the most impressionable and navigating adolescence. In the time of emotional heights of victories, winning wrestling matches, and in the emotional depth of defeats losing wrestling matches, they were there to lend significant emotional support.

A little-known fact; as a high school junior, I applied to the United States Military Academy (USMA), known as West Point, which overlooks the scenic Hudson River in Upstate New York. Growing up in the Fort Monmouth community, my locale certainly influenced my teenage aspirations. West Point accepted my attendance at the USMA

Prep School at Fort Monmouth for one year to gain enrollment at West Point. Of course, I decided to take a different path.

Sometimes life comes full circle. As a retired officer, I was honored to serve as a panel member on Congressman David Trone's (Maryland's 6th District) Service Academy Nomination. In addition, I had the honor to provide leadership work with Congressman Chris Van Hollen, who serves Maryland's 8th District. The blessing was working with Sol Graham to establish an MCPS mentoring program to increase Black and Brown candidates interested in attending service academies. We all recognized the need to attract qualified Black and Brown future leaders for nomination to the U.S. service academies. The highest honor is to serve the country; the opportunity to attend a service academy is a bonus.

When I reflect on whence I came, the witness of God's hand was upon me through the many experiences that shaped my life and set a trajectory for perseverance and service above self for a greater purpose. I recall Langston Hughes's poem entitled "Mother to Son." It reads: "I can tell you that life for me ain't been on crystal stairs. Instead, it's had tacks, splinters, and boards torn up." Amid some successes, I have had my share of disappointments, setbacks, heartaches, hurts, resignations, denial of awards, and promotions passed over. I have experienced just what others have experienced throughout my life journey.

In my senior year, I worked extremely hard as a student-athlete to defend my regional championship from the year before. As an upperclassman, I focused on where I would spend the next four years in college.

Although I didn't repeat as the regional champion, I received several college scholarships offers. I received offers from Temple University, Bloomsburg University of Pennsylvania (where our second daughter Dreka received her undergraduate degree in Pre-Optometry in 2012), and Montclair State College (now University) of New Jersey, to name a few. After evaluating my options regarding financial support, college major, and campus environment, in-state or out-of-state options, I selected Rider College (now Rider University) in Lawrenceville, New Jersey.

Rider University Undergraduate – Youth Development Taken Shape—Education Top Priority

After I accepted the student-athletic scholarship to represent Rider's Division I Wrestling program, I arrived on campus in the fall of 1976. At this time, my parents were unaware that I had met a guardian angel named Lawson McElroy. He was the Assistant Director of Financial Aid and Admissions at the college. I didn't realize then that McElroy would play a critical role in my life's journey. As my parents signed the financial aid documents, my dad repeated the message I had heard many times to Lawson, "Donald is here to earn a college degree." Lawson helped my family navigate the complexities of financial aid resources every semester. We became a team; he said, "Just tell your parents to sign here and make sure you get that degree." He became a trusted advisor, role model, and friend to my family.

A STORY WITH A KEY MESSAGE:

This is a perfect time to share with high school students about looking in the mirror and self-examination as you begin a new chapter in your life. Here is a message about knowing whose you are and who you are. Here's my story about visiting my parents in Wilmington, North Carolina.

As I arrived in town, I stopped by the gas station to fill up before heading to my parent's home. An elderly gentleman engaged me in conversation and asked whose boy I was. The translation was "whose family do you belong to?" I responded with my name and shared that I am the son of Donald Williams. He looked at me puzzled, so I continued with the name of my great grandfather Arthur Duncan McDonald whose parents were born during slavery. I shared that he probably knew my grandmother Hazel McDonald-Williams who had two sons. My dad and his brother Duncan lived with my great-grandfather at 1108 South 6th Street on the south side. Immediately the elderly gentleman smiled because he was able to make the connection to my father's family. He stated that he remembered me when I was a little boy and called the name "Donnie Boy." He said, "you are a spitting image of your father," saying I was my father's twin because we looked like each other. As fate would have it, my dad shared that he had recently spoken with the man at the grocery store.

As a sidebar for historians, slavery officially ended in the United States on December 6, 1865, after the 13th Amendment to the Constitution was passed to abolish slavery nationwide. My great-grandfather experienced what slavery felt like in his youth. We now know from Dr. Henry Louis Gates, Jr.'s "Many Rivers to Cross" series that African Americans were forced to move across the Middle Passage chained as slaves. His research highlighted the practices of slavery that continued for some time after the 13th Amendment was passed and ratified. Just think about it, this was 90 years after the Declaration of Independence was adopted by the Continental Congress, affirming that "all men are created equal." By now they did not intend it to mean individual equality for Black Americans.

Sharing my story, I remember former President Barack Obama's book entitled **"Dreams from My Father,"** where he describes his adolescence and challenges in his youth. A visit he made to Kenya as a young man to meet his African relatives following the death of his father helped him discover who he was as a young man became clearer and shaped his future.

A key message for today's youth is that you should know your family history to understand where you came from, and who you are. You should know where you are headed; it is all connected to your family history and legacy. I ask you this, who are you and to whose family do you belong?

Knowing my family history gave me a sense of purpose and direction because I knew who I was and where my family came from. I learned that I came from a family with a great work ethic, a sense of family purpose, and a willingness to do what is necessary to be overcomers like my ancestors and many other families from the South.

I end with this family story that occurred when I was between the ages of 11 and 13. I helped with putting my great-grandfather to bed. I remember seeing a series of number "markings" on his upper thigh. I asked my dad what those numbers were on his leg? I remember a series of numbers strung together (35 and 10 through 13) branded on his leg. I was told to "hush, boy." I never forgot what I saw. Although we will never know the whole story of slavery, I can surmise that great-grandfather, Arthur Duncan McDonald was enslaved. Thinking back, I never heard anyone in the family talk about slavery and what great-grandfather endured in his lifetime. As I reflect, this experience gave me a sense of purpose and pride even today when I hear the phrase: "Honor the past, celebrate the present, and inspire future leaders!"

A GAME CHANGER'S PURSUIT

RIDER COLLEGE WRESTLING TEAM PICTURE

In the Fall 1976, I arrived at Rider College on scholarship. The major events that year included the elections of President Jimmy Carter and Vice-President Walter Mondale. Carter was the first candidate from the deep south to win since the Civil War.

The average household income was about $16,000.00 and the cost of a new home was approximately $43,000.00. Inflation was soaring, and the top songs were "Best of My Love," by The Emotions, "Float On" by the Floaters, and "Got to Give it Up" by Marvin Gaye, and Shalamar's "Uptown Festival" medleys were the top R & B hits.

Top TV shows in 1976-1977 were Happy Days, Sanford and Son, Good Times, What's Happening, and The Jeffersons. The stamps cost 15 cents. The Roots TV mini-series based on Alex Haley's 1976 novel was aired on ABC in January 1977.

With all that was going on in the world, I do know that my dad had recently retired from the military a few years before my arrival at Rider, and he was working three jobs to make ends meet. His specific instructions to me as the family dropped me off at Rider, "I am proud of you. I want you to have fun." Those last few words came with a stern menacing Mike Tyson look that said "don't" forget why you are here, to earn a college degree. We have chosen to invest in you as part of the family plan to achieve a higher standard of life."

Attending Rider College in 1976, during the Bicentennial year, was a life-changing experience. I entered Rider as a young boy and left as a young adult positioned to take my place in the world as a military officer. And four years after stepping foot on campus as a student, I became the first male in my family to earn a Bachelor of Science in management in August of 1980. In 1989, I earned a Master of Business Administration in Management from Golden Gate University, based in San Francisco, California.

Rider University Undergraduate – Significant Persons of Influence on my Education Journey

My College Roommate, Brother, and Friend - Todd (T.K.) Murray

I decided to attend Rider for three reasons: receipt of an NCAA Division I scholarship offer to an in-state college (one of the best business schools on the East Coast). Also, my choice aligned with the goal I expressed to my dad, to become a businessman like Earl Graves. The third influence, there were several classmates from Neptune High already in attendance at Rider (Garry "Moe" Keel, Rudy "Allen" Johnson, and Todd T.K. Murray).

Garry (eh Moe Keel, class of 78) was a friend to all, highly respected, and a role model for many who attended Neptune High School and then at Rider. Johnson, my teammate from the high school championship wrestling team and good friend, became another "guardian angel" at Rider. When I arrived, he was already a sophomore who had completed his first year at the school. Rudy shared and showed proven practices and strategies that helped me successfully transition to college. I was a good student who listened and heeded his advice on what he suggested. As a result, I did not spend much time trying to figure out by trial and error what best practices were, nor freelancing on how to survive a rigorous first year at a predominantly white college. In addition, he provided helpful guidance that helped identify fair and reasonable professors and which professors to stay away from. This allowed me to select a well-balanced, manageable course load while adjusting to a rigorous academic environment as a student-athlete.

My "brother from another mother," Todd was my college roommate for the last three years. We both graduated from Neptune High as student-athletes and shared the same mindset for maintaining a positive attitude; never quit, and you can always do better no matter your circumstance. Although our experiences in the late '70s and early '80s at Rider weren't always kind nor gentle at times, we learned that all people, regardless of skin color, can do better because we know better! Message for today's youth, stop making excuses, change your attitude, and focus on what you can control – giving your best effort! At Rider, we learned so much about ourselves, resiliency, and positive attitude, and above all, we learned to value relationships and authentic friendships.

In addition to being a student-athlete, my college career included extracurricular activities such as the Reserve Officers Training Corps, (ROTC), which provided extracurricular activities on the weekend to train college students for future service in the U.S. Military. I learned so much about myself participating and providing leadership in extracurricular activities such as intramural sports from basketball and flag football to campus organizations such as Gentlemen Dedicated to Business (G.D.B.) and Third World Organization. I also participated in ushering in entertainment for Black and multicultural students and Black Greeks, specifically the Iota Gamma Chapter of Omega Psi Phi Fraternity, Inc.

Again, my college experience was a "game changer" that changed my life's trajectory. I learned so much from the maturation process on so many levels. I always learned to strive to do my best in all assignments, and no matter what the perceived obstacles may have been at any time, to give a winning effort. I also learned that when you're faced with challenges, barriers, or obstacles, find a way to overcome them, find a way to "see it through," and pursue the best course of action for a favorable long-term outcome in life.

I learned to incorporate the serenity prayer as a part of my being, *"to accept things I cannot change and courage to change the things I can and the wisdom to know the difference."* This prayer I share with students who cross my path. I encourage my mentees when they are up against trouble, challenges, and uncertainties that surely will come their way always to do their best, display a positive attitude, and trust God to do the rest!

The good Lord is indeed a provider! He had always provided guardian angels who impacted my life and helped me through difficulties, giving directions when there seemed no way. I am grateful and blessed to have a circle of friends that supported, encouraged, challenged, pushed, and desired the best for each other. These lifelong friends provided a supportive network, relationships, and connections that helped each other succeed, survive, and thrive in an environment that was difficult for many African American students. These persons were difference makers and helped shape my life in a critical season!

RIDER CAMPUS CORNER IS DEDICATED TO
THE HONORABLE LAWSON R. MCELROY

The picture above is from Saturday, June 10, 2017. That day it celebrated the 40th Anniversary of Omega Psi Phi Fraternity, Inc., on the campus of Rider College (University). The 40th Anniversary included reuniting with friends, a celebration recognition breakfast, and a tree planting and bench dedication ceremony in the name of the Honorable Lawson R. McElroy. It was wonderful to renew lifelong friendships.

The Honorable Lawson R. McElroy (now resting in Omega Chapter) was the most influential person at Rider. He single-handedly was responsible for increasing the diversity of Black and Hispanic minority students attending Rider in the early '70s. Lawson was the "Guardian Angel" who changed the trajectory for so many first-generation and underrepresented students with endless opportunities. He ushered in the first Omega line at the school named "Five to Survive," where

Omega men were known for their work in the community in and around Trenton, New Jersey.

Anyone who attends college understands the transformative experience has on a person's life of adjusting from high school to a higher education environment. To my readers, at the heart of UCF's purpose in mentoring students is the following message. First, no one can achieve anything significant by themselves – it takes teamwork!

Be intentional to surround yourself with winners, those positive people who want to see you win. Second, a college education changes your life. Even if you attend college part-time, each course experience and interaction with your professor and peers shape who you become. And if you are blessed enough, you gain valuable knowledge imparted by a professor; you gain a mentor guide and encourage you to achieve your fullest potential resulting in a better version of yourself. Attending college transforms your life quality whether you attend for a semester, four semesters, or long enough to complete a degree. Your life will be forever different!

Rider University Undergraduate – Significant Persons of Influence on my Educational Journey

I learned to put into practice what I heard many times from my parents, coaches, and mentors; surround yourself with those who make you believe in yourself and know that you can achieve greatness. Surround yourself with those who want to improve and improve themselves. Surround yourself with those who strive to achieve something more significant and those who push you to be better to raise your standard to a higher level. I share with our young people the importance of selecting your friends wisely. I ask them to "tell me your top five friends and I will show you your future." I also tell them, "show me your grade point average and I will tell you your future." We all should encourage students to take their education seriously.

A GAME CHANGER'S PURSUIT

LEGACY AND LASTING IMPACT

The Honorable Lawson R. McElroy (pictured above) left a legacy and a huge impression on many. He was placed at Rider for "such a time" to be a "guardian angel," not only for me but for several first-generation college students who are forever indebted. We affectionately called him "Mac," and there are just so many stories told and untold about the effect Lawson's life had on them. As a young man, he was an advisor, mentor, and friend who modeled Black Excellence throughout his life, especially during the decades of the '70s and '80s. I cannot begin to describe his colossal footprint, and all his good deeds that left an impression on so many people. He literally and figuratively transformed the lives of thousands of students, regardless of ethnicity across New Jersey. He believed in one race, humanity! His legacy lives on in the many lives he touched, as we experienced Mac's love and saw goodness put into action. His love continues as we emulate what he did for us. God called him to change the world by shaping the lives of future generations.

Lawson single-handedly was responsible for increasing the diversity of students at Rider College, changing the fortunes of underrepresented students by providing copious opportunities to obtain a college degree.

He recruited across New Jersey, going into economically depressed communities, high schools, recreation centers, and parks from the inner city to the suburban communities. Lawson provided social and emotional assistance, and financial aid pathways, and wisely advised so many first-generation students that otherwise would not have been able to have a college experience.

Surrounded by alumni supporters, Kathy McElroy, and Rider President Gregory Dell'Amo.

While serving at Rider as the Assistant Director of Financial Aid and Admissions from 1974 until 1985, Lawson earned his Juris Doctor from Seton Hall University Law School. He was an extraordinary man who was an example for so many. He opened his law practice, became prosecutor in New Jersey's capital city of Trenton, and was later appointed a Municipal Court Judge; a position he would later retire from. Lawson left a huge blueprint for living a life of excellence that many have emulated. We saw Lawson live his creed by putting good into action, we saw humility and compassion, we saw him treating others with respect and dignity, and always providing uplift and positive guidance towards all students. He always had a golden nugget as you crossed his path; I remember the poem entitled, *"Excuses are tools of the incompetent, They build monuments of nothingness. Those who choose to use them seldom amount to anything."* This poem with a powerful message was etched in the minds of students that knew the Honorable Lawson R. McElroy *(Omega Chapter, Omega Psi Phi Fraternity, Inc.).*

He passed away on September 9, 2013, and the alums established an Endowment Fund that provides educational opportunities to African-Americans and students of color —leaving a legacy of service through Omega Psi Phi Fraternity, Inc., Rider University, and the surrounding community.

A few years ago, my life seemed to come full circle. Thirty-eight years after graduating in 1980, I was nominated by colleagues, peers, and friends (Terry and Wanda Rogers, and Dr. Keel) to receive the first-ever award that honored the legacy of Judge McElroy.

On Saturday, June 9, 2018, at the annual Rider Reunion, I was honored to receive the first Lawson R. McElroy Alumni Award for Engaged Learning, (picture above). This was a humble honor to be the first recipient of this permanent alumni award. It is now given every year to a deserving Rider Alumnus who exhibits the same attributes that Lawson shared and supported in engaging and encouraging young people to reach their fullest potential. It is for any Rider alumnus or alumna who has demonstrated extraordinary leadership, dedication, and commitment to students and career development. The person must work in either the private or public sector to support students or employees learning outside the formal classroom.

The words on the award citation that touched my heart and soul today read: "He honors himself and the legacy. We are pleased to present Donald Williams II with the 2018 Lawson R. McElroy Award in Engaged Learning at the Alumni Awards Ceremony." I try to live each day to the standard of excellence that my mentor and friend established for so many. In addition to the annual award, a conference room named after Judge McElroy was completed in the newly built

Center for Diversity and Inclusion in the Bart Luedeke Center. I am proud to be a part of the Rider – Rider for Life alumni!

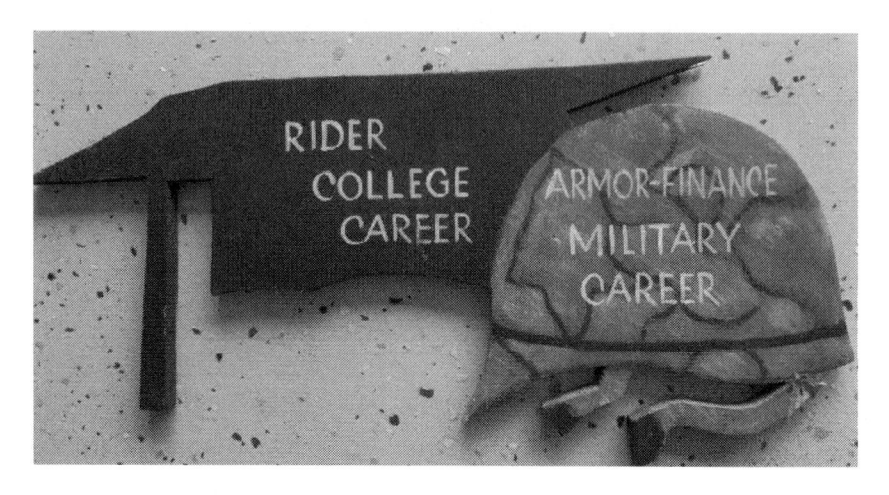

QUOTE:

"I shall pass this way but once, any good that I can do or any kindness I can show to any human being; let me do it now. Let me not defer nor neglect it, for I shall not pass this way again."

— Etienne de Grellet

SCRIPTURE:

[11] "For I know the plans I have for you," says the Lord. "They are plans for good and not for disaster, to give you a future and a hope. [12] In those days when you pray, I will listen. [13] If you look for me wholeheartedly, you will find me."

Jeremiah 29:11-13: New Living Translation

CHAPTER 5

Mona Senreka (Hodges) Williams: My Nubian Queen

"Whatever you've done so far is not enough."
— President Barack Obama

Two of my favorite passages are the perfect introduction to this chapter. **Proverbs 18:22,** "He who finds a wife finds a good thing and obtains favor from the Lord." The second passage is **Proverbs 31:28,** "her children arise up, and call her blessed; her husband also, and he praises her." Every time I hear this passage, I think about my wife. To honor someone means you care deeply about and respect them for she is more precious than jewels.

The most precious gift in my life is being Mona's husband, Dad to my two daughters, and Poppy to our two grandchildren. Mona is my crown's diamond with grace, beauty, inner strength, intelligence, and wisdom. She fulfilled a lifetime of unconditional love and made me a better man. Born in Spring Lake, North Carolina, we share core values from the same humble beginnings and upbringing in North Carolina, yet we went around the world to meet! That's why it's <u>crystal</u> clear that God directed our paths to intersect in a foreign land. Our meeting was no accident; rather — more specific than anything else—it was indeed the good Lord that brought us together in 1984. I believe " fate " brought us together as God set motion a predetermined course of events thousands of miles away from our home state in a little country town called Ansbach, Germany. I was working at my duty station and serving my country, looking forward to returning to the stateside. Mona was a federal government employee on assignment as the Central Accounting Officer for Moral Welfare Support, supporting the 1st Armored Division. As divine providence would have it, we were married two years after we met.

She has been my lifelong partner as a wife for 37 years, mother to our two lovely two adult daughters, Mrs. Deidra Long and Dr. Dreka Williams, and grandmother to our two sweet grandchildren. Nothing makes Mona and I prouder than watching our daughters grow into the incredible people they are becoming.

Mona has been an exemplary model for our daughters—leading by example— as a strong, intelligent person whose life was shaped by humble beginnings. Hailing from Spring Lake just outside Fort Bragg, North Carolina. Mona was raised by her grandparents who lived in Spring Lake while transforming from segregated schools to her family, being the first to attend an integrated school.

Mona is an overcomer who survived despite the tremendous obstacles that crossed her path. From an early age, she learned how to face and manage the challenges of integration, cross barriers, build relationships and get along with others from different nationalities.

From the very start, she has been an integral part of the maturation of the mentoring organization that recognized the need to expose at-risk youth to opportunities they may not otherwise have. She has used her unique interpersonal gifts to connect with everyone. Our signature heart logo was designed and hand-drawn by Mona to represent the branding of Unity Christian Fellowship, Incorporated (UCF) in the community.

She has a kind, understanding heart that allows her to relate to many people from all walks of life. Mona encourages young people to maintain their trust in leading a life based on the teachings of God—no matter what obstacles or perils they may face! Back in Spring Lake, lots of community problems were solved around the kitchen table. She often tells young people, "if you are the smartest person in your group, get a new group."

She continues this family tradition today by cultivating young people around the kitchen table at our monthly youth engagement meetings. And now—because of the COVID health crisis –via our "new normal" virtual meetings. She is affectionately called "Mommy Two" and "Mother" by many young people from the community who have sat at our kitchen table to receive counseling.

She has been by my side throughout my adult life, where she shared the successes and challenges of a military and federal government career, a college and AAU (Amateur Athletic Union) basketball coaching career and my journey into becoming a community leader in Montgomery County.

My wife and I taught our daughters about love, that love will always prevail over hate. To love your neighbor as yourself. We taught them that everyone would not love them as their parents love them. They will not love you because of your skin color, intelligence, brilliance, and the threat of your great potential and what you do. Love is like a light in a dark room that will shine brightly. We modeled love and faith through actions, so they knew what it looked like. We showed them what love feels like, so they recognize it. What is needed now more than ever before is love in the world.

We instilled in our daughters an exceptional work ethic and emphasized that God has placed greatness inside them. It's their responsibility to cultivate and develop their gifts to the fullest. We believe that God has a specific assignment that He gives everyone for a designated time to be used to glorify Him in His kingdom. Their job is to let no one outwork them—no one who is dead, alive, or yet born. No one can deny your performance; outwork them in all undertakings. Everyone must purposely work smarter, not harder, and use their intelligence to work through the process or assignment.

I always say, "can anything good come from a little town," and Mona is an example. We are so proud of Mona for letting God use her strengths for balancing family responsibilities and her love for her sorority, Delta Sigma Theta Sorority, Inc. God has gifted her with the "it" factor. If you have met her, you have seen and felt it as she gives 120% of her best self with her love, guidance, and kindness to touch and shape lives that cross her path. God has gifted her with leadership, integrity, grace and dignity at every station, assignment, and position. The "IT" is her ability to focus on the right things at the right time and promote love to improve relationships.

Like me, she loves people and one true thing – she has given her all and everyone the benefit of the doubt—even with "our" folk. And we know sometimes, this isn't exactly the easiest thing to do.

One of her favorite quotes is from Dr. Dorothy Height, the 10th National President of Delta Sigma Theta. "Greatness is not measured by what a man or woman accomplishes, but by the opposition he or she has overcome to reach their goals." What that means on this mentoring journey is that success will not be easy because there will be many barriers that you will have to overcome to achieve it.

In this global pandemic we have already demonstrated that we can overcome barriers because of the adjustments made to navigate virtual platforms daily to learn and conduct business successfully. Mona is committed to teaching and equipping this generation to overcome the challenges faced on the sidewalk to success where there is social injustice, health disparities, inequality, education disparities and other forms of discrimination.

Mona and I are products of the civil rights period where those who fought in the trenches firmly believed that love prevails over hate every time. We believe in promoting peace instead of violence. There are many good people from all walks of life regardless of race, creed, ethnic and religious groups. We are surrounded by those who purpose to do good in all ways, to all souls, in every place, and always to help others.

Dr. Martin Luther King Jr. helped us to think differently about pursuing education and striving for excellence with the gifts and talent one possesses. I am reminded of a particular moment early on my mentoring journey in the church at First African Methodist Episcopal Church of Gaithersburg. One of my mentees was assigned to recite the two greatest Commandments passage (Matthew 22: 34-40). He got a little nervous and stated, "the second is like unto it, Thou shalt love thy neighbor as thyself." Then he said, "thou shalt love your neighborhood." From the look in his eyes, I could tell in that moment he thought he had made a huge mistake. I hugged and assured him that it was okay and whispered in his ear that God does not make mistakes! Our God wants us to love everyone, including folks who didn't look or act like you and didn't grow up in your neighborhood.

UCF is laser-focused on serving students by building partnerships with like-minded people who meet the real needs of children and their families. We are committed to lifting as we climb to work together to increase success stories in the community.

Mona hand-drew the UCF logo below. The colors were deliberately selected to reflect our focused belief, values, and walk with Christ. Taken from the Rainbow Bible, UCF colors represent the following:

Yellow — family, marriage, children

Ephesians 5:3`, "For this reason a man will leave his father and mother and be united to his
wife, and the two will become one flesh."

Green — love, joy, and kindness

1 John 4:7, "Dear friends, let us love one another, for love comes from God. Everyone who loves has been born of God and knows God."

Red — discipleship, obedience, and praise

John 12:26, "Whoever serves me must follow me; and where I am, my servant also will be.
My Father will honor the one who serves me."

QUOTE:

"Do all the good we can, in all the ways we can, to all the souls we can, in every place we can and at all the times we can and as long as we can to as many people as we can."

— Anonymous

SCRIPTURE:

"Love your neighbor as yourself into one universal commandment. Jesus says: "You shall love Lord your God with all your heart, soul, mind, strength. This is the greatest commandment. The second is like it. You shall love your neighbor as yourself. On these two commandments hang all the law and the prophets."

Matthew 22: 34 to 40

CHAPTER 6

Military Service and Career —In My Father's Footsteps

"There are no secrets to success! If you are going to achieve excellence in big things, you develop the habit in little matters. Excellence is not an exception; it is a prevailing attitude."

— American Hero Colin Powell

From the onset, let me say there is no higher form of service than volunteering to serve your country in the United States Armed Forces. As you know, a lot is happening this season with the discord in our great country. Even with all that is going on, I pray and thank all those who have answered the call to serve – in all its forms. I pray daily for our military families and members of the Army, Navy, Air Force, Marines, Coast Guard, and Space Force serving daily in harm's way worldwide.

    I am a second-generation military member who's retired from the United States Army. I come from a legacy of service to our great country, with first my father who enlisted in the U.S. Army, and his brother enlisted in U.S. Marines, respectively. My mother's brother Edward Robinson served in the U.S. Coast Guard. I married into a military family, with all of Mona's uncles serving in the Air Force. We are all in; we have lived and breathed service to our nation. I greatly appreciate what the military does and what spouses and families endure daily. I don't know if many people, especially our young people, understand the benefits serving in the military offers.

Again, serving this great country is the highest form of community service. We live in an America where anything is possible, and we can't say that about anywhere else. We live in a country with endless possibilities, and if you are willing to put in the work and give a winning effort to realize your dreams, anything is possible. You can come from nothing, rise above life's circumstances, overcome obstacles, and achieve anything you put your mind and effort into.

I have encountered men and women from all walks of life and nationalities, and there is something about the service member's DNA. A "sense of duty" is crucial where service members live, work, and raise their families. It has been my experience that service members are the first to serve and help in their community. The one thing I learned early on about the military is that if you see a problem, you are obligated to try to fix it, find a better way, and provide a solution. The outcome is to make things better for families and neighborhoods.

As stated earlier, I am my parents' and Father's dream because I followed in his footsteps. My father truly enjoyed serving our country in the United States Army. He loved offering advice and sharing stories from his 21-year career as a Non-Commissioned Officer (NCO) in the Signal Corp (1954 to 1975).

My dad's advice was to consistently raise your hand to volunteer for duty and always perform your best regardless of the assignment. For instance, as a Cadet during the first two bivouac exercises when leadership Cadre asked for K.P. volunteers during the training exercise, I enthusiastically raised my hand high not knowing what K.P. entailed. I remembered my dad's advice and message. Oh my! Etched in my mind forever were the first Bivouac and FTXs.

I learned that the P38 was one of the most valuable tools in the field. A P38 is a can opener to open the canned food served in the field. I still have one on my keychain. Military Bivouacs and FTXs were training exercises designed to provide leaders with memorable experiences to boost individual and team confidence, create a readiness mindset, learn first aid, basic skills, and build team camaraderie. My learning was accelerated under field conditions, where I learned K.P. volunteers were for Kitchen Patrol Duty and worked under the kitchen staff. This team was the first to get up early in the morning to prepare meals for soldiers. This was a weeklong duty that also entailed going to bed long after everyone else to ensure the pots and pans were cleaned in preparation for the next day's meals for everyone. I also learned P.T. was Physical Training that occurred daily, every morning before daybreak, consisting of stretching exercises, calisthenics, and always ending with three to five-mile runs in military boots. This created a lifestyle and mindset to maintain healthy bodies and minds.

The G.I. parties my father attended every Friday detailed cleaning the barracks from top to bottom, baseboard to baseboard. Barracks were living quarters that housed soldiers in living facilities, (like college dormitories). As the saying goes, the Army provides "three hots and a cot." The translation means the military offers its members three meals daily, a place to sleep, and excellent training opportunities.

I could go on and on with my experiences. All in all, like my dad, I truly enjoyed serving our country in the U.S. Army.

FIELD TRAINING EXERCISE (FTX) IN FORT RILEY, KANSAS

I earned several awards and decorations as a military officer in two decades: 12 years on active duty, eight years in the Army Reserve, and retired as a Lieutenant Colonel. Many memorable life experiences shaped the maturation process of who I am as the effective community leader you know today.

Throughout my military career, I have been blessed to work and learn from some of the world's most dynamic leaders across the country, shaping my servant leadership style. I have learned organizational effectiveness by assessing the organizational environment, command climate, listening, and identifying critical skills, abilities and knowledge that affected and impacted positive change. A key life lesson I learned and now share with the readers of this book, whatever your assignment, perform the best that you can, no matter the assigned job. To drive home the point, I remember the recruiting slogan of the United States Army for 20 years was "Be All You Can Be."

Again, do your best in your job in all assignments. I have always tried to leave all assignments better than when I found them. I took what I inherited and built upon it to improve the organization and its members. Another tremendous benefit I received while serving in the military was meeting, working, and serving with all ethnic nationalities from across the globe. In the military, your ethnicity and race don't matter, what matters is a shared sense of purpose for the team, organization, and community in which you live and work.

I began my military career as a Reserve Officers Training Corps (ROTC) program member at Rider College, (Rider University). In May 1980, upon graduation, I was commissioned as a Second Lieutenant in the Armor Branch where I spent my first two years. After completing the Armored Officer Basic Course at Fort Knox, Kentucky, I was assigned to my first duty station, Fort Carson, Colorado, as a Platoon Leader.

Although I served 20 years overall, your first assignment always stands out as the most unforgettable experience in your life. The first assignment is the one you measure and judge all assignments against. I discovered my self-worth, developed higher confidence, and what today's young people call "manhood swag."

In the spring of 1981, I reported to scenic Fort Carson, nestled in the Rocky Mountains. I woke up every day viewing Pikes Peak and Cheyenne Mountain. The blue sky appeared so close as if you could reach up and touch it. The weather was beautiful for most of the day. I soon learned that if you wait 10 minutes, the weather will change instantly from sunshine to a foot of snow or even hailstorms or rain in a moment. Folks would say, "just go with the flow."

This was a similar saying that I grew up with as an army brat, "roll with the punches," meaning to keep moving forward. It also refers to my belief that the dreams that God put in you will not come to pass without opposition and speed bumps.

I reported to my assigned unit as a Platoon Leader, Alpha Company, 4th Battalion, 40th Armor, 4th Infantry Division (Mechanized), Fort Carson. My first Company Commander's name was Captain Peter

B. Marion who was a builder of men leaders. Standing 6-foot-4 with blue eyes, he had such a presence, and his favor says we "Soldiering is a Contact Sport." He was a West Point graduate with a great strategic tactician's mind for battle planning and warfighting. He was highly competitive with the outcome of being first in every mission from tank qualifications, health and welfare of our soldiers, all inspections, weapon cleanings, and yes, G.I. parties.

My first meeting with the Company Commander and First Sergeant was memorable. The Company Commander assigned me as the 2nd Platoon Leader with approximately 25 soldiers and five tanks. He shared the 3rd Brigade and Battalion's historical background, leadership expectations, chain of command, and organizational structure.

As I recalled, the immediate blessing of the assignment to Alpha Company was the organization's composition, which included a diverse demographic. Alpha Company had three unique Second Lieutenants with different backgrounds: Second Lieutenant Michael Smith, an Officer Candidate School (OCS) graduate was the senior Platoon Leader who graduated from Morgan State University in Baltimore, Maryland. He enlisted first in the Army and then became an officer by completing OCS. He was the senior platoon leader and was promoted shortly upon my arrival. Then there was Second Lieutenant Carl Vroman, a graduate of West Point, and me, the youngest officer who represented the Reserve Officers' Training Corp (ROTC).

Again, God surrounded me with guardian angels who had my best interest at heart and showed me the way as a Combat Arms Officer, specifically Second Lieutenant Smith and fellow Second Lieutenant Les Wilkerson from California. They were the only Black officers in the Battalion.

The conversation with the First Sergeant was different. In addition to discussing that my assigned NCO was the Senior Platoon Sergeant in the company, he shared the 60-day training plan including two

A GAME CHANGER'S PURSUIT

field exercises, formation times and his military experience. The First Sergeant's message started with the statement: "Sir, you can't get rich, and you can't stay in the Army! Sir, you can't plan on becoming rich because of the consistent monthly payday. Sir, you can't stay because circumstances might dictate your departure. If you make bad decisions, if we go to war and become a casualty and if life's priority changes." He added, "When it is time for your service to end, you cannot stay in the Army!"

His message as I understood at the time translated into the following three life lessons:

1. No person should be satisfied or comfortable with where they are in their station in life.
2. Make good decisions because one wrong decision can alter your life. Your crew, posse, and friends you surround yourself with can be detrimental and the group decisions can change your life forever!
3. Tragedies or significant emotional events can change whom you become and derail your dreams and what you worked hard to achieve, thus, shifting your priorities.

BRIGADIER GENERAL COLIN POWELL

One of my memorable experiences was the honor of serving with then Brigadier General Colin L. Powell, Assistant Division Commander (ADC), for operations and training. The first experience occurred during a field training exercise (FTX) downrange in the foothills of Colorado. General Powell observed our simulated tactical battle. I will always remember when he came to the battle position where I was leading my tank platoon on tactical maneuvers just as we achieved the objective.

I dismounted from my tank and saluted him. As he reminded me not to salute in the field, the following words blew me away. He complimented me on the tactical warfighting leadership and team building that he witnessed. He shared a golden nugget of wisdom always to take care of the troops, and they will take care of you. Wow! The affirmation from General Powell was huge! That meant a lot to a young Second Lieutenant learning to be a warfighter.

Another memorable experience as a young officer occurred at a formal dining-in where I served on behalf of the Brigade as Mr. Vice (picture above). The dining-in is a traditional formal dinner for members of a military organization. Mr. Vice, as it is affectionately referred to, is assigned to the youngest officer in the unit and serves as one of the key planners for the formal dinner and making toasts.

At that time, I had the privilege of presenting then Brigadier General Powell an award citation on behalf of the Command. As you have read in the history books, he became the first African American to be Chairman of the Joint Chiefs of Staff (1989-1993) and Secretary of State (2001-2005).

Another life lesson I learned in the military is that no one ever made it to the top of their professional career by never getting into trouble. I share this moment of my encounter with Colonel Robert G. Muscatelli, the Brigade Commander, who taught me a valuable life lesson about decision-making. It is amazing that I still remember his name, perhaps because he left an indelible impression on me.

A GAME CHANGER'S PURSUIT

I was running late for the morning formation roll call. I made a poor decision to park close to the Alpha Company area in an unauthorized parking area designated for Commanders only. On this particular day, guess whose inspection team conducted a random inspection of the company area and found my Privately Owned Vehicle (POV) parked? I intended to move the car after the completion of the formation. I drew unwelcome attention to my entire chain of Command, including my Battalion Commander, Sergeant Major, Company Commander, and First Sergeant, to meet the new Brigade Commander, who possessed an intimidating reputation.

In addition, my decision caused embarrassment that reflected poorly on the entire chain of Command because the Brigade Commander viewed this as a failure of leadership.

Although the length of my punishment was excessive, the message sent was clear that a new commander was in town. My punishment was to conduct inspections of the parking area to ensure no unauthorized POVs were parked in the "Commander" designated parking areas every four hours, including weekends, for two months. I persevered and couldn't wait for the two-month life lesson on "leadership responsibility" to end! As a mentor, my students have often heard my departing message after our embrace and handshake. I always say, "make good decisions and choices."

As a Combat Arms Platoon Leader, I was entrusted with meaningful leadership responsibilities right out of college. These experiences early on served as a launching pad for mentorship and helping others navigate life's challenges. I was responsible for high-value resources such as five M60A1 Tanks and associated equipment. I was responsible for the lives of countless soldiers who were high school graduates of different nationalities and ages, just starting their lives as young adults. They looked to me as their leader, mentor, coach, and a person to give proper advice. I learned early on that leadership is about solving problems. The day soldiers stop bringing you their problems is when you stop leading them.

I learned that soldiers love to win! They want to be part of a successful team. They respect a leader who stands with them under all circumstances and a leader who holds them to a higher standard, and pushes them to achieve what they didn't think was possible to accomplish

meaningful objectives. My leadership was about finding ways to reach down and touch the hearts and minds of everyone in the platoon. I had some soldiers with behavior challenges and bad attitudes, which were undisciplined but were excellent under field conditions. And yes, I would go to war with them any day.

As a leader, it's your responsibility to make each person feel valued, a part of something larger than themselves, the team, and the staff. The organization comes first, similar to being a squad, platoon, battalion, or brigade member! Leaders are responsible for creating a winning team everyone feels a part of.

The warfighting training, I received was an outstanding experience. Three weeks of each month were spent either in gunnery-qualified training to become an expert tank gunner or downrange honing tactical and leadership skills and learning to operate as a fighting team. Training

was second to none, from attending Armor Basic Course at Fort Knox, being a Combat Platoon Leader learning armor tactics from a skilled tactician in Captain Marion, working collaboratively with the other platoon leaders, other support units, and the seasoned, dynamic Non-Commissioned Officers (NCO) in the maintenance motor pool during monthly FTXs exercises, gunnery firing ranges, road marches, competing in unit sports to learning Armor tactics in the Mojave Desert in California.

Shortly after being promoted to First Lieutenant, approximately two years into my military career, I applied for a branch transfer. The branch transfer request had to be approved by my chain of Command, who knew me quite well enough. I was surprised to learn that this was an earnest request that had to be signed off by the first General in the chain of Command! As a result, I met Brigadier General Collin Powell personally in his office for a closed-door advisement session.

Although I was as nervous as one can be to meet a General Officer up close and in person, I believed this was the right thing to advance my career as a military officer. With the meeting scheduled, I practiced my salute before reporting to General Powell, wondering how this meeting would turn out. The wait was so nerve-racking, as I recall!

General Powell served with grace, dignity, and devotion to service, reflecting that leadership must be about something greater than yourself. I was blessed to have several personal encounters with General Powell at Fort Carson. Another memorable encounter occurred, as mentioned earlier, at a formal dining-in. There were other encounters, but the one that left a footprint on my life was a closed-door meeting when I requested a branch transfer from Armor Branch to the Finance Corps.

A good friend who served as the Aid-to-Camp to General Powell provided excellent advice on reporting before I met with him. He told me to make sure that I reported early to his office. After he announced my presence to the General, he added that I should knock on the office door and listen for him to tell me to come in. Once I entered his office, I should then walk three feet and stop in front of his desk and render a proper salute and wait until the General dropped his salute first, then wait for instructions.

I remember it like yesterday; he had such a commanding presence and voice. After saluting, I heard the next words, "Lieutenant, please close the door." Again, my reaction was, "oh my God." He asked what was my "why," and I provided a well-rehearsed response that connected to why I attended Rider University, one of the best business colleges on the east coast. My branch selection was to serve in finance, personal or medical careers. I was surprised that his consultation was so uplifting as he encouraged me to become the best officer, I can support the warfighters when they seek financial support. I will always have fond memories of Fort Carson, developing leadership skills, and meeting Brigadier General Powell, who approved my branch transfer request (I would cross paths with him in Germany later). I left Fort Carson with a renewed sense and clear purpose to pursue excellence as a Finance Officer.

I also ran into General Powell when he served as Secretary of State (2001-2005). I adopted the General's three rules as guideposts for my life. First, in an officer's call, he shared that a part of his philosophy was to focus on outcomes, meaning that a comprehensive strategic plan

must encompass an entrance and exit plan. This included implied tasks with a detailed checklist – check the small things!

Second, as a mentor, you must have a vision, be able to express optimism, and demonstrate a positive attitude and consistent effort – the marks of a Force Multiplier! Third, surround yourself with compassionate people with a heart to serve beyond what they think they can – these people are called winners!

Paying tribute to an American Treasure
– General Colin L. Powell

A GAME CHANGER'S PURSUIT

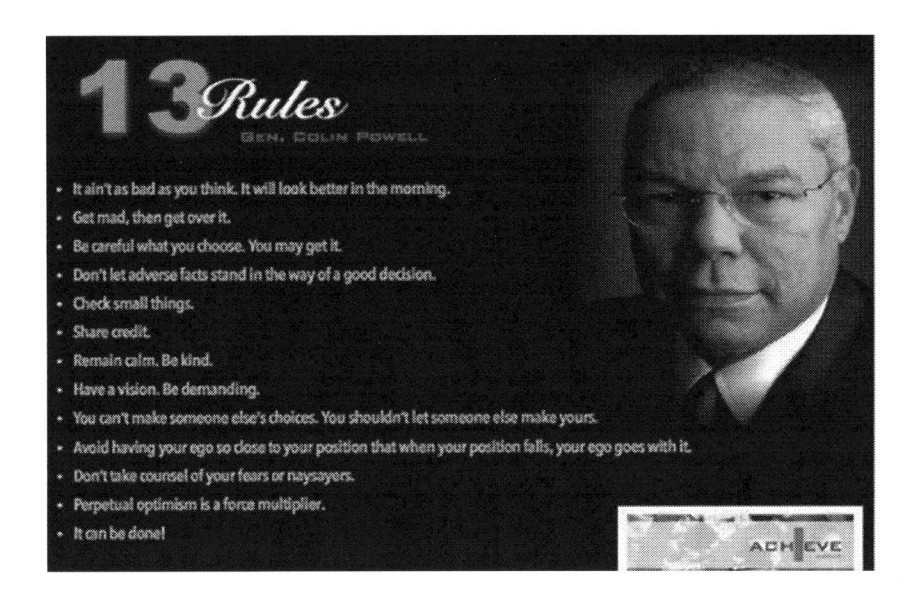

13 Rules
GEN. COLIN POWELL

- It ain't as bad as you think. It will look better in the morning.
- Get mad, then get over it.
- Be careful what you choose. You may get it.
- Don't let adverse facts stand in the way of a good decision.
- Check small things.
- Share credit.
- Remain calm. Be kind.
- Have a vision. Be demanding.
- You can't make someone else's choices. You shouldn't let someone else make yours.
- Avoid having your ego so close to your position that when your position falls, your ego goes with it.
- Don't take counsel of your fears or naysayers.
- Perpetual optimism is a force multiplier.
- It can be done!

What a privilege to have served with a trailblazer and role model who was proud to live the American Dream as an immigrant. He cherished the opportunity to serve with the common purpose of making lives better for all Americans.

On Monday morning, October 18, 2021, I woke up to breaking news that General Powell had passed away from complications of COVID-19. Once again experienced the heart-wrenching news that another great American servant departed Mother Earth. It felt like a hard punch to my mid-section. When people talk about great Americans with integrity and leaders who achieved great things in so many key positions, they talk about General Powell. Like my dad, he was a Vietnam vet. He also was the first General who looked like me, who rose to four-star General, the irst Black Chairman of the Joint Chiefs of Staff, national security adviser, and one-time Secretary of State whom Americans and our allies trusted.

He was such a model of excellence in every way at every level and was a role model for so many. You need not look far for a trailblazer and American hero who was allowed to rise to heights based on performance, intelligence, high character, and reputation for being a problem solver. As a young officer trying to find my way, this is what servant leadership looked like and I wanted to emulate it as I moved along in my career.

In 1982, after completing the Finance Officer Basic Course at Fort Benjamin Harrison, Indiana the home of the Finance Corp, I was assigned to the 1st Armor Division in Germany. In the first 18 months of a three-year tour, I served at my first Finance and Accounting Office in Nuremberg, the second largest city in southern Germany, (after Munich), had a full staff of finance officers.

In the second half of the tour, a position became available to serve as Deputy Finance Officer in Ansbach under the leadership of Major General Crosbie E. Saint. This was an excellent career move in so many ways that spurred my personal growth and development as a Finance Officer. I was soon promoted to Captain and supported the Finance Account Holder by providing leadership for the finance operation.

I was involved in several community activities, including payday operations, office automation implementation, Reforger support, town hall meetings, community festivals, and unit sporting teams. I even served as a high school assistant wrestling coach who trained and coached a European champion. This was a great experience as I developed my leadership skills, where lifelong relationships were cultivated among approximately 65 soldiers who supported combat commanders and soldiers in three communities (Crailsheim, Illesheim and Ansbach).

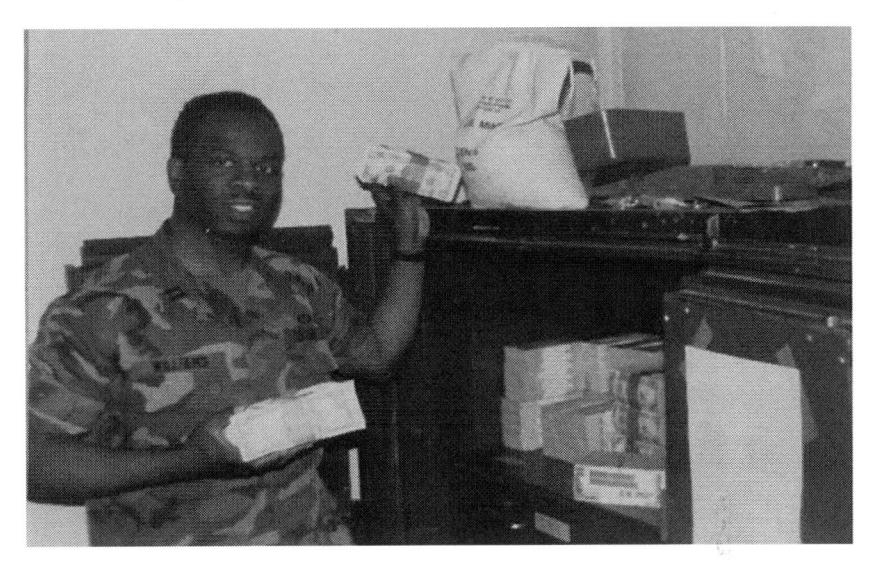

THIS IS WHAT A MILLION DOLLARS LOOKS LIKE IN A VAULT!

My primary focus at the end of the three-year tour was returning to the States. However, something unexpected happened along the way. I met my soulmate, Mona. She was serving as a civilian in the federal government hired by the Finance Account Holder, Major George B. Morton, who was excited to introduce us. I was the Disbursement Officer for the 17th Area Finance Support Command in Ansbach.

In 1986, I returned to the home of the Finance Corp at Fort Benjamin Harrison to attend Finance Officer Advanced Course, followed by successful Airborne training at Fort Benning. This set in motion a wonderful uplifting, life-changing experience in many ways.

I was excited to be assigned to the premier military installation, Fort Bragg, the Home of the 82nd Airborne Division, the primary fighting arm of the XVIII Airborne Corps. In addition, the military installation was near Mona's hometown of Spring Lake. We were married there on August 16, 1986, in a double wedding, joining Mona's grandparents, who renewed their marriage vows on their 50th anniversary. We enjoyed a wonderful planning season and wedding day like no other, witnessed by our closest friends and family nearby.

In the first two years, I was assigned as a Budget Officer for the 525th Military Intelligence Brigade, which I enjoyed immensely due to the unit's real-time mission. I had a great, technically knowledgeable staff motivated to work together as a team. I was a staff officer on a high-performing headquarters staff under the dynamic leadership of a Brigade Commander, Colonel Patterson. I had completed two years of exceptional leadership, as reflected on two outstanding officer's evaluation reports, with approximately two years from the Major promotion board for my year group.

525TH MILITARY INTELLIGENCE BRIGADE LEADERSHIP TEAM

At the time, things aligned on all fronts, and life was good in many ways, personally, professionally, and spiritually. These were indeed the best of times! We purchased our first property, a lake-view townhouse, in a new development. We fell in love with the Cosby Show sitcom, which led to buying our first pet dog, a Chow Chow breed. We named the pet after the Cosby Show character Kenny, who played Rudy Huxtable's friend (nicknamed "Bud"). So, we named our dog "Budd" with the extra letter d. Mona loved that dog so much (that's another story)!

Our first child Deidra was born in July 1987, and it was a special moment for Mona's grandparents, who provided childcare for our baby daughter. We were committed to using our time wisely during this military assignment to pursue scholarship aspirations. I attended night school and completed my MBA from Golden Gate University, and Mona dedicated herself to passing the CPA Exam to become a Certified Public Accountant. In addition, I was initiated into the greatest fraternity known to humankind, The Omega Psi Phi Fraternity, Inc., on May 6, 1989, Beta Chi Chapter in Fayetteville, North Carolina.

Military careers are based on performance reflected in the annual Officer Efficiency Report (OER). I was a senior Captain with an outstanding officer performance record preparing for the next promotion board for my year group (15 months). My experience at Fort Bragg changed suddenly with a reassignment to the Finance and Accounting Office. I made an ill-advised decision to seek reassignment to my primary specialty with the Corps Finance and Accounting Office. At the time, without a mentor, having an OER that reflected an assignment in my technical specialty would solidify promotion to the rank of Major. I learned that having a mentor makes a significant difference in your life journey.

I had my eyes on positioning myself for the promotion board. I served in my secondary specialty excellently as a Budget Officer with two outstanding OERs. I initiated and sorted counsel with Colonel David Parrish, the account holder and Commander of the Finance and Accounting Office that supported the XVIII Airborne Corps. The office was an integrated operation with civilians and military soldiers who worked as a team to ensure soldiers were paid on time. Colonel Parrish worked out a successful reassignment where I was well received for the first 14 months (April 1988 to June 1989) as Chief of Pay and Examination.

Peggy Smith, the deputy finance, and accounting officer was my first civilian rater with many years of service coming up through the civilian ranks. I performed exceptionally based on all performance indicators, leadership, annual inspections, and timeliness reports. In our weekly meeting updates, she affirmed that my performance exceeded her expectations and was pleased with my service-oriented and team-building leadership style.

This position suited my performance-oriented leadership style and technical abilities gained in Germany. Things were going well based on exceeding all performance metrics, internal reviews and keeping the civilian deputy informed every step of the way.

Approximately two months after the verbal evaluation performance, things took a drastic downturn because of philosophical differences with the civilian rater. I found myself attacked with an all-out effort to marginalize, diminish, and minimize my exceptional data-driven performance during the rating period.

The first civilian promotion opportunity in many years occurred right before my OER was due. My responsibility was to improve the organization and fill the position with the best-qualified candidate. My civilian supervisor assured me that the promotion decision was all mine, and I didn't have to worry about her influencing the decision. I took her at her word.

I had to choose between two knowledgeable women who had worked in the finance office for over 20 years. One demonstrated her personal sacrifice by attending night school for self-improvement to earn a college degree.

The other was an equally hard-working woman who did not invest in self-improvement. I was unaware of an outside personal relationship between my civilian rater and one of the candidates. I decided to promote the best qualified person to the GS7 position who invested in her education, made personal sacrifices, and served the finance office wholeheartedly.

That is when all the questionable practices began, and I reaped the consequences from the chain of command! My position was a just decision, this was the right decision resulting in me standing my ground and living with the consequences. I experienced character assassination, where my judgment was questioned, and my leadership was undermined.

And the exceptional office performance metrics that were applauded earlier were minimized.

The civilian rater retaliated against me by submitting a poor OER evaluation that immediately derailed my chances for promotion to Major and guaranteed the end of my active-duty career.

Military careers are based on performance and reflected on an annual Officer Efficiency Report. An officer's career and future aspirations depend on the written statements and boxes checked. As one becomes a senior officer, one understands the method used to end careers is

reflected with code words in the narrative evaluation. For example, there are three boxes, one box reads to "promote ahead of peers," another reads "promote with peers," and the third reads "do not promote." Yes, I met with the senior rater, Colonel David Parrish, the account holder and Commander who took no action to change his rating and supported the false civilian rater. I remember that he later apologized, but the damage had already occurred.

As you may have suspected, although race shouldn't have played a role in the selection process, this instance lent itself to speculation that it could have played a significant factor–you be the judge.

I selected the person that put in the work professionally and academically. She was rewarded with the promotion and happened to be African American. The other person in the relationship with the rater happened to be white. If I had to make the decision again, I would maintain my core values and the selection would be based on the merit of the best-qualified person.

This painful experience taught me that unsuccessful people make decisions based on their current situations. Successful people make decisions based on where they want to be in God's Kingdom. Also, decisions become easier when your will to please God outweighs your will to please the world.

It was interesting to note that one of my hero's books, "My American Journey" by General Powell, had a similar experience (located on page 270 of the book). Colonel Parrish's support of the OER didn't reflect my actual performance, and he knew the rating would end my career.

My only recourse was to change duty stations, which took me to Seoul, South Korea. I had one last opportunity to perform at a high level and achieve the outcome of an OER rating that would counter the previous report before the Major promotion board.

Trusting and standing on God's word, I requested a two-year assignment to try to recover with another Officer Evaluation Report (OER) to offset the one I previously received.

I was granted my final overseas assignment to 8th Army, Finance Command located in Seoul under Colonel William Palmer, Commander, Finance and Accounting Command. I took my family to South Korea, which was a tremendous blessing. We made lifelong friendships that remain even to this day. While there, Mona gave birth to our second daughter Dreka Denise, who was born at the Yongsan military installation in Seoul on September 11, 1990.

I was assigned as Chief Pay and Examination Officer by the Finance Accounting Officer, LTC John Paul Jones who I will never forget. After working and excelling under LTC Jones' leadership, (a God-Fearing Christian), I received an outstanding OER, but it wasn't enough to counter the OER from Fort Bragg. I share for the first time my inner-emotional feelings of pain, embarrassment, disappointment, hurt and humiliation for a predicament out of my control. What have I done to deserve this?

Have you ever trusted God? As I race to a corridor of my mind at the time, I believed that God would intervene and turn the situation around to show others in that moment that He's in control and leave others wondering, "what happened – I thought we got him!" So much I wanted to believe that would become an eventual scenario and that I would experience a positive outcome. I will forever hold LTC Jones in high esteem. As my first-line supervisor and rater, he was responsible for the one-on-one counseling session upon receiving the results of the promotion board.

I remember the session like it was yesterday; LTC Jones started the session with the scripture from Roman 8:28. He said, "Captain Williams, I want you to know that all things work together for good to them that love God, to them who are called according to his purpose."

At that moment, I wasn't expecting to hear a familiar scripture. I was puzzled and taken aback by LTC Jones' remarks. What was he telling me? That the positive outcome I'd prayed for had come through? Or was he telling me that no matter how optimistic you are, fair treatment eludes some? Maybe some things are not right, there's no silver lining and sometimes, situations and outcomes outright suck.

As I digested the moment, this Christian officer shared that God is in control even in this moment of disappointment for not being promoted to the Major rank. He shared that God has plans for your life, plans not to harm you but to prosper you so will be prepared for a greater blessing.

You can't comprehend this moment because you are in a place of hurt and pain. God has a greater vision and purpose for your life. This counseling session helped make sense of the painful moment that certainly didn't seem right or just and was unfair. In that moment, my thoughts were to trust in the Lord and let Him lead and guide me, for He reigns from heaven above and is still on the throne!

LTC Jones played a significant role in helping me through this painful time in my life's journey. I recalled him saying, "Captain, you must take the long-term view when it comes to all things working together for your good in His kingdom." He then prayed with me and every day we would meet in his office for a wellness check and share God's moment. I learned as I pressed through to lift my eyes to the hills which cometh my help.

Yes, I asked many of those same questions you would have asked. I felt like the biblical character Job that struggled with the "why of his predicament: God why have you allowed such sadness and hurt to happen to me? What have I done to deserve this? An intentional mean act by Peggy Smith and her leadership team turned into a positive divine redirection. I couldn't see it then, but God uses believers' lives to reveal His glory to show others that your setbacks are connected to a greater divine purpose. God sees your whole life and has something more significant for you in your future. He used this experience to redirect my life for a greater kingdom-building purpose.

Honestly, it was the best and worst of times; God's wisdom prevails with the emotional conflict between love and hate, good and evil intentions, just and unjust. God gives us encouragement to press and move forward. We know that all things work together for the good of those who love God.

How will they know if you've never gone through anything? I learned that God uses you as an example to reveal His glory to someone else of what He can do. Your life experiences have a part to play in someone else's life. I tell you; I don't know where I would be if it had not been for the Lord on my side!

The best times in this South Korea overseas assignment stretched the family to new heights on all levels. Both Mona and I grew together spiritually, professionally, and personally. We were active leaders with the church, our family bond strengthened, and God blessed us with our second child.

In addition, we thoroughly enjoyed being active with our respective Divine Nine organizations and operating in a community where everyone supported each organization. In the two years in Korea, I served as Keeper of Finance for Lambda Xi Chapter of Omega Psi Phi under the leadership of Chapter Basileus S. Earl Wilson, (International Chairman for the Fatherhood Initiative and Mentoring Committee) and more importantly, a lifelong friend.

We saw and experienced the model for community organizations working effectively to support each other's organizations, including The Order of the Eastern Star, the National Pan Hellenic Council, and the church. The goal was to work collaboratively to enhance the overall community experience for families on the island. Mona and I even formed our home-based business, Williams Associated Finance Services (WAFS), where we conducted audits and helped others start their small businesses and provide tax services.

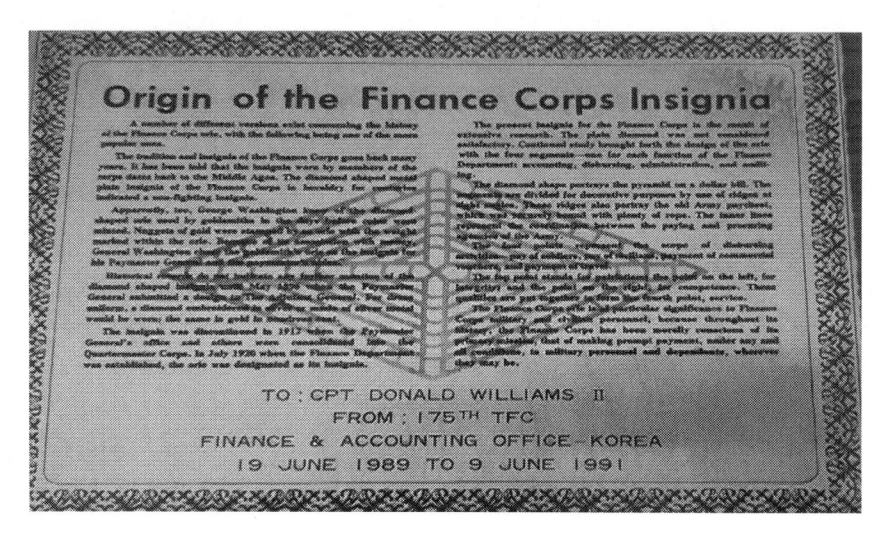

Origin of the Finance Corps Insignia

TO: CPT DONALD WILLIAMS II
FROM: 175TH TFC
FINANCE & ACCOUNTING OFFICE - KOREA
19 JUNE 1989 TO 9 JUNE 1991

I return stateside and was assigned to a beautiful scenic mountainous installation near Camp David, Maryland. The installation was in the western part of the state, nestled in the Catoctin Mountain region, with a golf course in the center of the installation. My last duty installation was at Fort Ritchie, where I transitioned from the Army in August 1992. This was a wonderful assignment where I could travel in support of the command.

Reflecting on my many years of service, it was a blessing to have experienced the best of both worlds serving on active duty and in the Army Reserves. Serving in the Army Reserves was different; however, rewarding, gratifying, and indeed an unexpected blessing where I continued my growth and development as a military leader. My reserve command was the 2122 U.S. Army Garrison Support Unit in Baltimore, Maryland. I was promoted to the rank of Major shortly upon arrival and was placed in a senior-level position responsible for performing management analysis of command activities that included reviews of organization missions, programs, and internal management control to develop a qualitative evaluation. The senior rater provided glowing comments on my potential and checked the top box on the evaluation. I was accustomed to receiving this before the last assignment at Fort Bragg. After three years, I was reassigned to 5115th USAREUR at Fort Meade, Maryland, as Deputy Director of Resource Management.

1999 Promotion with Colonel Michael T. Masnik

In 1999, I was promoted to Lieutenant Colonel and assumed the duties of Director of Resource Management for the command. I was excited to work in a brigade-level position under Colonel Michael T. Masnik, who worked for the same federal government agency as me (U.S. Nuclear Regulatory Commission). My mission was to provide financial service support to the 7th Army Command (7th ARCOM) and mobilize units to support Germany during peacetime operations and wartime deployments.

I was grateful to return to Germany for the annual two-week training at Grafenwohr army installation. I had the opportunity to visit Ansbach, where I met my lovely wife and recalled many other fond memories. I retired as a Lieutenant Colonel in August 2002 after completing 20 years of honorable service to the country.

1984 Visit to "The Berlin Wall" in Germany
The official purpose of this Berlin Wall was to keep so-called Western "fascists" from entering East Germany. The wall represents so many things on so many levels, reshaping the modern world and ideology systematically of keeping people out versus letting people in.

As I reflect on my life and pierce through my spiritual lens, I'm reminded of the early days of the Globe Positioning System (GPS). I understand that God rerouted, reset, and redirected my life's path and destiny for a greater purpose in His kingdom.

I have stopped asking the questions many people ask themselves. "Why did this happen to me?" Why was I denied an active-duty career? Being initially passed over for a promotion to Major was a painful life experience; the circumstances crushed me to the floor. I had no control over the outcome; my family had to alter our life plan as the future was uncertain. I learned to trust God and to put my faith in His hand as he wove a masterpiece using my life as a servant leader! I am grateful for God's grace and mercy daily and shepherding throughout my life.

Another critical message I want you to understand regarding mentorship. This is the same message to those who have served in the military as sailors, soldiers, marines, airmen, coast guard, and space force, the newest branch formed. Americans must see you!

To uplift and inspire the next generations of Americans behind us, Americans must see us in our uniform, out of our uniform, and in the community. Our young people must understand the benefits and life-altering opportunities of joining the armed services. In my time in the military, I experienced all military persons standing together. In the service, you'll meet fellow service members who want to help you develop your skills and advance your career and will be there to hear you out and see you through life experiences.

Too many of our young people are unaware of the great experiences the military offers because we don't share the pride and joyful experience as members. I encourage you to share information and inspiration to encourage families intentionally, the next generation of young people, and their parents of the tremendous benefits of military service. We must educate the public and share our experiences so young Americans can grow into strong leaders daily and develop skills like you and me. All military members have a role in ensuring our military remains strong. It is incumbent upon each one to do the following:

Tell your story so that it will inspire others. Your story must be told about how the military made your life better (as well as the lives of your family).

1. Tell them what your experience being a military member is all about, the pride you have, and what service means to you. The sacrifices you and your family made in service to our country. Your commitment to sharing your wonderful experiences will help dispel negative stereotypes, misconceptions, and mixed messaging.
2. We need Americans in our community to understand that serving our country is the highest honor of service. We need to share the pathway to establishing a higher quality of living that the military offers. We need to share the pride of serving, learning a skill set and vocation that's transferable to the private sector, the fun we had while serving overseas, and the many installations throughout the United States. Your influence in our community will help a new generation to see the many opportunities for our sons and daughters.
3. This is the same key message I want mentors to understand, the importance of what you do every day, late at night when the phone rings or unexpected lifeline conversations occurs. Mentors, military, and other professionals, we must tell our unique personal stories of how we defied the odds, the personal struggles, sacrifices, and extraordinary circumstances and situations to show today's generation of young people the copious options to help turn your situation around. This is the mountain top or rooftop perspective for them to be successful in the 21st Century.

So many have served and continue to use the unique experiences that the military services offer to enhance their personal life, church life, and communities where they live and work, even serving on county commissions and boards.

Many military members have used their experiences to enhance their personal life and improve where they live, work, and raise their families in communities, townships, neighborhoods, boroughs, and cities worldwide. Leadership is about helping others be better because of your presence! Lastly, our country is grateful to all who gave some, especially those who gave all!

Years of Progressive Experience as a Financial Professional

I have been truly blessed and grateful for the successful 40-plus years of progressive experiences and accomplishments in the financial resource management career field. I worked in three sectors: military, public, and private, as a leader, manager, and decision-maker, lending my gifts and interpersonal skills as an exceptional communicator and a consensus team builder.

I retired as a proud public servant on December 31, 2020, from the Nuclear Regulatory Commission. I served as a senior program analyst responsible for formulating the annual Presidential budget to achieve the program's goals and objectives for the agency for more than a decade. Before that, I worked for the Department of State Diplomatic Security Division as a Financial Management Officer. I enjoyed traveling worldwide to administer the Local Guard Program (LGP), totaling more than $290 million. Then the LGP was the third-largest budget in the State Department. Our team provided summary reports to senior level foreign service officers at various Embassies. LGP provided approximately 40,000 guards under contract to 163 embassies and 100 consulates for Residential Security Upgrades (RES) and Emergency Security Supplemental (SSP) guard service programs that protected U.S. citizens and their residents.

In addition to working in the public sector, I work in the private sector for an 8(A) Firm as the Chief Financial Officer for Interior Systems, Inc., Washington, D.C. This job was a challenging but fulfilling one connected with my entrepreneurial spirit. I wrote and implemented the business objectives in the organization's business plan and helped an entrepreneurial 8(A) Government Contractor gross more than $9 million annually over four years.

As stated earlier, my last duty station as a military officer was at Fort Ritchie, located in western Maryland. When I transitioned from the military, I entered an uncharted and unknown space regarding a path forward. I relied on and trusted God to plant me in a meaningful

environment that would use my leadership gifts and talents to benefit the Black community.

I always made it my business to visit local colleges, regardless of what state I found myself in. On a trip to Johns Hopkins for a medical doctor's appointment while still in the army, I visited Morgan State University in Baltimore, Maryland.

Wow! You cannot tell me that there isn't a God! I found myself on the Morgan State campus at Truth Hall and met the Associate Vice President for Finance and Management, who conducted an informal interview. He asked for my resume! Tell me where I would be if it had not been for the Lord on my side! God sees your whole life!

I remembered my Dad's advice always to be prepared. He said, "success is when preparedness meets opportunity." Two weeks later, I received a call to meet with the Vice President of Finance and Management from Morgan State University, and he made an offer to serve as his Special Assistant. This was the perfect job to transition to in the public sector. I thoroughly enjoyed every moment of this experience. I embraced the opportunity to provide senior-level leadership from September 1992 to August 1998. It was an honor to serve under the dynamic Dr. Earl S. Richardson, the 9th President of Morgan State University (1984 to 2010).

The exceptional professional staff at the school worked tirelessly to advance the university's goals and improve its students' quality of life. All the staff recognized this was a special moment during the university's unprecedented growth and development. As Special Assistant to the Vice President, Finance and Management, I led a diversified team of technical professionals during phenomenal growth that saw a rapidly improved and refurbished campus physical plant.

We exercised our faith and worked together to develop and execute the capital operations strategy and master plan for relocation for more than 25 departments totaling more than 300 personnel and conducted small-scale facilities renovation over three years. Highlights during this time included the new Hill Field House, the renovated football facility and track at Hughes Memorial Stadium, acquiring and converting Monticello Hospital into a one-stop center for student services, a new bookstore, the building of the Earl G. Graves School of Business, James E. Lewis Museum of Art and the Clarence M. Mitchell Jr. School of Engineering, new dormitories and host of other building transformations occurred under my leadership.

As I close this chapter, two points of emphasize my friends Americans must see you in your community! And when a person says "thank you" for your service. I suggest your response reflects the response of a five-time Purple Heart recipient from Tennessee! "You are worth it" because fighting for freedom, liberty, and justice for all is worth it for every generation!

Second, the experiences gained throughout my life as a military family member in my youth and the army in my adult life were invaluable to shaping the mentoring work I am now known for. I have experienced segregation, being bused out of our neighborhood for integration. I have experienced racism and setbacks; however, on the other side, the joy was raising our children to experience diversity in the 21st Century. I have traveled worldwide—living, working, playing, and engaging with many nationalities and ethnic communities. I have experienced cultural diversity like never before. The sheer beauty of this is that many of those same relationships I had in those countries I still maintain to this day!

This land, the Lord's land—belongs to all of us. Diversity is all about a rich "mix" of differences and respects encompassing all the dimensions that make us unique in our ethnicity, race, style, personal belief, and experiences. Meeting and engaging with <u>so many</u> different cultures that I met while traveling around the world was one of the most life-changing and essential benefits of my life and career—benefits that I no doubt would not have been able to attain otherwise at that level had it not been for the military. Diversity is such a measurable value to so many facets of life.

A STORY WITH A KEY MESSAGE:

You ought to live within a standard of excellence that sets the direction for your life with civility, integrity, professionalism, and high expectations. To all who have served, Americans must see you!

There is so much going on today as we continue to pursue fair and equitable treatment for all citizens regardless of race, color, religion, and creed. I encourage you to always pray for members of the military wherever they serve in the world. Let's pray for our service members who continue to be in harm's way today. Also, pray for those who answered a call to serve - in all its forms.

Secondly, prepare yourself to develop successful winning habits on your life journey. You should work smarter and not harder, and at the end of your assignment, you salute smartly for a job, position, or project well done. Then move on to your next challenging growth assignments. There comes a time in everyone's life when you prioritize what is most important. Leadership is about preparation.

My mantra used during my lifetime is always to be prepared. Be sure to get in shape before the night of the championship. I challenge you to improve yourself every day, find an area where you don't do so well, and work on strengthening and improving that area so that you will be prepared when the opportunity comes your way. Preparation is essential for living an impactful and meaningful life. The acronym I learned during my time in the military was the 5Ps—Proper Planning Prevents Poor Performance (actually, there are 6 Ps that old soldiers know well).

Finally, God is always with you when things appear perfect in your season of life; He is with you. He is with you as you enter life's storms and with you, as you go through challenging times. He goes before you to walk and talk with you side by side. He will never leave you. Will you leave him? I encourage you not to walk away when life gets rough. God will bring you through the difficult days and around life challenges for a greater purpose. He will use past experiences to shape and form you for His good! Leadership is about people with the right skills, knowledge, and abilities. It is about relationships and motivating people to get the job done, to accomplish the impossible and extraordinary. A leader must be people centered. Also, as a leader, it is about your preparation, presence, and service. I heard an old soldier put it this way, "when you see a problem or something that needs to be fixed, it is your responsibility to step up and try to fix it, no matter what." I encourage you to make a difference and influence a positive outcome. As a leader, your presence should make a difference in relationships and how you relate to helping other people with their challenges and issues. Practice service above self and strive to be a "helping hand" by lifting those most in need, the lost, the least, the left behind, and those traveling in the wrong direction because they may have lost their way!

DONALD WILLIAMS II

I AM AN AMERICAN SOLDIER.
I AM A WARRIOR AND A MEMBER OF A TEAM. I SERVE THE PEOPLE OF THE UNITED STATES AND LIVE THE ARMY VALUES.
I WILL ALWAYS PLACE THE MISSION FIRST.
I WILL NEVER ACCEPT DEFEAT.
I WILL NEVER QUIT.
I WILL NEVER LEAVE A FALLEN COMRADE.
I AM DISCIPLINED, PHYSICALLY AND MENTALLY TOUGH, TRAINED, AND PROFICIENT IN MY WARRIOR TASKS AND DRILLS. I ALWAYS MAINTAIN MY ARMS, MY EQUIPMENT AND MYSELF.
I AM AN EXPERT, AND I AM A PROFESSIONAL.
I STAND READY TO DEPLOY, ENGAGE, AND DESTROY THE ENEMIES OF THE UNITED STATES OF AMERICA IN CLOSE COMBAT.
I AM A GUARDIAN OF FREEDOM AND THE AMERICAN WAY OF LIFE.
I AM AN AMERICAN SOLDIER.

QUOTE:

"Write down what happen so no one will forget – Get it all on record now – get the films – get the witnesses because somewhere down the road of history someone will get up and say it never happened!"
— PRESIDENT DWIGHT D. EISENHOWER

SCRIPTURE:

"Do not be anxious about anything, but in every situation, by prayer and petition, with thanksgiving, present your requests to God. And the peace of God, which transcends all understanding, will guard your hearts and your minds in Christ Jesus."

PHILIPPIANS 4:6-7

CHAPTER 7

Order Our Steps in the Lord

MY CALLING TO INSPIRE & SAVE OUR YOUTH

Someone once said the two most important days of your life are "the day you are born, and the day you discover your purpose for living." Keep walking in faith! The incredible joy of my life is loving my wife, being a dad, and raising our family together. We were embedded in our community for approximately 30 years. We found a church in the community with loving people who welcomed our family with open arms–First African Methodist Episcopal Church-Gaithersburg. It was a close-knit church that allowed us to grow spiritually and raise our children with Christian values alongside other believers, which was equally important to us on our spiritual journey.

Our family was intentional about developing our Christian character that would reflect Christ's ministry of selfless service. Along the way, Mona and I discovered we had a heart for service to the Lord and humanity to help others improve the quality of their lives. Spiritual renewal and maturation played a significant role in shaping and molding our faith and connecting with other believers from local area churches, which was just as important to us. Our family was all in, supporting worship services, men's ministry, singing in the men's choir, serving on the usher board, and planning youth activities with Mt. Calvary Baptist Church in neighboring Rockville, Maryland. My family's faith was strengthened with developing and cultivating relationships with other believers with the commitment to improve the community where we lived, worked, and raised our children.

Mona and I have always had a heart for youth. Years ago, we recalled First A.M.E. Church's first mentoring session for girls conducted by the Women's Missionary Society. The church members and women were excited to plan, organize and gather the young girls together. Our daughters, Deidra and Dreka, attended the girls mentoring program's launch. They had to be about ten and eight years of age, respectively.

After the first three sessions, we asked our daughters if the experience was enjoyable and meaningful. Their response resounded, "We are not enjoying it," and why are we making them attend? Being parents raised with old-school values, we drilled down in our conversation with the girls and asked them what the mentoring was like and what fun activities that were announced during church did they do. We will always remember their responses because they shaped the future program.

Our daughters shared that first, the program wasn't fun. They added, "We were sewing, knitting, and ironing clothes. They are training us to be homemakers." As a mentor, you can build a program based on your experience, as many of us do to get started. However, you must be willing to adjust and expand your thinking and launch past your comfort zone. It is imperative to connect with children where they are. You should be relatable, relevant, innovative, and creative in introducing activities that interest young people and prepare them for a future world.

On Facebook, I read a quote that conveyed a key message to parents and mentors: "We appreciate you informing me about when you were in your youth and events that occurred but don't prepare me for that world. Prepare me for the new world that is emerging."

UCF intentionally equips, empowers, and educates youth with the three "ships;" Leadership, Scholarship, and Citizenship. These are life skills that will sustain you throughout life. As a mentor it is important to incorporate leadership development opportunities to help our students grow and discover leadership attributes to become future leaders.

Scholarship will always be synonymous with education. Once you achieve your education, no one can take it away from you. You need to develop a "knowledge base" to earn a living (learning is earning). No matter where you come from, education will always be a great equalizer. As the world transforms itself, the ability to earn a degree or technical certificate, HVAC or electrician training, plumbing licenses, computer programing certifications etc., can level the playing field and position you to succeed in the real world. It provides a higher standard of living for you and your family. Citizenship is another word for community service. Today's young people must develop a civil mindset and be engaged in the community in which they live and go to school.

Several relationships, events, and encounters led to the launching of the Unity Christian Fellowship (UCF) youth development organization. These encounters were explicit confirmation from God and helped shape the UCF's mission, strategic focus, and resolve every step of the way. UCF's mission promotes student success by connecting them to their destiny with positive outcomes that literally shape and save lives!

FIRST A.M.E. MISSIONARY DAY PICTURE

First A.M.E. Church was our family's home church where Mona and I became members and served faithfully starting in 1993. I am a third generation African Methodist Episcopalian and Mona was raised Methodist in her youth as well. We both were active church lay leaders raising our two daughters and mentoring countless children who crossed our path. Mona served as a trustee, and a lengthy term as Superintendent of Church School, raising the profile of First A.M.E. in the 2nd Episcopal District with a robust youth engagement program.

I served as a Steward, Commissioner for Youth, President of the Sons of Allen Men's Ministry, Sunday School Teacher, choir member, and the entire family enjoyed serving on the Usher Board, Young People and Children's Division and Sunday School. The family was thoroughly immersed in developing our spiritual walk with the Lord. We continue to be grateful for the A.M.E. church's influence in our family's lives as the third generation of my family continues to adopt

Christian values. We were blessed to have many Christian friends who have poured into our family.

As the Commissioner for Youth at First A.M.E., I enjoyed working together with a group of like-minded young adults who desired to make a difference in young people's lives in the community, such as our youth minister Reverend Ayanna Newton, Reverend Moya Harris, her husband John Harris III, Maurice Hamilton, Kareem Johnson, and Adrian Burnim to name a few. We enjoyed working together to plan kingdom building youth programs. Our focus centered on outreach to youth who lived in the surrounding neighborhood and invited them to outings to learn about the Christian lifestyle, such as Vacation Bible School (VBS), revivals, church picnics, youth lock-ins, and other church activities in and around the community. I love the quote by former First A.M.E. member, Reverend Abraham Smith, who summed up this season, "We were saved to serve."

Mona and I attended our home church every Sunday. However, approximately 15 years ago, on July 4, 2008, we decided not to attend First A.M.E., instead, visiting Ebenezer A.M.E. Church of Fort Washington, Maryland, Mona's sister's church. The worship service's message and several other encounters planted the motivational seeds to launch the UCF Youth Development Organization.

Ebenezer A.M.E. is a well-known, thriving church led by Reverend Dr. Grainger Browning, and Co-Pastor, Reverend Dr. Jo Ann Browning. Reverend Grainger began his sermon that day with a speech from Frederick Douglass entitled "What to the Slave is the Fourth of July," an address given in Rochester, New York, on July 5, 1852. The speech highlighted the American Day of Independence from a Negro perspective, highlighting the injustices African Americans experienced in the 19th century.

Reverend Browning's sermon centered on the book of Esther about a Jewish queen. She had to be reminded of God's divine purpose for her life and why she didn't become queen by herself. For such a time as this, God worked behind the scenes orchestrating events lining up the right people at the right time, to bring about His divine purpose to save the Jews. At this point, I want to share several encounters that preceded the worship service that day, propelling us to launch UCF.

At this time, Mona and I continued to grow our home-based finance and accounting service business that we started and operated in Korea to help provide financial counseling to families. The first encounter occurred over a weekend when my wife gave me an assignment to help one of her tax clients. The client had a first-generation wide screen television and was upgrading to a newly purchased flat screen. Mona had arranged for another family to receive the television. Of course, she promised to have me pick up the television to be delivered to another family's home. I gathered some young males from the Towne Crest neighborhood near First A.M.E. to help pick up and deliver the television. The television was delivered to the Simpson's home, where we became surrogate parents and mentors to the family, that included four girls and one boy.

As part of God's master plan, the Simpson family experienced the loss of their parents at an early age. The father passed away shortly after his only son was born, and the mother passed away before the three youngest children graduated from high school. As a Steward at First A.M.E. and representative for the church family, I was at their mother's hospital bedside with the family when the Lord called her home. I will never forget her struggling to remove the oxygen mask to look me in the eye and say, "Sir, take care of my family." Again, I will never forget that moment!

Before Sister Simpson's passing, in another encounter, I attended parent teacher meetings starting when her son Ray was in middle school. A circle of adults and our family availed themselves to help the children succeed. During this time, I recalled his mother, a single woman who raised her children the best she could while being a faithful member of First A.M.E.

As members of the church, the family was supported primarily by Sister Jackie Rhone, the Williams family, and a few others. We all looked out for the Simpson family and connected them to community resources and youth opportunities. Sister Simpson was a committed woman who wanted the best for her children.

She ensured the family attended every church activity offered and walked the family to church every Sunday. We were connected to the family in many ways throughout their adolescence into adulthood. So, it was only natural to go by the Simpson home to pick up Ray for him to help with the task of hauling the television to be delivered to his family's home. This was my way of teaching, modeling, and showing Ray a man's responsibility for taking care of the house. Ray was excited to spend time with me. Our relationship continued to grow. I took him under my wing to teach and provide guidance and advice through mentorship.

The task of picking up a TV and delivering it to the Simpson house should have taken an hour. I picked up Ray, Antwuan Meekins (the first UCF Graduate- high school class of 2009) and two other friends from the neighborhood and off we went, enjoying conversations until we arrived at the client's home. The man of the house greeted us and then we explained to the boys what needed to be accomplished. The instructions to the young males were to take the television down the stairs and load it in the van.

It should have taken at most 15 minutes for the entire process. However, it wound up taking at least one hour! We witnessed the lack of critical thinking skills and the limited understanding of angles required to navigate from the top of the stairway, that had a slight curve, to the bottom of the stairway and out the front door. At 14, these boys did not understand how to load a large item out of the house into the van. We watched three near misses that would have required repairs to the drywall. The young males, without adult help, finally accomplished the task an hour later. They were so proud of themselves when the television was delivered to the Simpson home that I treated them to pizza. My takeaway was – "wow! These young males should have been further along in their growth and development in reasoning, critical thinking, and decision-making."

The second encounter that caused us to start UCF occurred about two weeks after the first encounter, at a McDonald's near the Flower Hill Shopping Center in Gaithersburg. This encounter helped shape the focus of the youth development mentoring work that continues today. Anyone who knows me well knows how I love fishing outings. A few of my friends had just returned from another great day on Chesapeake Bay. The grill was ready to receive the fresh rockfish that I had caught. All that was needed was french fries from McDonald's with the grilled fish. I told Mona that I was going to McDonald's and would return to put the fish on the grill. Upon entering McDonald's, I witnessed frightened customers due to approximately eight to 10 young males from the First A.M.E. basketball ministry playing "fake football" in the restaurant. The young males were playing and "just having fun," commandeering the restaurant. What I saw in the face of each customer was fear. They were terrified that one of the guys would bump into them, and then what?

As I assessed the situation, I met the restaurant manager's eyes. His eyes reflected being terrified and his next step was to call the police to remove the boys from the restaurant. Also, as our eyes met, he welcomed my presence in the restaurant as the young high school-age males greeted me with ", Hi, Brother Williams!" I took the guys out of McDonald's to talk about their perception of them and their activities.

This was a teachable moment for the young males participating in the summer Christian Youth Basketball Ministry. Outside of the restaurant, I conducted a mentoring session about the right time and place to conduct "just having fun" sessions, which never should be in any restaurant.

I recapped the perception; if I didn't arrive when I did, the outcome would have been very different. The young males were very respectful and acknowledged that just playing fake football in the restaurant was the wrong place to do so. They honestly didn't realize that they were frightening the patrons. At that moment, I shifted the conversation to ask the following question to each of the ten males, "what do you want to be when you graduate from high school in three years?" I was shocked that only two young males could express themselves and articulate their goals. The others were clueless and had given any thought to their future aspirations.

As shared earlier in this chapter, these encounters appeared to be clear communication from God to trust him. That is precisely how we responded to establishing the youth organization that has impacted, shaped, and saved thousands of young people.

As I return to the spiritual influence shared by Reverend Dr. Browning's 4th of July sermon about Esther the Jewish queen, his account and effective delivery of God's word convicted us. It was an uplifting, emotional and inspirational worship experience for me. Reverend Dr. Browning took a familiar message from the biblical story of Esther and related the text to our community and events that occur with our young people. Mona and I sat in the balcony listening to every word the Pastor delivered; we related to every word of his sermon that challenged and expressed that the sense of urgency is now! This message stirred something inside me when the Pastor asked: Why do you think you have been blessed? When he suggested to those in attendance that they substitute Esther's name with their names and achievements, that was it. How did he know what we were experiencing back in Gaithersburg?

I asked myself, "Why do you think God has kept you through adolescence, made way for you, and blessed you with two college degrees, a wonderful family, and a military and basketball coaching career?" The answer is, "It is for such a time as this!" Mona's eyes met my eyes with every illustration. It was as if Pastor Browning's message was meant for me.

Now is the time to step out on faith and lend our leadership gifts, talents, skills, and resources to help uplift the community to do something extraordinary. To give hope, inspire and impact young people's lives and be a helping hand for their families is "for such a time as this." On that day Reverend Browning became my mentor from afar! I can still recall my emotional state from that worship experience and the restless nights of tossing and turning.

I will always remember the look Mona gave me! That sealed the conviction to trust God and take actions to use the gifts He blessed each of us with to walk in faith to accomplish the assignment to glorify Him! When you experience success, you think you can relax, stay the course and do less. As I reflect, the opposite must occur; you must work harder to sustain excellence for the generation behind you.

When people ask, how did we start UCF? This is the whole story, the complete story that inspired us to act for a higher level of meaningful and purposeful service. My response always starts with, "This continues to be a faith journey," inspired by God. One of our mentees, now a young adult says it this way: "Only God" could have saved his life by using ordinary persons to accomplish His will and purpose for a community to save and shape lives.

Mona and I committed to a life of service and shaping the lives of countless young people. For more than 25 years, we've focused on African American youth—specifically at-risk male youth—mentoring and sometimes taking them into our home. UCF's goal is to change lives in the community—one student at a time by empowering youth to gain confidence, be productive community contributors, and engage them, their families, and communities through educational, social, Christian fellowship and enrichment activities.

Proud History since April 1988

Spanning more than twenty years of Christian Brotherhood!
Can anything good come from "First A.M.E. Church in Gaithersburg
Absolutely!

Like Queen Esther (who had to be reminded of God's divine purpose for her life that she didn't get to the position of a queen by herself), Mona and I have witnessed God's orchestration. We have experienced his signs, wonders, and miracles for ourselves. We know that if God gives you a vision, He will show you the way and provide the provision. He will make way for you that you could have never imagined. The Sons of Allen (S.O.A.) men's ministry was a blessing for the church's men in many ways. The African Methodist Episcopal Church (A.M.E. Church) denomination was founded by Bishop Richard Allen in Philadelphia, Pennsylvania, in 1816, and the men's ministry was named after him. The monthly meetings were a safe place for men to share their spiritual convictions and express themselves about the daily issues and challenges impacting their spiritual growth and development. S.O.A. provided inspiration, meaningful wellness information, and social, emotional, and spiritual support for all participants.

The S.O.A. even tried implementing a mentoring program for young males in the church. To gain insight, we invited a young Reverend Tony Lee, (Pastor of Community of Hope A.M.E. Church in Hillcrest Heights, Maryland), to conduct a workshop on things to be aware of implementing mentoring programs.

I felt the movement as God equipped and ordered my steps and the journey to be in His will. For many years, the men enjoyed a special bond in learning to be obedient, love their families, and improve their prayer lives. We enjoyed working together on the various outreach projects around the church by planning and organizing to enhance the spiritual climate at First A.M.E. The church was known throughout the district for having an active S.O.A. ministry that brought glory to God with iron sharpening iron.

In 2009, I was blessed to be invited by the 2nd District Leadership (which included Reverend Richard S. McNair, Jr., and Reverend Donald Marbury) to present annually at the S.O.A. Retreat. A goal of the retreat was to encourage men across the A.M.E. connection to be doers in the vineyard, seek God's will, and uplift others. My presentation centered on sharing what an effective S.O.A. program looked like to encourage other churches to start their own men's ministry. The picture above was the first in the slide deck that depicted bonding and unity. Behold, how good and pleasant it is for brethren to unite together! (Psalm 133:1)

A memorable experience at the retreat was a tag-team presentation with Adrian Branch, the retired National Basketball Association player, whose message was the following:

> **You are not born a winner or a loser - YOU are born a CHOOSER!**
> **- Adrian Branch**

Looking back from the beginning, I believe God has ordered my steps and shaped my life. Since adolescence, He brought me through countless good and bad experiences. He allowed me to succeed as a Division I student athlete, career military officer, family man, college basketball coach, and community leader. More importantly, He used my life to show His love, by loving God's people! God has been so good to me as He continues to work behind the scenes, orchestrating events and aligning the right people at the right time to bring about His divine purpose.

Presiding Bishop Adam Jefferson Richardson Jr.,
and wife Connie S. Richardson
African Methodist Episcopal Church 2ND Episcopal District, Women's Missionary Society Washington Conference 62ND Annual Luncheon – Celebrating Partnership, April 23, 2012.

Mona and I realized our purpose for being in the world. We continue to be blessed to have essential and trusted relationships to influence, impact, change, shape, and save lives in the community, one person at a time. UCF theme since inception: Building Youth Success—*Changing the Landscape and Leveraging Opportunity!*

As a result, we pulled together our closest friends to share God's vision to do something greater than ourselves to help the young people in the community. Our friends were encouraging as we shared the powerful sermon about the Jewish Queen Esther and the message. They provided immediate support to move forward with first launching UCF as a non-profit youth organization.

We will forever be grateful to God for surrounding Mona and me with Christian friends for life: Wanda "Hit Dog" Sims, Sister Jackie "Mother Teresa" Rhone, Sister Pervy V. Broady (RIP), who was my spiritual leader, French Pope II, Clifton McKnight, John Tucker (my mentor), and Damita and Cliff Green (otherwise known as the Green Team). We agreed that our first action was to look up to God and pray. The second action was to look forward to developing a strategic action plan while trusting God for specific direction and next steps. Working together, we learned that God will provide the pathway forward when he gives you a vision.

When my friends came together to research how to start a non-profit organization, it was one of my memorable experiences forever etched in my UCF journey. We worked together to complete the IRS documentation for submission to the state of Maryland. The energy level was so high that we almost pulled an all-nighter to satisfy the IRS forms that officially established UCF as a 501 c 3 non-profit organization.

It is refreshing to have like-minded people who believe in the greater good in your corner. In Colossians 3:23 it says, "whatever you do, work at it with all your heart, as working for the Lord, not for human masters." The UCF journey has placed the right people at the right time with enough resources in His perfect timing. We learned that there is no limit to the kinds of work you can do for Him and the places where this work can be done. Mona and I will forever be grateful to so many who encouraged us to step out of our comfort zone, go beyond the church walls, and put our trust in God, for He will take you places that you never dreamed possible.

"All Gave Some, Some Gave All, and We Honor Our Veterans"

November 8, 2020 Veteran Day Worship Service -
The Christian Soldiers'
Reverend, General R. Scott Dingle,
45th United States Surgeon
General, and Commander MEDCOM

The unexpected blessing as we pressed through the COVID pandemic occurred at First A.M.E. Church, our home church in Gaithersburg, Maryland. The military veterans who served our country and continue to serve in the local church worked together to celebrate all veterans. It's indeed been an honor to serve on the Veteran's Ministry throughout the 2020 global pandemic that claimed more than a million lives. I am grateful to the Presiding Prelate, Bishop James L. Davis, for appointing Reverend Dr. Chaplain J. Elizabeth Pinkney to launch and ignite The Second Episcopal District Veterans Ministry Celebration.

The ministry celebrates the men and women who wore the uniform in our Army, Navy, Air Force, Marines, or Coast Guard and the newest Space Forces, for this is the highest form of service. Together, our leadership team raised awareness, educated parishioners, and increased the number of local churches that established veteran ministries. Equally important in the last three years, Churches across the connectional showed love to many veterans who went unrecognized while continued service long after active duty service.

Many people ask how I came to be in The Second Episcopal District, African Methodist Episcopal Church veteran ministry. My response is "Only God." My father is a member of the historical St Stephen A.M.E. Church in Wilmington, NC. He was so disappointed and didn't understand why the church never recognized veterans throughout the year, let alone on Veterans Day and Memorial Day. One day, I received a phone call from Reverend Pinkney, First A.M.E. Church, where we were members. God will make a way; when Bishop Davis called Reverend Pinkney to establish the veteran ministry, she invited me to join her team. My response,

"Only God."

I want you to know that being a member of the leadership team for the last three years has been an enriching experience. My father served 21 years in the United States Army as a Non-Commission Officer and is a Vietnam War Veteran who served two tours (1967 and 1970). The Vietnam War was the longest in American history at the time. The war lasted from 1964-1975, a war that claimed millions of lives. "All gave some, some gave all, and we honor our veterans." My father also served two tours in Korea. My Dad is 88 years young, still driving himself to church, and stays strong! For those veterans who served in The Vietnam War, we also say, "**Welcome Home!**"

The last three years' impact on the local Churches has been a labor of love to the 2nd District.

Shoutout to team members past and present, Reverend Dr. J. C. Chandler USAF, Reverend Abraham Smith USAF, Reverend Herman Gladney Navy, Major Chaplain Jumanne Green, USAF, and Sarah Hall, our Gold Star family member whose husband died on active duty. And the many churches that established Veterans Ministry during the last three years.

We pray for those who are in harm's way every day! The Second Episcopal District of the AME Church honors you, and our Nation is grateful for your noble service. We Salute you!

I've told you these things for a purpose: that my joy might be your joy. This is my command: Love one another the way I love you. This is the very best way to love. Put your life on the line for your friends. John 15:11-13

A STORY WITH A KEY MESSAGE:

"Unity Christian Fellowship has been a blessing in my life, my family's life, and the community in teaching young people to reach their full potential. UCF has guided my siblings towards success to stay on track to graduate from high school and go on to college. UCF has gifted my family with educational support, spiritual support, emotional support, financial support, life skills activities, leadership training, college road trips, scholarships, resources, and networking opportunities.

In April 2006, my mother, Dinah L. Simpson, passed due to breast cancer at 49. At the time, I was 25 years old, Crystal (23), Melissa (17), Dinah (16), and Ray (14). Unity Christian Fellowship jumped right in with friendly and caring support during the most challenging experience in our lives.

In October 2010, the Lord released me of my responsibility in raising my family, and with the support of UCF, I moved to Greensboro, North Carolina. I moved in with Deidre Williams-Long for a few weeks then the Lord blessed me with my own home. I then began to look for full-time employment. I started a long journey in temporary work, where I experienced the highs and lows of finding full-time employment.

In 2011, I joined Love and Faith Christian Fellowship Church and the Ministry of Encouragement. In 2012, I joined Love and Faith Christian Fellowship Church – Eagles Nest Bible College. Eagles Nest Bible College has allowed me to effectively develop a spiritual ear to hear the Word of God while building a personal relationship with Jesus Christ. In 2013, I joined StepUP Greensboro, a year-long job readiness and life skills training program for adults transforming through employment. In 2011, Melissa went on to graduate from Johnson C. Smith University with a degree in communication. In 2016, Dinah went on to graduate from Bowie State University with a degree in nursing. Crystal, Ray & I went on to join the workforce. In 2015, I was hired as a temporary employee at The Center for Creative Leadership as Facilities Maintenance Coordinator. In Spring 2016, I was hired as a full-time employee. The Center for Creative Leadership is a leadership development research non-profit organization.

I am truly grateful that Mr. and Mrs. Williams allowed the Lord to use them in birthing Unity Christian Fellowship! Romans 8:28 reads: And we know that all things work together for good to those who love God and are called according to His purpose. My siblings and I are grateful that Unity Christian Fellowship assisted in planning for our future in demonstrating good character towards Christian leadership and living a healthy lifestyle." —Anitra Simpson

QUOTE:
"To be yourself in a world that is constantly trying to make you something else is the greatest accomplishment."
— Ralph Waldo Emerson

SCRIPTURE:
"The Lord is my light and my salvation; whom shall I fear? The Lord is the strength of my life; of whom shall I be afraid."
Psalm 27

CHAPTER 8

My Basketball Story

"Practice makes perfect; find a way to strive for excellence on every possession."

—Source Unknown

Hagerstown Hawks Coaching Staff with Head Coach Jim Brown

The above picture is at Hagerstown Community College, where I listened intently to legendary head basketball coach Jim Brown issuing instructions for team success. I was blessed to coach basketball for 25 years. It has taken me on an incredible odyssey across the country, meeting people from all walks of life. I love teaching the game of basketball, championship principles, developing players, and mentoring students to believe in themselves. I love promoting accountability and teaching players to be the star in their roles to help the team succeed. I love coaching student-athletes, showing them what goal achievement, work ethic, confidence building, and teamwork are all about!

I've worked with many people, coaches, athletic directors, college administrators, support staff, community leaders, trainers, and players. I thank all these people for their support and for being part of my basketball coaching career. Most of all, I am grateful for your loyalty and friendship! It has always been about student development to encourage them to make good choices consistently and to stay on the right path.

There isn't a better feeling than leading, guiding, and teaching the game of basketball to people who love to learn about the importance of teamwork, team effort, discipline, hard work, dedication, and determination to develop skills to play smart, hard, and as a team. The game of basketball might look like an easy game to play, but it's a challenging game to play well together.

Here is a little-known fact about the man who invented the game of basketball in 1891. Dr. James Naismith served as a Chaplain in the Army National Guard and volunteered in France during World War I. I'll bet many sports fans didn't know about the Canadian-American physical educator, physician, Christian chaplain, and athletic coach (November 6, 1891 – November 28, 1939).

Also, a little-known fact is about the first Black Coach, John B. McLendon Jr., who studied under Dr. James Naismith. As a pioneer, he's recognized as the first Black basketball coach at a predominantly white university and the first head coach in any professional sport. Coach McLendon invented basketball's fast break, zone press, and four corners offense. He has been enshrined in the Naismith Memorial Basketball Hall of Fame and inducted into the National Collegiate Basketball Hall of Fame. Though not allowed to play on the varsity team at Kansas University due to the university's color line, he would go on to an impressive career as a basketball coach. (April 5, 1915 – October 8, 1999).

Like Dr. Naismith, who made working with young people his life's work, basketball has taken me places I never dreamed possible. Shortly after being named interim head coach for the Morgan State University women's team (during the 1994-95 season), I shook hands at center court with legendary coach Geno Auriemma from the University of Connecticut in the fifth annual Hartford Courant Connecticut Classic tournament in November of 1994. At a Sons of Allen Men's Retreat, I conducted a tag-team presentation with Adrian Branch entitled "Searching for Excellence." Branch was a second-round draft pick of the Chicago Bulls in 1985 after a successful collegiate career at the University of Maryland. At the WNBA Washington Mystics training facility, I coordinated a tryout for my star player at Montgomery College, 6-foot-8-inch Tiffani Williams, the pride of Trinidad and Tobago, who went on to play for Hampton University's Mid-Eastern Athletic Conference championship team under coach Patricia Cage-Bibbs. I could go on; it was an amazing journey!

It has been an incredible experience coaching youth recreational basketball, establishing the Fast Break Basketball Camp with former local high school coach Nathan Lewis and his family. The five-year camp was tremendously successful because it brought a diverse community together. It was a positive experience for the campers who learned listening skills and how to receive instructions to execute different basketball skills. It was great for campers to be around other students. In addition, it was a positive experience for the teenage counselors, as they were placed in leadership positions. Also, the Lewis and Williams families learned to operate a camp interacting with families dealing with young people of all ages and colors. We taught fundamentals to students who desired to learn to play the right way. I was grateful to teach my daughters how to play and confidently compete in the

Maryland Flames' AAU program. I perfected championship principles while helping to change young people's lives by teaching basketball skills that led to winning National Junior College Athletic Association (NJCAA) regional championships, earning multiple trips to the national tournament in Corning, New York. On our first trip to the Division III "Elite 8," our team finished fifth in the country with student-athletes affectionately known as "Fantastic Six." Although winning championships was fun, I believe establishing a program where students consistently earned Associate of Arts degrees every year was the greatest accomplishment. As a mentor, Dr. George B. Thomas always said, "Education is the great equalizer for every generation."

To those who desire to pursue a coaching career, you must be willing to be a student of the game and put the required work in by increasing your knowledge base by reading books. I pursued knowledge and hung around successful, knowledgeable coaches. I attended several basketball clinics and camps during the summer with legendary coaches such as former DeMatha High coach Morgan Wootton at Mount Saint Mary's University in Emmitsburg, Maryland, and former University of Maryland head coach Gary Williams, who won an NCAA title in 2002.

Wootton was a very personable man of faith that shared wisdom about the coaching profession (good and bad). His camp was an overnight operation. The coaching staff stayed in the dormitory with the students, where we shared the same summer experience without air conditioning, which made for a memorable experience for all.

The development of my coaching intelligence came from these experiences, combined with tape reviews of systems run by my favorite coaches, such as Dean Smith, Rick Pitino, Jim Boeheim, and Mike Krzyzewski. My passion for being a positive influencer in the lives of young people peaked when I coached women's basketball at Morgan State and Montgomery College.

A GAME CHANGER'S PURSUIT

At Morgan, I was blessed to enjoy the best of both worlds as a senior administrator and coach. In the 1994-95 season, I assumed the reins as interim head coach for the Lady Bears' program. At the time, I brought a wealth of experience from the military and the junior college ranks. I completed three years as an assistant men's coach under the legendary coach Brown at Hagerstown Community College.

At Montgomery College, I served as an assistant coach under coach Lesley Lougy (1996-2000) and took over the program as head coach in the fall of 2000. I was blessed with the opportunity to build a championship program from scratch, where players received scholarships. These experiences deepened my relationship with God and combined with my love for improving and impacting our youth's social, emotional, and athletic skills. Additionally, these experiences gave me the volition to involve our youth in Unity Christian Fellowship.

I stressed performance value over winning, as winning would become the long-term result. My coaching staff and I challenged players to reach their potential and to be the best they could be on each possession. As the championship program was being built, our players enjoyed developing skills to play an aggressive style. We emphasized reading passing lanes, playing multiple defenses with an up-tempo style on offense, and dominating space for rebounding and running assigned fast break lanes. This high-energy and effort approach also included attacking the hoop at every opportunity, shooting the three-pointer, crashing the boards, and hitting free throws to seal the game!

I will always be grateful to the many players, parents, and high school coaches who entrusted me with their students throughout my career. The game of basketball parallels the game of life. You must "put the work in," and your progress, skill development, and improvement will directly relate to your positive attitude and consistent effort! It is the same in life; you must compete and do the necessary work to get better every day, no matter what path you choose.

My players have repeatedly heard me repeatedly repeating this motto, "positive attitude plus consistent effort always equals success in giving a winning effort!" My nephew, David Anderson II, says this: "there are three things that people lack and you have control over, effort, discipline, and consistency." These are the fundamental cornerstones for young people to succeed today. You don't have to be the smartest person in the world to succeed, but no one can deny your performance if you give maximum effort.

I encourage you to make good choices every day! I reminded my mentees that it is their choice alone, they are the ones to control their performance and effort for developing themselves. The two questions: Are you putting in your best performance? Are you giving a winning effort in all areas of your life?

Many people have asked me over the years how I ended up with an affinity for coaching basketball, especially since I was an outstanding wrestler in high school and college. I respond by saying, "what do Michael Jordan and I have in common?" We both were cut from our respective high school basketball teams in our freshman year. We both love basketball and just as he was fueled to be the greatest basketball player he could be, I took the same attitude in coaching.

A STORY WITH A KEY MESSAGE:

I always shared the MJ story with my students by asking them what they think the greatest basketball player ever lived and what I have in common. A wise-cracking youth always responds with "not your bank account," and everyone laughs.

Once they would stop laughing, I would respond, "now that I have your attention, what MJ and I have in common was we both were cut from the basketball team as freshmen." Yes, some friends and I tried out for the varsity basketball team at Monmouth Regional high school. I made it to the final cut and found that my name wasn't on the final roster. I know MJ was disappointed when he didn't make his team. However, I don't recall being disappointed about being cut. I was no MJ; I just moved on to "door number three," which was the wrestling team. This is where I discovered increased confidence, and with the encouragement of the coaches, I developed skills and abilities to compete at a high level on the mat.

When my dad retired from the Army at Fort Monmouth, we relocated to Neptune Township in New Jersey. However, before moving to a new community, I completed all but the last marking period of my freshman year at Monmouth Regional High.

When we moved to Neptune Township, I quickly learned that everyone in my new community who played basketball had remarkable skills. As the new kid, with the pressure of being accepted in the community, I set out to work hard, learning and excelling in the sport on the playground and in gym class.

I attended two high schools that exposed me to two physical education curriculums. In my experience at Monmouth Regional and other DOD schools, the curriculum was centered on exposure to all sports. We learned and played a different sport every three weeks in gym class. However, at Neptune High, the gym teacher would roll out the basketballs during gym period. The gym teacher would be assembled to play three on three, four on four, and five on five during class – with a strong desire to compete and show off our basketball skills.

Fort Carson was my first opportunity to coach the company team and teach the game to our soldiers who played against other teams in the battalion. Throughout my military career, I coached basketball teams ranging from soldiers in Colorado to Korea, coaching the Young People's Division.

In Korea, I recalled advice from a senior officer who encouraged me to become a college basketball coach because of my expertise. He believed that I was natural at coaching. In my military assignment at Fort Ritchie, I pursued becoming a college coach once I was settled into my military position. I was fortunate to meet Coach Brown, my first mentor outside of the military.

Coach Brown was the highly respected and legendary head coach of Hagerstown Community College (then known as Hagerstown Junior College), located around the corner from Fort Ritchie. He and his staff had established a respectable Division I junior college program in the Maryland Junior College Conference (JUCO) and Region XX of the National Junior College Athletic Association (NJCAA).

I had the pleasure of participating in this championship pedigree from 1991 to 1994 and was blessed to learn how to coach and run a college program with integrity. I was an assistant coach for the Hawks' men's program under Brown's tutelage. He was one of the winningest coaches in Maryland during a 27-year career with 525 wins. Hagerstown Community College and fellow western Maryland rival Allegany Community College would compete annually for spots in the NJCAA national tournament.

Coach Brown respected me for reaching back to volunteer while serving in the military. He took me under his wing, and he and I developed an excellent relationship. He agreed to teach me everything he knew about being a successful coach but warned me there could only be one head coach! His first rule was always to be yourself in all personal interactions. As a coach, you must be comfortable in your skin, and with who you are as a person. He challenged and taught me the complexities of being an effective coach, managing the study hall, the locker room, staff meetings, and interacting with school administrators. Coach Brown had assembled an outstanding coaching staff exceptional in performing their assigned duties: Barry Brown (lead assistant and son), Kenny Keyes, Rob Kline (analytics), and Academic Advisor Dr. Marie Nowakowski. Coach Brown assigned me to the third-string team to develop players' skill sets to improve their performance. In this assignment, I learned the value of building relationships with players working to improve their skills to break into the first-team line-up.

My first recognition from the coaching staff came when the starting shooting guard and another player suffered injuries. I helped prepare the substitutes for the starting line-up, where they played effectively.

HAGERSTOWN COMMUNITY COLLEGE

Coach Brown taught me many nuances for coaching the right way from recruiting talented student-athletes, player development, booster members engagement, to mentoring the young men to help them reach their full potential.

You cannot be anyone but yourself, our children know fake anything when they see it. Student-athletes recognize when you sincerely care about them, when you have their best interest and well-being at heart.

While at Hagerstown, I acquired a once in lifetime experience. I left the program with a thick notebook, and lots of tips, reflections, stories, and strategies from what I learned from Coach Brown.

Hagerstown earned plenty of success during my time there. We were Maryland JUCO Conference Tournament champs for the 1990-91 season with an 18-15 record. The following season, we won the regular season title (25-6). In 1992-1993 and 1993-94, we won the state JUCO crown regular season and tournament back-to-back with records of 25-5, earning a national ranking in 1994.

God only gives you a season or two where he will align you with the right people and the right time to accomplish your goal. My engagement with the Hagerstown community was a blessing. I will always be grateful to Coach Brown, a true advocate for me, helping secure employment at the college. I always learned to keep an eye on the future because all season's end, and a new season begins every year. This personal season ended when I was hired at Morgan State University as Special Assistant to the Vice President, Finance and Management in the fall of 1994. The time was right to leave the excellent support structure and many friendships in the Hagerstown community.

Morgan State University: Lady Bears

While I left a comfortable coaching environment in Hagerstown, I was fortunate to procure my dream job at Morgan State University as a Special Assistant to the Vice President of Finance and Management. It was a blessing to lend my leadership gifts to serve at an HBCU (Historically Black College and University). I can honestly say that being a staff executive under President Dr. Earl Richardson's dynamic leadership during unprecedented campus growth during the 90's was a joy. I was excited every day to wake up and drive an hour to Baltimore to help achieve the university's goals and objectives for campus-wide improvement. I always desired to work in the African American community for an African American institution. I met exceptional leaders from all walks of life and learned much about operating in an environment with a long-standing history of being under-resourced and underserved.

I was afforded the opportunity to replace former head coach Anderson Powell for the 1994-1995 season, as I jumped at the chance to coach the "Lady Bears." What an opportunity this was to combine my gifts for leadership and team building to impact a professional staff by day and after hours, developing a team of student athletes.

I was grateful to lead an NCAA Division I program. My head coaching journey began two weeks before Thanksgiving Holiday with a trip to Storrs, Connecticut, to play the first game of the season against a national powerhouse, the University of Connecticut. I met coach Auriemma at center court and shook hands wishing him good luck – he just smiled! After the game, I was asked what I thought of the game at the press conference. I paused and responded, " well, we got our butts whipped soundly. You saw two different programs headed in different directions regarding talent, resources, and support."

As a former assistant coach at Hagerstown, it was a challenge stepping in as an interim coach at another school, implementing a system I learned at Hagerstown. The experience was like being a substitute teacher for the season. We were challenged to discover each player's strengths and prepare the team for a competitive season. I quickly established a foundation and promoted a program with integrity that stood on the merits of academic excellence.

COACHING THE LADY BEARS DURING THE 1994-1995 SEASON

My focus throughout the season was to establish a structure and create and foster an atmosphere conducive to success at the highest level. The Lady Bears improved with each game to the highest season ranking in fifth place Mid-Eastern Athletic Conference. For the season, the team won its first postseason game in the school's previous five years, finishing 5-20 overall, 5-13 in the conference. Season highlights included competing against UConn, LaSalle University (Pa.), Santa Clara University (CA), Boston University, and cross-town rival Coppin State University.

After the season opening game with UConn, I stated that my claim to fame was starting the Huskies on its way to capturing the program's first national title led by 6' 4 center Rebecca Lobo in 1995 with a 35-0 record.

In 1996, after I completed my tenure at Morgan State University. I joined the Montgomery College-Rockville women's basketball staff as assistant coach to coach Lesley Lougy. My focus was on player development. After four years, while serving in the Army Reserve, I was named head coach of the Lady Knights in the fall of 2000 and stayed until 2007. I was excited to take the helm for the program, a Maryland Junior College Conference member and Region XX of the NJCAA. It was an honor to inherit the responsibility for operating the full scope of the women's intercollegiate basketball program: recruiting, academic liaison, scouting, and program evaluation. I must thank coach Tom Bichy, a founding father for athletics at Montgomery College who spent 37 years at the school, including 24 years as Athletic Director. He was a mentor, friend, and wonderful man who provided an opportunity for me to contribute to student success. I remember sharing countless conversations, getting to know each other, and sharing his vision for building the program. I was saddened to learn of his passing in 2014.

MONTGOMERY COLLEGE: LADY KNIGHTS

Assistant coach Tarlouh Gasque and I built a "non-scholarship" program to compete with scholarship programs at the conference. We devoted countless hours to building a program from scratch into a national championship-level program highly respected in Maryland

and recognized throughout the country as one of the top women's basketball programs. Several players from area high schools benefited from our holistic program centered on building confidence, self-esteem, player development, and academic confidence for long-term success in the real game of life!

I was extremely proud of our student-athletes graduation rate. The women's basketball program became a stop for four-year college coaches to recruit our student-athletes. Some of the institutions of higher learning our students attended upon earning their associate's: Adelphi University, Bowie State University, Hampton University, Virginia Union University, Virginia Wesleyan University, University of Maryland, East Tennessee State University, Howard University, Towson University, Temple University, North Carolina A&T State University, and West Virginia Tech University.

I was extremely proud of approximately 15 student-athletes who earned all-Maryland JUCO Conference honors and the 18 who achieved all-Region XX honors since 2000. We won the Region XX Championship five times: 2000, 2002, 2003, 2004, and 2005. Three teams competed in the NJCAA National Tournament: 2000, 2002, and 2005. I received coach of the year honors twice, 2002 and 2005, and advanced to two final fours. I represented Montgomery College at a Maryland Conference Ethics and Standard Hearing in September 2005 to defend the program for some of our students' poor choices on the national stage.

In addition, I had the privilege of coaching three All-Americans who were recognized as Women's Player of the Year: Tope Ogunniyi, Virginia State University and East Tennessee State University, Williams at Hampton University, and Rachel Dumont, Shepherd University (W.Va.). In 2005, I secured a Washington Mystics tryout for Williams. She is Montgomery College's first female professional basketball player to try out for a WNBA team.

Montgomery College: Lady Knights

Timeout with Coach Lesley Lougy

Coaching Philosophy: Play Hard, Play Smart and Play Together

My coaching philosophy emphasized teamwork, tenacity on the court, and academic excellence off the court. In all my years of coaching basketball in the military, recreation leagues, AAU, and college, I urged my student-athletes to perform well in their classes and on the basketball court - because these attributes could lay the foundation for them to become future leaders.

For example, I recruited and taught these well-rounded students to play hard, play smart, and play together every possession. My philosophy was designed to build their confidence to compete, apply leadership skills as student-athletes, and give back to their community.

"Perfect Practice Makes Perfect vs. Practice Makes Perfect!"

A coach's aims to use practices and regular season games to build team winning habits and to determine how to place players in the best possible position to experience success on and off the court. On the court, a coach must determine how to use players' skill sets to maximize the team's success. Today's coaches must always emphasize the value of winning as a team and have players understand that they can be stars in their assigned roles to help the team succeed!

Today's student-athletes must strive to be the best version of themselves in the role assigned by the coach to help the team perform at its best and win. Since 1891 when Dr. Naismith invented the game of basketball, present-day coaches, and players must understand that it's about teamwork versus promoting and creating Most Valuable Players. Coaches are responsible for creating a team culture where players excel. For example, if I am accountable for rebounding, let me be the best rebounder to help the team win games. My message to the players who make basketball a top priority at all costs—be sure to make plans for the day the air will go out of the ball (when your playing career is finally over). It would be best if you had a plan to go professional in something other than basketball. The late Kobe Bryant once said, "to strive to be the best in all areas is to rest at the end, not in the middle."

My players enjoyed playing aggressive defense and up-tempo offense, using 94 feet of the floor and making free throws at the end of the contests. I stressed improving individual performance value over winning. Basketball tenacity and savvy were achieved by improving each player's

performance value. Players were challenged to reach their potential and to be the best they could be on each possession. **Perfect Practice Makes Perfect vs. Practice Makes Perfect!" The key is consistency. Training the mind to make quick decisions leads to winning plays in the moment of "winning time!"** For my Lady Knights, winning became the long-term result!

MONTGOMERY COLLEGE: REGION XX CHAMPIONSHIP TEAM

The team pictured above epitomized true teamwork and hard work using everyone's skill sets. This was the first team of my tenure that experienced success by advancing to the NJCAA Division III National Championship in New York. I learned that it's not about how many members you have on a team, it's about developing team chemistry, team culture, work ethic and a thirst to put in the work to improve every day. Our major accomplishments were the result of the many relationships that played a significant role in helping young student-athletes succeed in the real game of life!

2002 REGION XX CHAMPIONSHIP TEAM

I placed a high value on positive relationships, surrounding myself with compassionate people who understand what young people are going through. I valued trusted advisors with different perspectives who would speak up, be willing to sacrifice and work toward a common goal of putting students first.

Our goal as coaches is to help young people develop, resulting in them reaching their full potential. I believe God brings the right people in the right season to help others succeed, work for a common goal, and to make a more significant impact. I always believed in developing the total person, student, and player. I am so proud of the people that God surrounded me with who provided unwavering and unconditional support for our student-athletes while also helping ensure the holistic development of the next generation.

Together, we worked as a team to help young people develop minds, bodies, and spirits that are interdependent. Our success came by working together to help our students build confidence in themselves, resulting in them taking pride in their academic and athletic achievements. This is what I do know, the fact that we have yet to get to where we are by ourselves.

Assistant Coach Tarlouh Gasque and I built a "non-scholarship" contingent into a championship program that impacted and influenced lives.

The above coaching team effectively consistently developed a championship program for many years. It continues today under Coach Gasque who eventually took over the helm at Montgomery College. I'm so proud of the investment we made together to focus on meeting students where they were to build each student's character, increase self-esteem, and confidence that resulted in hundreds of students earning a degree.

I enjoyed sharing motivational stories that help prepare our student athletes mentally to compete at a championship level. These stories reinforced championship principles that we instilled during the week of preparation and served as guidepost in the actual game of life. Life comes at you quickly with unexpected challenges that each must confront and navigate.

A STORY WITH A KEY MESSAGE:

One of my favorite pre-game motivational stories that prepared our team for a higher level of competition was "the donkey in a well" and "shaking off and stepping up."

The story occurred on a farm in North Carolina where it was common practice to have water wells. One day a loud noise was heard coming from the well that provided water for the community.

It was discovered that the screeching, high pitched, piercing sound was a donkey that somehow fell into the well. The donkey was frightened to death. As community members gathered around the well to see what the matter was, a conversation ensued about what should be done. Someone said, "Let's save the donkey." The question was how the donkey could be saved, as he cried out even louder.

Someone came up with the idea to work together as a team to save the donkey. One team would use shovels to dig from the nearby dirt pile, and a line was formed to pass the bucket of dirt from person to person, and the person at the end of the line would pour the dirt down the well. As the dirt hit the back of the donkey, the screeching, high-pitched, piercing sound got louder. The donkey simultaneously became alarmed and resilient, thinking they were trying to bury him. As the team worked together with all their heart and might, passing the bucket of dirt from person to person, the noise from the donkey ceased! After about 45 minutes, some looked down the well and noticed that with each bucket of dirt that hit the donkey's back, he would concentrate on shaking the dirt off his back and step up a level. The donkey adjusted his focus to the current situation and condition of each bucket of dirt. He stopped crying and screeching and began taking meaningful action: "shaking off the dirt and stepping up!" And soon afterward, the donkey stepped over the well ledge and trotted off into the open area.

As we prepared to compete for a championship like the donkey, the lesson was for our team to adapt in the face of adversity. They needed to trust their abilities to play together, play smart and hard as a team, thus increasing their chances of success. In the moment, the key is to trust one another to make winning plays down the home homestretch of the game. The only guarantee in championship contests is that both teams will give a winning effort. The team that responds in the moment, that copes with the ebb and flow and the ups and downs that come with competing will have an advantage in making winning plays. A team 100% invested is better than one talented player carrying a heavy load. In basketball, as with most sports, "there is no I in the word team."

There are moments in every game that determine the outcome. These plays are called "game changers." Sometimes they are made by individuals or by the whole team, pulling together on one play that transforms the entire momentum of the game. The team at that moment will make winning decisions and plays when the game is on the line. Let's do what we have done all season, each player can step up and make a play that ultimately affects the game's outcome.

I have received many accolades, awards, and titles, but my greatest honor besides the "Dad" title was to be called Coach. I am so grateful for the many players, trainers, academic advisers, Montgomery College professor Cliff McKnight, and all the relationships and partnerships with people who wanted to see me win, achieve, and prosper. I recognized early on that God works through people to expand His reach in kingdom building. I was blessed with many memorable moments and memories during my basketball coaching career with a network of wonderful people who gave purpose to my life! My faith in God caused me to see and learn that I am responsible for you. I was just an instrument, a "dot" connector so the people would know it was the Lord – don't miss the signs!

I am so grateful that God connected me to wonderful people in my life and a network that fulfilled His purpose. I have been blessed that the people in my circle committed themselves and helped me succeed. I thank them for walking in with their purpose, supporting me, and participating in my journey. My family, especially my wife, was the impetus behind all my success in basketball, my career, and my life.

We were not limited to yesterday, because we believed tomorrow was another opportunity to enhance the students' academics and basketball. Moreover, I had humble people in my life who believed that the best was yet to come if we worked to succeed in the next game, the next class, the next semester, etc.

GOD'S PROPERTY – FIRST GIRLS TEAM COACHED
BACK ROW: UPPER LEFT: DEIDRA WILLIAMS,
NOVLETTE AKINSEYE, COR'TNIE BUSH.
FRONT ROW: TORIA FELDER, DONITA ADAMS, JESSICA,
KIM ADAMS, AND STEFFI THOMPSON.

One of the most euphoric experiences during my coaching career was coaching my two daughters.

The picture below shows a picture of my oldest daughter and her teammates when they were a part of the Montgomery County Recreation Department's sports program. The girls selected the team name – God's Property!

MARYLAND FLAMES AAU BASKETBALL

To an outsider, basketball seems like an "easy" game. However, teaching athletes the fundamentals of the game, enhancing their skills, teaching them to play as a team, and changing mentally is needed to produce winners. The game of basketball is bigger than any one person and must be viewed that way, as it is a privilege to play the game we love and respect. Whatever position you find yourself in, coach, player, or support staff, you should always play to win with grace and lose with dignity. To the next generation, always line up at the end of each contest to fist bump, exchange high fives or shake hands to show respect for the game.

As mentioned, I have always believed in developing great relationships and surrounding myself with the right people. An unexpected blessing came from the memorable experience of serving as head coach for the Maryland Flames AAU Basketball program while simultaneously manning the head coaching position at Montgomery College. My wife had connected with the Flames organization while I was building MC into a championship program. She encouraged me to take our youngest daughter Dreka to the Flames tryout. I was so impressed with the number of students and families in attendance.

I was impressed with how well the tryout was organized and run by the owner/director Bill McDermott and his staff of coaches. This was my introduction to the AAU basketball scene that exploded during the same time a new Women's National Basketball Association team came to town. The Washington Mystics attracted many fans in the early 2000's during the initial branding of the sport – a perfect storm! The Williams family became season ticket holders for the first ten years when professional women's basketball was at its apex.

This was a special time as an AAU coach because I enjoyed coaching my daughter, shaping her character, and developing her basketball skills. In addition, I gained lifelong friendships with many of the families that joined the AAU journey. My trusted assistant coaches were also wonderful dads.

Maryland Flames Heat – AAU Travelling Team

Lower Row: Coach Williams, Dreka Williams, Vicky Lisle, Melanie Owens, Sammie Kroll
Back Row: Samantha Callahan, Sabrina Mangat, Brittany Persaud, Shaday Doyley, Kerry Lane, Coach Larry Kroll Raquel Coronado and Coach Dan Lane

Maryland Flames Heat - Timeout!

Play hard, play smart, play together
and have fun on every possession

A GAME CHANGER'S PURSUIT

Larry Kroll and Dan Lane started the voyage from the beginning when our daughters tried out for the Flames' traveling team and weren't selected. I learned so much from my coaching staff, and they will say they learned a lot from me. Together we taught the young girls how to compete as they learned basketball skills and how to play as a team. It was gratifying to witness their growth and development as students and athletes from middle to high school. I will always remember the early struggles that led to breaking a long losing streak and the feeling that initial win brought to our entire program.

It was a joy to teach the young girls what I have taught my teams about being winners, on and off the court. Our most significant achievements were incorporating championship principles beyond the game of basketball, and that in life, like basketball, there are moments in every game that determine the outcome. Sometimes they are made by individuals, other times by the whole team pulling together on one play to transform the entire momentum of the game.

As a person and a player, each has control of the following: their attitude, staying positive, giving a winning effort, and striving for consistent performance while having fun. A wise person once said the outcome of team sports is to compete to win with humility, lose with grace, and do both with dignity." As a player, leader, and mentor, you will always control commitment, effort, and energy.

Again, I believe God brings the right people in the right season to help make a greater difference in the lives of others. Thank you coaches for sharing the wonderful life-changing experiences that we all cherish. Below are thoughts shared by coach Kroll during his time coaching with me with the Flames organization. Coach Kroll has also shared a church exercise describing the Williams family's influence on the team and his family.

"[I] got the call from coach Williams – When my daughter Sammie was ten years old, she attended a tryout for the Flames AAU Basketball Club. She was very excited and nervous. Later that evening, coach

Williams called and told me, 'Congratulations, Sammie made the Flames team.' We were so excited. I found out later that the Flames told the fathers at the tryouts that there were enough girls for an additional team and needed a coach. Coach Williams volunteered to ensure these kids were able to play. This was when he also was Head Coach for the Women's program at Montgomery College, Rockville. He wanted very much to coach his daughter's team (Dreka).

I got drafted as the assistant coach, otherwise known as the 'team mom' – soon after we started. Coach Williams told me that he needed me to be an assistant coach. There was no saying 'no.' I never played basketball in high school, so he must have been desperate. I soon took the 'team mom' role of organizing tournaments, collecting fees, and uniforms, and providing directions to gyms before there was GPS. I was so glad to be a part of my daughter's experience. Coach Williams's philosophy was centered around the whole person concept, (being responsible at home, school, practice, family, and faith). As a basketball family, we were together for 11 months out of the year for six years, playing many tournaments and leagues.

We learned so much from coaching and motivating 12-year-old girls to be competitive as they learned how to play basketball correctly. I remember one game against our [rival] team, The Classics, where we lost the game. Coach [Williams] felt we needed to motivate the girls with hopes of increasing their energy and effort to a higher level. During the next foul call, he told me, 'I am going to argue with the referees excessively and get intentionally thrown out of the game on purpose. This will motivate the girls to step up their intensity down the stretch to win the game.' The problem was that the strategy backfired! The girls were so concerned and distraught about Coach Williams getting kicked out of the game, they completely fell apart the rest of the game. This tactic worked with the college team, but not so much with sixth grade girls.

Another great memory was how practices were conducted, especially at the end of every on-court practice. Coach Williams would say, 'Great practice, now let's have a seat in the "living room."' Most practices were held at Gaithersburg Middle School over many years. At the end of each practice, Coach would bring all the girls to center court which he called the "living room." The girls would sit on the floor (the couch). He would talk about the girls focusing on schoolwork, their families, character-building attributes, and everything except basketball.

Our Flames-Heat AAU team was exposed to many experiences that aided in the growth and development of every student-athlete. When the kids were about ten years old, we took them to a Washington Mystics basketball game. Coach Williams had connections to the team and got the Flames to play during halftime of the pro game. The girls wore different color Mystics t-shirts and participated as part of the pre-game ceremony for the pre-game introductions. The announcer over the public address system announced each girl by name as the youth players gave a ceremonial basketball to Mystics' players. This was a special moment for the girls and their parents to hear their child's name being announced. After the game, we also took a team picture with Chamique Holdsclaw (the number one draft pick for the previous year in 1999).

Another far reaching impact of our AAU experience: our girls came from all ends of the socio-economic spectrum. The team's diversity proved to be one of its strengths, as the kids became life-long friends.

When I reflect on the impact of the "Flames Family" years, they significantly impacted my daughter Sammie's [life] and my life. For Sammie, she made life-long friends with the core group of girls (Kerry, Dreka, Vicky, Shaday and Brittney) and others that came and went over the years. She also made friends with diverse cultures, backgrounds, experiences, family situations and economic opportunities.

MARYLAND FLAMES TEAM MEMBERS ATTENDING A
WASHINGTON MYSTICS HOME GAME.

It was a blessing to be with my daughter, talking in the car, just the two of us while driving to practice, games or tournaments. It was a very special time for our relationship. Watching her develop a relationship with coach [Williams] was also fun. He was able to have discussions with her that I couldn't have about basketball or even life. When my other daughter was in college studying kinesiology, she had a project to interview someone and to reflect on a person (sports related) that has impacted her life. Sammie wrote in a paper in response that Coach Williams was the most influential person in her life.

This was a special time in our lives in developing and building a competitive program where student-athletes reflected academic achievement and athletic excellence. Our students always gave a winning effort in all relationships to help others on and off the court. Our student-athletes learned to excel at doing the little things to help the team compete. Every player consistently made smart hustle plays, winning plays, and getting tough rebounds or loose balls to keep the possessions alive. Our players were taught to make winning plays with the game on the line. It was safe to say that our students earned respect from teammates and classmates for being positive role models in the classroom and on the court. They learned to balance responsibilities as students, athletes, family, and community while maintaining excellent and high scholastic achievement."

Lastly, so much love and respect for Coach Williams and their family. Together they operate a non-profit Christian and community-based youth organization. That mentor's young black males to be successful in life, as family members, and eventually be good fathers. UCF conducted a fundraiser and stated, "we saved 21 young males from going to prison, doing drugs or joining a gang. This was a different perspective for the privileged white guy. Coach Williams lives a life of faith in action through service to the community. He's the first person I have ever met that lived his life with Christian confidence.

KEY MESSAGE #1:

From legendary coach Brown, "Coaching, like mentoring (using a metaphor) is like a two-edged knife that will cut you at some point and keep you up at night." In a teachable moment with Coach Brown, I took in a valuable mentoring lesson. Coach Brown stated that 98% of student-athletes will listen to you, follow instructions, play by the rules, and compete in the classroom and on the court. They will go out on the court to give you 110% effort in execution and following the game, play and abide by team rules. He proclaimed it is the 2% that will keep you up at night, wrestling with what you could have done better to prevent an undesirable outcome for the student and the basketball program.

KEY MESSAGE #2:

Be intentional about being in the presence of people with greater professional experience in the field you are pursuing. The good Lord wanted me to become a basketball coach, and I pursued how to accelerate the learning process. I learned to surround myself with compassionate people who understand what young people are going through. I have experienced people from all walks of life, local and out-of-state who may show you just one thing that isn't aligned with your core values. I learned to acquire their best practices while noting what needed to be improved for my toolbox. Whatever profession you pursue, you can benefit by developing relationships with the top professionals in your local community.

Now that we are in the virtual world, you will accelerate your experience base by attending seminars, conferences, and meetings where they speak in front of an audience!

I experienced this when I was stationed in Germany. I sought out and met with a higher-ranking officer and asked what I needed to do to become a Colonel. He was candid and shared that I needed to stop pursuing being an all-around sports person. I excelled at volleyball, football, wrestling, and basketball. I needed to shift my focus toward promotions to advance to the highest rank possible.

So much of my life has been shaped by the experiences in the military. Whatever your profession, thinkers, doers, dreamers, and leaders are required for "next level" achievement.

The Colonel looked me in the eye and said, "Captain Williams, to advance as an officer you must pursue a master's degree and score high in performance and assignments in senior-level positions (i.e., Executive Officer, Company Commander, Brigade level positions, etc.).

I applied the same life lesson to become a head basketball coach. I relocated to Fort Ritchie, Maryland and once I settled into my new senior-level assignment, I looked for the top basketball programs in the area. I met with Mount St. Mary's University's men's assistant coach Don Anderson, who pointed me to Coach Brown at Hagerstown Community College. Coach Brown was my shepherd, mentor, and friend that taught me how to think about the game, develop my mindset, helped with my employment of game-time strategies and with the development of a high-performance program. My advice is to surround yourself with professional high achievers who will take you to another level in a shorter time.

Using other people's experiences to advance and learn how to be an effective leader to deal with a new generation of youth and thinkers was essential. If you desire to be a coach in any sport and become a mentor and leader in any community, you must be willing to invest your time, talent, and treasures to realize the dream of becoming the very best!

QUOTE:

"Talent wins games, but teamwork and intelligence win championships."

— Michael Jordan

SCRIPTURE:

"Listen to advice and accept instruction, so that you may gain wisdom in the future."

Proverbs 19:20

CHAPTER 9

Fraternal Brotherhood

The most amazing life-changing experience I have ever been a part of is being a proud member of the greatest fraternity known to humankind, Omega Psi Phi Fraternity, Inc. For more than 111 years, Omega men have influenced thousands of men, women, boys, and girls throughout the world.

Omega Psi Phi Fraternity, Inc. (ΩΨΦ) is the first African-American Greek-lettered international fraternity founded on a Historically Black College or University campus. The fraternity was founded on November 17, 1911, by three Howard University juniors, Dr. Oscar James Cooper, Professor Frank Coleman, Bishop Edgar Amos Love, and their faculty adviser, Dr. Ernest Everett Just. The Honorable Founders are shown below:

Dr. Oscar J. Cooper (1888-1972)   Professor Frank Coleman (1890-1967)   Bishop Edgar A. Love (1891-1974)   Dr. Ernest E. Just (1883-1941)

Our fraternity was born out of the friendship of three young men and a young college professor.

Let us always remember that when you choose your friends, friendship is always motivated by love! The fraternity was derived from the Greek phrase, Philia Ophelema Psukism, meaning *"friendship is essential to the soul."* The phrase also was selected as the fraternity motto. Our cardinal principles: Manhood, Scholarship, Perseverance, and Uplift, are the guiding principles in which we live and raise our families. There are more than 200,000 members of our fraternity and more than 750 chapters worldwide in North America, Europe, Asia, Africa, Bermuda, The Virgin Islands, and Panama. This fraternity, like none other, promotes the bond of friendship, builds the brotherhood of men, and uplifts their communities. We are trusted messengers who strengthen families in every community. We mobilize, invest resources, and pool our collective efforts, time, and talents to help the least of these, the left out and left behind in the community.

The words that inspired me to lead and serve were from beloved Founder Bishop Edgar Amos Love: "I want Omega to be a shining light among all the fraternities among us, with the highest ideals, and we must first serve before we can lead." Our immediate past Grand Chaplain, Reverend Dr. Walter T. Richardson, shared that the founders of Omega Psi Phi Fraternity were men of faith, believed in godly character, and made Christian manhood a central principle. Each of the Founders ascended to the top of their respective professions. They were Christian men who sought to attract and select men whose lives would reflect the character of Christ. In the early years of the fraternity, the vision was to tap into the potential of Godly men who had a heart for service to the Lord. Our fraternity continues to seek men of like-mindedness, high achievement, and next-level forward thinkers to serve and lead all humanity.

Omega Men are Praying Men

THE 81ST GRAND CONCLAVE WAS HELD
JULY 20-24, 2018 IN NEW ORLEANS, LOUISIANA

I am glad to be counted in the number of Omega men who are praying for men. For our generation, these are some exciting times in our fraternity. With all that is happening in the world, Omega men set the example in our communities and this world directly with our works. At this pivotal point in the 21st century, our fraternity continues to play an integral part in uplifting our communities and strengthening our families. We are the beacon to communities across the world. I am excited to join this generation of Omega Men committed to transforming our beloved fraternity by working together for a greater cause. We are purpose-driven to provide hope, encouragement, and solutions to help families and youth deal with the social, economic, and medically debilitating ramifications of this current worldwide pandemic.

Our acts of service are reflected in the many programs geared towards improving African Americans' quality of life in health and wellness, housing, social injustice, civil rights, and disparities in education. The pandemic has taught many to base decision-making on science and to think about doing things differently. We are not defined as Omega Men by the royal colors worn (purple and gold) but by what we do in the community! We have dedicated professional men "with the highest ideals" who work tirelessly to lift the downtrodden. The new generation of Omega men will fulfill the hope of our Founders. I encourage this generation to be intentional about mentoring the selection of new initiates and college students.

Furthermore, I want to encourage this generation to be intentional about authentic relationships. I care about you; you care about me and together we care about making Omega shine every day throughout the world. The way you communicate and treat people impacts a person's effectiveness. Let's always operate from a place of friendship!

Omega Psi Phi Fraternity, Inc., has truly shaped my life into the man I am today. I was initiated into the fraternity in Fayetteville, North Carolina (by the Beta Chi Chapter of the 6th District) on May 6, 1989.

At the time, I was serving at Fort Bragg, North Carolina, as a Captain in the U.S. Army. My line included four other men seeking friendship. This was my second opportunity to become a member of our illustrious fraternity. I am grateful to have completed the mission that started at Rider University when I was a junior. As I reflect over the past 34 years, it was one of the best decisions I've ever made.

Membership Intake

From Left to Right: Donald Williams II, General Bernard McGeachy, Terry V. Price, John J. Becton Jr., Charles Emory Harris Jr.

Shown with Dean of Pledges Brother Perry Robinson

DONALD WILLIAMS II

THE VALUE OF OUR FRATERNITY IS NOT IN NUMBERS, BUT IN REAL MEN, IN REAL BROTHERHOOD. EIGHT MEN THOROUGHLY IMMERSED IN THE TRUE OMEGA SPIRIT ARE FAR GREATER ASSETS THAN EIGHTY WITH LUKEWARM ENTHUSIASM.

The first Omega man I witnessed living the creed was my brother-in-law, role model, and mentor – David Anderson. He was raised in a little country town called Vienna, Georgia. As a college student pursuing an engineering degree, David was initiated at Savannah State University (then College) via the Alpha Gamma Chapter, 7th District, on December 4, 1970. He was dating my older sister when I was just a youngster (around 12). My awareness was heightened when I noticed that he was different in terms of work ethic, discipline, focus, perseverance, and scholarship. He was the first Omega man I saw who displayed the fraternity's cardinal principles.

I wanted to emulate his sense of purpose. He would tell you that "success" is about the difference you make in people's lives and how you work together to illuminate our community. He shared a valuable life lesson used in his life, to always speak with facts and data, develop a decision tree that says – "these are the facts, and here is the supporting data behind the facts that lead to the decision."

A GAME CHANGER'S PURSUIT

The second heightened awareness of the shining light of Omega was on the campus of Rider University in New Jersey, where the Honorable Lawson R. McElroy, known to many as

"Guardian Angel" increased the diversity of Black and Hispanic minority students attending Rider in the early '70s. Omega men were known for their work in the community in and around Trenton, New Jersey.

I SERVED IN THE 13TH DISTRICT, LAMBDA XI CHAPTER AS KEEPER OF FINANCE, LOCATED IN SEOUL, KOREA.

Our fraternity exists to serve and help uplift people in the community. I am grateful to lend my gifts, talents, and treasures to improve our beloved fraternity at every station and position served.

Serving in three districts has been an amazing experience: I was initiated in the 6th District while serving in the Army. In addition, I served in the 13th International District of Omega Psi Phi Fraternity as Keeper of Finance, Lambda Xi Chapter located in Seoul, Korea—"The District that makes Omega truly International," and comprised of men who serve around the world and whose chapters are located outside the continental United States.

There are 20 chapters across this District, and we maintain an international presence in Bermuda, Canada, China, The Dominican Republic, Germany, Ghana, Hawaii, Italy, Japan, Korea, Mexico, Panama, The Bahamas, The Netherlands, St. Croix VI, St. Thomas VI, St. Maarten, the United Arab Emirates, and the United Kingdom.

After Korea, I relocated to Maryland (2nd District) to raise my family. As my children grew older, the time was right to connect with Mu Nu Chapter, Montgomery County. I stepped up to provide leadership as the chapter's Chairman for Social Action, a natural fit for my passion for community engagement and working with other community stakeholders.

I have always advocated the importance of community engagement and collaboration with others to improve the quality of life in the community. Our youth need to see adults working together. We are a better community with our young people joining in to work together. Students need to see a community that interacts with county officials, public school district leaders, the NAACP, and other racially diverse groups.

I am reminded of an excerpt from my favorite poem: "Live Your Creed,"

"...For I may misunderstand you and the fine advice you give, but there's no misunderstanding how you act and how you live." - Langston Hughes

A little-known fact is that First A.M.E. Church-Gaithersburg played a significant role in many ways. Our small church was blessed to have three Omega men who provided active servant leadership as we worked on our spirituality together. I recalled after a church meeting, we agreed to attend the next fraternity chapter meeting together. My mentor Brother John Tucker provided an example of Godly leadership for both Larry Melton and me. We reunited with Mu Nu before the 100-year Centennial celebration by attending the chapter meeting in Silver Spring. Also, we agreed not to raise our hands to volunteer for any leadership positions. Well, of course that backfired, and the rest is history.

MENTOR BROTHER JOHN TUCKER EPITOMIZED CHRISTIAN MANHOOD

Since then, I have been "all in" by lending my gifts to improve the quality of the chapter, community, and the 2nd District. We found a chapter that operated from a place of friendship that shares their joys and sorrows. It was refreshing to find camaraderie, common loyalty, sense of pride and witness the men of Mu Nu Chapter working together as a team to assist the community.

For 53 years, the chapter has believed it's vital for Omega men to be engaged in the community, such as holding leadership positions such as Board of Education, PTA, county-wide, Commission, House of Delegates, etc. Omega's presence in the community gives hope and inspiration to African American families, young males, and educators.

It is imperative to see men leading out front in their homes, church, and community, interacting with other organizations, sororities, fraternities, and other ethnic groups that make up this diverse county of 1.2 million residents where we live, work, and raise our families. Our young people, especially our young males and young adult dads must see us in the community to show them the way.

PRESIDENT BARACK OBAMA (FLANKED PICTURE LEFT BY 39TH GRAND BASILEUS DR. ANDREW RAY AND PICTURE RIGHT BY 40TH GRAND BASILEUS ANTONIO KNOX) POSES FOR A PHOTO WITH THE LEADERSHIP OF THE OMEGA PSI PHI FRATERNITY AT THE WASHINGTON CONVENTION CENTER IN WASHINGTON, JULY 29, 2011. (OFFICIAL WHITE HOUSE PHOTO BY LAWRENCE JACKSON)

Omega Psi Phi Fraternity, Inc. hosted its Centennial Grand Conclave celebration on July 27-31, 2011, in Washington, D.C. The nation's capital was where our great fraternity celebrated 100-years of extraordinary leadership and community engagement. The 39th Grand Basileus of Omega Psi Phi Fraternity, Dr. Andrew Ray, (2010-2014) was the host for showcasing Omega centennial excellence!

An extraordinary number of high-ranking military men, spiritual leaders, well-known business people, accomplished entertainers, political leaders, and exceptional pro athletes joined the milestone celebration.

President Obama inspired Omega leadership to increase our "next level" community engagement by mentoring young males and strengthening families with male engagement. What a joy it was to be connected to the historic former 44th President of the United States and his Fatherhood and Mentoring Initiative that spotlighted the critical challenge of the absence of fathers in the lives of children, families, and communities across the nation.

Omega Psi Phi Fraternity, Inc. has engaged communities for a very long time with meaningful parenting and mentoring programs across the nation. We continue today as the only Greek strategic partner under the Fatherhood and Mentoring Program. It is more vital now than ever with the recent attempted efforts to roll back the success of African Americans, with the COVID-19 pandemic, and the world's rapid transformation in the 21st century. We must persist in increasing the awareness of the importance of responsible fatherhood and expand our partnerships with as many like-minded community organizations, public agencies, schools, and advocates of responsible parenting. We must work to solve the problem of paternal absenteeism, deconstruct negative stereotypes, and celebrate those who are engaged in their children's lives--both the children in their families, and the children of their communities. Our future is only as bright as what we as parents invest in children – all of them, not just your own, so that they as the next generation can be a light to this world.

I share the words of Grand Basileus Ray (a mentor to all), his metaphor of running a relay race is advice for all men to govern themselves. Omega leadership at every level, district and chapter is like a relay race. When you come out of the blocks and then receive the baton, your focus must be on running your leg of the race to the best of your ability. He warned that a time will come when there will be a baton handoff, which is the critical part of the race, don't drop the baton or miss the handoff.

I share the words of Grand Basileus Ray (a mentor to all), his metaphor of running a relay race is advice for all men to govern themselves. Omega leadership at every level, district and chapter is like a relay race. When you come out of the blocks and then receive the baton, your focus must be on running your leg of the race to the best of your ability. He warned that a time will come when there will be a baton handoff, which is the critical part of the race, don't drop the baton or miss the handoff.

Left to right: 28th District Representative Benjamin Jeffers, 39th Grand Basileus of Omega Psi Phi Fraternity Dr. Andrew A. Ray, (2010-2014).

If you drop the baton, you lose, and the whole team loses. We stand on the shoulders of courageous past leaders who worked diligently to move the fraternity forward into the 21st century. Dr. Ray said, "you don't have to cross the finish line yourself, just give the team a chance to win!" Do thy duty that is best; leave unto the Lord the rest.

Brother Ben Jeffers' focus is displaying friendship and respect everywhere you go, to everyone you meet, and in all the places you can. He encourages everyone to do great things. However, it is important to first focus on being a great friend to all that cross your path. He challenges each one to demonstrate acts of kindness to improve a person's life. To pour out love in your community, pay off rent and utilities, give away gift cards, and go into laundromats and grocery stores to show acts of kindness. These two men epitomize authentic friendship and have supported my leadership in the district.

Mu Nu has a storied and proud history of community engagement, working collaboratively with community partners for greater results. The chapter was chartered on May 23, 1970, and has led by example in leadership excellence and community engagement for five decades and counting, reaching all of the over million citizens of Montgomery County, Maryland--one of the most diversified counties in the country and one of the most highly educated and accomplished workforces over the age of 25.

The first Basileus during the fraternal year of 1970-1971 was the late Brother Rudolph W. Snowden. An Assistant Principal at Gaithersburg Middle School in the early 70's, Brother Snowden was the founder of the Montgomery County graduate chapter of Omega who also put in so much work organizing the chapter. He set the chapter's course for heavy engagement in Montgomery County Public Schools (MCPS). It has been amazing to me that despite the challenges of the county's history, the chapter was able to overcome obstacles and experience phenomenal accomplishments. We collaborated to make a difference in the community, changing the narrative on black lives, shaping, and impacting young people, especially young males, and adult fathers.

We can't tell of all the incredible work accomplished working together as a team over the many years. An example of this work is the widely acclaimed Dr. George B. Thomas, Sr. Learning Academy (GBTLA), known as "the Saturday School program," founded by C. Arthur Eubanks from Mu Nu Chapter. The first Saturday school class began in 1986 with 19 students ready to learn and improve their academic performance. Omega men first started tutoring students with the Housing Opportunities Commission (HOC) in Olney, Maryland, run by Ms. Deloris Cole.

The success resulted in the expansion of MCPS, which helped set up 12 sites to help close the academic achievement gap with Black and Brown students. The chapter provided mentoring and tutoring for hundreds of students in grades 1 through 12. In addition, Mu Nu Chapter has raised financial resources to provide significant scholarships to support hundreds of young people attending colleges and universities across the United States.

I am so proud to be a part of such an outstanding chapter respected throughout Montgomery County and Omega Nation. I'm also very proud of the men of Mu Nu for being consistently visible in their homes, serving in local churches, and providing leadership in the community. I can truly say Mu Nu Chapter believes in promoting friendships and brotherly bonds, and we celebrate each other's joys and accomplishments.

The chapter has stalwart role models and men who lead the way to include our very own "legends" in former First Vice Grand Basileus Dr. Adam E. McKee Jr., Dr. Leonard Haynes, Dr. George B. Thomas Sr., Reginald M. Felton, C. Arthur Eubanks, Richard Tyler, Dr. William Powell, two District Representatives; 34th District Representative, Milton D. Harrison, and 37th District Representative, Kelvin Ampofo, and several District Chairmen and many more members who gave of themselves unselfishly and excellently. Today, we continue to stand on their shoulders.

In this pivotal time of the 21st century, it is an exciting time to be an Omega man. We must persist to play an integral part and role for uplifting our youth and strengthening families. I heard an elderly brother say, "if serving is below you, then leadership is beyond you."

My life has been enriched because of my love for people and desires

MAY 25, 2019 - THE INAUGURAL MU NU-MCAC COLEMAN-LOVE BBQ!

In October 2017, it was indeed a blessing to be elected and serve as the 25th Basileus of Mu Nu Chapter (2017-2019) in the same period as my wife Mona's election to serve as the 17th President of the Montgomery County Alumnae Chapter of Delta Sigma Theta Sorority, Inc. My wife and I provided leadership simultaneously in one of the most affluent counties in America. It was a blessing to witness God ordering our steps by using our leadership gifts to bring people together to bless the community where we lived, worked, and raised our family.

It was a privilege and honor of a lifetime to have served as Basileus, the 2nd District Chairman for the Fatherhood Initiative and Mentoring Committee, and the fraternity's International Committee. I am grateful to the brotherhood for allowing me to serve passionately and promote the precepts of Omega Psi Phi Fraternity during the past decades.

As a leader, I try to do God's will, lead by example, and inspire other men to live by the Cardinal Principles the Founders envisioned. Together we raised awareness of equal and equitable access to education. Together we galvanized the community stakeholders, providing a higher level of leadership across Omega nation and specifically community presence in Montgomery County and five states: New York, New Jersey, Pennsylvania, Delaware, and Maryland.

Mu Nu Chapter men, past and present, have led the chapter with honor, dignity, and integrity. I am excited about the future direction of the chapter. We are grateful for the brotherhood that embraced, encouraged, and supported my administration, operated from a position of love

of humanity, and promoted friendship, community-based collaborations, and partners. I am grateful that my brothers embraced my servant leadership style to let my light shine. Like the poem **"Our Greatest Fear" by Marianne Williamson, together, we unconsciously permit other people to do the same. As a servant leader, I believe that love unites, binds, and unifies us to fulfill a greater purpose.**

We affected the community with teaming arrangements such as the annual Game Changer Conference for male youth and Bridge Builder Middle School Mentoring. We launched a podcast called "Ques on the Move," connecting to a new generation of listeners about incredible mentoring stories. Mona and I were proud to plan and organize the first-ever Montgomery County "Coleman Love" cookout that brought together more than 1,000 families and friends, community leaders, and dignitaries from across the state of Maryland (see picture above).

We are so proud of the Ques on the Move podcast initiative that started in 2017. Its rollout was facilitated by using the WBGR studio in Hyattsville, Maryland the first four years. Shoutout to Dr. Lionel Green Owner/CEO, as well as Tim Day and Stacey Jordan, host of Real Husbands of Largo.

The "Ques on the Move" podcast spotlights the incredible work that Omega Men are doing across the 2nd District with mentoring our young people, especially our young males. The podcast also helps give strategies to help men become more effective fathers who stay engaged in their children's lives!

In the sixth year of the podcast, we pivoted to a new production team during the pandemic. We want to give a shout-out to the Stanton Group, Inc., under the leadership of Darius A. Stanton, executive producer of the "Peace in the Morning Show."

We are grateful for the many chapters of Omega under the teaming arrangement, along with guests and supporters who tuned in to support

"Ques on the Move" every Tuesday. Together we have impacted the world with meaningful conversation for our community.

Mentoring is more vital now than ever before, as there is no denying that students were negatively affected by the pandemic. Some students excelled with virtual learning and others were unsuccessful for many reasons. The academic gap has widened, and the "love gap" for teachers inspiring students to rise above barriers and obstacles to succeed in the 21st century has also increased. The greatest gift is love, agape is the love of mankind. And what the world needs is love more than ever before. We must help our students get back on track. The Divine Nine Greek organizations have a role to play with meaningful mentoring programs that meet students where they are to help them reach their full potential, and to assist fathers with effective parenting strategies.

Some like-minded organizations seek Omega as partners because of our intentional commitment to mentoring young people and men to be better fathers and positive role models. Encouraging "partnerships" with your local township's social service agencies, housing authorities, fatherhood organizations, and organizations like Big Brothers and Big Sisters that share common interests are vital to helping parents, especially men, to help their children grow into healthy young adults. This will result in stronger families.

In March 2022, Ques on the Move Podcast featured educators across the district who addressed a topic hardly anyone is talking about, the "Silent Crisis in Education." Co-host brother Jeff Diggs asked the guests to share their insights on what they are seeing regarding academic performance, mental wellness, school security, and safety.

Dr. Carlton Lampkins, a retired Deputy Superintendent of the Delaware Public School System, shared that the last two years affected our young people more than we like to admit. Dr. Lampkins, who retired in 2016 after 36 years as an educator, believes a part of student development is interacting with their friends and adults teaching them.

The importance of social interaction centers on how children learn, grow, and develop into future leaders. The issue is "learning loss," the challenge is how do we catch our young people up from the two years students lost in the pandemic!

PLEASE CHECK OUT THE YOUTUBE STATION TO LISTEN TO A FULL CONVERSATION ABOUT "THE SILENT CRISIS" IN EDUCATION. (HTTPS://FB.WATCH/BVRZL_YILO/)

For the past decade, Dr. Gorman Brown, the Principal of Charles Herbert Flowers High School (Prince George's County, Maryland), echoed the above sentiment. He also noted that we are in a "silent crisis." The ultimate education goal is to prepare young people for college and career readiness. The two years of learning loss have arrested the development of all students, even if they did well academically. The last few years (2020 through the present) stunted students' natural development because of limited interaction in a school setting. Students are struggling with learning, organization, social-emotional, and conflict-resolution skills needed to function effectively in a learning environment. The reality is, the last time students learned those skills mentioned above, they were in middle school and now struggling in high school! We are indeed in a silent crisis and will not get to educate students to standard until we address these mental wellness issues.

Dr. Leroy Evans, the Principal of Col. Zadok Magruder High School in Rockville, Maryland, experienced the first-ever student shooting in MCPS in January of 2021, where a student was gravely wounded. As a result of this shooting, his school was put on lockdown for more than three hours. Dr. Evans stated that wellness and safety go together.

Wellness is born out of a nurturing environment that is safe and resourceful. School safety is important because education and learning can't occur without students in a safe environment. This includes physical wellness as well as creating a safe place for learning.

Schools must go beyond emergency practice drills. The same goes for mentoring. In school, establishing trusted and meaningful relationships with adults, pre-K through 12th grade, is most important for students. All of us must be concerned with having a safe school while providing the most educational resources for our youth to win at life!

Just Click: (ARCHIVE FOR ALL PODCASTS OF QUES ON THE MOVE)

https://youtube.com/channel/UC8NhHyTWVywssxPgo68tphw

It is a great honor and privilege to provide leadership and to serve under four Second District Representatives as the 2nd District Chairman for the Fatherhood Initiative and Mentoring Committee (FIMC). I was groomed under the 34th District Representative, Milton D. Harrison, who conducted his first Leadership Conference at Solomons Island, Maryland, spotlighting mentoring in 2014. The conference began to raise awareness about the importance of mentoring work with fathers and young people.

In 2016, I was appointed District Chairman under the 35th District Representative Sherman Charles, who strategically separated the sub-committee from the social action committee. He established the Fatherhood Initiative and Mentoring as a stand-alone committee which changed the trajectory in the fraternity. He charged me to develop a meaningful program with strategic direction. I was totally surprised to be recognized at the annual Achievement Award celebration for earning Chairman of the Year in 2017.

MU NU CHAPTER IMPACT IN THE 2ND DISTRICT
2ND DISTRICT, CHAIRMAN OF THE YEAR (2017)
FATHERHOOD INITIATIVE AND MENTORING COMMITTEE

District Representative Charles whispered in my ear at the award presentation, "continue to keep working to take this committee to next level achievement." We continued to work to improve and develop new initiatives under the 36th District Representative, J. Kendall Smalls. As the COVID pandemic disrupted the world, innovative, effective, and creative mentoring occurred using virtual platforms under the 37th District Representative and Mu Nu Chapter Brother Kelvin Ampofo. I am extremely grateful to serve under four District Representatives administrations, including the current 38th Second District Representative, Delrecole "Rico" Gales. He's very supportive of "Next Level" mentoring initiatives now that the brotherhood (at the 83rd Grand Conclave) voted to make the committee mandatory to all 750 chapters worldwide.

A GAME CHANGER'S PURSUIT

MENTORING MATTERS AND MENTORING SAVES LIVES!

PICTURED AT THE ANNUAL DECEMBER 2016 NEW JERSEY STATEWIDE FATHERHOOD SUMMIT, (LEFT TO RIGHT): MATTHEW STEVENS, PHI UPSILON, DARRELL EDMONDS, UPSILON ALPHA, AULA SUMBRY, DELTA UPSILON (OMEGA CHAPTER), DONALD WILLIAMS II, FIMP CHAIRMAN, JEFFREY DIGGS, MU RHO FORMER BASILEUS; SHAUN RATLIFF, MU NU; THABITI BOONE, OMEGA PSI PHI FRATERNITY INTERNATIONAL REPRESENTATIVE.

The conference theme that year was *"Celebrating Fatherhood! The Difference a Dad Makes – Incorporating 2-Generational Approaches."* Witnessing the state-sponsored commitment at the 4th Annual Statewide Fatherhood Summit in New Brunswick, New Jersey, was so meaningful. What if every state committed to supporting dads and making Fatherhood programs a top priority?

As a fraternity, we must persist in raising awareness of the importance of responsible Fatherhood and expand our partnerships with as many like-minded community organizations, public agencies, schools, and advocates of responsible parenting as possible. We must continue to work to solve the problem of paternal absenteeism, deconstruct negative stereotypes, and celebrate those who are engaged in their children's lives, the children in their families, and the children of their communities. Children are the future! Our future is only as bright as what we as parents invest in them – all of them, not just our own.

QUILTED GIFT PRESENTED BY THE INTERNATIONAL COMMITTEE FOR FATHERHOOD INITIATIVE AND MENTORING TO DR. DAVID E. MARION, 41ST GRAND BASILEUS (AT THE 83RD GRAND CONCLAVE) FOUNDERS BANQUET.

On July 21-26, 2022, the fraternity celebrated the significant accomplishments of Dr. David E. Marion, 41st Grand Basileus, the fraternity's Chief Operating Officer (2018-2022). He intentionally made the Fatherhood Initiative and Mentoring Committee the centerpiece of his four-year administration to encourage greater results. Consequently, mentoring and community engagement reached new heights while navigating the pandemic.

During the Conclave, the baton passed between the immediate past Grand Basileus, Dr. Marion to Ricky Lewis, 42nd Grand Basileus. In his first message, Brother Lewis said, "Our fraternity is well-positioned to become the premier mentoring organization in the world." He shared that our goal is to impact the world through mentoring men to help them become better fathers and help our young people, especially young boys, reach their full potential. Omega Nation will roll out a mentoring program in local communities across the globe.

As the country continues to work through COVID, the question was asked, "What is 'next level mentoring?'" The key message and charge from our newly elected 42nd Grand Basileus Lewis, is for our generation to "perfect our presence" in communities nationwide!

The message that "you cannot escape the precious moment of today" was echoed by the Grand Chaplain, Reverend Dr. Richardson, in his keynote delivery during the Founders Banquet. Now is the time to use influence, improve, and take advantage of 'our now!' Now is the time to be innovative, on the cutting edge, ahead of the curve, and to be the point of the spear. We must be powerful and be believers and doers to help the generation here and now achieve greater heights.

As I learned from my experiences as a military officer, professional career, and basketball coach, it's truly about teamwork. I am grateful for the opportunity to serve and work beside some of the most educated, compassionate, caring, and dedicated men anywhere on this earth. In the current crisis with absent fathers, the fatherhood description is much more than being "related" to a child. It is about influence, being a resource, lending a helping hand, and lifting as you climb. We want youth to know that people beyond their circumstances are looking out for them.

We want to be model examples to share our knowledge, wisdom, gifts, and talents to strengthen and uplift families and communities. I have met many men who sacrifice their time to ensure that others are successful. These men give of themselves just because they care. They sacrifice to be great role models and pay the price through unselfish acts of losing free time, to reach back and grab a young person's hand. Everyone wants to be great and good, but only a few are prepared to sacrifice to help a young person succeed!

I am grateful to serve the past four District Representatives to launch a comprehensive, strategic, and focused program. In addition, I appreciate the two International Chairmen, S. Earl Wilson and Robert Fairchild, and White House staffer, Thabiti Boone for their leadership, mentorship, and friendship. I would be remiss not to recognize the committee members who support a robust, bold, strategic, and focused 2nd District Fatherhood Initiative and Mentoring Committee, (FIMC). Together we have accomplished so much to make mentoring a top priority across the five states that represent approximately 85 chapters from across the district.

I am also very proud of my purpose-driven teammates for providing outstanding leadership in their respective states: Jeff Diggs, Deputy Chairman, FIMC (my accountability partner), and my friends who have a servant's heart in their community are the state chairmen for their respective states: Harry Watson and Anthony Sheppard, New York; Matt Stevens, New Jersey; Brian Twyman and Anthony Jones, Eastern Pennsylvania and Carlton Heywood, Western Pennsylvania; Vince Stutts, Delaware; and of course, my home team Mu Nu Chapter, Social Action Chairman past and present, Shaun Ratliff, Dr. Lorenzo Prillman and Jason Miller representing the state of Maryland. All brothers who have crossed my path in support of this meaningful, impactful mission of grassroots community engagement should be aware that I am grateful for your contributions and equally proud of our generation that's intentional about being difference-makers in these critical times!

At this moment, all men, (members of Greek-lettered organizations and non-Greeks) are challenged to roll up their sleeves to help the next generation. Join in this meaningful mentoring work by putting your hands on the plow to work together to lend your gifts and abilities to strengthen families in the community who are without a man in the house.

There's just so much happening in the world today with social justice issues, the Black Lives Matter struggle, voter suppression, education equity and access--underlying issues all occurring in a global COVID-19 pandemic.

I ask you, firstly, what are **you** doing individually and secondly, how many young people are you working with this month and/or plan to work with this year to make the community better?

A government report before COVID-19 reflected the African American high school graduation rate was 69% nationwide. Seventy-three percent of Hispanic youth have earned high school diplomas, and the graduation rate for whites is 86%. In addition, another report reveals that our students are reading below the 4th-grade level, and 85% of students need help to do 8th-grade level math. The gap has widened, not just the academic gap but the love gap for inspiring students to rise above the barriers and obstacles of this generation to meet future challenges.

In April 2020, Dr. Leonard Haynes, former HBCU President, and White House Executive warned at the beginning of the pandemic that there will be a crisis with education. The pandemic negatively impacted our students, although some successfully used Chromebooks and laptops in the virtual learning environment. For many reasons, many needed to be more successful in learning under those conditions.

Our fraternity must provide leadership in the community and be advocates and "helping hands" on the other side of the COVID-19 pandemic. You must know that mentoring and education are like gloves – they go hand in hand! Many of our chapters across the district partner with the public schools in their respective communities to help students reach their full potential. The pandemic has impacted mentoring relationships with students and learning loss due to the isolation of students.

As I close this chapter, I hope our founding fathers are smiling down and proud of the community engagement and partnerships we continue to build. We aim to keep doing the meaningful and impactful work envisioned when our fraternity came into being over

112 years ago at Howard University. I encourage you to keep doing what you do to make a difference where you live and work in your community. This outreach ensures that our legacy lives in future generations. I recall during the planning of the 2022 District Youth Leadership and Game Changer Conference, I was asked, "What does fatherhood mean to you?"

FATHERS MATTER
CREATING POSITIVE MEMORIES

For me, fatherhood is the journey of a man when he accepts the responsibility for raising a child throughout his and that child's life. It is the planting and nurturing of seeds that grow with a child and bears fruit when that child accepts the journey of fatherhood (or motherhood) for children that will one day come into their lives.

And this means those persons whether biologically or by choice, parent a child. Fatherhood is a lifetime commitment that evolves. It's about being present, keeping them safe, protecting, nurturing, disciplining them in love, celebrating achievements, and providing teachable moments when things don't go as planned. It's beyond financial supporting and giving gifts in the absence of not keeping a promise. It's there to teach them how to read, drive a car, tie a tie, be properly measured for a suit, show love to others, respect themselves to overcome obstacles, and believe in themselves. It helps to guide them through every facet of life. It's knowing when to step back and step in. It's an advocate. It's helping them develop their individual gifts and talents to grow into their God-given purpose. Fatherhood is a fraternity of its own. It's a shared responsibility that we as fathers need to lean on each other to be our best. To help lift not only the children, but one another.

Omega Psi Phi Fraternity, Inc., has engaged communities for 11 decades with meaningful mentoring of young people nationwide. My friends, I have learned the most precious gift God gives us are children. The most important responsibility God gives a man is to nurture and protect those he's blessed to father! Children want their fathers in their lives! Our daughters learn from their dads what a healthy, loving relationship with a future boyfriend/husband should look like by how you treat their mother. Our sons learn how to be a man who loves, respect, and protects those he loves by watching their fathers navigate the trials of life.

Lastly, the difference dads make is immeasurable! Too often I hear narratives that seem to diminish and marginalize the role of fathers in their children's lives. This is the rhetoric that society seemingly echoes. Both fathers and mothers seem to underestimate the importance. There are various factors, including socio-economic factors that feed this narrative. But it's simply untrue. As important as mothers are in children's lives, fathers are equally important. It takes both parents to raise children. The balance they get from each aid in the healthy growth and development of children. Both parents are valuable in raising a child created by you.

The first Fatherhood Initiative and Mentoring workshop held in Atlantic City, New Jersey was a success. The International Committee under the leadership of Brother S. Earl Wilson and Brother Robert Fairchild showcased mentoring activities. I was honored to be a part of the Dr. Moses C. Norman, Sr. Inaugural International Leadership Conference at Harrah's Resort in Atlantic City, NJ from July 9 through July 14, 2019. This event brought together thousands of Omega Men, young males, and chaperones to the area for mentoring activities, meetings, training, community action programs, entertainment and all the city has to offer.

2019 Dr. Moses C. Norman, Sr. International Leadership Conference

A STORY WITH A KEY MESSAGE: Divine Nine Opportunity

A story is told about a brickmaker. The Divine Nine Greek fraternal members assembled at a brickyard site where men made bricks. There were members from Alpha Phi Alpha, Kappa Alpha Psi, Phi Beta Sigma, and Iota Phi Theta Fraternities on site, watching or working where the men made bricks. An Alpha brother asked the man, bending down, what are you doing? The man replied I am making bricks. There were also brothers of Sigma, Iota, and Kappa present. A Kappa brother asked another intensely focused man, "What are you doing?

As the man rose to answer, he wore a purple and gold T-Shirt and proclaimed that he was building a kingdom to change the world. All the Divine Nine organizations have put in yeoman's work with other community and civic organizations. We must link arms together to solve this challenge; we have a role in making our communities and world a better place for our children and families. When we mentor a young male, he grows to become a young adult man. He then takes a wife and becomes a father with children and is charged with raising his children into young adults. This is what our perspective must be.

We as a community, must be all in with all that's occurring in our communities today, especially with the U.S. Supreme Court rulings intentionally "turning back" the hands of time to the civil rights era. Their ruling targeted students of color and impacted diversity, access, and equal opportunities for gifted, talented, and intellectually qualified students to attend nationwide higher education institutions. It has been stated that affirmative action was not about taking unqualified students and putting them in Ivy League Colleges. Affirmative Action was about identifying qualified students with exceptional academic credentials such as high SAT/ACT scores and G.P.A. that have been overlooked. These students we would never know existed and putting them in Ivy League Universities. What do these rulings mean to our Mentoring efforts and programs nationwide?

We must intentionally do the meaningful work of mentoring, nurturing, and instructing our young people and families to reach their full potential! The community engagement work that we do is bigger than you can think or imagine. It goes beyond one-on-one mentoring, and mentoring impacts the economic base trajectory of families.

That is why I cannot emphasize enough that Mentoring work is meaningful, purposeful, and impactful, and together we can make a greater impact when we put our might and resources into action - building a kingdom to change the world! This duty is what we must do now in the present day! We must do this duty specifically, persistently, and honestly now in the present day!

I am excited that God chose you to be a legacy builder, create new pathways, and turn new ideas into opportunities for young people. Let me be clear Mentoring Leadership and Scholarship Matters at the local community level is more critical now than ever. There is no better investment than our young people and we are stronger working together to make "hope happen" in young people's lives!

75TH SECOND DISTRICT CONFERENCE, FOUNDER'S BANQUET IN PITTSBURGH, PA., AMAZING NIGHT OF CELEBRATION DONALD WILLIAMS II RECEIVED THE 2ND DISTRICT, 2023 COMMITTEE CHAIRMAN OF THE YEAR AND WALTER NEIGHBORS RECEIVED RECOGNITION FOR BASILEUS OF THE YEAR, SHOWN ABOVE CURRENT 38TH DISTRICT REPRESENTATIVE, DELRECOLE "RICO" GALES AND THE 37TH DISTRICT REPRESENTATIVE AND CHAPTER BROTHER KELVIN AMPOFO, (APRIL 22, 2023)

The sense of urgency is NOW!
If not now, then when?
If not us, then WHO?

A STORY WITH A KEY MESSAGE:

Our leadership presence makes a tremendous difference in uplifting African American families, ensuring fair, equal, and equitable access to resources where we live, work, and raise our families.

Now is the time to work, use influence, and be bold and innovative to connect with today's youth to help the generation behind us achieve greater heights. As COVID-19 state mandates are relaxed, our fraternity must be well-positioned to come out on the other side of the global pandemic with a collective plan on several fronts. We must close the gap on education equity, we must mentor young people to provide social emotional and literacy support, advocate for economic empowerment with the backing of Black businesses, address the disparity between health and wellness, and vote in every election to honor our ancestors. All these things are essential in the Black community. We must get behind President Joe Biden's American Family Plan, which ensures investment in young people and families as the economy rebounds with growth and opportunity creation through education and workforce readiness development.

I am grateful for the men leading in their homes, churches, workplaces, and the community. We have some, but we need some more men to make an impact in doing something bigger than yourself. I encouraged you to serve on a county council and working groups, become House of Delegates like Greg Wims, board of education members, run for PTA President and NAACP leadership positions, and join other stakeholders' initiatives. Inside the fraternity, find a committee that aligns with your passion. You should serve as a Corridor Representative, District Chairman, and Committee Member, and work at the international level. It is important to have leaders from your local chapter at the district level to serve the community. It is also important to collaborate and interact with other sororities, fraternities, other community-based organizations, and other ethnic groups in the community.

As men, we are responsible for shaping, nurturing, and modeling love and teaching our children to value themselves. As fathers, we must equip, educate, empower, and encourage our children to have confidence and self-esteem, to be positive in the face of adversity, and maintain faith. To do this we must first love ourselves, and then our brothers and sisters. I challenge you to ask yourself the question that was posed to me, "what does fatherhood mean to you?"

We are not defined as Omega men by what we wear and the hop choreography, but by what we do in the home, church, and community. Our fraternity must be men of Impact and Influence!

Mu Nu Chapter in Montgomery County, Maryland was chartered on May 23, 1970, and has been a model of leadership excellence and community engagement for five decades and counting. The home of two District Representatives, 34th Milton Dewy Harrison, and 37th Kelvin Ampofo. Mu Nu provides scholarships, founder of GBTLA (Saturday School), Bridge Builder Mentoring for Middle School students and a robust Fatherhood and Mentoring program.

QUOTE:

"Whatever you do, strive to do it so well that no man living and no man dead and no man yet to be born could do it any better."

—BENJAMIN E. MAYS

SCRIPTURE:

"For we are God's handiwork, created in Christ Jesus to do good works, which God prepared in advance for us to do."

Ephesians 2:10

Part 3 - Trees

Branches and Fruits of a Dynamic Mentorship Program

ELSP Overview - Saving Our Youth One at a Time

- Chapter 10: UCF Program Launched 2006
  – Aim High Education Life Skills Program Overview

- Chapter 11: Dream Chaser College Tour Program

- Chapter 12: SAT/ACT Boot Camps

- Chapter 13: Basketball Ministry

- Chapter 14: Leadership and STEM Enrichment Programs

- Chapter 15: What Leaders do in a Crisis?

- Chapter 16: The Game Changer Conference for Young Males

CHAPTER 10

UCF Aim High Educational Life Skills Program Launched 2006

A Divine and Driven Purpose

The Early Beginnings

KEY MESSAGE: Be Intentional and Stay Engaged

The Lord has positioned this organization as a premier youth development organization that has consistently engaged youth, families, and communities through educational, social-emotional support, spiritual renewal, and enrichment activities.

Mona and I have committed ourselves together to a life of service and shaping the lives of hundreds and thousands of young people. For more than 25 years, we've focused on African American youth and other young people of color —specifically underserved, marginalized, and at-risk children who we refer to as "at-promise youth"—mentoring and sometimes taking them into our home.

Our organization was formed with the following scripture in mind: "For if you remain silent at this time, relief, and deliverance for the Jews will arise from another place, but you and your father's family will perish. And who knows that you have come to royal position for such a time as this?" Esther 4:14

We use the scripture from the book of Esther 4:14 as our north star and guidepost for this ministry. Family and friends, our community, can no longer afford to sit on our blessings, we must build on our blessings to stay connected and engaged with today's generation. Recent events have made it clear: we must fight harder to create a more just and equitable society for young people.

God's vision calls for the right people to do his good works. I am mindful of one of my favorite stories from the Bible, the story of Nehemiah shows that God blesses the work of those who work faithfully. It is refreshing to have like attainment people in your corner at all levels who believe in the greater good. Colossians 3:23 says, "whatever you do, work at it with all your heart, as working for the Lord, not for human masters." The UCF journey has placed the right people, at the right time and resources intersected in His perfect timing. We learned that there is no limit to the places and kinds of work you can do for Him. I learned that God wants you to live fully committed to serving Him. Whatever you do as a servant leader, work at it with all your heart!

There have been many challenges along the way, and there have been speed bumps that challenged the collective effectiveness of the program in the community and the youth it serves. When God is for you and some people are against you, it strengthens your resolve. Like others before me, I have learned perseverance and to focus forward, keeping the main thing the main thing – positive youth development.

A GAME CHANGER'S PURSUIT

I recall a conversation posted on Facebook from Reverend Al Sharpton where he shared how God blesses everyone with gifts and talents.

Some He gives big dreams and others small dreams as your assignment to work. When the haters come--and they will--one thing you can bet on is that everyone will be engaged. There will be some working with you and some working against you. If you offer your heart to lead and bless others correctly, this will help maintain your focus. You can't fit big dreams into small minds; some might not understand your ministry or purpose. Don't let that distract you from what you were called and instructed to accomplish. God gives each person a dream with their name on it. It is up to you to exercise and put your resources and actions into making a difference. Let's celebrate and support each other regardless of your assignment.

NOVEMBER 11, 2014, DONALD AND MONA WILLIAMS, JACKIE RHONE, EXECUTIVE BOARD MEMBER AND LEONARD GRANT, UCF FIRST YOUTH PRESIDENT ARE INTERVIEWED BY SHEILA OGILVIE ON MONTGOMERY COMMUNITY MEDIA CHANNEL 21.

The above picture shows Sheila Ogilvie, the host for Transforming Lives spotlighted Unity Christian Fellowship, Inc., for "Giving Back to the Community." UCF, a nonprofit youth organization, provided enrichment activities throughout the year. The show's surprise highlight came at the end when Debra Thomas, President of Potomac Valley Alumnae Chapter of Delta Sigma Theta Sorority, Inc., presented a monetary check to support the annual Game Changer Conference for Young Males.

We never dreamed that UCF would become a "community champion" for positive youth development and a premier youth organization that proudly serves Montgomery County families and young people with year-round enrichment planned activities. As we celebrate 18 years of promoting student success, our youth development program engages youth, families, and communities through educational, social, emotional, and spiritual renewal, life-long learning, and enrichment activities.

As leaders in any organization, you should have a vision that propels your team, branch, division, or organization to the next level. A leader's vision is having foresight and awareness about the future. Vision is said to be able to see things other people's eyes cannot see. A leader can see things so clearly that they must describe them to those who can't see the vision. As a leader, you must think about or plan the future with imagination, creative agility, discernment, and wisdom. A vision is a way to evaluate and assess where you are and where you want the organization to be in six months, a year, or even two years. The vision for UCF was to connect with young people to elevate their thinking. We encouraged them to make better choices daily and give a winning effort to do their very best on their life journey.

On a personal level, it is a way to answer your purpose. It gives you the reason for your actions, choices, and decisions to make hope happen for others. The best way to find yourself is to lose yourself in service to others. Make it your mission to create a better neighborhood, township, and community. Everyone can do something to help young people be better in this post-pandemic era.

In my life, this approach has provided a sense of meaning and purpose every day. In the youth development space, I think about how to impact this generation of young people so that they can help others and, as a result, leave a legacy for tomorrow. I think about all that is going on, the uncertainty of the future, and how it shapes and affects the minds of young people ages 10-21. How can our team open a door for young people? How can our team make a difference in someone else's life in the times we live today? I want young people to have a vision for themselves and identify steppingstones to accomplish their objectives and goals.

End of the Sidewalk

UCF aim to counter the challenges students of color experience in our communities to ensure the success of all to reach their fullest potential. UCF kicked off our Aim High Educational and Life Skills Program, entitled initially "You Got Skills Workshop," on September 20, 2006. The program began as a vehicle to get young men of color in the community off the streets and into a structured program to promote their ability to dream and achieve those dreams. Over the years, the program evolved into monthly life skills meetings and exposure trips, SAT/ACT preparation, Dream Chasers Campus visits, and STEM activities. The activities are designed to develop not only male students but all students into responsible adults that achieve success and give back to their communities. Countless students have journeyed down the sidewalk of this life's skills program that successfully graduated from high school. Ninety-five percent of those students enrolled in college, and the remainder joined the military, became entrepreneurs, or work in the private sector. Our students have become doctors, educators, engineers, counselors, tradesmen, and mentors.

Although the first four to five years focused on young males, the growth came with including our young girls, as many of the young males had sisters. The primary focus areas we teach are life skills, educational strategies, and leadership skills. UCF's goal is to change lives in the community —one student at a time—by empowering youth to gain confidence, be productive community contributors; and engage them and their families to be active participants in countywide programs.

From our inception until now, we have wanted to teach children to dream again. We tell them to close their eyes and dream, for there's a dream with your name on it. We encourage them to do the necessary work to move toward greatness. You must put in the required work and stop being scared to take challenging courses to learn at a higher level. Here is the message to young people if you want to get paid you must listen, learn new things, read books to acquire knowledge. I grew up with the saying: knowledge is power, only when applied to your life journey.

The world is constantly changing, and your journey of excellence must start and end with the three "ships," Scholarship, Leadership, and Citizenship. With Scholarship at the forefront parents and young people prepare for the future as the world transforms. I encourage you to

prepare for new employment opportunities rapidly emerging in artificial intelligence, robotics, science, technology, engineering, and mathematics, and unknown opportunities not yet discovered.

Leadership, we ask students to think of innovative pathways and create new business ideas that will help your community. Be a leader that genuinely cares for your family, others, and the community in which you work and live.

Citizenship, do good deeds! Students are encouraged to find ways to conduct or participate in community projects to do all the good they can, in all the places they can, and in all the ways they can. I want young people to compete and create the best version of themselves as the world transitions. As with one of my favorite movies and plays, "The Wonderful Wizard of Oz." I want young people to use their youthful energy to find their yellow brick sidewalk like Dorothy. Set goals, objectives, and milestones, and use persistence in discovering answers within yourself. Young people must understand the answers that they search for are always within themselves to achieve their goals.

Our Rollout: Early Beginnings of a Game-Changing Divine Movement

2013 Scholarship Dinner Celebration

In its early inception, the group met frequently to keep the young males engaged through exposure activities and off the streets. Anyone who works directly with young people learns right away that students today face unprecedented challenges in a rapidly changing environment with shifts in culture, social media, family values, and family structure. The students who crossed our path mainly came from households headed by single parents, i.e., mothers and grandmothers. Many of our young people, especially our young males come with anger issues due to abandonment, rejection, absentee fathers, separation of parents where the father no longer lives with his children, and blended family relationships create additional challenges. It's not that it's impossible. If a child had two parents in the house, both parents spent more time working to make "ends meet" than they did with their children. My point is that both parents must work together in their children's best interest for their healthy development when they reach adulthood. The absence of a father can be for various reasons, and it is difficult for a young person to understand and process, so they act out, demonstrating unacceptable behavior.

My dad was raised by a single mother when his dad died when he was six months old. My grandmother raised two young boys with the help of her father, so I get it! The key message is that our children need both parents working together for healthy development. I salute the single mothers who are raising their children by themselves. No one should have to be strong all the time. Parents need one another to lean on to show strength and vulnerability. It enables children to have balance by seeing healthy displays of love and support modeled. Women shouldn't bear the sole responsibility alone to raise children alone. And men shouldn't be made to feel their role is limited to providing financial support. And as a community, we should remember the concept of developing a safe, supportive community that a village offers families.

I have observed that today's parents seem to be disengaged in their children's development. These parents defer to delegating and letting someone else raise their children, i.e., coaches, teachers, day-care providers, etc. Too many of our students show up in the school building unprepared, with incomplete homework assignments, a lack of reading comprehension, writing deficiencies, and overall, just aren't ready to learn.

On the UCF journey, providing emotional support and establishing a safe space to implement a meaningful structure from the beginning was critical. Once that was in place, the real work began as we shared knowledge, inspired, and encouraged young males to look beyond their current circumstances to take marginal steps to improve academically.

The young males were taught transformative life skills such as responsibility for one's actions, keeping your word, maintaining good character, the four P's of Manhood (becoming a provider, a producer, a protector, and a priest in the home), communication skills, eye contact, and a firm handshake. We used role-playing to improve their communication skills, which proved crucial in the boys' lives when the police stopped them. It was emphasized that it's their responsibility always to communicate respectfully and use this skill in all areas of their lives.

Another role-playing example we used was called, "What If?" A scenario would be presented, and then the question would be asked, "what if you found yourself in this situation?" Or "what if someone said that to you, what would be your response?"

You often hear that our young people aren't this, and they aren't that, so I connected with friends and other men and invited them to speak and share their stories of overcoming life circumstances.

I was convinced the exposure to working men in the community would be a "game changer" for the young males. Our young males must see that men came from a legacy of overcomers. Our young people must understand and learn that they are descendants of kings, queens, and tribal warriors. They must also learn that despite the obstacles our forefathers, they can still ascend to become community leaders and pillars in the community.

We must teach our real history and encourage young people to learn about their family history to find their purpose. We must teach them to learn from their family history that there have always been barriers and obstacles to overcome. The struggle and perseverance made your family into who you are today. Every day, our young people must understand that they have greatness inside of them and are worthy of being excellent in all areas of their lives. Our young people must know that their lives count; there is strength in adversity and being overcomers. I have shared with young people that they must live purposefully and be persistent, passionate, and productive in whatever they pursue.

As a student-athlete and coach for many years, the game of basketball parallels the game of life in this generation and must learn not to imitate but to innovate. They must "put the work in" so that their progress, skill development, and performance improvement will yield greater outcomes. The world is ever-changing, and our young people must get in the game, compete, and do the necessary work to improve every day, regardless of their path.

My student-athletes have often heard me say, "positive attitude plus consistent effort always equals success!" My nephew, David Anderson II, says it this way: there are three things that people lack, and you have control over "effort, discipline, and consistency." These are the fundamental cornerstones for young people to succeed today. You don't have to be the smartest person in the world to succeed. However, no one can deny your performance if you give maximum effort.

Many of us come from situations of limited possibilities, starting from the bottom and rising to greatness by learning to operate in a spirit of excellence! There is no greater gift in life than the ability to learn, for learning is lifelong. I encourage you to pursue lifelong learning with excellence, leave your comfort zone, take some risks, and keep pressing to become the best you can be. The winner in life is not always the person who succeeds; it is the person who gets knocked down and keeps getting up, pushing, and pressing to gain one more step further than expected.

Most people will experience failure most of the time. In these moments, you can flip the script if you adjust your attitude and approach to pursue excellence. Challenge yourself by asking if you are living up to your opportunities. Are you saying to yourself that failure is not an option?

It would be best if you prepared for life in the 21st century. To adapt to changes, you must keep learning, pressing forward, and finding new, creative, and innovative pathways in this rapidly transforming world. If you prepare yourself for success, are disciplined with staying on task, and can be counted on to perform to the best of your abilities daily, you will succeed.

How are you managing your life experiences? You are facing just what others have encountered. Persevere, never give up and never quit! The bottom line of success is knowing how to recover, getting up when knocked down, and learning from a failed experience.

I wanted the young males to see responsible men concerned about them. More importantly to see and hear from men who have distinguished themselves in every profession, at home and abroad.

I wanted to expose the young males to adult men outside their circle of influence, to help them realize that they will face just what other young men have faced from generations prior. Although life is unpredictable, despite life challenges, I have learned that most men are responsible, committed, and persevere when confronted with obstacles. Men think through challenges; they take positive actions and try to do the right thing to navigate life when confronted with obstacles.

I intend to expose the young males in every meeting to speakers that look like them to share their personal stories from a teenager's point of view. The young males heard about the benefits of making good choices from every speaker. They listened to the consequences of making bad choices. They heard about the ramifications and lasting impact of bad decisions and the challenges of recovering from those choices.

Lieutenant Eric Burnett,
Montgomery County Police Department

My friend, Walter D. Neighbors, Jr., a criminal attorney with a wealth of experience, says it this way. What does seventeen seconds mean? It is all the time it takes to make a bad choice that you must live with for the rest of your life. On the other hand, the good news is in the exact seventeen seconds, and you can make a great choice that will be impactful for the rest of your life.

It takes a man to teach a boy how to think like a man! A young boy needs a man to show him how to act, talk to him about overcoming poor choices, and provide a roadmap to follow. In life, it is not about what you have done; you can self-correct and learn to think in a new way. Young people must understand that one bad decision doesn't mean the game is over!

Young males must intentionally prepare for the future and equip themselves with meaningful skills. Although the speakers came from different upbringings, backgrounds, cities, counties, states, and countries as well as generations, there were still lots of things in common that every one of us shared.

The life-changing impact resulted in young males understanding that education is a must. Young people can apply the lessons of determination and perseverance from our ancestors who helped them have a better life. Education is the great equalizer because it can level the playing field. Education will always be the great equalizer for every future generation.

Young people in every generation must have the ability to learn--they need to acquire knowledge, skills, and abilities to change the trajectory of their lives. It is so encouraging and refreshing to witness the results of mentoring. To see a drastic change in young males' behavior when they realize that a circle of adults cared about them and were there to walk the path to adulthood.

Once we instilled a sense of accountability, they positively conducted themselves in school and family settings. The consistent encounters served as a compass to guide the young males. The critical message to our mentees continued to be to surround themselves with positive people (thinkers and doers) and be committed to doing the necessary work to achieve their goals.

I knew in my heart that if God provided the vision, He would make a way to connect me to the right people at the right time and provide resources for positive results. I also knew that I had to connect with respected community leaders that would lend their support. I knew the local churches, sororities, and fraternities (especially Omega men from Mu Nu Chapter) had a significant role to play. I also knew that many people were in meaningful positions to play their roles in a positive outcome. Many just sat, watched, and wondered how this would work out.

I learned through my Christian upbringing that God's ministry was always community-minded! He honors those who intentionally work together to accomplish something greater than themselves.

He knew the purpose, the destiny, and the impact before he planted the seed in your heart and that it was bigger than anyone could think or imagine. God is the master of facilitating a blessing by using you so that others may be fully blessed. Although the vision was daunting and seemed impossible in the beginning, He always had something more significant in mind!

As I conducted an environmental scan to assess who was mentoring in the community, I learned immediately that many mentors consistently engaged 10 to 20 students throughout the month. Many of these organizations included local youth ministries, athletic coaches, and other mentoring organizations.

I thought, "what if I employed the Officer Professional Development (OPD) model used throughout my military career to develop leaders?" It is designed to meet and develop the soldier's needs, growth, training, education, and experience. The OPD program's objective is to maximize a person's potential and willingness to succeed. The heart of the philosophy is about shared responsibilities among stakeholders.

I further pondered, "what if more young males outside of UCF meetings could be impacted with a major exposure experience that put them in the same place with community stakeholders, such as black men, educators, church leaders, coaches, and community leaders to inspire and uplift to show the young boys that they matter and their lives count?"

September 20, 2006, was the birth of the UCF Youth Development Organization. Montgomery College Professor McKnight led young males through an ice-breaker exercise that set UCF strategic trajectory: "you must reach beyond what you think or imagine achieving your goals as a person and student." It's about stepping out on faith and doing the required work to improve yourself by learning new skills and earning a certification.

The Journey-Early Beginnings

Aim High In Life
Educational and
Life Skills
Program
1st Meeting

If you can dream it, you can reach it.
Mr. McKnight stepping out on faith!

Professor Clifton A. McKnight
Ice Breaker Reacfor your goals

In 18 years, our growing programs have been structured to enhance high-achievers success and help all youth excel academically and socially throughout middle and high school. Our efforts are positively impacting the lives of our students and the community. UCF's top priority will always be working with families and students who want to achieve college and workforce readiness. We want all students to experience educational success. We want all students to work to increase their learning ability and be willing to improve their learning skills. Our community must understand future earning power is in educational achievement!

The heavy lifting occurs in monthly youth engagement meetings where the hearts and minds are touched by youth and parents alike. UCF focuses on education and life skills activities that will teach students how to navigate life challenges on the way to degree completion. Overall program opportunities include mentoring, promoting positive attitudes, teaching responsibility, reinforcing positive behavior, and self-esteem, rewarding academic improvement, and raising grades and test scores. It also challenges students to perform better and rewards academic performance.

We met monthly with approximately 15 young male students actively participating in the program. Their grades ranged from 7th through 12th, as well as college freshmen.

From the beginning, our theme continues to the present day "building youth success, changing the landscape, leveraging opportunity." Our Educational and Life Skills Programs evolved to include SAT/ACT Boot Camps and preparation sessions, summer leadership, and enrichment camps, the USTEM Program, the National Society for Black Engineers (NSBE), Jr. Chapter, Dream Chaser College Tours, hospitality camps, summer book clubs, summer athletic activities (golf, lacrosse, and basketball) for boys and girls as well as community volunteering such as The March of Dimes and Flags for our Heroes supporting Rotary Club activities. Also, before the COVID pandemic, we launched new initiatives such as home improvement and repair, the Toastmasters Public Speaking unit, Math Homework Club, and the 2022 High-Level Virtual STEM Pilot Program.

UCF connects our youth to their destinies and creates necessary pathways to help them achieve and succeed in life. And through this engagement commitment — with all the collaborative and interactive efforts— we were able to successfully reach, encourage, nurture, coach, challenge, and reward students to strive for excellence and to be extraordinary!

We will forever be indebted to you all for teaming with our beloved Unity Christian Fellowship (UCF), Inc. Youth Development Organization. We cannot express appreciation enough to you for being an intrinsic part of this extraordinary positive youth development journey.

From the beginning, the youth organization was successful due to the circle of caring adults who were determined to be a "helping hand" who assisted and linked young people to their destinies by teaching educational strategies and life skills. We impressed our students that they have skills, talents, and abilities to improve. To help achieve our objective, we helped to boost the confidence, competencies, and values they need to become healthy and productive adults.

We invited guest speakers, police officers, community leaders, and business owners to speak to our youth with the expectation of planting seeds. Students walked away with the thought, "I can do this if I just improve my grades, correct my behavior, and take education seriously."

The overall program's direction provided opportunities that included promoting positive attitudes, teaching responsibility, life skills, and reinforcing positive behavior, self-esteem, improving grades, and grew into teaching test-taking skills for achieving higher scores on standardized exams.

We desire our students to take ownership of improving their quality of life. In addition to focusing on education, we took students on cultural field trips such as Harpers Ferry, West Virginia, and the Blacks in Wax Museum in Baltimore. This gave students a sense of worth, purpose, and desire to change their mind maps!

Motto:
We will have fun and get our work done! Sister Jackie Rhone setting the ground rules.

JackieRhone's Overview (1Meeting)

Our group of students at-promise were often marginalized, left behind, counted out, and excluded from the mainstream as young students. Like many young organizations, we experienced some incremental praise reports. However, many challenges placed us on the front lines of the realities of our community in and around the Emory Grove 124 corridor. We experienced youth with gang pressure avoidance, teen pregnancy, drug abuse, robbery and assault, and families in crisis.

These were just some challenges our young people faced from the start of UCF's early existence. As a circle of caring adults, we learned together what at-risk, underserved access, and equity disadvantage truly meant. We learned about the everyday stress and trauma that young people go through, which impacts them as they attempt to navigate a challenging adolescent process.

As we approached our second year of the Educational and Life Skills Program, entitled "You Got Skills," we were reminded why UCF existed through our guiding scripture, Esther 4:14.

We learned that our young people were struggling and searching for relief, alternatives, and deliverance elsewhere. The shaping of UCF's mission took place with each meeting and building trusted interactive relationships with students and skeptical parents who only knew what they knew. Many families are stuck in a "space" where they experience limited success or victories during their lives.

Many of the young people who cross your path were wounded with anger and bad attitudes and their behavior translates as disrespectful. We all go through disappointments, betrayals, unfair situations, and life circumstances. We don't realize the impact of our wounds. How much do our personal wounds sour our attitude, drain our energy, limit our creativity, and derail future opportunities?

It's a new day, and the stakes are too high, young people you must get good at managing and letting wounds go. Young people don't be the one to live out of a wounded place over how they were raised, or what their mother and dad didn't do for you. How you learn to deal with life circumstances will determine whether you move forward and new opportunities. If you're going to fulfill your destiny, move forward with a positive attitude to see new pathways, options, and favors for your life, let go and redirect, rethink, reset, and refocus to win your future! And in our 18th year UCF focus continues to create options and competitors.

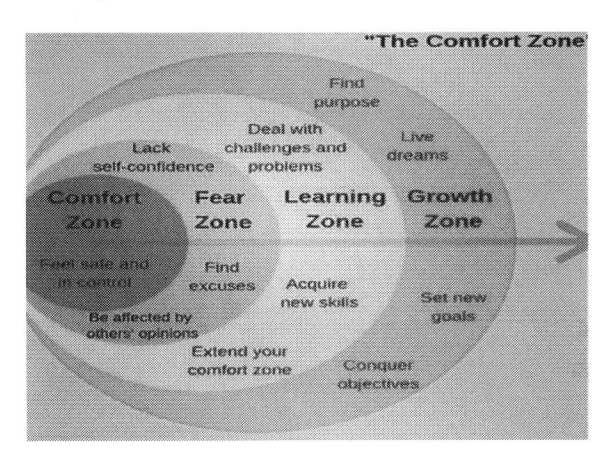

![The Comfort Zone diagram showing Comfort Zone (Feel safe and in control, Be affected by others' opinions, Lack self-confidence), Fear Zone (Find excuses, Deal with challenges and problems), Learning Zone (Acquire new skills, Extend your comfort zone, Find purpose), Growth Zone (Set new goals, Conquer objectives, Live dreams)]

UCF created an environment to improve academic performance so that upon graduation from high school, youth will have options, a path forward to either enroll in college or vocational/ trade school to earn a trade certificate or pursue a career in the military/federal service.

As we reflect on the early days of the UCF Educational and Life Skills Program, we learned many lessons. I know several young adults who desire to start mentoring programs. They have asked about how to create a mentoring program in my community.

With our human lens, honestly, it's never an easy thing to leave one's comfort zone (where the focus is on just your home and family) to navigate the fear zone (where you look inward and start making excuses) and internalize what others might think and say behind your back, (why are you doing this? Look at them, it doesn't take all of that, etc.).

When moving out of your comfort zone to deal with the anxieties of the fear zone, remember the best is ahead of you. Everything you want to pursue is right outside of your comfort zone. As a coach, I shared that you must grow, learn, and improve or you can't stay here in practice, and so it is with life's journey; you can't stay the same.

When moving to the "learning zone," one must deal with the unknown challenges of receiving buy-in and bringing people together to move in the same direction of providing hope to students and families who are living in survival mode and need a morale boost to know others care about them.

You need to understand it's about your heavenly assignment! The master wants you to walk with spiritual confidence and to operate according to the kingdom's purpose. I encourage you to stay connected with prayers. The creator will give you the authority and the confidence to ignore what others might say about you. He will provide you with everything you need to accomplish the assignments given to you!

I recall an encounter with a dad in the neighborhood who asked to speak with me after I dropped his three sons off at his house in the first year. I believe he was going to share his appreciation for the mentoring work that we had started by conducting monthly meetings with the boys.

Instead, he admonished me, asking, "Mr. Williams, why are you raising these boys' hopes to include my sons?

"Why are you providing experiences and having speakers share success stories that get these boys to believe they can succeed? You are just like the schools. You will eventually abandon them and just let the boys down." I wasn't expecting that kind of conversation from a parent in the neighborhood who attended all the high school sporting events.

He caught me off guard, so I listened attentively and then extended him an invitation to join the youth meetings and participate in the journey to change lives. Guess what? He never showed up!

This was an awakening that mentoring is so much more than "pep talks" from celebrities. This exchange strengthened my resolve as it provided a realistic insight into the thinking of some parents' social, emotional, and psychological impact to make ends meet for their families. Today's parents and young people deal with so many challenges every day.

In the "growth zone," I learned that there are two sides. Many parents appreciate mentors for being "helping hands" in their children's lives. On the other side are parents who are resentful for many reasons; perhaps in their youth there weren't any positive influences when they were adolescents. I have learned a lot about using negative encounters to improve the mentoring impact by including parents and redoubling efforts to reach out to fathers to be a part of the mentoring experience. I believe it takes a village, and everyone can lend their gifts and life experiences.

The sense of urgency is now the "all-hands-on-deck" approach is needed to help shape the next generation of future leaders. Many hands make light work to make a difference in our community. No one person can do everything, but everyone can do something. I have learned that men might feel threatened by another man being involved with their children's life due to a broken relationship with the child's mother. The relationship may be strained because of life's circumstances or economic situations, having to work two to three jobs to make ends meet and provide for the children.

With proper care, the rift between you and your mother's child can heal your relationship so the child can witness a healthy parent relationship. After attending many conferences and forums where men shared that they felt guilty about the limited opportunity to be more involved in the children's lives, many men wanted to be more active. However, some felt guilty that they should be able to do more in their children's lives. They think "the best I can do" is to appear at their children's birthdays, extracurricular activities, and sporting events like football and basketball games. They say to themselves, "I showed up, and that should be enough!"

My friends, your presence is vital in the lives of your children. Showing up at the front door with gifts now and again can be detrimental to your children's development. Your children's character development takes shape by your consistent presence. They'll learn life lessons and values from the information you present. As you impart lifelong lessons, they gain a new perspective. Don't take the easy way out; become a "gift giver" to compensate for your absence or get back at the child's mother. I know it isn't easy; however, your focus must be on the outcome of developing a healthy young person who grows to become a successful adult!

Your children will reflect and say, "my parents had their differences, but my dad was present every step of the way. I am a healthier adult because my dad and mother were committed to working together to help my life make sense and my future secure. I have gained valuable life skills, and perspectives, and have been given meaningful information that opened my eyes to something new and enhanced my decision-making as a young adult."

I do know that when you pierce through the spiritual lens that God gives each one an assignment to fulfill, the scriptures come alive! A mentor's power is in the words they use to communicate with young people to inspire, uplift, and equip them. There is power in your words! I try to do my best to lead by example and use my gifts to unite people to work on positive outcomes.

It is clear with all that is happening in the world and the challenges of the family structure and dynamics, we need many more mentors in our community who will establish trusted relationships to reach and connect with today's young people. Our young people need you to be there for them. Mentors, like parents, have information to share with young people and a historical perspective. It is said that vision is the ability to see things other people's eyes cannot see. Mentors help young people open their eyes to something new that will benefit them.

Mentors should stay the course and stay in faith because you might be the only positive person that crosses a young person's path to make a difference in their lives. Mentors, the principles you have in public must be the same in private. Young people always look at you and will instantly recognize " fake " by what they see and feel. Young people need to see a person of principles! Children don't care how much you know or even about the number of degrees, you may have until they see that you sincerely care about their well-being.

For mentors to grow, it is all about acquiring new skill sets to manage the many different types of encounters, relationships, and family situations. On this mentoring journey, you must continue your education by attending conferences and connecting with other like-minded youth organizations. I encourage youth leaders to continue to learn how to stay relative to connect with today's generation of young people. Learning strategies for collaboration with other like-minded youth leaders and teaming with other youth organizations is important.

Early on, we believe caring adults make a more significant impact working together, building relationships with like-minded individuals from MCPS educators and counselors, local churches, and businesses to bring the community together for a common purpose – to save our youth!

UCF represents faith in action, a true faith walk aimed at doing God's will to shape and save young people's lives. An organization that was initially funded out-of-pocket and later grew to donation-only funding, in its first seven years, UCF was successful in nurturing, assisting, and linking young people to their respective destinies by teaching educational strategies, leadership, and life skills.

From the beginning, we realized the focus must center on instilling hope, uplifting, and teaching life skills. We learned quickly that our children have various social, emotional, and family situations and circumstances. Our children faced different family situations and structures when we grew up in the 70s. We were clear on the focus to teach children to dream small dreams and then implement plans. We want to teach them to believe in themselves, strive for excellence, and take ownership to achieve their dreams. Later, we tell all our students to dream big dreams, for there is a dream with their specific name on it. We also emphasize trusting that God will connect you to your destiny in the kingdom!

FRENCH POPE AND DONALD WILLIAMS AT MARCH OF DIMES EVENT

UCF IN ACTION -MARCH OF DIMES - TEACHING COMMUNITY RESPONSIBILITY & ENGAGEMENT

Our focus centers on helping students build confidence, develop a positive self-image, high esteem, and a positive attitude that says "YES" I can do anything but fail. We encourage students to stay out of trouble and use their youthful energy to invest in themselves and the circle of adults who can help prepare them for life after high school.

An objective is to provide a support structure to give young people opportunities they may not otherwise have. We expose them to cultural, educational, and economic opportunities. An example was French Pope Jr., a proud member of Alpha Phi Alpha Fraternity, Inc. provided young males with the first two significant community engagement experiences that helped develop their leadership growth and understanding of community involvement.

FRENCH POPE JR. MAKES POINT

French Pope Jr., a UCF executive board member known as "Mr. March of Dimes" in Montgomery County, took the opportunity during a worship service at First AME- Gaithersburg to request prayer for the premature birth of a church member's child. This act changed his life forever, as he dedicated his efforts to raising awareness of premature births.

Since witnessing and experiencing God's miracle with the child's birth, French loves with his heart and has been "all in" since h. His drive has been fueled by the compassion and commitment to promoting the annual March of Dimes campaign. He singled handedly brought together meaningful annual drive by recruiting local churches and Divine Nine Greek sororities and fraternities to join the Alpha Phi Alpha Fraternity, Inc. to participate with resources, helping is worthy cause.

In April 2012, French and the UCF were recognized by the African Methodist Episcopal Church's 2nd Episcopal District Women's Missionary Society Washington Conference 62nd Annual Luncheon – Celebrating Partnership. French has single-handedly promoted and introduced to the African American community the importance of supporting the March of Dimes for Babies.

The March of Dimes for Babies was a popular community event that drew thousands of residents from across Montgomery County. UCF youth helped support the following efforts with the march: site set-up support, tent assembly and disassembly, hauling equipment and route set-up with directional signage, and whatever else was needed to contribute to the event's success.

Another exposure experience that gave the students a sense of purpose was serving as ushers for the Memorial Prayer Breakfast that honors Reverend Dr. Martin Luther King Jr., also conducted by the Iota Upsilon Lambda chapter of Alpha Phi Alpha Fraternity. Our students participated as ushers, assisting more than 1,200 patrons to their tables. We prepared our youth for success at the event by conducting a class on etiquette, dress for success, and hygiene workshops. special event planner Mrs. Deidra D. Williams-Long conducted etiquette seminars at youth meetings to prepare students to help serve as ushers for the event.

I enjoyed taking the boys to shop for clothes at Marshalls and JC Penney. I taught them how to read the tags to determine their sizes for shirts and pants. The UCF's uniform for all formal and semi-formal outings is black pants, white shirts, and their favorite ties. We refer to the UCF uniform as their "BDU" (Best Dress Uniform) for all events. This might sound simple, but the reality for many young males is there's no man to show young boys how to dress properly. This was first for my guys to experience selecting and purchasing the proper-sized shirt, pants, and belts.

As UCF was birthed, we were reminded of the old gospel song, *"Through It All I Learned to Trust in Jesus ...I learned to trust in God!"* And by trusting in God, you learn to walk in your purpose!

1ST REVEREND DR. MARTIN LUTHER KING JR. MEMORIAL PRAYER BREAKFAST Preparing to Serve – Jan 15, 2009 at Marriott Hotel

An expression of gratitude is deserved for Pope, who, through his leadership, is bringing the community together for a greater purpose. He is a native of Norfolk, Va., who graduated Cum Laude from Norfolk State University with a degree in business management and pledged Alpha

via NSU's Epsilon Pi chapter. He is happily married to Zenobia Pope, and through this union, they have three children, French III, Jasmine, and Imani. They are also the proud grandparents of French IV, Alexander, and Kyah.

French is a proud and active member of Alpha Phi Alpha Fraternity, Inc. Iota Upsilon Lambda chapter of Montgomery County, where he is Chairman of the March of Dimes Committee, sings with the IUL ensemble, and serves on the chapter's Health Affairs Committee. His desire to aid the March of Dimes extends into his community.

French orchestrates the annual Walk for Babies by inviting his church family, local chapters of fraternities and sororities, and other organizations he was associated with to form teams, donate to his website, and participate in the walk.

**Sharing Knowledge and Wisdom
Monthly Meeting at
Upper County Community Center**

DEFINING MOMENT IMPACTING LIVES

In the first six months of launching UCF, we experienced a "game changer" moment. The picture above was a milestone on the UCF journey because it shifted the focus to academic improvement for all participants. In all meetings, even today, students must introduce themselves by standing up, sharing their full name, school, principal's name, grade, and what they want to be when they grow up.

Over the many years of mentoring, when you ask students what they want to be or ask their goals, 90% will respond with either of the following: a football player, basketball player, singer, or a rap artist.

In the picture above with the basketball in his lap was 4 foot 2, Derrick Akuoko who dreamed of playing NBA basketball from an early age of nine years old. In the front row seated next to him was Jonathan Onasanya, wearing the Magruder High School blue sweatsuit.

These young males represents so many of our children even today with aspirations and dreams of playing NBA basketball.

This was a special moment in the growth of the UCF youth program that encouraged young male students to aim higher in life and take their education seriously. The "game changer" moment came when Jonathan (a sophomore at the time) stood up and proudly announced that he had a 3.4 grade point average (GPA). The young males directed their inquisitive looks toward me because they didn't know what GPA meant or represented. To my amazement they thought GPA meant Garage Parking Attendant. The conversation that ensued shifted the program's trajectory as we learned that all students are competitive in nature, especially young males. All students, whether in sports, student government activities, bands, choirs, or the classroom, possess competitive DNA inside them.

I explained that GPA stands for Grade Point Average, and you go to school to demonstrate your ability to learn. It is crucial because that is how you will be defined in the academic journey. It represents how high you scored in your courses on average and assesses whether you meet the standards for degree completion. The UCF journey in the early years was about helping students improve their attendance, behavior, and learning ability. It was a challenge to help them understand what "winning" looks like. Taking ownership and being responsible for arriving in the school building ready to learn and staying out of trouble.

How do you get kids to want to win when they are used to losing? As a leader and mentor, you must engage with them to help, show, and help them determine what success looks like. How can we help students connect, pursue their dream and be successful as opposed to documenting student's successes or failures?

UCF truly believes that there is a dream with each person's name on it. We are conscious about not being dream snatchers. However, we intentionally show students and parents alternative ways to invest in children by preparing for the future to raise their standard of living.

Our desire will always be to promote student success by helping them believe in themselves. We desire to raise post-generation competitors for the 21st Century. Secondly, help them increase their confidence and equip them with strategies to assist with navigating adolescence. We encourage them to do their absolute best in school and prepare for life after high school: college and workforce readiness. UCF wants to assist students and families with the realities of today's industries and the confidence to pursue realistic meaningful professions that currently demand intelligent, gifted, and talented students of color.

I have found on the mentoring journey that our young people want to be successful but don't know how to go about it. Our children want the same thing you and I had growing up. They want adults to be present and engaged in their lives. Young people wish to have parents, mentors, and teachers who genuinely care about them. They need a "listening ear," with wise counsel and advice to help them reach their full potential and possess sound judgment. UCF is intentional to show parents and students alike a different pathway forward. UCF has redoubled our efforts to engage parents in their 30's and 45's. UCF provides Parent Academy seminars led by Mr. Donald Wharton at monthly meetings, HBCU College Fairs, STEM Expo, and the Game Changer Conferences.

The strategies and corrective measures you and I grew up with and used in the 70's is less effective, as reported by today's parents. UCF conducts round table discussions with parents; I called these meaningful sessions "new school parenting for old school issues."

UCF cultivates an environment for young people and parents to shift their thinking to help students pursue their purpose with the passion of their ancestors. We encourage young people today to give 100% of their very best and "go pro" by living purposefully, so they can make a good living in the right profession.

Our approach shows students that if they can change their attitude to be intentional about learning and apply themselves – all things are possible. Along the way, they will discover through exposure experiences: purpose, passion, and practices for unlocking what drives a person to achieve their best life (how to pursue a favorable outcome). Students benefit from experiences that include exposure to various career fields, broadening their thinking to endless possibilities. Exposure experiences unlock energies and helps them discover who they want to become and the sacrifices to be made to achieve their goals.

What amazes me is the countless hours and resources our parents devote to their children pursuing sports. As a basketball coach for many years, it is incredible how super-invested parents and students are in pursuing becoming professional athletes. In our community, parents invest and bank on sports from an early age. They devote every hour to training, practices, and road trips for their children, hoping they will become the next "lottery pick" or the next "chosen one" in the pro ranks.

In his workshop entitled "School is Cool," Dr. Joey Jones highlighted the analytics of professional sports odds where the average length of career is between 3 to 6 years. Your sports career will end in six years at age 26 or 27, barring injuries, roster cuts, politics, and unforeseen occurrences. Best case, you will make a lot of money in a lifestyle that requires a lot of money to maintain and sustain. Now what?

The same question remains, what will you want to be when your career ends? Please consider The following analytics by sport. Basketball is the second most popular sport to play in the United States (counting amateur levels) after football. There are approximately one million high school students that play basketball annually. According to the National Federation of State High School Associations in the United States, over 545,850 boys and over 438,900 girls play basketball in high school. Millions of people play and practice every year. For many of those who play in high school, their dream is to become a collegiate basketball player or to receive a scholarship so they can go to college.

Every year there are 60 draftees' positions in the NBA. The odds of going pro is 3%, meaning 3 out of 10,000 collegiate players can go PRO in the National Basketball Association, with those 60 slots available for 30 NBA teams annually.

The odds of going pro in women's is 3% meaning 3 out of 13,000 have an opportunity to make the Women's National Basketball Association for only 32 positions available for 12 teams. The average career is 4.5 years in the league barring injuries. Plus, the pay is often not as lucrative as the available positions to play pro women's basketball overseas.

In the most popular sport football, more than 1.1 million boys play high school football nationwide. There are approximately 67,887 football players in college. The odd of going pro is 8%, meaning 8 out of 10,000 players have an opportunity to go pro in the National Football League with 32 teams for only 224 draftees position available annually. The average career is 3.3 years in the league barring injuries.

I encourage you to shift your thinking for family planning to encourage your children to pursue meaningful and sustainable professions for raising the standard of living. Stop focusing limited resources solely on sports to go pro. It takes work to become a lottery pick in your favorite sport. You must put in the required work and stop being scared to take challenging courses to learn at a higher level. I encourage young people to use their youthful energy to do hard work, take difficult courses, and take education seriously. I encourage you to exhibit good behavior, operate with leadership and citizenship, put in the time to prepare for a profession other than professional sports.

We want all students to be successful in a profession to help raise the quality of life for their families. We want all students to give 110% in pursuit of realistic goals. We want them to be the best "PRO" in underserved career fields such as education, business, healthcare, artificial intelligence, computer science (information security analysts, robotics, genetic programmers), attorneys, law enforcement, accounting, plumbing, and electrical engineering. You can still go pro in all these professions!

In September 2012, at the beginning of the school academic year, UCF provided incentives to promote good conduct and academic excellence. We were excited about the newest initiative that sparked and encouraged attendance, positive behavior, educational improvement, and attendance at 80% of the UCF education and life skills planned activities throughout the year.

The Academic Performance Contractual Agreement yielded immediate positive outcomes that were remarkable for our students who were labeled as having behavior problems. The incentive program shifted focus from disruptive behavior to students taking responsibility for their education and putting forth winning efforts for their future.

In 2008, while the D.C. Public Schools Chancellor Michelle Rhee was being attacked for launching pilot program paid for grade incentive, it was a "game changer" for UCF students. It was the best part-time job in the county that kept students focused on securing their future. It was imperative to build UCF's foundation by instilling high standards of character, excellence, and instilling the overall expectation pillars below:

24/7 Performance Objectives:

- Pursue Excellence in all areas of your life by Staying out of Trouble
- Make Good Choices/Decisions Daily
- Turn in all homework assignments! Study for unit quizzes, tests, and exams!
- Lead by Example in the classroom, extracurricular activities, and team sports
- Model Good Behavior doing what is right and not succumbing to peer pressure

- Give a winning effort, stay on task with assignment completion no matter what
- Perform good deeds and do something good for someone else
- Join extracurricular activities as a team member or team leader

It was extremely important to undergird students not only with social-emotional support, but to help them understand the benefits of success. UCF rolled out an incentive to shift students' thought processes by paying for academic improvement and positive behavior as a student. This

incentive aligned with UCF's mission to "promote student success and change lives in the community one student at a time" by exposing young people to positive experiences they otherwise would not have.

We desire to create and nurture competitors that are equipped for a world that is transforming itself in plain sight. We wanted to increase the number of success stories from our community to boost high school and college graduation rates in our community, especially amongst our male students.

Our primary goal is for all our students to improve their academic performance before graduating high school so they will have options and a successful path forward, whether it be college, vocational training, military, private sector, or federal government employment. We help our students build the confidence, competencies, and values they need to become healthy and productive adults.

UCF Goals and Priorities

- Transform Lives of Young People, especially our Male Students
- Booster High School and College Graduation Rates for youth – particularly boys

- Promote greater school community businesses collaboration through partnerships
- Develop Leaders, Teach Life Skills and Educational Strategies
- Increase Numbers of Success Stories from our community

Tom Scherer, Vietnam Veteran,
Planned UCF Hiking Excursion
"It is not what you leave for someone...
as it is what you leave in someone."

Have you ever considered that God chose you for an assignment only you can perform? He loved you so much that you were chosen to be his hands, feet, and mouthpiece to love others. God allows each person to walk with Him; this will lead to the scriptures coming alive in your life. If you walk away from God, know that you chose to walk away. He indeed, will never walk away from you because of His love for you. God chose me to use as a living testimony in a world that has lost its way.

We don't always realize just how precious life is until we experience a significant life-threatening situation. Sometimes, it takes a moment of danger to remind and awaken something inside of you. And once that moment occurs, you never come out the other side quite the same. I have experienced two significant emotional events that occurred once in my youth where I almost drowned at the Fort Monmouth post swimming pool in New Jersey. The second event as an adult approximately two years into the UCF journey, as I suffered a cardiac event on Saturday, October 31, 2009.

At the time of the publishing of this book, it will be another Halloween that marks 14 years since my encounter with God. I had a heart attack at the age of 51. As the story goes, I had to be rescued from Harpers Ferry Mountain in West Virginia at 5:30 p.m. on Halloween. I am reminded of the old gospel song, "Through it All, I've learned to trust in Jesus ... I've learned to trust in God! As I share my personal account, I advise you to trust God, and you will learn to walk directly into your purpose!

A good friend, Vietnam veteran, and Federal Government servant Tom Scherer excitedly planned a fall exposure outing for UCF that Saturday. An avid hiker, Tom planned a great midday trip for a few of the UCF's young males to Harpers Ferry National Historical Park. The plan included easy walking trails up a mountain to the signature position where the Shenandoah River and Potomac River converge along where West Virginia, Virginia, and Maryland meet.

Tom was excited to plan this two-hour trip up the mountain. This was perfect so we could all return to our homes to participate in Halloween festivities. We had just arrived at the signature position on the mountaintop site where the rivers meet. I had just taken the picture above and given the boys trail mix snacks.

The warning signs and symptoms of a heart attack differ for each person, but that doesn't mean they're any less dangerous. I was blessed to be surrounded by others because many people are alone when they suffer a heart attack without help. The person whose heart is beating improperly and who begins to feel faint has a short time before losing consciousness. However, you can help yourself by coughing repeatedly and very vigorously. You can take deep breath before each cough, and each cough must be deep and prolonged. I understand that deep breaths get oxygen into the lungs, and coughing movements squeeze the heart and keep the blood circulating. This helps to regain a normal rhythm. People should check with their cardiologist, stay in tune with their bodies and see a doctor at the first sign of irregularity.

I have often been asked, "did you feel any pressure: intense pain, shortness of breath, or fatigue?" I recall feeling terrible nausea in the stomach, and a general feeling of unease or discomfort came over me. At that moment, I knew in my heart something was wrong. As I attempted to climb up the trail connected with the path to go down, I collapsed. This is when Tom and the boys jumped into action. The Vietnam vet took charge by sending the boys down the mountain to get help while he administered first aid by covering me up with leaves and asking everyone that passed by us for aspirin.

Thank God for my young males who took lifesaving actions. Keith Foster and his friends, Marcio Davenport and Richard Pineda were the young males who found help from a nearby West Virginia fire and rescue team that rescued me from the mountain.

I will never forget lying on the mountain floor bed among the vegetation. I remembered having a conversation with God while trying to remain conscious by reciting and repeating over and over the 23rd Psalm!

"The Lord is my Shepherd; I shall not want He maketh me to lie down in green pastures. He leads me beside the still waters. He restores my soul: he guides me in path of righteousness for his name's sake. Even though I walk through the valley of the shadow of death, I fear no evil, for you are with me; thy rod and thy staff comfort me. You prepare a table before me in the presence of my enemies. You anoint my head with oil; my cup runneth over. Surely goodness and mercy shall follow me all the days of my life; and I will dwell in the house of the Lord forever."

HARPERS FERRY NATIONAL HISTORICAL PARK - WEST VIRGINIA

If you don't climb the mountain, you will never see the view or vision for your life!

I was given a second chance in my encounter with God, and his instructions were crystal clear. He said to go back and redouble your efforts: 1) to love God's people and 2) be a person of impact who brings people together to save our youth and bring back my glory! It is so clear even today for me to remain obedient. We are in it to win the hearts and minds of our young people to guide, direct, coach, and encourage them to do the necessary work to reach their full potential. Our youth and our parents must do the hard and essential work now to win the future that is rapidly shifting and transforming into a new society.

I was carried from the top of the mountain on a stretcher to an all-terrain vehicle which took me to level ground where a truck was waiting to deliver me to the base of the mountain, where an emergency ambulance was waiting to take me to the hospital. On-site, the emergency medical technician (EMT) administered an EKG. He shocked me by saying that I was having a heart attack and that getting me to the hospital was imperative. I was in disbelief as the sense of urgency intensified at the site. I was strapped in as the ambulance drove toward the Frederick Memorial Hospital.

My life is a testament to God's presence, love, goodness, power, and promises. My parents raised me to be a blessing to others, and all this now comes full circle on the mentoring journey. I will praise the Lord always, and his praises will continue to be in my mouth. I pray and thank God for providing a "second chance" in my life. He continues to provide more than I could have thought or imagined. I am grateful for His abundance of blessings with protection, promises, power, and, most of all, his presence in my life as I travel along the way. I couldn't perform this mentoring work, building alliances and trusted friendships without the Lord on my side.

After meeting my cardiologist, Dr. John Vitarello, he explained that I was a "miracle man." I was told other doctors gathered to see this person who survived a major heart attack. Dr. Vitarello showed on the monitor my "heart valve" that was subject to a close. He stated that if that occurred between the mountain rescue operation and the operating table, my life would be over! He gave me some analytics for those people that survived similar conditions. He always celebrated when I attended follow-up appointments with an announcement that "the miracle man is here!" God is so good, and every time I hear the 23rd Psalm, my emotions are moved, and I tear up. I know God spared my life for a greater purpose!

One "yes" from God will change the trajectory of your life. I cannot explain it! It's about trusting God, for He has "greater works" for you with just one yes. To be obedient and to have the courage for what He assigned you to do in this season. I never dreamed or envisioned that my purpose in life would be to empower, engage and raise awareness about the importance of mentoring work in the community. In addition, it impacts, shape and equip young people's lives, especially young males.

CHERYL CROSS GIVES YOUNG MEN A
MOTHER'S PERSPECTIVE FOR SUCCESS

I recall attending a conference at Bowie State University where Congressman Steny Hoyer, 5th Congressional District, was representing the University President with significant funding. I will never forget his message that struck me differently, but after reflecting on the following statement, it has some truth. He stated that funding resources can be disbursed to our community. However, he can't wake children up, take them to school or inspire them to do their best-earned quality education. It starts in the home with parenting and surrounding students with mentors who make a difference in the lives of future generations. My translation of the message was that there's no military cavalry coming to our community to rescue our young people. We all have a role to play; parents, teachers, mentors, coaches, and the village must be accountable for raising children to the best of our abilities. I am so proud of the mentoring work, working side by side with like-minded parents, educators, coaches, and community leaders to be difference-makers.

UCF experienced explosive blessings in the first five years with three primary programs: Aim High In Life Educational and Life Skills

Program (ELSP), the Christian Youth Basketball Ministry (CYBM), and the Game Changer Improvement Program (GCIP). These programs were designed to serve minority middle and high school students who are underserved and economically disadvantaged in the metropolitan DMV region.

Education and Life Skills Program (ELS) - Changing the Mind-Map

This program includes promoting positive attitudes, teaching responsibility, reinforcing positive behavior, self-esteem, improving grades and standardized test scores, job shadowing opportunities and fieldwork, and quality of life. This program was accomplished by inviting speakers to conduct workshops highlighting their personal journeys and sharing their career fields. This strategy showed the students that if they changed their attitude to work to learn a new skill and apply it themselves – anything is possible.

Adrian Burnim, Clearinghouse Manager
& Senior Youth Policy Associate

Several men from the community volunteered to mentor each of the young males in the Aim High In Life Education Life Skills Program. A mentoring workshop was conducted by Adrian Burnim, Clearinghouse

Manager; Senior Youth Policy Associate, National Clearinghouse on Families and Youth JBS International, Inc. He served as the public voice and face of the Clearinghouse at the time.

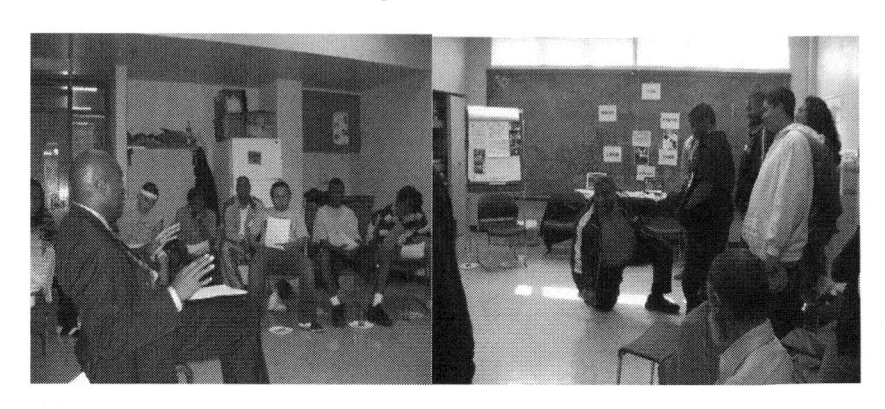

Dr. Larry Frazier Retired Naval Officer/ Professor Cliff McKnight Montgomery College Professor & Academic Advisor

The Educational and Life Skills Program enjoyed a day at the National Institutes of Health

Students benefitted from experiences that included exposure to various career fields, field trips to cultural and art events, sponsorship of enrichment programs, and participation in a mentorship program. In addition to focusing on education, activities teach students how to navigate financial aid resources for higher education and trade school entry with the expectation of degree completion. Reaching out to our community is central to our mission and vision.

SUMMER OF 2009 – FIRST BOOK CLUB
LED BY OUR DAUGHTER DREKA

The young males in the ELS Program met several times over the summer. Sessions were conducted on 'How Do You Feel About Yourself?' followed by 'How Do You Think Others Feel About You?' Each student took a 'Personality Quiz', similar to the Myers-Briggs test administered in school. The Personality Quiz gave students some ideas of how much their thought processes and future goals have changed. The young male students watched and discussed the documentary "The Pact," a book about three African American doctors from Newark, New Jersey. These young males made a pact that together, they would make it out of the projects, and when they became successful, they promised to return to the community and open their practice. As parents, we were so proud of our daughter Dreka for leading the first summer book club. The following year, our college students also lead the summer book clubs. "The Other Wes Moore," a work about the current Maryland governor, was the second book read during the summer. Thank you, Jasmine Pope, Kaifa Boyce, Tolu Onasanya, and other college students who returned to provide literacy leadership. We also introduced the young males to the game of chess during the book club sessions.

A STORY WITH A KEY MESSAGE:

Here is another story about the "water wells" where a family of frogs lived for many years. One day while swimming around the well deep below the ground, one of the baby frogs asked the mother frog, "what is that light way up there?" He went from family member to family member asking that question and was brushed off and ignored. This baby frog proclaimed that when he grew older and stronger, he would find out where the light was and what it was about. That day came when the baby frog became older and more assertive and started climbing and clinging to the side of the well wall, reaching, and climbing as the light was getting closer and closer. Finally, the frog reached the ledge, exhausted. Then, with all his might, he pulled himself over the ledge and lay on the ground to recover from the climb deep down in the well.

The frog turned himself over and was amazed to find a pond. He really enjoyed swimming in the pond. While swimming, he noticed a creek that led to a lake and went swimming there. "Wow," the frog said to himself, "I can't believe this is better than the well; this is better than the pond. The creek and the lake are fantastic!" He then noticed a path to another creek leading to a river with rushing water full of twists and turns. The frog exclaimed that this was certainly better than the still water in the well, the sitting pond water, and the lake. He absolutely loved swimming in the river water. It was unbelievable!

The story contains so many messages for today's young people. The key message is a wonderful world awaits each generation to explore. Make your life count by doing the hard and difficult things using the energy of your youth. Please do not limit yourself, do not make excuses, do not settle, and live your life with purpose. You are the world's most precious resource. Stop being afraid to discover something new today. Act today with confidence and challenge yourself to do the unthinkable things. You might be the only one in your family to spark and shift the trajectory for an entire generation. You are responsible for investing in yourself to change your family, school, neighborhood, and community. It is what each generation must do!

UCF youth activities: One of our students had an opportunity to attend a professional golf tournament featuring Tiger Woods, several went on a trip to Anacostia in Southeast Washington, D.C. to visit the Frederick Douglass Home while later attending a Washington Nationals' baseball game.

You have not because you ask not! Ask and you shall receive… We asked Waldenbooks in Lakeforest Mall for support in obtaining books from our booklist. Once we received our nonprofit status, UCF then presented it to store manager Delunte Lewis, who entered the ELS Program in a book drive. The bookstore asked patrons to purchase a book and donate it to The UCF's program.

PARTNERSHIPS <u>WALDENBOOKS, LAKEFOREST MALL (2008-2010)</u>

KEITH FOSTER – FIRST UCF STUDENT TO ATTEND LEADERSHIP DEVELOPMENT INSTITUTE (LDI)

Alpha Phi Alpha Fraternity, Inc.

The Montgomery County Chapter of Alpha Phi Alpha sponsored Keith Foster to attend its June 2009 Leadership Development Institute at the University of Maryland, Baltimore County. UCF supporter French Pope Jr. was instrumental in Keith's selection for the program. French has also been instrumental in providing venues for young men to earn community service hours to complete the requirements to graduate.

UCF is grateful to "team together" for the past 14 years to assist in the growth and development of over 100 plus young males who have passed through our youth organization. This is the UCF capstone camp for our leadership program. The camp equips and prepares young males for manhood instructions and college campus experiences.

THIS IS THE SECOND GROUP OF STUDENTS TO ATTEND THE 2010 LEADERSHIP DEVELOPMENT INSTITUTE

Youth church visitations have been a welcome blessing. The above picture was taken at Clinton AME Zion Church in Rockville. We met former NBA great Grant Hill father's Calvin Hill, a former NFL star and senior executive pictured with national gem Jim Madison (age 100), an Ohio State University graduate and college track and field teammate of four-time Olympic gold medalist Jesse Owens.

Exposure Experience - The National Great Blacks in Wax Museum in Baltimore, Maryland

UCF partnered with the Upper County Community Center's Club Friday for three years.

This effort gave our young people an outstanding opportunity to gain entrepreneurial experience. Our students learned practical business applications and related skills by operating a concession stand. This initiative provided students with a tremendous year-round experience and hands-on learning opportunities. They learned about customer service skills, math aptitude practice, marketing, etc. Our student enrollment exploded in four years, resulting in the outgrowth of meeting spaces, classes, and banquet halls. Experts say now is the best time to start a business, but most people don't know how.

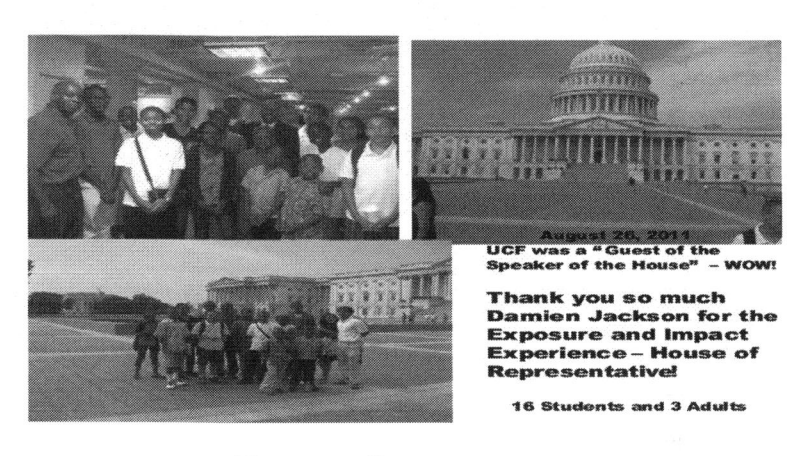

August 26, 2011
UCF was a "Guest of the Speaker of the House" – WOW!

Thank you so much Damien Jackson for the Exposure and Impact Experience – House of Representative!

16 Students and 3 Adults

HOUSE OF REPRESENTATIVES

Maryland Eastern Shore University
Hospitality Summit for Students - Tony Pearson
Summer 2012

Also included in the summer enrichment program for children were golf and basketball camps, SAT/ACT Camp, Hospitality Summit Camp with Donald Wharton, and team building camps hosted by Kappa Alpha Psi Fraternity Inc. for middle school boys. The UCF program helped countless young people, especially our male students build the confidence, competencies, and values they need to become healthy and productive young adults.

SEVEN SUMMERS LACROSSE ORIENTATION CLINIC (2013)

From the beginning, our theme continues to the present day "building youth success, changing the landscape, leveraging opportunity." Our Educational and Life Skills Programs (ELS) evolved to year-round summer activities to include athletic enrichment programs, such as, the Lacrosse Instructional Clinic resulting in several students playing for their respective high school teams. This was a tag-team initiative where students attended practice and the summer reading program. It was going strong until the pandemic. UCF was blessed to have two committed families to launch and sustain the lacrosse program. The angels who provided leadership for operating this program before the COVID-19 pandemic were executive board member Jon Metrey (along with his family members), Metrey's co-worker April Parker, and her son Caleb Atabong, who drove from Harford County, Maryland every Saturday. Caleb, at the time, attended and played the sport at John Carroll High School, a Baltimore area lacrosse powerhouse. Volunteers reported every Saturday to teach skills along with Jon's daughter Mary and son Jack. Also included in the summer enrichment program for boys and girls were golf and basketball camps, SAT/ACT Camp, Hospitality Camp with Donald Wharton, and team building camps hosted by Kappa Alpha Psi Fraternity Inc. for middle school boys. The ELS program helped countless young people, especially our male students build the confidence, competencies, and values they need to become healthy and productive young adults.

Washington, DC - On September 25, 2013, the George Washington University men's lacrosse team hosted a group of several young men from the Unity Christian Fellowship Youth Organization at the Mount Vernon Athletic Complex in Alexandria, Va., for a free lacrosse clinic. "It was an honor and a blast to teach such a great group of kids. It was clear that they enjoyed and appreciated learning from college players and coaches," said GWU assistant coach Patrick Rigney.

GWU coaches and players led the young men through a series of drills focusing on the fundamentals of lacrosse - ground balls, passing, catching, dodging, and shooting. Following the clinic, the young men enjoyed pizza while they soaked in the sights of a college lacrosse practice. Head Coach Joe Opron added context to the event's significance, stating, "for the past two seasons, it has been our goal to become a 'virtual varsity' program. Part of being a student-athlete is using your talents to give back to the community. Thus, today marks an important step in our program's development. I'm so proud of our team because today they proved that our motto, borrowed from George Washington himself, 'Deeds, not words,' is more than just a saying."

THE EMORY GROVE / EPWORTH UMC BASKETBALL CLINIC
(2016-2020)

UCF partnered with community churches with multicultural congregations for approximately four years before the COVID-19 pandemic. These efforts included Pastor Tim Warner and Reverend Mackessa Holt of Emory Grove United Methodist Church, Pastor Jennifer Fenner, and Derek Harps of Epworth United Methodist Church. The goal was to unite two communities using soccer and basketball as a hook to connect youth to Christ.

Mr. Donald Wharton provides leadership by preparing UCF students for success and navigating the interview process that has resulted in four winners. Although Katherine Ortega was UCF's first POSSE winner in 2017, we have had five other student finalists and one Meyerhof winner.

MAGRUDER HIGH SCHOOL COACH RICHARD HARRIS, 2017 MARYLAND STATE GOLF COACH OF THE YEAR GAVE INSTRUCTION ON THE GAME'S FUNDAMENTALS / CARLA DICKERSON, THE SCHOLARSHIP LADY, PROVIDING PASSION FOR THE YOUTH

UCF TEAMED WITH SARAH BROWNER OF ST. MARK UNITED METHODIST CHURCH SCHOLARSHIP RECIPIENTS IN 2015 AND 2017, RESPECTIVELY.

HYATT HOSPITALITY CAMP AT UMES
CAMP DIRECTOR MR. DONALD WHARTON (JULY 9 -14 2017)

A STORY WITH A KEY MESSAGE:

We impress upon this generation of young people that life is like a running clock. Make use of the time the good Lord grants you and make your life count!

Using a sports analogy, we want students who cross our path to learning to compete using their gifts and talents to become the best competitor they can become as a person and student and excel in a meaningful career. Young people believe they have all the time in the world to live their lives, and I want to encourage you to live your life purposefully and make your life count.

I heard CBS sports analyst James Brown refer to life like the game of football. To become the best at anything, you must develop a different mindset to put in the required work to "break the huddle and run the play!"

As a basketball coach for 27 years, I flipped the script to my favorite sport. There are four quarters in the basketball game (except for men's college basketball). There are two quarters in the first and two in the second half.

You may have a lot of time ahead of you. How many of your young people are 15, 16, 17, or 18 years old? If you are 18 or younger, you are in the **first quarter** of your life. That means you need to get together at the tender age of 18. It would be best if you focused on making good choices and pursuing your education like the passion of our ancestors (the warriors, kings, and queens). Look in the mirror and say out loud, "get it together!" You must put in the necessary work to live up to your family name. Like in basketball or any other sport, listen to the instructions so you can play the rest of the game knowing who you are and whose you are.

We don't need any bench warmers. At 18, you are supposed to be planning and preparing for life in your 30s at the EXECUTION stage!

By the end of the **second quarter**, how old are you? That's right! By the time you turn 36, you are at the "halftime" of your life! Can you believe that? At 36 years of age, we have lived half our lives. This is when you are supposed to be preparing and running your play to live out your life in your 40s! That's right, life in your 40's begins with preparation in your 20's; the "execution" phase of life starts in your 30's!

By the end of the **third quarter**, you will be 54! That means by the time you reach that age, you are at the end of the third period and preparing for the final quarter of your life! This is the "sustainment" phrase of life. I don't want any of my friends to say the following, "where has the time gone?" Or "I should have, could have, and would have, if only I knew." Again, life is like a running clock; live a purpose-driven life. I challenge you to prioritize the main things in your life because time really does fly by so fast, and by the time you look up – time has moved on.

By the **fourth quarter**, you will be 72 years old. It's not too far from the end of the game. It is the end of regulation time, and you are looking in the rearview mirror in the kaleidoscope of your life. A few more years beyond the age of 72, you are in overtime! I tell young people and young adults that they don't have time to waste. You are on the clock. Life is a RUNNING clock!

I put it this way from the poem entitled Excuses. "Excuses are tools of the incompetent. They build monuments of nothingness. Those who choose to use them seldom amount to anything." I learned this powerful poem from the late Lawson McElroy during my college days at Rider.

Our most precious resource is that your generation matters. This truly is a pivotal point in the 21st Century. We are counting on you to prepare yourself to be extraordinary. There's greatness in each young person, whether you have lost your way or are on the right track! You need to understand to whom much is given; much is expected! In this century, you belong to the generation with the most gifts. Your generation grew up with iPads, cell phones, Facebook, Instagram, Twitter, and TikTok.

I encourage you not to fall prey and become a victim of the false narrative that says, "we've lost another generation." Don't be the generation that does less with all that has been given to you. You were given so much more than the generation before yours. This generation needs to become "dream makers" and walk in faith and love. If you can do this, you will accomplish so much more. It's not what you can get but what you can give!

I need young people to recognize their purpose, don't get scared, don't settle. There will be speed bumps on your journey. Don't let the setbacks, the temptations, and the shortcuts sidetrack you. The stage is set for you to pursue your promise and destiny. "Break the Huddle and Run Your PLAY to be a person of IMPACT!"

Family and Friends Day
Title Boxing with Master Fitness Trainer French Pope,
Jr Certified Group and Personal Trainer

Motto Have Fun but Get Your Work Done -
Hands on Paint and Chat Youth Initiative

UCF Youth Initiatives

Upper County Community Center	4 Years	First Community Partner 2006
Leadership Development Institute (LDI) (Alpha Phi Alpha Fraternity, Inc.	14 Years	Dr. Joseph A. McMillan - 60 Students (2009)
Dream Chaser College Tour	14 Years	Carla Dickerson, Known as Scholarship Lady (2010)
SAT/ACT Boot Camps	14 Years	Carla Dickerson, Known as Scholarship Lady (2010)
Game Changer Conference for Young Males & Families	13 Years	Community Collaboration Model (2012)
KAMP KAPPA Kappa Alpha Psi Fraternity, Inc.	13 Years	Chairman Will McLeod (2011)
Posse Scholarship & College Planning	12 Years	Donald Wharton (2012)
Christian Youth Basketball Ministry	9 Years	DMV Churches (2007-2017)

HBCU College Fir (MCPS) & Mt. Calvary Baptist Church, Rockville	9 Years	Reverend Barry Moultrie (2014), Felica Williams-Palmer
USTEM/NSBE	8 Years	Indian Banks 2022 Brain Harris - 2017 Randy McCain -2015 Charles Hopson Jr. 2014
Lacrosse Summer Program	7 Years	Jon Metrey, April Parker, Caleb Atabong (2013 -2019)
Hyatt Bridge Program	5 Years	Mr. Donald Wharton (2012-2017)
Golf Instruction Summer Program	5 Years	Coach Rich Harris (2015-2019)
Professional Career Day	5 Years	Community Professionals (2014 -2019)

QUOTE:

Someone once said that the best ideas are in the cemetery because the people died with their ideas, because they didn't live pursuing their dreams. Dr. Myles Munroe was an evangelist, author, and speaker.

"Our graveyards are filled with potential that remained potential. Buried beneath the soil of those sacred grounds are dreams that never came to pass, books that were never written, songs that were never sung, ideas that were never shared, paintings that never filled a canvas, visions that never became reality, plans and inventions that never went beyond the drawing board of the mind, and purposes that were never fulfilled. What a tragedy."

SCRIPTURE:

Don't lose your grip on Love and Loyalty. Tie them around your neck; carve their initials on your heart. Earn a reputation for living well in God's eyes and the eyes of the people. Trust God from the bottom of your heart; don't try to figure out everything on your own. Listen for God's voice in everything you do, everywhere you go; he's the one who will keep you on track."

Proverbs 3:4-6 (MSG)

CHAPTER 11

Dream Chaser College Tour

2ND YOUTH DEVELOPMENT INITIATIVE

First Dream Chaser College Tour to North Carolina (2010)

A guiding principle for UCF centers on providing students and their families with experiences that create meaningful memories. Our experience has been that many students have forgotten how to dream and don't know how to pursue their dreams because of current life circumstances.

Our primary objective will always be to connect students to their dreams and provide leadership opportunities supporting the pursuit of their goals. Our circle of adults offers social, emotional, and academic support so that every student can get better as a person and a student.

The Dream Chaser College Tour was created to address the decline of African American students, especially male students attending universities and colleges. In a recent study, colleges and universities have experienced significant enrollment declines of men of color during the pandemic. For instance, community college enrollments for Blacks and Native American men dropped by 26% and 24%, respectively. Many colleges need help to return enrollments and retention to their pre-pandemic levels. This reflects significant implications on so many levels for the future of Black male leadership. As the world adjusts in the post-pandemic period, this isn't the time to be left behind or say I am taking a gap year. Mentors let reach back and grab a hand to coach, nature, mentor, and motivate young people to persevere in the face of challenges to achieve their goals. I remind those that work directly with young people that the entire world might be just one person, but to one person, you might be the entire world and key to the future. Again, the world continues to transform itself, and this isn't the time to be left behind!

In a county hearing prior to the pandemic to acquire funds for the college initiative, my wife stated that in our community, students don't wake up believing they can attend college, which is why the spring break college tour is important. UCF provides families with options for students to see beyond their current circumstances and envision their future graduating with a college degree.

The college tour has grown in many ways, positively affecting hundreds of students and families over the last 13 years. The picture above is from the first trip in 2010. UCF rented a 15-passenger van with 11 students and three chaperones. My wife Mona and I, Lillian Dangerfield and Jackie Rhone served as chaperones for the next two years. During the tour, we visited six universities and colleges over three days during Spring Break.

In our communication and messaging, we share with families and students that this program is a business trip, not for recreation. We impress them that "education is the passport to the future," and everything we do on the three-day trip will be geared toward that end.

REVEREND DR. CLAY S. GLOSTER JR., SCHOOL OF TECHNOLOGY CHAIR – NORTH CAROLINA A & T UNIVERSITY -
THE FUTURE IS AT HAND!

His inspirational message on POP uplifts our students annually: Young people start today to live your life with PURPOSE, for there are OPPORTUNITIES for you to make a good living in the right career fields. Pursue your PURPOSE with the PASSION of our ancestors! Of course, do here in Aggie Nation!

UCF encourages partnerships with other community organizations that work directly with young people (using their chaperones). We encourage youth organizations to invest in their students by conducting campus visits. The UCF campus tour experience is unique because we have seen the actual results since our inception. The young people who have been a part of our program from an early age are now enrolled in college and have even graduated and moved on to various careers. Our students give back by conducting tours of their college campus upon arrival. They also stay in touch with the students interested in their college or university.

After the first trip, we had parents pick their students up at our house. As we gathered on the front lawn to pray before their departure, we asked the parents and students to commit to three future actions. First, to pray that God will lead them and bless them with the spirit to do the necessary work to improve academic performance. Second, at the first opportunity, to meet with their academic counselors to register for advanced courses that align with the college curriculum. Finally, promise to participate in the upcoming SAT/ACT Boot Camp.

2019 Dream Chaser College Tour
(Last trip before COVID-19)

Campuses Visited:
UNC-Greensboro, North Carolina A&T University,
Bennett College,
Greensboro College, Fayetteville State University,
Campbell University, East Carolina University,
Shaw University,
North Carolina Central University,
Virginia State University
and Virginia Union University.

In the fourth year of the Dream Chaser College tour, we teamed with Mr. Ludley Howard, Executive Director/CEO of Pride Youth Services, Inc., for a more significant effect on families and Students. His support of this collaborative youth initiative began an excellent teaming partnership with other county initiatives, such as the My Brother's Keeper Engagement initiative.

We are proud of the staff members who worked tirelessly and diligently to promote student success at all Montgomery County Public School-based Health and Wellness Centers. Noteworthy contributors to this effort included Gaithersburg High Director Veronica Stroman, and fellow Gaithersburg youth specialist Donnell King. These two connected with all students and the other wellness centers, including Watkins Mill, Northwood, Wheaton, and Seneca Valley High Schools during a seven-year period. Donnell King, a great organizer, and mentor who sincerely cared for so many students supported by the wellness centers would collect the monies, help identify students with realistic financial challenges, reviewed report cards/transcripts, and ensured parents and guardians completed permission forms. These annual spring break college trips truly motivate students to perform their very best to be eligible to get on the bus to North Carolina.

UCF and Pride Youth Services worked collaboratively to impact students with a desire to win their future. We would conduct candid parent meetings to keep everyone in the loop with program goals, objectives, and expectations. The goal was to encourage our students to be committed to doing the necessary work academically, stay focused and stay on track to graduate to increase the number of success stories from the community.

Too many of our young people are unaware of the great experiences the military offers because we don't share the pride and joyful experience as members of the armed forces. I repeat the key message to our parents and future leaders. Regarding mentorship, I want you to understand the tremendous opportunities and benefits that our community remains uninformed about. This is the same message to those that have served in the military as sailors, soldiers, marines, airmen, coast guardsmen, and the newly formed Space Force guardians. Americans must see you!

The goal was to expose students to higher education institutions to encourage our young people (especially our male students) to the endless possibilities of pursuing a college degree. The expectation was to return to school and sign up for honors courses. And like our first group of students in the van, the expectation was for students to attend our SAT/ACT Boot Camps and UCF Youth Engagement Meetings to expose them to 30-second interviews and learn how to communicate in networking scenarios and resume writing.

In addition, to our students, another aspect that makes our college tour unique was an outstanding team of chaperones. The UCF team was led by Jasmine Adkins, responsible for engaging the young ladies on the trip, Jason Miller, the lead male chaperone, and Chester Hardy, who provided academic enrichment questions by categories that kept students engaged. Students were rewarded for giving correct answers to the questions. They were also taught how to evaluate the colleges and universities they visited by learning key data points such as demographics, student population, etc.

CHAPERONE JASON MILLER, MU NU CHAPTER MEMBER OF OMEGA PSI PHI SHARES WISDOM AND KNOWLEDGE ABOUT HIS COLLEGE EXPERIENCE DURING THE APRIL 2019 TRIP.
THIS WAS THE LAST TRIP BEFORE THE ONSET OF COVID-19.

In year four of our annual tour, we transitioned to a beautiful 52-passenger bus owned and operated by Ricardo and Lorain Roach. Grace Transportation provided exceptional service and became a part of the mentoring team. We are also grateful to our mentoring team from the wellness centers and UCF core, who every year made personal sacrifices, taking leave from work to take high school-age children out of their comfort zone to visit college campuses.

According to the Congressional Black Caucus Foundation, exposing our young people to college at a young age is imperative, especially for our young males. Black males ages 18 and older comprise just 5.5 % of all college students. Only one in six black males who attend college will receive a degree. As you see, the implications are dire, which is why more youth organizations must conduct college visits.

UCF's experience mentoring young people shows that it continues to be vital in changing their mental outlook, instilling confidence, and coaching young people to help increase minority college enrollment.

David Hayes, Virginia Union Ambassador

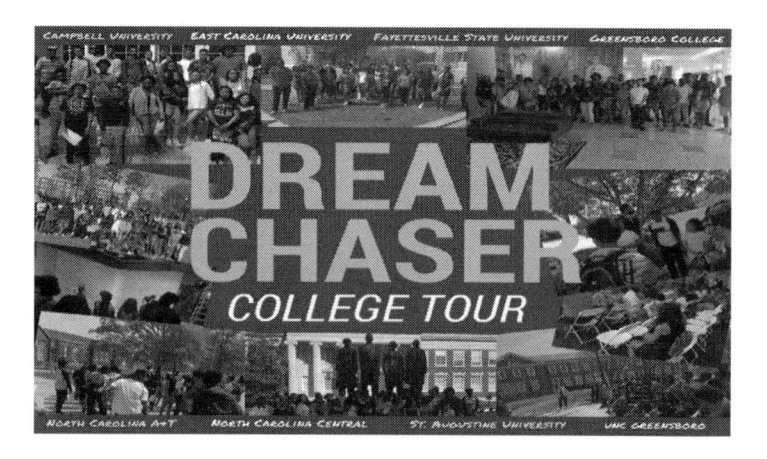

Six Questions You Should Ask On a Campus Tour

The spring and summer seasons are when families tend to visit college campuses, either because a student has been accepted or are considering applying. When you visit, most campus tours will focus on the amenities (modern dorm rooms, number of dining facilities, new library buildings, state-of-the-art gyms), and the prestige factors such as the number of Nobel Laureates on faculty, how old the college is, or the names of famous alumni. But as a parent helping a student with one of their life's most important choices, here are some questions you should be asking at a campus tour.

January 26, 2017

Lifelaunchr is a regular contributor to the Edmodo Blog. With articles written by Venkates Swaminathan, Founder/CEO of LifeLaunchr, the site provides parents and students with virtual and in-person coaching for all aspects of college planning, starting as early as freshman year. Watch for a new post regularly on the Edmodo blog and find out how you or your student can better prepare for a life-changing experience in college.

Six Questions You Should Ask on a Campus Tour

1. What percentage of students have jobs or go onto graduate school after they graduate?
2. What is the student-faculty ratio?
3. What is the campus culture like regarding the student body?
4. What percentage of students graduate in four years?
5. How diverse are the cafeteria menus?
6. Bring up specific points about your desired major.

CPT (P) Chelsea Frazier (ROTC Commission Officer)

I will never forget Friday, March 13, 2020, for that was the day that our lives changed dramatically due to the Coronavirus. All Maryland schools were closed, and students were sent home for an unknown and undetermined period. This order impacted several of UCF's planned activities, such as the Dream Chaser College Tour (April 5-8, 2020) to visit ten institutions over MCPS spring break and other youth engagement planned activities. The UCF leadership team huddled, regrouped, and pivoted to using "virtual platforms" to stay connected to deliver youth engagement initiatives to encourage them to stay positive in the unprecedented health crisis. I was so proud of our team, led by Jasmine Adkins and Jason Miller, who planned and executed an outstanding virtual experience in 2021 and 2022. The above picture featured CPT promotable Chelsea Frazier, Morgan State University graduate who received ROTC Commission. She was a standout basketball student-athlete at Gaithersburg High School in Gaithersburg, Maryland.

The first post-pandemic in-person college tour occurred April 2-5, 2023. As the colleges began to allow visitation, UCF was excited to return to the bus to re-start the campus tour. The life-changing experience impacted 20 students and five adults and achieved the outcome of changing students' future outlooks. Upon returning, we visited ten colleges in three days over Spring Break and several students stated, "Now they now believe" there's a college for them! They promised to meet with their academic counselor and do the necessary intellectual work to achieve their college dream! They were grateful to have chosen to attend the Dream Chaser College Tour over Spring Break.

ELIJAH BLACK SHARING INSIGHT ABOUT THE UNC CHARLOTTE CAMPUS WHERE HIS SISTER WAS A 2021 GRADUATE

VIRGINIA UNION UNIVERSITY

NORTH CAROLINA NC A&T TOUR GUIDE SOPHOMORE ARIEL THOMPSON IN FRONT OF THE NEWEST ENGINEERING HI-TECH FACILITY - AGGIE PRIDE!

The Dream Chaser College Tour on April 2-5, 2023 was a phenomenal and fantastic success. The life-changing experience impacted 20 students and five adults and achieved the outcome of changing the mental outlook of our students. On this business trip, we visited ten colleges in 3 days over Spring Break, and several students stated "now we believe" there's a college for them upon returning! They promised to meet with their academic counselor and do the necessary academic work to achieve their college dream! That's what success looks like!

QUOTE:

"Success isn't about how much money you make; it is about the difference you make in people lives."
　　　　　　　　—Former First Lady Michelle Obama

"It isn't a calamity to die with dreams unfulfilled, but it is a calamity not to dream. It is not a disaster to be unable to capture your ideal, but it is a disaster to have no ideal to capture. It is not a disgrace not to reach the stars, but it is a disgrace to have no stars to reach for. Not failure, but low aim is sin."
　　　　　　　　—Dr. Benjamin E. Mays

SCRIPTURE:

"I will praise thee; for I am fearfully and wonderfully made: marvelous are thy works; and that my soul knoweth right well."
　　　　　　　　Psalm 139:14

CHAPTER 12

SAT/ACT Boot Camp Program

2010 Inaugural SAT/ACT Boot Camp

UCF Partners with Carla Dickerson,
known as the Scholarship Lady US

3rd YOUTH DEVELOPMENT INITIATIVE

The above picture was the first SAT/ACT Boot camp held in our home in September 2010. UCF Youth Development celebrates its 14th year teaming with Ms. Carla M. Dickerson (thescholarshipladydc.com), known as the "Scholarship Lady US," and her team of certified instructors to offer SAT/ACT Boot Camps for students. The Scholarship Lady U.S. is recognized as a national college scholarship consultant, educator, and leader in the academic field and significantly impacted our community in this 13-year partnership. The partnership is a demonstrated labor of "love" and our desire to collaborate with parents and students regarding position outcomes. The overall goal of the "boot camps" continues to prepare students to learn exam methodology. And to equip students with a better, easy, and understanding of standardized test-taking skills. We want the students to know how to select the correct answers during the exam. The partnership generated over $1 million in scholarship monies for students participating in the Boot Camps for the 2015-2016 academic year! Seventy-five percent of students reported at least a 70% percentile score or higher on the SAT or ACT Exam.

LAUNCHING SUMMER BASKETBALL MINISTRY

In 2010, I received a phone call in the middle of the workday from Ms. Dickerson that would change the trajectory for UCF families and students across Montgomery County. She shared that she visited our website and was excited to learn that UCF was laser-focused on increasing graduation rates among young African American males. Her next statement touched my heart and soul, "what can I do to be a part of this effort to help students to gain confidence in passing standardized exams by teaching test strategies?"

We agreed to meet at a restaurant across from Montgomery-Blair High School in Silver Spring to discuss and shape a teaming arrangement. I was impressed with her passion for working together to grow a vision for winning with academics and athletics, and any former athletic coach such as I understand the many dedicated hours used to inspire students to higher heights. I listened to Ms. Dickerson share her story of a 20-year commitment to education, starting in high school and then departing to step out on faith to pursue her purpose in life. She always shares that **God** purposed her to dedicate her efforts to helping students and families succeed in passing standardized examinations. As I looked through my spiritual lens, it was apparent that this was another confirmation from the Lord of what the educational component of UCF is all about.

In the summer of 2010, we rolled out the SAT/ACT Boot Camp in the Christian Youth Basketball Ministry, which served approximately 450 families and students annually. Since then, we have expanded the growth and development of the camp connected to other UCF signature youth initiatives, such as the Game Changer Conference for Young Males and The Dream Chaser College Tour. Remember, the first college tour was earlier over the 2010 spring break, with students promising to attend the inaugural SAT/ACT Boot Camp at our home. Sharing the announcement at the summer basketball ministry seemed like a natural path forward. We desire to impact the community through education on SAT/ACT test-taking strategies, writing winning essays for scholarships, life skills, and developing the student in student-athletes.

Ms. Dickerson and UCF have continued to work together. We conduct workshops annually starting in the summer through the fall months every year. These sessions are for students who are serious about achieving high scores on the SAT/ACT exams. Students learn how to apply the strategies taught, reduce test anxiety, and increase their test-taking confidence.

INAUGURAL 2010 BOOT CAMP WITH CERTIFICATED INSTRUCTORS: DR. JAMES FRACTION, NASA ENGINEER, MOREHOUSE COLLEGE, AND RECIPIENT OF THE JACKIE ROBINSON SCHOLARSHIP AND MR. JACK SMITH, HOWARD UNIVERSITY, (ENGLISH PROFESSOR)

As we celebrate a decade teaming together, we have found extreme satisfaction in aiding several hundred students from seven MCPS high schools who have participated in the program. They have learned strategies to improve test scores and pass standardized exams. The good Lord has blessed this meaningful youth initiative with increased growth, practical understanding, and, more importantly, raised students' test-taking confidence.

When we gathered before the COVID pandemic, working with MCPS schools, camp sessions for serious-minded students were held throughout the county at Bethesda-Chevy Chase, Springbrook, Clarksburg, Rockville High Schools, and Forest Oak Middle School.

UCF provided a light meal for students and parents and held parent roundtable sessions on navigating the college's progress. The parent conversations occurred while students in a separate classroom would receive three days of intense practical exercises, test-taking strategies, and personalized, hands-on instruction from the staff.

IN THREE SHORT YEARS, THE CAMP GREW TO 30 STUDENTS BY 2013. A TOTAL OF 18 MALE AND 12 FEMALE STUDENTS ATTENDED THE THREE-DAY SESSION. THE BOOT CAMP CONTINUES TO BE VITAL PART OF UCF PRIMARY UNIT THAT PRODUCES POSITIVE OUTCOMES.

COLLABORATION MODEL THAT REFLECTS WE ARE STRONGER WORKING TOGETHER! TEAMING ARRANGEMENT PRIOR TO COVID-19

The 2019 SAT/ACT Boot Camp was paid forward by a generous donation by Michelle Taylor that created an explosive registration of more than 110 students. The camp was hosted at the Fire & Rescue Training Academy (FRTA) on Snouffer School Road in Gaithersburg.

UCF will forever be grateful to the community leadership of Captains David Kennedy and Ty Dement, along with Lieutenant Irvin Smith. UCF benefited from the MCFRS EEO/Diversity CE services on several occasions. NAACP Youth Director Kimberly McClurkin Harris, Linda Plummer, and Carla Dickerson came together to help our Boot Camp reach unprecedented levels.

This is what a collaboration model looks like. We're grateful to Michelle Taylor, President, and CEO of BETAH Associates, Inc., in Silver Spring, Maryland. We are stronger working together! What does it look like for you to increase your level of commitment?

2018 THE UCF HAS PROVIDED A COLLABORATION MODEL THAT HAS SPENT A DECADE TRANSFORMING LIVES.

QUOTE:

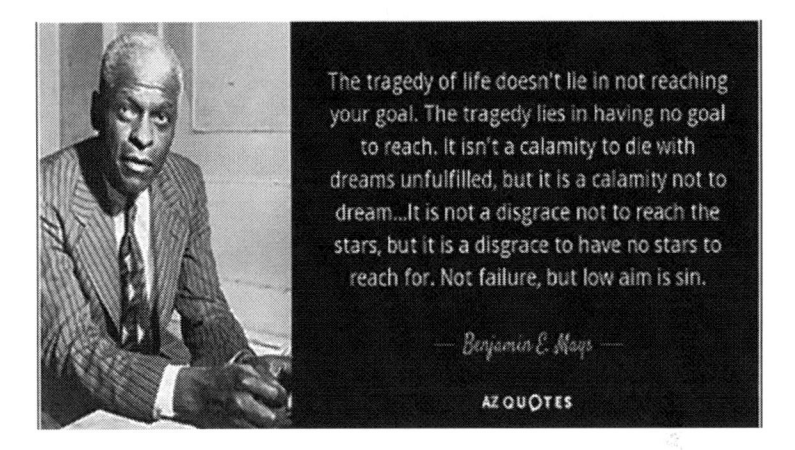

> The tragedy of life doesn't lie in not reaching your goal. The tragedy lies in having no goal to reach. It isn't a calamity to die with dreams unfulfilled, but it is a calamity not to dream...It is not a disgrace not to reach the stars, but it is a disgrace to have no stars to reach for. Not failure, but low aim is sin.
>
> — Benjamin E. Mays

SCRIPTURE:

"Don't lose your grip on Love and Loyalty. Tie them around your neck; carve their initials on your heart. Earn a reputation for living well in God's eyes and the eyes of the people. Trust God from the bottom of your heart; don't try to figure out everything on your own. Listen for God's voice in everything you do, everywhere you go; he's the one who will keep you on track."

PROVERBS 3:4-6 (MSG)

CHAPTER 13

Basketball Ministry (2007 -2017)

"Let me say there is not a better investment than our young people!"
—Donald Williams II

Christian Youth Basketball Ministry

I was blessed to experience success in coaching on several levels for over 25 years. In the several years, I coached while in the military, recreational league, Amateur Athletic Union (AAU) traveling teams, and the collegiate level at Hagerstown Community College, Montgomery College, and Morgan State University.

I have a passion for young people and the game of basketball that provided excellent "teachable moments" that parallel life! There is no more incredible feeling than being instrumental in young people's growth, development, and success.

Maurice Hamilton, co-labor in this ministry, a good friend and fellow Steward at First A.M.E. Church approached me about becoming the Commissioner for the previously named A.M.E. Church League in the winter of 2007. I told him I would have to pray about assuming leadership. I had to talk to my wife and family about taking on this tremendous responsibility for the 2nd District of the Washington Annual Conference of the African Methodist Episcopal Church.

Maurice had been involved in the league for more than four years prior. When I asked him how my name surfaced to be commissioner, he shared that they asked him to be commissioner for the 13 churches participating in the A.M.E. League. He immediately declined and said he knew the perfect person to take over before volunteering as an assistant commissioner. Maurice explained that he believed in my heart for service, organizational skills, integrity, demonstrated faith walk, and interpersonal skills to communicate a vision and strategic plan needed to enhance the ministry. Maurice, a high school and collegiate basketball referee, had responsibilities for scheduling and managing the officials for the ministry. There is a scripture that references God speaking to each of us in dreams. It says, "In the last days, I will pour out my Spirit on every kind of people. Your sons and your daughters will prophesy; your young men will see visions, and your old men will dream. I will pour my Spirit on those who serve me (Acts 2:17)."

A LABOR OF LOVE – Commissioner and Assistant Commissioner Maurice Hamilton – SERVANT LEADERS serving the Community. "God's Legacy Builders."

Maurice didn't know that God spoke to me in a dream earlier that year while enjoying championship success at Montgomery College. I dreamed about establishing a basketball ministry to teach the game I love and share God's principles with the next generation of young people outside of the four walls of the church. There is a need in every generation to introduce God's message and words to keep it fresh, understandable, and relevant in a way that engages young people right where they are.

The Lord through a dream led me to accept the mission of serving the community through athletics. From the beginning, I prayed that churches would embrace this ministry to work directly with their congregation's youth and their communities to introduce Jesus Christ.

It was a blessing to experience God's influence on my life and trust him to be a way maker. The Basketball Ministry's objective was to use basketball as a "hook and lure" to attract young people, and then use our time together to introduce them to "GOD's Principles…" winning and bringing souls closer to GOD – Kingdom Building!

Brother Maurice Hamilton and I were truly blessed to work with two wonderful men of God, our spiritual leaders from the 2nd District, A.M.E. Church: our beloved Presiding Elder Louis-Charles Harvey, (retired) of the Potomac District, and the late Presiding Elder Goodwin Douglas, (RIP) of the Capital District.

Brother Hamilton presented the appeal at the Washington Conference before the Bishop and district churches to seek official approval and support that the Washington Annual Conference of the African Methodist Episcopal Church officially recognizes the Christian Youth Basketball Ministry (CYBM), Co-Ed. On Friday, April 17, 2009, at the 59th Session of the Washington Annual Conference, the CYBM was officially recognized, supported, endorsed, and sanctioned by the Right Reverend Adam J. Richardson, Presiding Bishop and the two Presiding Elders: Reverend Harvey and Reverend Douglas.

CYBM COACHES MINISTRY
"God's Legacy Builders"
Have you ever wondered why God created Coaches and Athletes? No body impacts our lives more than a Coach!

It was an amazing blessing to be recognized by spiritual leadership. It was a remarkable blessing for approximately ten seasons. So proud of the support received by churches and their coaches who worked year-round planning to bring their community together using basketball to keep children off the streets during the summer for eight weeks by engaging in a positive fitness development program.

I was clear about my assignment in this season of CYBM ministry which was to pleased God. It was much like the Jewish leader Nehemiah who was clear about his mission to rebuild the wall. My mission was clear for providing leadership – to shift the focus from the church basketball league to a church co-ed basketball ministry that used coaches as the ministry's "first line" - coaching God's way! I shared with Brother Hamilton that we will focus on doing the challenging work of ministry.

I had been active supporter of my friend Mark Stephens, the State of Maryland Director for Fellowship of Christian Athletes. UCF and FCA had started around the same time and were supportive of each other's ministry. What a beautiful partnership in which FCA provided inspirational video messaging by celebrities who professed their faith and whose messages connect with young people. Hearing professional athletes whose messages appealed to young people was impactful.

A GAME CHANGER'S PURSUIT

LET'S BUILD A LASTING "LEGACY" BY:
— CONNECTION TO CHRIST
— CONNECTING THE BIBLE TO COACHING
— CONNECTING WITH OTHER COACHES
— CONNECTING OUR YOUTH TO CHRIST!

GOD LEGACY IS IN YOU - WHAT LEGACY WILL YOU LEAVE?

For approximately a decade, the Christian Youth Basketball Ministry's mission was to prepare young disciples for Christ, to nurture and raise up Godly young people to send into the world to serve. The

CYBM was an outreach ministry that allowed us to share Jesus Christ with our young people and coaches!

Coaching to win God's way is about "authentic discipleship," to be a servant leader so that others see God's Legacy in you. Our primary focus was to work together to bring churches from across the Washington/Maryland/Virginia metropolitan area together to provide our young people and church families with a fun, safe, exciting recreational activity that kept our children off the street and involved in a positive Christian base ministry during the summer months. Approximately 500 student-athletes enjoyed this wonderful community activity at the height of the basketball ministry. The CYBM instilled community pride between pastors, church members, and supporters. Throughout the ministry, approximately 3,500 sports bags were purchased for all participants. Seeing the smiles on the faces of the young people and volunteers was a blessing. All Coaches, referees and team winners received trophies, bibles, and coaches' plaques. The Fellowship of Christian Athletes provided "The Competitor's Devotional Bible for Athletes" that was easy to read and use and provided daily inspirational sports stories. These stories engaged, encouraged, and equipped youth and adults with engaging topics such as: How to Pray, No Excuses, Fuel Up, Going Halfway, Living Sacrifices, Choose Love, and Playing for the Lord. Having countless Black men involved as servant leaders was indeed a blessing. You know that Coaches have a greater influence and impact on our young people in many ways. Are you aware that one coach can influence more people in one year than the average person will do in a lifetime? The issue is how you will influence individuals on your team.

Have you ever wondered why God created coaches and athletes? The Answer: We are raising up the next generation of coaches and leaders! I encouraged all adult leaders to recognize the ministry work was important, meaningful, and impactful. The reality is that you may be the only bible your players ever read! Our coaches were the heart of our basketball ministry where we worked together and positively affected the lives of countless young people. Once we received the buy-in from the young athletes, I believe we made God smile.

CHRISTIAN YOUTH BASKETBALL MINISTRY

God's word says train up a child in the way they should go and they will never depart!
We are seed planters!!

LET ME SAY THERE IS NOT A BETTER INVESTMENT
THAN OUR YOUNG PEOPLE!

CHRISTIAN YOUTH BASKETBALL MINISTRY (2007 – 2017)

As the CYBM grew, we were proud of all the men and women who rolled up their sleeves to work with our young people. What a joy it was to see and witness the dedication and commitment of "people builders and Christian builders." They ensured young people participating in the basketball ministry received not only basketball instruction but, more importantly, biblical instructions through bible lessons at practices and before playing a game we all love.

The interdenominational summer basketball ministry had a record number of ten Churches participating at the height of the CYBM's growth: Reid Temple A.M.E., Metropolitan A.M.E., Shiloh Abundant Life, Turner Memorial A.M.E., First A.M.E., Faith A.M.E., Embry A.M.E., Young Life Ministry, Israel Baptist, and Mount Ephraim Baptist.

The picture above centered Sister Iris Akwara of Faith A.M.E. Church, Eric Burnett, Victory Christian Church International, Donald Williams, Maurice Hamilton, First A.M.E. Church, and Joel Leigh, Church of God in Christ. Sister Akwara was responsible for developing a "devotional focus" guide for the basketball ministry. We devised a theme every summer such as "Be a Shot Caller for God." At the local churches, coaches presented bible lessons to players every week at the beginning or end of every practice. They were provided talking points to center their discussion around the devotional focus. The outcome was a standardized ministry devotional focus shared with the young people before play on Saturday.

Building a basketball program from scratch into a championship program was one of the best experiences in my life. I was wrong. For the record, there is no greater feeling than to provide leadership for ministry in the Kingdom, changing culture by touching the hearts and minds of others. It is a blessing to speak faith into others and show them how to use their God-given gifts and efforts to coach God's way.

There was no better experience than working with Black men to impact the community in a positive way and to lead and organize an excellent experience for our children. It was wonderful to see coaches doing the necessary work for the community. It's amazing to focus your efforts on building young people up and establishing a support team of adults to help guide, nurture and direct collective efforts and energy to find ways to invest in others.

CHRISTIAN YOUTH BASKETBALL MINISTRY
Servant Leader
Giving the best of yourself

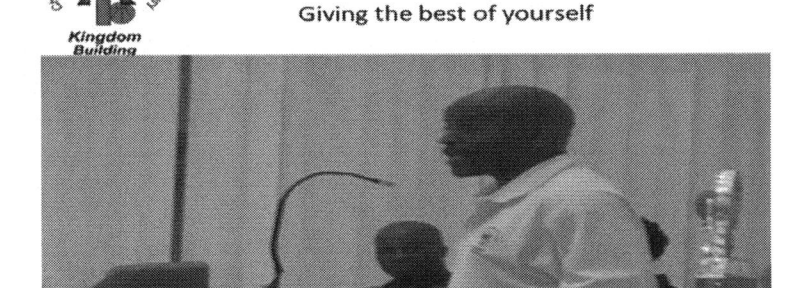

UCF - Basketball Diaries - SUMMERTIME

Tim Alston

Summertime usually brings about the end of the school year, family vacations, and jobs for the under-18 crowd that UCF (via the Christian Youth Basketball Ministry) supports. However, summertime also brings about a few other activities that aid in developing individuals spiritually, culturally, and socially.

As an aspiring basketball official, the CYBM was a training ground for me to work on my skills and techniques as a basketball official. Moreover, the CYBM allowed me to develop into the basketball official I wanted to become with my spirituality intact and use it to view the game with a set of spiritual lenses (filters).

One of UCF's focuses was to develop the spiritual characteristics of young men and women. Although that was one of its focus areas, it impacted everyone involved, especially me as a basketball official. The CYBM allowed me to include my spiritual side to officiate the game competitively and compassionately. My focus in the game was to ensure safety and security but to teach various aspects of the game which the youngsters could incorporate into their respective developing games.

The CYBM summer league was a local cultural phenomenon as well. It brought together multigenerational persons where folks learned about significant individuals in the community contributing to the growth of the African American diaspora. As a result, the youngsters in the basketball league received increased knowledge, awareness, and self-discovery. I channel that culture into a more teachable officiating skill set enabling respect for calls made during the games.

As a basketball official, it is typical for the person officiating the game to be less inclusive in how calls are made. However, the CYBM, because of its focus on spirituality, opened the fabric of communication between staff, players, coaches, and parents/guardians. The game became a window where I could teach and socialize the reasoning behind such calls. I believe it gave an appreciation to all of those involved and a better understanding of what is transpiring on the court. As the colloquium states, "knowledge is power." Having that additional information about what is occurring on the court allows the groups of people to better mentor and coach players about the game and life. It allowed me to gain the trust of those people in the social fabric of the hard court to win the lessons learned needed beyond the court as well.

The run was great! I always looked forward to each season, along with the end-of-season ceremonial luncheon. UCF grew the spiritual, cultural, and social behaviors of all involved while making significant strides in youth development.

TIMOTHY L. ALSTON JR. (OFFICIAL IN BLUE SHORT SECOND FROM LEFT) DEDICATED OFFICIALS THAT CONTRIBUTE TO THE MINISTRY SUCCESS FOR A DECADE

(L TO R) TROY PINCKNEY, DONALD WILLIAMS II, JOHN HARRIS III AND ADRIAN BURNIM

The church's Youth Advisory Council inspired the First A.M.E. Church-Gaithersburg Basketball Ministry. At a 2002 meeting, John Harris III mentioned to Maurice Hamilton that he felt that the sport of basketball would perhaps be a solid vehicle to draw more youth to the church. The original conversation sparked a movement that started a decade-long ministry at First A.M.E. (2003-2013) that provided a safe, holistic outlet for recreation, fitness, sportsmanship, and a venue to learn more about our Lord and Savior Jesus Christ.

After a brief discussion with Youth Minister Rev. Ayana Newton and the rest of the YAC (Mona Williams, Rev. Moya Harris, Yolanda Lindo, Donald Williams, and Brothers Hamilton and Harris), Rev. Newton brought the idea to Pastor Barbara Y. Glenn and Assistant Pastor Marvin T. Glenn for approval. The eventual support paved the way for the ministry to begin with an original group of children ages 11 to 15 to register to play in the original Washington Conference Youth Summer Basketball Ministry, a ministry started in the early 1990s by Rev. Michael Henson of Turner Memorial A.M.E. Church.

To start the First A.M.E. Ministry, boys and girls were recruited from the church only, and eventually children from adjacent neighborhoods in the Washington Grove area were invited to join the church ministry as well. There was some early trepidation about who to consider for the First A.M.E. roster, as the church was not 100 percent knowledgeable about the rules regarding recruitment. As blessings would have it, the Conference Ministry considered it highly important to evangelize throughout the areas where the participating churches were located. While this was unfortunately realized after our initial winless season (including a season-ending one-point loss to one of the league's best teams), the original seeds were planted for a burgeoning ministry at First A.M.E. Church.

In that first season, First A.M.E. recruited approximately 15 children for its inaugural team to play in the Washington Conference's 12-15 age group, hosted at Sligo Middle School in Silver Spring. They were coached and mentored by Brothers Harris, Hamilton, and Albert Thompson. A practice facility was procured less than 2 miles from First AME church (the Washington Grove Center).

All but one of the players attended the church, and while the team failed to win a game for the entire season, the players, coaches, and First AME's ministerial leadership felt that the season was a rousing success. Everyone immensely enjoyed the fellowship, camaraderie, biblical education, spirituality, and the game of basketball. Longtime bonds, friendships, and mentorships were forged during the process, and the ministry developed a solid launching pad for its future.

Equipped with further knowledge and understanding of the Washington Conference Ministry rules, the coaching and administrative staff of the First AME Basketball Ministry began to take off. In 2004, players and coaches began to reach out to the youth of the church's surrounding neighborhoods. They brought together over 30 children from ages 8-15 to play on two separate teams, one in the 8-12 division, and the other in the reformatted 13-15 division. Because of our growing numbers, we were forced to find a facility to help house our practices/study sessions. The ministry procured Shady Grove Middle School to become our new longtime home. Later, Forest Oak Middle School also served as a reserve practice facility for the ministry. Both neighboring middle schools were gracious partners in our efforts to serve the Washington Grove-Gaithersburg community.

The summer of 2004 was a standout campaign for the ministry on and off the court, as the 13-15 team went from last place to win the regular season championship. The 8-12 team won nearly half of their games that season and were always a threat to upset the league's top teams in their division.

In addition to the on-court success, the ministry's evangelistic approach encouraged friends and neighbors to become a part of the ministry. The serious players found a brand of basketball that they enjoyed. At the same time, the children who needed a venue to go and enjoy themselves and become further acquainted with an organized brand of basketball were also pleased just to become a part of a team. The blend of abilities and attitudes on these two teams meshed perfectly. It became the ideal laboratory for now expanded coaching staff to begin to mentor and coach these children in the game of basketball and in life.

While Sligo Middle School could no longer hold the Washington Conference Ministry games in its gym, Albert Einstein High School in Kensington, MD, stepped up and allowed the ministry to host the 2005 season.

After that season, the ministry had to move to southern Prince George's County to be housed at a middle school and a community recreation center. Nonetheless, with a growing coaching staff (with the additions of Brothers Adrian Burnim, Kareem Johnson, Troy Pinckney, Greg Sydnor and Lee Black) the First AME basketball ministry witnessed unprecedented growth, and in its first four years, had already served over 100 youth from across the greater Gaithersburg area.

By 2007, both the First AME basketball ministry and the newly named Christian Youth Basketball Ministry (CYBM) found a new home in Silver Spring, this time at spacious John F. Kennedy High School. The move to play games at the site allowed the utilization of two gyms in one facility, enabling the rapid growth of the overall ministry. Also, by that time, First AME had grown to 4 teams, an 8–12-year-old squad, two 13-15 teams, and a 16-18 team. By then, the ministry included student-athletes from as far north as Frederick, Maryland, and as far south as Silver Spring.

The growth of both the CYBM and First AME basketball ministry caused growing pains and painful departures. After many years of coaching in the league, Brother Hamilton moved to the front office as Assistant Commissioner, providing leadership with referee management. He established an excellent network with referees who wanted to be a part of the ministry with a heart to give back to the community. In addition, he helped with officiating games in the CYBM. An original assistant coach with First AME, Brother Williams' expertise in leadership, management and public relations were eventually tabbed as the eventual commissioner of the CYBM.

On the court, the overall success of the First AME Basketball Ministry can also be measured by the amount of hardware it earned, as the church collected over two dozen regular season and postseason tournament first-place trophies throughout the four age groups from 2004 through 2013. However, the "FAME" ministry could also be lauded as an oasis for young men and young women on spring and summer weekends for an entire decade.

The ministry served scores of youths from around Montgomery County and were able to absorb the ministry's coaching, teachings, and mentorship. As players age out of the 16-18 teams, many went on to post-secondary education and earn college degrees. A few even earned athletic scholarships (in football, basketball, women's basketball, and track and field) from schools such as the University of Pittsburgh (Manny Williams, football), the University of Buffalo (Imani Chatman, football), Howard University/University of Portland (Natalie Day, women's basketball), North Carolina Central University (Bethany White, women's track and field), Mount St. Mary's University (Jonathan Onasanya, track and field), Guilford College/Salisbury University (Justin Taylor, basketball), and Mount Olive College/University of Maryland-Baltimore County (Marcus Foster, track and field).

One ministry veteran is now the head coach of the boys' varsity basketball team at Albert Einstein High (Taylor). Day has played professionally in Europe for several years and participated in the Pan-American Games and the FIBA Americas Zone Championships as a veteran member of the United States Virgin Islands Women's National Team. Plenty of young men and women were a part of the ministry who went on to college and earned degrees from schools such as Morgan State University, Bowie State University, University of Maryland-Eastern Shore, Fayetteville State University and Virginia Union University among others. More importantly, there have also been just as many former participants who absorbed the teachings of the First AME Ministry to become solid citizens of society and in the world of work. One longtime participant of the First AME Ministry credited the organization for putting him and an older sibling on the right path after considering a trip on the wrong one. As a teen, the young man admitted that he and his brother had considered joining gangs while in school. He enthusiastically noted that both him and his brother's involvement with the First AME basketball ministry gave them an activity that allowed them to be among positive Christian male role models (and teammates) and helped to launch both into solid careers after high school with a government agency and in the automotive industry, respectively. This type of example served as the original mission for the First AME Basketball Ministry; leading youth to Christ, helping them stay off the streets, and learning teamwork, sportsmanship, and overall life skills.

—Reflections by John Harris III, former Director, First AME Basketball Ministry

LET ME SAY THERE IS NOT A BETTER INVESTMENT THAN OUR YOUNG PEOPLE!

I would be remiss to conclude this chapter without sharing that the CYBM was a game changer across the DMV communities. The ministry was a microcosm of the community at large and the dynamic challenges of any community. CYBM experienced everything in your community such as fighting, the tragic loss of two young males, players and coaches being disciplined and suspended, etc. Just because CYBM was a ministry didn't absolve us from environmental, social and cultural influences that communities experience every day.

Coach Stephen Brown of Shiloh Abundant Life Church shared that grace is when God gives you good things you don't deserve. Mercy is when He spares us from the bad things we deserve. In a moment of trepidation, he provided uplift stating that God's blessing is when He is generous with both. This ministry's impact across the state was amazing and changed hearts, saved souls, and inspired another generation to realize their potential. God's word says train up a child in the way they should go, and they will never depart!

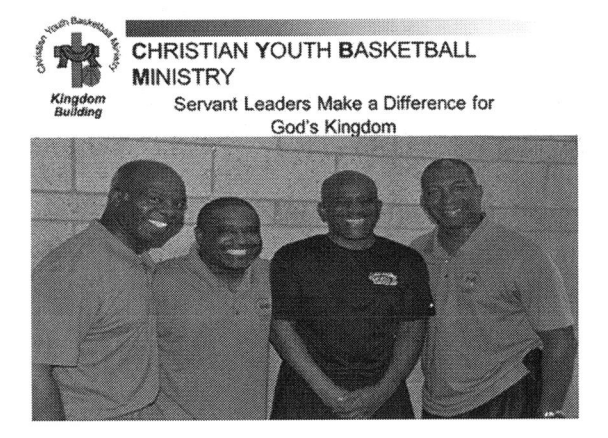

(LEFT TO RIGHT) FAITHFUL SERVANTS: DONALD WILLIAMS, VINSON HILL, MAURICE HAMILTON, ERIC BURNETT

As stated earlier, we were clear about the ministry's mission to use basketball as a "hook and lure" to attract and position young people to be introduced to "God's Principles and bring souls to Christ. As stated, we were committed to being seed planters, dream releasers, speak faith, hope, and blessings into young people's lives. Prepared scripts for coaches to read and review with their students at practices were provided. Coaches were given talking points and life application stories to help make devotion relevant to students. On Saturday, teams attended the ministry room before playing their game. I conducted the bible lesson review, and prizes were given to students who demonstrated knowledge of the lesson on game day. We wanted to provide young people encouragement, confidence, and uplift to awaken the greatness inside of them. An example is below:

Spiritual Muscle

Our Definition: Do you have the *muscle* to *muscle* your way to the top? *Muscle* is both a noun and verb associated with strength, power, or the use of physical force.

Life Application: In addition to biological muscle, like the biceps in your arms, *muscle* can refer simply to power or authority, as in "We have the *muscle* to get the job done." *Muscle* can also refer to a hired thug. In a similar sense, *muscle* is used as a verb to mean «use force.» A bully might muscle someone out of their lunch money, or you might muscle your way through a crowd by pushing people out of your way.

Scripture Lesson from Acts 4:13, Message Bible

13-14 They couldn't take their eyes off them—Peter and John standing there so confident, so sure of themselves! Their fascination deepened when they realized these two were laymen with no training in Scripture or formal education.

Peter and John were supernaturally equipped. Everyone around them marveled at their boldness, at their ability. They recognized them as companions of Jesus, but with the man right before them, seeing him standing there so upright—so healed!—what could they say against that?

They knew there wasn't anything special about them. This power and wisdom could have only come from one place - the presence of Jesus.

<u>Read the Story and add/incorporate your life experience (Colossians 2:6-7)</u>

It seems like only yesterday that I was in my high school weight room pumping weights with the music cranked. I do not doubt that the thousands of hours I spent in the weight room as a high school, college, and professional athlete paid off. As a young man, I wanted not only to get big and strong but also to excel in my sport. Lifting weights built me up and strengthened me to be the best athlete I could. The added muscle helped me perform better and kept me from injury. Too bad my mom didn't like that my clothes weren't fitting anymore. Paul wrote that we must be "rooted and build-up" in Christ. The Lord desires for us to develop spiritual muscles. In 1 Timothy 4:7, Paul wrote, "train yourself in godliness." He challenges us to work out and produce spiritual sweat.

What does it mean to be strong in the Lord? I have a detailed, specific workout routine when I am in the weight room. We may need the same thing spiritually. God desires for us to invest time to develop spiritual muscles – not for our gain, but for His glory!

What does it mean to work out spiritually? What is your spiritual routine? It was beautiful to hear students provide examples of how to build their spiritual muscle, such as praying, having quiet time, reading the bible daily, and maintaining a positive attitude and effort in your relationship with God. In addition to attending Church school, vacation bible school, etc.

First A.M.E. Church Youth Ministry

QUOTE:

The greatest "legacy" is not what we leave for people; it is what we leave <u>in</u> people. Be a dream releaser, a seed planter, speak faith and blessings into a young person life. Let's pay it forward! …to give our young people more encouragement and confidence to achieve greatness! I believe dreams become God ordained destiny when you are in pursuit of your dream.

SCRIPTURE:

No eye has seen, no ear has heard, and no mind has imagined what God has prepared for those who love him.

1 Corinthians 2:9 NLT

Our Youth Committing to Christ

Jabril Rhea gives his father Calvin Rhea a hug

Team Williams A Labor of Love

CHAPTER 14

Leadership and STEM Enrichment Programs

5TH YOUTH DEVELOPMENT INITIATIVE

In the early launching of the UCF Youth Development Organization, it was imperative to undergird students with social-emotional support and equip them with skills to earn a living. We have steadfastly inspired students to take ownership by making opportunities for themselves while building confidence in a different learning environment! Making hope happen!

We encourage our young people to level up and acquire a good education. At the same time, in high school, go to college and pursue a degree in a meaningful career profession, or get certifications, gain experience, and try to use your education to improve your quality of life and make life better for your family and others by giving back.

We recognized that it was critical to introduce students to new pathways to learn new skill sets that lead to employment opportunities.

Young people, especially males, must be committed to continuous personal growth and development. The desired outcome was to show students as many future options as possible. To have them accept responsibilities for managing their great experiences, self-development, improvement, and ownership of their maturation process. The UCF journey is about encouraging, uplifting, and inspiring students to increase their commitment to doing the necessary work to become providers and producers so that one day they will grow into responsible young adults. During the emergence of UCF in 2006, two significant events in 2001 provided a perfect storm that caused the organization to embrace the transformation for promoting careers in science, technology, engineering, and mathematics (STEM). Congress under President George W. Bush, on January 8, 2002, passed the "No Child Left behind Act." Also, a significant shift occurred with Universities and the National Science Foundation (NSF) administrators introducing and promoting a curriculum that centered on STEM. Studies have shown that after being introduced to STEM, student confidence increases and spurs them to want to learn more. Some students will be inspired to pursue majors and careers in STEM fields, thus increasing the number of minorities available to enter this part of the workforce.

UCF has been intentional with introducing students to potential employment and career opportunities. We have held annual professional career days that help students think differently, shift, and consider new possibilities. We invited professionals from various careers to share their stories, including returning citizens who've served their debt to society. We want young people, especially young males, to view their lives in terms of where they will be in two to five years.

A GAME CHANGER'S PURSUIT

BRYAN LEE, (FORMER) DEPUTY FIRE CHIEF FROM
THE DISTRICT OF COLUMBIA

"Teach me, and I'll forget. Show me, I may remember. Involve me, I'll understand and may pursue!"

The above picture began introducing students to new thinking and different pathways they might not have experienced. A question was asked of the students what they wanted to be when they grew up. A middle school student named David Hayes said, "I want to be a fireman." It was important to keep David motivated and engaged and to show the other students something different by putting a firefighter in front of them.

In its first eight years, UCF exposed youth to STEM professionals by inviting guest speakers to monthly meetings. There were many programs, such as the U.S. Naval Academy's 1-Day STEM Camp for young girls, Game Changer Conference for Young Males, and remote racing car competitions.

In the beginning, I leaned on several fraternity brothers so the students could see passionate, caring men with different attitudes who pressed through obstacles and roadblocks to becoming success stories. Former D.C. Chief Bryan Lee was the first Omega man I asked to speak with the young males in uniform. The facial expressions on the student's faces were priceless when he entered the meeting room. Their eyes lit up as he shared his teenage story of not being a perfect student and not making the best decisions. He was asked what transpired in his life that caused him to change course to advance to becoming a success story – "I started listening to advise."

He discussed his childhood friends who kept getting in trouble and said he wanted something different. He challenged young males to make better choices as they navigate their adolescence. He impressed upon them to work now to make their lives count. In addition, he planted the seeds of how he was led to pursue a STEM career such as firefighting.

STEM PROGRAM LAUNCHED EXPOSURE TO PROFESSIONAL MEN

Larry Melton Jr.
– Purple Line Light Rail Project Engineer Leader

This session with the young males heightened UCF's overall profile in building a meaningful STEM program that would help hundreds and thousands of students over the years. The UCF's STEM journey has evolved from conducting professional speaker forums to developing the U-STEM Fun Zone and the National Society of Black Engineers consistently meet monthly. UCF speakers shared wisdom and knowledge with students monthly about principles, decision-making, and educational strategies including building positive relationships with teachers, improving academically, and selecting a meaningful career.

It was essential to build UCF's foundation by instilling high standards of character and excellence and instilling the overall expectation pillars below:

- Pursue excellence in all areas of your life
- Make good choices/decisions daily
- Lead by example in the classroom, extracurricular activities, and team sports
- Model good behavior, do what is right, and not succumb to peer pressure
- Give a winning effort, stay on task with assignment completion no matter what
- Perform good deeds and do something good for someone else
- Join extracurricular activities as a team member or team leader

The UCF MOTTO since 2006 has been to "Have Fun and Get Your Work DONE – If it is to be, it is up to me."

Winning the FUTURE with Math and Leadership Skills
Ken Mott is an Electrical Engineer for the Nuclear Regulatory Commission

At the center of the UCF's philosophy is equipping students with life skills such as situational awareness, teaching educational strategies, navigating adversity, difficult relationships, and promoting leadership. We impressed upon students to not only do good but to be good and choose to do good at everything they are involved with. We tell students not to let anyone tell them that they can't achieve and won't amount to anything – put forth a winning effort and prove them wrong! We advise students on their academic journey to pursue excellence to be aware of the "Dream Snatchers and the Dream Makers!"

During the early years of our youth meetings, we encouraged young males to flip the script by working harder to exhibit a higher level of commitment, improvement, and excellence in the classroom.

The student engagement meetings helped young males focus on making good choices and share how bad decisions can derail their dreams. A key communication exercise that encouraged young males to "speak up" and discuss real-life challenges involved two young males with an adult male in discussing current events and topics of the day increased student's confidence and helped them maximize their potential in school.

There will be people who serve in positions that are not "all in" to help young people succeed. We wanted to ensure that students were equipped to recognize those situations. We taught them strategies that encouraged them to put forth their best effort even when they struggled.

We encouraged them to give a winning effort in every undertaking. We wanted our students to be overcomers who rise above systemic barriers and traps and learn from disappointments, setbacks, and failures.

It was crucial to undergird students with social and emotional support and introduce them to new pathways in learning new skills that lead to employment opportunities so that young males can grow and take care of their responsibilities as adult men. UCF rolled out an incentive to improve academic improvement and student behavior.

24/7 Performance Objectives:
1. Good behavior/ good grades/perfect attendance/ model citizen/ become a leader!
2. Turn in all homework assignments! Study for unit quizzes, tests, and exams!
3. Stay out of trouble, demonstrate a positive attitude, and stay on track to GRADUATE!
4. To grow into strong adults who will give back to the community and make a positive contribution to society.

From 2008-2012, UCF intentionally introduced students to potential employment opportunities. Our community was already behind in STEM exposure (essential for competing in the 21st century). UCF was committed to equip students with increased awareness and understanding of specific STEM proficiencies in the methodologies.

CHARLES HOPSON JR., STEM PROFESSIONAL

In 2013, a young STEM professional and Bowie State alum named Charles Hopson Jr. briefed the UCF Executive Board and launched the first STEM workshop at the annual Game Changer Conference. He was convinced early in his professional career that students must be exposed to STEM careers by any means necessary. He was committed to giving the best of his service to his community, where he grew up in Germantown, Maryland.

UCF has been working diligently to increase student exposure year-round with hands-on learning opportunities in our underserved community. In early c UCF established a new educational unit that challenged students to become critical thinkers and pursue new STEM occupations.

TEACHING CRITICAL THINKING SKILLS & TEAMWORK

Randy McCain Teaching and eaching Students

In January 2015, UCF took a big step by teaming up with the Metro Warriors STEM Organization. Randy McCain, the CEO/Founder of Metro Warriors STEM organization from Prince George's County, provided instructional leadership to launch our program (www.mwso.org).

Our initial meeting with McCain lasted past midnight. This late-night encounter between community leaders reflected a passionate conversation about being a willing vessel to be used by God to provide leadership for our community. We believed in a shared vision that God inspired us to work together to close the gap in our communities.

Collaborating with a like-minded person was so exciting to address an urgent national need for more young people to pursue careers in STEM.

It was Ernest Hemmingway in a letter that reflected these words, "this is what we do when we are at our best; we make it all up and make it up so well until later it will still happen that way." We didn't have all the answers but were willing to work together. We took an inventory of access, relationships, resources, and a commitment to work together for the greater community good. We recognized that both youth organizations could be the catalyst for encouraging youth (male and female) to go to college, major in meaningful career fields, and positively contribute to society, thus, achieving our mission of closing the gap.

We desired to collaborate, believing we were stronger working together than apart. We wanted to connect the two youth organizations in two counties to improve science and math education starting in the third grade through 12 to prepare more students for these fields in college and graduate school. McCain was excellent at interacting with students and introducing them to the hands-on program, building racing cars, teaching students to work as team members, and developing business and marketing plans.

The students learned to work as team members, and leaders, solve problems, and develop critical thinking skills. An encounter with introducing students to STEM terminology drove home the importance of early intervention. In the picture above, Randy held up the object and asked the students to name the object.

We were shocked as our eyes locked to hear students yell, "hair drier, blower, cake maker!" He was holding a drill, a tool for making round holes or driving fasteners. It is fitted with a bit and used to bind together the sections of the race car. This experience reinforced that we had much work to accomplish to close the knowledge gap!

Later during the session, two remote control STEM building kits were used. This concept unlocks and explores children's imagination and exposes them to engineering and physics at an early age.

The RC cars came with a simple kit that required students to put together and control a design that made the car easier to move in all directions and quickly turn while driving over obstacles. Students were assigned positions such as drivers, pit crew members, engineers, spotters.

**SENSE OF URGENCY AND PURPOSE
NOW IS THE TIME TO IMPACT A NEW GENERATION**

Team Self-Discovery, Self-Development, and Problem Solving!

There have been so many success stories and highlights of the U-STEM/National Society of Black Engineers (NSBE) journey of excellence that we can't share it all. The signature outings before COVID-19 were the Organization of Black Aerospace Professionals (OBAP) expos hosted an annual "Passport to Aerospace" Youth Day, the National Society of Black Engineers (NSBE) Convention being held in Pittsburgh, PA, Bechtel Corporation Career Day, and the Brookhaven National Laboratory trip. It has been an amazing transformational journey partnering with parents and community partners!

"Passport to Aerospace" Youth Day

Randy McCain arranged the first field trip. He invited and registered U-STEM students for the journey on August 13, 2015. Joyce Walker and I transported ten middle school students in our cars to a hotel in D.C. where the OBAP hosted an annual "Passport to Aerospace" Youth Day. The organization aimed to increase students' excitement and awareness of STEM Professions (Career Exploration). The day was filled with excitement from start to finish. At 8 a.m., our ten students participated and competed in the Remote Control Cars competition with other youth teams. It was an eye-opener for our students to see other Black and Brown students from the Maryland/Washington D.C. area competing. There were approximately 150 STEM peers who participated in a race car competition and wore team shirts.

Remote Control (RC) Cars competition

The second two hours of the Expo included meeting one of NASA's superstars and special guest Dr. Aprille Ericsson, NASA's first female astronautical/aeronautical engineer. After she spoke, students were introduced to a drone demonstration by Fly Robotics and experiential group learning activities facilitated by various aerospace engineers and aviation professionals. The hands-on learning activity focused on a team-building competition that required teams to design a simulated vehicle to carry and land an egg from a 6-foot ladder to the floor without breaking the egg. The picture above and below was our team with a bag of material issued with missing items to assemble the craft and document process steps. This was an excellent hands-on and team-building experience that resulted in the students interacting with other students, trading parts to build their aircraft, and working as a team to solve for "X." Ms. Nia Walker provided the student impact perspective in response to the event. At the luncheon, more than 500 hundred dignitaries, students, and mentoring group leaders were in attendance.

THIS IS WHAT SUCCESS LOOKS LIKE!

After the hands-on learning activity, the job/career fair allowed students to participate and hone their networking skills. In preparation for the expos, as part of our Wednesday classroom instructions, students had to demonstrate career readiness skills by writing and rehearsing their 30-second elevator speech. This included learning how to respond to their questions by repeating them, listening to formulate an answer, and then responding. The beauty of the learning experience was that their peers provided positive, constructive feedback in a classroom setting.

It was amazing to witness each student's transformation of classroom instructions after school on Wednesdays at Forest Oak Middle School during the 2014-2015 school year. The students increased their confidence and understanding, followed instructions, carried out multiple tasks, and showcased the ability to execute the instructions provided. Just as importantly, they worked together to solve problems as teammates.

UCF equipped the students with business cards before the expo. We paired them up with a team member and gave them a control bingo card. A competition was created with the bingo cards where they had to have four or more signatures for each interview they would conduct. The student with the most interviews completed won a prize of their choosing—approximately 50 aviation and aeronautics showcase booths and exhibits at the career fair expos.

A two-star General approached UCF from the U.S. Air Force Academy who wanted to learn more about our community-based organization while encouraging us to stay the course. He noted that we must produce more students of color to keep up with the 21st-century workforce demands in the STEM career field. In our initial competition, UCF scored a huge upset by taking second place in a field of 50 other teams.

UCF MEETS NASA SUPERSTAR -
Dr. Aprille J. Ericsson,
(Innovative Technology Partnerships Office)
Second Place Team Finalist – August 2015

Pictured with NASA, Dr. Aprille J. Ericsson, Dr. Melvin Stallings and Joyce Walker

National Society of Black Engineers
2018 Convention

In 2017, I connected with Brian Harris, a former co-worker at the Nuclear Regulatory Commission who's a successful nuclear engineer. He possesses a giving heart to help young people succeed by increasing their understanding of STEM as it relates to everyday use. Our strategic goal was to provide a rich, out-of-school learning experience to advance STEM learning and career exploration around the themes of robotics, graphic design and programming, leadership skills, business management, and marketing systems. The program continues to thrive because of his outstanding leadership for the U-STEM Fun Zone over the last five years and the tremendous support from parents working collaboratively to ensure students have unlimited pathways to pursue college and a career.

He immediately launched the National Society for Black Engineers junior chapter that has benefited the students and kept them excited to learn about this underserved career field. This was a life-changing experience for our students who participated in the community program. To connect and keep students engaged with learning and developing "critical thinking skills," students met on Wednesday at Forest Oak Middle School before COVID-19. Student teams were formed and sent to participate in local STEM conferences, expos, and race car competitions. Creating a higher-level learning environment that encouraged students to use problem-solving and team-building skills was refreshing. Students were exposed to new terminologies and math applications related to building RC cars. They also learned new applications resulting in increased confidence, high self-esteem, and intelligence.

Witnessing the students' growth from planned exercises developed by Brian Harris and Joyce Walker was so exciting. A breakthrough occurred when students started incorporating technical language in their communication, explaining learning points, exchanging ideas, and learning to operate as a problem-solving team. The planned activities centered on increasing students' interest in STEM literacy. Students participated in math competitions, evidence-based, hands-on, fun educational activities using remote-controlled (RC) cars, robotics, design programming, and business management and marketing systems.

Students working with Remote Control Cars

National Society of Black Engineers (NSBE) Convention in Pittsburgh, PA

The team, under the leadership of Director Brian Harris and Joyce Walker, Parent Liaison for U-STEM and NSBE Jr. Adviser, has provided extraordinary experiences for the youth. The picture above represents the second capstone outing with students attending the National Convention in Pittsburgh, Pennsylvania. UCF rented a 15-passenger van and traveled to Pittsburgh during the winter of 2018. After countless hours of classroom instruction, we exposed our students to aspiring and practicing engineers.

This trip to the 44th NSBE Annual Convention was for the NSBE Jr. U-STEM chapter members. The purposes of the trip were: to improve our Ten80 racing challenge experience through feedback and instruction from outstanding engineering professionals who have a passion for STEM, to experience premier STEM workshops, activities, and events led by high-profile speakers and high achievers in STEM. In addition, students learned about pre-college summer programs and internships, college scholarships and admissions, and global workforce opportunities through visits to the NSBE Convention Career Fair of more than 200 academic institutions, government agencies, corporations, and nonprofit organizations.

These objectives support UCF's vision of exposing, growing, and enhancing educational opportunities in STEM for our students. We were excited to provide this opportunity to our hard-working students to leave the neighborhood and travel to a major convention to see black professionals competing, networking, and being interviewed by various companies.

The second exposure experience was the NSBE Region II Fall Regional Conference (R2FRC) at the Bethesda North Marriott Hotel & Conference Center in Bethesda, Maryland, hosted from, November 16-18, 2018. The theme for that year was "R2FRC: Explore. Engineer. Elevate."

This experience equipped our students with leadership skills, team-building skills, and network exposure at the fair and, most of all, inspired them to have fun while making "hope happen."

BECHTEL CORPORATION CAREER DAY, APRIL 22, 2019

Bechtel is an American engineering, procurement, construction, and project management company known for building scores of infrastructure projects worldwide, such as power plants, transit systems, construction projects, etc. The company is a significant employer committed to hiring a diversified skilled workforce.

The inaugural U-STEM/NSBE Jr. Career Day at Bechtel Corporation in Reston, VA occurred on Monday, April 22, 2019. We were grateful to our parents that entrusted their students to us to create learning opportunities outside of the classroom. The event's theme, "Engineering Future Leaders," included approximately 25 students from UCF at Bechtel Corporation Headquarters in Reston, Virginia. The program was simply amazing!

This career day event reinforced my belief that access is critical to student academic development and that by working together, we are stronger and can achieve more significant outcomes working in unity with parents, students, and community partners.

Similar to coaches' and parents' relationships in AAU athletes and traveling athletic teams, parent engagement is meaningful. We truly value partnerships and look forward to providing future STEM youth engagement opportunities that inspire academic excellence, high school completion, college graduation, and success in career and life.

Our leadership team was so proud of the growth experienced during the 2018-2019 school year. The students worked hard in the after-school instructional sessions. Our students' unique talent and determination will positively impact the world when you dare to **Dream Big**!

The Bechtel staff was "all in," providing our students with an excellent experience, including hands-on enrichment activities. Students who participated in team-building exercises were given roles, titles, and materials to solve a mock situation. The students also briefed Bechtel staff members to finish their activities.

This was a game-changing experience with a full day of inspiration, motivation, and activation— **Create** a plan, **Believe** you can, and then **Do it!** Students were invited to **Dream Big** and to **Think** and **Do Great Things** in STEM —and in life—by engaging in activities that promote skills essential for to success — i.e., critical thinking, openness to learn and practice new knowledge, knowledge, collaborating with others, effective communication, perseverance, problem-solving, innovation, and learning from failure and mistakes (self and others).

Again, parents' support and participation in all UCF activities make the dream work regarding their commitment. This commitment includes time, energy, and personal sacrifices to complete students' waiver forms, help dress them in appropriate professional attire, and transport them weekly to instructional sessions and planned activities. In the words of Brian and Joyce, parent support makes a world of difference. It makes it possible to offer exclusive STEM learning and career opportunities in collaboration with one of the world's most respected engineering, construction, and procurement companies.

It is still remarkable that UCF, a community-based youth organization, made history as the first and only NSBE Jr. chapter to be hosted as VIP guests of a Bechtel Executive at its headquarters!

As I share with parents over the many years of being a community leader throughout my youth development journey, you must keep connected with your children's interests and help shape them. We suggest that parents and guardians keep an open mind and aggressively seek opportunities that aid their student growth and development. We have learned, raising our two daughters and grandchildren, that exposure to experiences outside the classroom is invaluable. These experiences help a child's cognitive development in terms of how a child learns to think, reason, and use language, which is vital to the child's overall growth and development. In addition, young people stay more engaged, interested in school and learn more when participating in meaningful activities.

BROOKHAVEN NATIONAL LABORATORY, OCTOBER 9, 2019,

Also echoed throughout this book is the value of sustaining meaningful relationships. I have intentionally surrounded myself with likeminded people and community leaders who want to work together for positive outcomes in young people's lives. We set our egos aside and work to make things happen for young people who desire to do the work required to succeed!

A proud moment occurred on October 9, 2019, when UCF teamed up with Mount Calvary Baptist Church in Rockville, Maryland, to take a one-day trip to Brookhaven National Laboratory in Upton, New York. Reverend Barry Moultrie, Youth Minister at Mount Calvary, and I collaborated throughout the summer to plan, organize, and meet in person with Brookhaven staff members. We identified resources, a date, and a time for the trip. I remember the skepticism of the staff when they asked about the size of our party. We told them that it was possibly 50, and they just smiled. Reverend Moultrie and I spoke about the trip into existence as we looked at each other without blinking!

It's difficult to describe the early morning excitement from the participants that loaded up on the 52-passenger bus that departed at 4:30 a.m. from Upper County Community Center with eight chaperones and 43 students. Anyone who works with youth development knows it is challenging at best to manage a big group. However, bringing two organizations together for a special moment is truly a ministry.

MONTGOMERY COUNTY COMMUNITY IMPACT
U.S. Department of Energy's Brookhaven Laboratory

On a personal note, it is an indescribable feeling working with friends, especially in the ministry, helping make hope happen! Working with my friend Reverend Moultrie was gratifying, refreshing, and uplifting. Although he couldn't make it for the 4:30 a.m. departure, he sent his wife, Glenda, to help in our efforts.

Noel Blackburn, Chief Diversity, Equity, and Inclusion Officer of the U.S. Department of Energy's Brookhaven Laboratory Chief, and Dr. Bernadette Uzzi, Supervisor of K-12 Educational Programs at

Brookhaven, led an outstanding team of scientists who engaged students for an exceptional research experience at Brookhaven National Labs.

The excitement-filled day included a tour of the NASA Space Radiation Laboratory, Nanoscale Science Research Center that housed the booster accelerator to simulate space radiation. Students donned safety equipment, eyewear, and "purple gloves" to participate in activities at the Science Learning Center. Students participated in a culminating group briefing to organize a presentation that captured learning points with examples from the day-long field trip. This was another amazing opportunity for students and families for years to come.

MCFRS Open House Tour of
Fire and Rescue Training Center

In the words of the Reverend Dr. MLK, "we are now faced with the fact that tomorrow is today. We are confronted with the fierce URGENCY of now." Under the leadership of Captains David Kennedy and Ty DeMent, along with Lieutenant Irvin Smith, a facility tour of the Montgomery County Fire & Rescue Training Center in Gaithersburg was given to UCF. We benefited from the MCFRS EEO/Diversity CE services that allowed the use of the training facility on several occasions. It was about community-building together and being community-center focused. This exceptional community leadership team added tremendous value through its presence in county communities. The group showcased fire truck equipment at the Game Changer's Conference for young males. It provided opportunities for one-on-one career conversations to an audience of more than 500 male students (of several nationalities) and adult community citizens. These individuals also gave personal testimonies of encouragement at UCF's annual Career Day meetings, allowed the use of classroom space to conduct SAT/ACT Boot Camp for almost 200 students, and a STEM Day (Science, Technology, Engineering, and Mathematics) for approximately 100 students meeting at the Training Academy.

This leadership team that grew up in Montgomery County went on to facilitate the first-ever 2019 STEM Community Day, partnering with STEM leader Melvin Stalling of Prince George's County's chapter of 100 Black Men.

IMPACTFULL EXPOSURE EXPERIENCES

NIH LABORATORY

These UCF field trips were life-changing experiences that our young people otherwise wouldn't have encountered. There is no better investment than our youth people, and these experiences don't occur without the support of committed parents and loyal supporters. We are grateful to community partners that received emails from aimhighinlife@aol.com over the many years, from attendees at the annual UCF scholarship dinners in November to those who contribute by

volunteering at youth conferences and sow financial donations no matter the amount – thank you! We are grateful that you have stood by us throughout the positive youth development journey.

This is what community engagement looks like and what a community can achieve by working together as good stewards for youth engagement. Our students and families have been affected positively and have benefitted from classroom experiences, after-school STEM instructional sessions, local competitions, and so much more.

In March 2020, the entire world was changed because of the global pandemic called COVID-19 UCF was forced to place all programs on hold as the country, community, and families were forced to reflect, reassess, reset, retool, redirect, and rejoice amid the health crisis.

It was our STEM leadership team of Brian Harris and Ed Reed who worked to pivot to stay connected with our students and families. While national and local leaders wrestled with the unknown health crisis, UCF's focus shifted to how to stay engaged with our students. The rejoicing came from learning how to use virtual platforms and receiving a significant grant to pour into our students and families.

A GAME CHANGER'S PURSUIT

A STORY WITH A KEY MESSAGE:

UCF's journey as a community-based organization committed to saving and shaping young people's lives has been about searching for learning exposure experiences.

I recently watched an annual recording of the V Foundation for Cancer Research, founded by former North Carolina State University head coach Jimmy Valvano with one goal: to achieve victory over cancer. I was reminded of my first pre-game pep speech as a head coach, where I incorporated a message from the Green Bay Packers football team. This reminded me of my coaching mentors, specifically legendary coach Jim Brown of Hagerstown Community College.

He always gave inspirational pre-game speeches that challenged and motivated the higher-level performance of everyone in the locker room. Coach Brown's main message centered around a team searching for excellence. In other words, everyone is responsible for being "all in" on this journey of excellence. If we wanted the team to be successful, it would take everyone to give a winning effort. He challenged us not to be fearful and afraid of the big moments when adversity showed up. He encouraged everyone, trainers, coaching staff, and players, to make good decisions in those moments.

In my pre-game speech, I incorporated both messages from Coach Brown and Coach Valvano about teamwork and searching for excellence together. I said, "all eyes are on me. We will be successful this season if we focus on three things only. Your family, your religious faith, and our basketball teams. The coach's message was that everyone has a role in making success happen.

My primary message, human connection is vital. We must collaborate, work together, and build trusted relationships as a new world emerges. To all stakeholders, community leaders, county officials, mentors, and parents, we must work together to make hope happen for everyone. Coach Brown message applies to everyone that works directly to create pathway for young people.

Everyone must be responsible for being "all in" on this journey to make hope and success happen for young people!

UCF- Monthly Meeting
February 18, 2012
John Tucker Black History Guest Speaker
Tennessee State University Graduate

As the world transforms itself, we must replace out-of-date practices and policies with implementing new policies and education models for greater effectiveness. As the world changes with STEM occupations, robotics, and artificial intelligence, we still operate with 130 years old academic model. Our kids use high-tech instruments at home and walk into schoolhouses needing more modernized classroom experiences and teaching practices. Let's reimagine education and implement new engagement models and methods that enhance learning. Our children are bright, brilliant, and have great potential; let's change with the times and provide them with access and opportunities.

Stakeholders must work together for a more significant impact with the assistance of young people to navigate the new realities. We must take the time to get to know students and their circumstances. We must return to demonstrating love for one another by inspiring success, genuine caring, and kindness and challenging students to perform higher.

I recall a popular song in 1965 song by Dionne Warwick, "What the World Needs Now Is Love." Sweet love, not for just one, but for everyone. It's the only thing that there's just too little of.

Your community will achieve greatness when we put aside petty differences and work together for real solutions for today's challenges. All stakeholders must focus on what is best to provide a social, emotional, and learning support system to help all young people succeed.

QUOTE:

"In this way, mentoring enables us to participate in the essential but unfinished drama of reinventing community, while reaffirming that there is an important role for each of us in it."

— MARC FREEDMAN

SCRIPTURE:

Let us not become weary in doing good, for at the proper time we will reap a harvest if we do not give up.

GALATIANS 6:9

CHAPTER 15

WHAT LEADERS DO IN A CRISIS?

Dr. Darryl Hill, Ed Reed, and Brian Harris

The historical novel by author Charles Dickens, "Tale of Two Cities," has a famous quote, "It was the best of times, it was the worst of times. In a blink of an eye, the world we knew was suddenly different!"

The COVID-19 global pandemic created unprecedented worldwide challenges for all sectors, especially with mentoring engagement efforts to help students process information. With all that has been going on since 2020, young people remain concerned about how their lives may be affected. I believed the pandemic at the time would alter the educational experience for millions of our students across the country, let alone in our community.

I knew in my heart this would forever be a "defining moment" for the community and country. This was a pivotal time in history when we continuously found ourselves in a period of unrest as a country on many levels. I was scared in the early days of the pandemic, and you were scared because of the unknown. The global pandemic created so much stress in everyone's lives due to the uncertainty.

In April 2020, approximately 30 days after Governor Larry Hogan's stay-at-home order, MCPS closed, public facilities restricted access, and we all had to shelter in place. The unpredictability of the ever-changing COVID-19 outbreak had everyone afraid of the unknown. The Governor's shutdown decision saved lives by avoiding unnecessary exposure to the Coronavirus.

Across the nation, many disturbing events would follow the same negative path of the global health crisis. The tragic death of George Floyd shortly followed which led to the worldwide social justice and Black Lives Matter movement protests during the pandemic. Across the nation and in other countries, the masses wore masks to demonstrate the tragic event. A toxic presidential election culminated with an insurrection on January 6, 2021. In addition, the world experienced unseasonal weather patterns, and suddenly the world we knew was transforming. History will indeed look back on how we responded to this time.

During this time, my phone rang with parents seeking guidance about the current events, advice for their children, and what UCF can do in this crisis. We were moved into action by taking the focus off ourselves to help and show others now what leaders do in a crisis.

After several calls from parents in the UCF family, Mona and I called together youth leaders to discuss how to move forward with developing an action plan for children and parents to connect and engage with them while they were sitting at home worrying about the unknown.

The above zoom picture shows Dr. Darryl Hill, MD, Coach Ed Reed, and Brian Harris kicked-off a series of youth/family engagement meetings. UCF was able to stay connected and engaged with students and families during this health crisis! These bi-monthly virtual meetings were our way to "check-in" with students' and family's mental wellness.

Although we could not meet physically in a building with our students, we were able to pivot and rethink mentoring engagement using virtual platforms. Our crisis leadership team consisted of Mona, Coach Harris our STEM/NSBE Director, and Ed Reed, MCPS Counselor. Reed possessed experience with operating in the virtual environment to deliver learning opportunities. We brainstormed and formulated an engagement strategy to include a theme that focused students to the possibilities on the other side of the COVID-19 pandemic. Ed Reed earned the title of Coach Reed because he helped to increase the learning curve by providing excellent instructions using the Zoom platform. He coached us on operating effectively using the Zoom application in the new virtual environment. Team UCF regrouped, reassessed, reset, retooled, and redirected our efforts to the learning intricacies of using Zoom for conducting interactive workshops to stay connected in this crisis with our youth and families.

What do leaders do in a crisis? Our UCF team researched the history books and found that this was not the first pandemic in our country's history. In 1918, the U.S. endured a pandemic, and ordinary people stepped up to provide leadership in their communities. Leaders gathered to share information that changed and evolved rapidly during the pandemic and worked together to keep everyone safe as best they knew.

During the pandemic of our lifetime, our crisis leadership team conducted interactive workshops enjoyed by the community. Our team intentionally provided consistent messaging that provided assurance, uplifted, encouraged, and presented meaningful information that served as a guidepost. This was important because no one knew what the participants were going through at home. As UCF operated from a place of love and concern, our organization was elevated to the forefront for being a community champion for young people and their families!

We are proud that UCF served the greater good in the community by delivering caring, thoughtful, and meaningful information in moments of crisis. The team actively listened to what students shared as they expressed their thoughts, concerns, and what they needed during interactive meetings. It wasn't about returning to normal, but it was about operating in a new reality using virtual platforms to navigate the current environment.

Our theme during the pandemic was "Raising the next generation of young leaders." We emphasized that you can't stay the same; you must grow to reach your true potential, even in a pandemic! The UCF leadership team developed the acronym W.A.L.K. to keep our students and parents focused on experiencing academic success during the pandemic. Ed Reed led this segment in the virtual meeting every meeting. What is W.A.L.K.? Wellness, Access, Leadership, and Knowledge.

We wanted students to shift focus on maintaining their wellness, both mental and physical. We wanted students to look around and determine what resources they could access, i.e., the nearest food distribution site. Our focus was always on demonstrating leadership skills and to educate students by reading books, learning, and acquiring knowledge on what other leaders did in a crisis.

Our overarching goal was to demonstrate to the UCF family network what leaders do in a crisis. My mentor from afar, Reverend Dr. Browning's first virtual sermon in the pandemic, reminded us of the biblical story about the ten men with an infectious skin disease called leprosy. Those with contagious diseases had to isolate themselves, keep their distance, and cover their bodies to prevent infectious diseases from becoming epidemics. His spiritual emphasis drew the comparison to the power and requirement of faith! The men with leprosy first acted by asking for healing and, second, followed instructions. In faith, the men obeyed and acted by walking to the priest, and the word says they were healed on the way to see the priest (Luke 17:11-19). The astonishing similarities between the biblical story and the pandemic we all experienced had similar protocols.

Does this sound familiar? No large gatherings of crowds, wearing a mask, keeping your distance, and washing your hands. Our national leaders issued guidelines, people asked for help, prayer warriors were in demand, and the best and brightest sought a vaccine to save lives. Some

followed guidelines and instructions from the Centers for Disease Control and Prevention (CDC), and others didn't. Overall, people worked together to keep everyone safe the best they knew how, and that's what UCF demonstrated throughout the pandemic. UCF leveraged relationships for the greater good to keep everyone connected, engaged, uplifted, informed, safe, and inspired. We encouraged our students and parents to be leaders in their homes and speak with friends and family members in other states. These actions resulted in deeper relationships.

The UCF Youth Development Organization's journey continued throughout the pandemic, meeting with explosive success in the virtual environment. The youth engagement meetings yielded record-breaking participation. During 14 months of inactivity (reopening in 2021). UCF introduced to our youth the virtual Zoom platform by conducting youth engagement meetings shortly after the stay-at-home order that prohibited the gathering of large groups. The best of times was that a new pathway was discovered to stay connected and engaged with our mission for positive youth development.

Shortly after the stay-at-home order that prohibited gathering large groups, UCF introduced and conducted virtual meetings. This experience delivered meaningful, inspirational, and important information. While unknown then, the virtual experience kept UCF families connected and engaged through the reopening of schools to the present. The unexpected blessings were impactful topics and workshop content, and the attendance increased from each previous meeting (growing to an estimated 250+ participants). It was a captive audience due to the unprecedented Pandemic, as we were all afraid while staying in our residences, not sure of what the future held.

UCF COMMUNITY ENGAGEMENT IN THE COVID PANDEMIC

Dr. Cynthia Turner-Graham, Psychologist

Students and families benefitted from the mentoring sessions, including scavenger hunts, ice breakers, history sharing, student interactive sessions, physical fitness exercise sessions, and mental wellness moments.

The organization truly benefitted from the collective efforts of presenters who shared meaningful messages of encouragement and important guidance for healthy living during the pandemic. Psychologist Dr. Cynthia Turner-Graham was a blessing, providing 20 minutes of mental wellness Moments at the start of every meeting throughout the pandemic. We thank God for sending the right people at the right time for a greater result in the community. Dr. Turner-Graham is the wife of renowned NIH Scientists Dr. Barney Graham, who laid the groundwork for the world to battle the pandemic. He and his team of scientists raced to develop a vaccine. Before retirement, the Grahams were members of Mount Calvary Baptist Church in Rockville Nd lend their gifts and knowledge to educate the community.

Dr. Darryl Hill, MD, shared health and wellness best practices for staying safe while we learned more about the virus. He encouraged everyone to practice physical distancing, the washing of hands, along with the proper way to wear masks while out in public. In addition, he provided strategies to establish a daily routine for physically exercising the mind, body, and soul.

Coach Reed provided inspirational messages that encouraged students to elevate their creative thinking to respond and find solutions during this pandemic as others did before us.

UCF COMMUNITY ENGAGEMENT IN THE COVID PANDEMIC

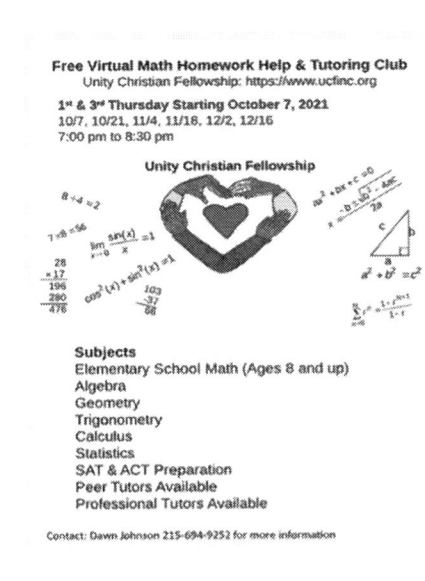

Coach Harris challenged students to intellectually expand critical thinking pathways and pursue new STEM occupations that the country will indeed be counted on in the future!

Dr. Aaron Johnson and family, hearing pleas from students needing math help, responded by stepping up to conduct the virtual Math Homework Club. The Johnsons, members of the Inter-Denominational Church of God in Gaithersburg, Maryland, pulled their friends to tutor students using the virtual platform.

Unscheduled Intervention: You Are Never Too Young to Lead

Can you imagine your mental state at nine, twelve, fourteen, sixteen, or older? All of us have been affected mentally over the past two years, not to mention a day that will go down in history as a dark day in our country, the insurrection of Wednesday, January 6, 2021.

UCF is committed to addressing real issues that impact this generation of young people. We designed interactive workshops to help our students and families "process information" that no one talks about in the community. The workshops prayerfully serve as a gateway for students to share their thoughts on the events that impact all our lives!

As a team, we conducted unscheduled intervention seminars during the past two years of the pandemic. In the pandemic, our young people were subjected to a toxic political climate at a level we have never seen, which included social justice news involving George Floyd, 25-year-old Ahmaud Arbery, and the tragic and senseless death of many others on the news and social media outlets. Young people experienced the deaths of loved ones from the pandemic, home evictions due to family members' loss of employment, food insecurities, no Chromebooks for themselves or their siblings, and little to no bandwidth or Wi-Fi connectivity.

Our purpose was to teach students to be leaders in moments of crisis! We encouraged students to shift their focus on maintaining their mental and physical wellness. We wanted students to look beyond their current conditions and determine what resources they could access (i.e., nearest food distribution site, hot spots for Wi-Fi connectivity). Our focus was to help our students to demonstrate leadership skills and to educate themselves by reading books. We challenged students to learn something new and acquire knowledge of what other leaders have done in a crisis.

Despite the challenges of the Pandemic, our USTEM program was forced to reassess and pivot during the summer of 2020 summer. At this time, a friend of the UCF encouraged us to apply for a Montgomery County grant in July 2020.

Left to Right: Brian Harris, UCF Director for STEM/NSBE, Tameka Williams and Tanye Coleman, MCAC-DST STEM Directors, Donald and Mona Williams, UCF Founders and former Mu Nu Basileus and MCAC President, Sidney Katz, 3 District, Greg Wims, Victims' Rights Founder and Regional Director at Germantown Regional Services Center Director, and Dr. Joey Jones, Principal Robert Frost Middle School (A National Blue Ribbon School).

In August 2021, UCF received a congratulatory notice from the Montgomery County Economic Development Nonprofits program. UCF was selected to receive a grant for $25,000. UCF decided to invest resources in a higher-level STEM pilot program to reverse the trend regarding the alarming and unfavorable disparities of African American families and minority students. The average conservative cost for STEM equipment per student is approximately $1,500. This pilot program impacted 25 students who actively participated. In the final virtual session, students shared feedback about being intimidated by STEM and soon found the building block approach fun while learning how to build a drone.

To bolster our operations, we teamed with the Montgomery County Alumnae Chapter (MCAC) of Delta Sigma Theta Sorority, Incorporated. In partnership, UCF and MCAC used grant funding to create a pilot program for middle school students.

Although this was a team effort, the most valuable person for the pilot program was Dr. Joey N. Jones, Principal at Robert Frost Middle School, who reached out to Principals who selected students of color to participate in the higher-level pilot virtual STEM Initiative to represent their school. We are so proud of the MCPS teaming arrangement, especially during the 2021-2022 academic year when our young people needed our attention the most.

On November 13, 2021, the UCF in collaboration with the Montgomery County chapter of Delta Sigma Theta greeted parents, students, and community leaders at Forest Oak Middle School to celebrate the launching of the newest 2021-2022 Virtual Science Technology Engineering and Math (STEM) Pilot Program, explicitly targeted to middle school students.

The UCF Founders were beyond excited to be selected for the first-of-its-kind county grant and to work together. Kudos to Bill Tompkins and his team, the Montgomery County Economic Development Corporation, for providing the $25,000 grant received to support the work of nonprofit organizations like UCF.

- We connected with approximately 25 MCPS students who shared a higher level of interest in the STEM career field. We believe our young people will transform the world and not conform to the world and be problem solvers!
- We were extremely excited about the response from principals who selected these students from across MCPS to participate in the next level STEM initiatives for middle school students.

- The STEM Planning team conducted pick-up/drive by celebration at Forest Oak Middle School at the end of November 2021 for parents and students pick up drone and science kits.
- Several County Officials and VIPs showed up to join in the celebration, including Councilman Sidney Katz, 3 District, Greg Wims, Victims' Rights Founder and Regional Director at Germantown, Dr. Joey Jones, Principal Robert Frost, Ed Reed Commissioner, Poolesville, USTEM/NSBE Director Brian Harris and MCAC-DST STEM Directors Tanye Coleman and Tameka Williams.

UCF supports Councilman Katz and Greg Wims

The STEM Planning Team conducted approximately 35 planning meetings Councilman Sidney Katz, 3 District, and Greg Wims, Victims Rights Founder and Regional Director at Germantown (Message: You have our support)

And then along came COVID-19, like a Blitzkrieg!!

Our team's vision and efforts in 2020 were to be hyper-focused on raising our engagement level to help young people reach their potential. We were three months into a new year, and then an epic shift in a new decade happened.

The UCF leadership team had to rethink early in the pandemic how to engage and stay connected with students during the unprecedented season. As shared earlier, our planning team pivoted to use a virtual platform to stay connected and increase the meeting frequency with our youth.

But as always—change was good because God is good at "nudging" us to that next level attainment—making us explore other possibilities and roads we may never have taken! This amazing challenge quickly evolved into a wonderful experience as we focused on keeping our primary goals front and center: mentoring, shaping, and saving lives! The Zoom platform allowed our team to adjust our thinking about mentoring our young people. It was also in line with maintaining our theme of raising the next generation of future leaders. We could reach our students and, more importantly, their parents during the crisis.

You alone must decide what your commitment and path will be in life. And, if you're fully committed to mentoring in your family, neighborhood, school, or even on a large-scale level, know that you don't have to do it alone.

The COVID-19 globe pandemic created unprecedented worldwide challenges for all sectors, especially with Mentoring engagement efforts to help students reach their potential. There was a plethora of assistance out there ready and willing to assist! UCF connected and engaged with MCPS staff members such as Office of Student and Family Support and Engagement, Mr. Everett Davis, became so beneficial to UCF families and friends early in the pandemic via Zoom meetings.

<u>2021 VIRTUAL Dream Chaser College Tour (COVID-19)</u>

This allowed UCF to stay true to our team's 2020 vision to help young people reach their potential— despite the pandemic. The UCF's community engagement during the pandemic using the virtual Zoom platform included bi-monthly youth meetings, a Math Homework

Club, the 2022 High Level Virtual STEM Pilot Program, two SAT/ACT Boot Camps, College Planning for Parents and Students, six-week seminars, POSSE preparations, two virtual Dream Chasers College Tours and two Game Changers Conferences for the entire family.

Brian Harris, Director STEM/NSBE for UCF and Donald Williams II, UCF Executive Director delivered fun STEM Engagement and Professional Development Activities

QUOTE:
"Show me a successful individual and I'll show you someone who had real positive influence in their life. I don't care what you do for a living- if you do it well, I'm sure there was someone cheering you on or showing the way. A mentor."

— Denzel Washington

SCRIPTURE:
Blessed is the man that trusteth in the LORD, and whose hope the LORD is. For he shall be as a tree planted by the waters, and that spreadeth out her roots by the river.

Jeremiah 17: 7-8, KJV

CHAPTER 16

The Game Changer Conference for Young Males

INAUGURAL GAME CHANGER CONFERENCE
HOSTED AT MONTGOMERY COLLEGE
(SATURDAY, APRIL 14, 2012)

Someone once stated that the two most important days of your life are when you are born and discover your purpose. When I had my cardiovascular event on Saturday, October 31, 2009, at the top of Harpers Ferry Mountain, I shared that I talked with my God. I repeated the 23rd Psalm, to stay alert and conscious "The Lord is My Sheppard." I remembered the conversation as clearly today as it was over 15 years ago. God's instructions were to return and redouble your efforts: 1) demonstrate love to God's people and 2) use your leadership gifts to unite people and save our youth.

People have often asked me many times what inspired the inception of the all-male Game Changer Conference. The why, young people, especially males, continue to be at risk. They are receiving different opportunities than others with the same academic performance, gifts, and talents.

The real story is that educators, churches, and community leaders recognized this as a shared responsibility. UCF stepped out on faith to provide student advocacy leadership for African American and minority students of color in Montgomery County. To encourage every student with a desire to improve their quality of life and reach their full potential by giving a winning effort.

I was blessed to have a supportive wife who encouraged and challenged me to do this meaningful, purposeful, and impactful work with mentoring young people. We also had a circle of Christian friends who encouraged us to run the race and keep the faith no matter what speed bumps appeared in the way. Their influence and faith made me think I could make a difference in the community.

My personal and professional experiences inspired the Game Changer Conference for young males. UCF Youth Development Organization was formed in response to significant problems existing in communities across our country: high unemployment rates and low high school graduation rates among underserved, minority youth, especially among black males, who are underperforming academically, emotionally, and socially according to research.

Indoctrinated with the military "can-do attitude," if you see a problem, you must fix it! I relied on my faith foundation and strong friendships to respond to this crisis by creating several youth initiatives. These youth initiatives created a "safe environment" to help parents keep their children in school, off the streets, out of trouble, and involved in year-round, positive, exciting youth development activities have made a remarkable difference in our community over the last ten years.

The Game Changer Conference for young males was designed to raise awareness among stakeholders. It addresses the critical need to find solutions to reverse the trend regarding the alarming and unfavorable disparities of African American and students of color in education. UCF has worked with churches, community organizations, and Greek-Lettered Organizations in the last decade to find solutions. Approximately 5,000 at-promise, (you call them at-risk) young males have been affected by this life-changing, one-day conference experience.

For the last 13 years working together, we have proudly served and impacted the Montgomery County Community for African American and Minority Students of Color! We have encouraged young males to compete academically and socially to reach their full potential, boosting High School and College Graduation. This has been an incredible experience working to make a difference in the lives of young males and families. Together, we conducted 17 conferences over thirteen years to shape the hearts and minds of young male students.

Specifically, the inaugural Game Changer Conference held March 12, 2012, saw approximately 175 young male students in attendance; in 2013, the attendance rose to 300 participants. In 2014, that number swelled to 600 young males.

This was an incredible community engagement experience with young males, adult men, volunteers, and parents who uplifted the community. On March 29, 2014, for the first-time bus transportation was provided for all the students and volunteers on a rainy day; we all were amazed! In 2015, 2016, 2017, more than 500 students attended, respectively. In 2018 and 2019, approximately 450 youth participated, not counting volunteers in the conference. In March 2020, the conference was canceled due to the pandemic, which prevented gatherings of large crowds for safety. On October 22, 2022, the conference returned to its in-person format and accommodated approximately 125 parents and students. The second in-person conference on March 25, 2023, saw an explosion of over 500 attendees, and volunteers demonstrated a caring community working together to help parents and youth regain social-emotional confidence, competencies, and values needed to reach the next level and become a Success Story!

What was the conference's objective? The all-male conference is a vehicle that helps accomplish this *collective* objective of *promoting student wellness, success, access, and positive outcomes for students and families. The conference reassures* our young males that the community cares about them succeeding and making good choices. The aim was to raise awareness and promote student success, especially amongst African American males and students of color, by providing strategies to win with academics and athletics.

Remarkable things happen when people care! More than a decade of looking back, we are a community that cares about helping families and children to win at life! As we put the pandemic behind us, it is more important now than ever to continue investing in the community and work together to make hope happen to help families and students navigate the ever-changing world. The observation from the first two in-person conferences is that our children are struggling, learning loss has arrested the development of all students, the family focus needs to be improved, and social and emotional well-being is paramount pressing forward.

I wanted the young males being mentored by UCF to see concerned men outside of their circle of influence being responsible and taking care of their families. The young males needed to see and hear from men who were overcomers and distinguished themselves in every profession, at home, and in the community.

I have learned to embrace the affectionately name of Game Changer, the "power of one" that develops trusted relationships, that allowed me to better impact the lives of youth and their families far beyond what I could ever do alone. I recognize that no one can accomplish anything of significance alone.

When I look back on life, I have always been directly involved with youth development as a student-athlete role model for younger students, as a military officer, basketball coach, and public servant in the federal government. I am passionate about young people, especially our young males, who lose too many to foolishness. It's about encouraging them to use their hearts and minds to make good choices. For mentors and those that work directly with young people, it's about passion, giving back, and saving our young people to do the necessary work to gain a competitive edge during their lifetime.

Many have asked how the Game Changer Conference was inspired, the vision, organization, and purpose. This was a divine vision that led to bringing the community together. The single purpose was to address the most serious economic and civil rights challenge faced by our generation in this century. We must find solutions to help empower Black males and students of color to reach their full potential. We must work together to ensure their future is secure. We can help motivate our young people to excel in school, stay out of trouble, stay on track to graduate from high school, complete college degrees, and join a workforce in meaningful, sustainable careers.

This is critical for the African American community, the American family and society's prosperity, health, and well-being. Whatever report you may read, you can find distressing analytics regarding the unfavorable disparities of Black males in education, employment, healthcare, juvenile correction, and the legal system. I am reminded of the Reverend Dr. Martin Luther King Jr.'s quote, "Our lives begin to end the day we become silent about the things that matter."

The conference allows young black males to assemble a meaningful forum to discuss male issues, and provide manhood instructions, problem resolutions, affirmation, and future aspirations. Our men have critical, meaningful, and important information to share with young males.

I attended several local conferences to gather best practices for conducting large-scale conferences. On November 20, 2010, a conference centered on young males was sponsored by Xi Zeta Omega Chapter of Alpha Kappa Alpha Sorority, Inc. at the Kelly Miller Middle School in Northeast Washington D.C. This was an outstanding conference, well planned and operated in an exceptional manner. My young male group was exposed to NFL players, community leaders, and engaging workshop speakers and received a nutritious meal. In early 2011, I connected with Basileus Joseph Harrison of the Pi Chapter of Omega Psi Phi Fraternity, Inc., at Morgan State University. The Omegas teamed with another organization to conduct an outstanding one-day conference for young males in the Baltimore area. I took 12 young males from the UCF to this event on a college campus where I had previously worked for approximately a decade on the president's staff. I captured best practices from both conferences to plan and organize a collaboration model to launch our inaugural Game Changers Conference in 2012.

The conference's overall objective is to prepare young people for a "game changer" experience by helping them build the confidence, competencies, and values they need to get to the next level to become healthy and productive adults. All our students can be successful with proper planning, guidance, positive affirmation, and follow-through.

The conferences at Montgomery College will be etched in my mind because of the leveraging of meaningful relationships established when I was the head women's basketball coach establishing a championship-level program. This was a special moment for the entire community, planning committee, volunteers, all participants, and community and church leaders who responded to the call for action meeting in January 2012.

The inaugural conference picture at the beginning of the chapter was of historical significance. The first Game Changer Conference occurred approximately one month after the tragic murder of 17-year-old Trayvon Benjamin Martin (February 5, 1995 – February 26, 2012). Trayvon was an African American high school student shot in Sanford, Florida, by George Zimmerman, a 28-year-old Hispanic American who was a neighborhood watch coordinator for his gated community where Trayvon was visiting his relatives. I sort counsel from the "greatest man I know," my Dad as to what to say and how to approach the tragedy with the young people.

My Dad profound statement drew parallels when he was a young man, my dad's friends were "emotionally rocked" and impacted by the racially motivated violence against and murder of 14-year-old Emmett Louis Till, who was abducted, tortured, and lynched in Mississippi in 1955. In 2012, the young people were impacted emotionally by the death of 17-year-old Trayvon Martin, who was fatally shot in Florida by a neighborhood watch captain who was acquitted. His counsel included:

1. Tell them that their life matters, counts, and is important, stay alive by any means necessary.
2. Tell them their communication abilities are a matter of life and death; encourage them to speak respectfully in all interactions. He asked me to convey to the young males that it is alright to use good manners: "yes sir/ no sir" and "yes ma'am/ no ma'am," along with "thank you, and no thank you."
3. First Impression is for every generation, dress the way you want others to see you – dress for success!

Our community is losing many young males to poor choices, ending up in prison, or dying early! In my youth in New Jersey, my exposure to being a "military brat" in a military community was much different; living away from the army community versus life exposed to street life, which appealed to some of my friends who wanted to be cool! As we navigated adolescence, developing from childhood into young adulthood as teenagers it was understood that you don't have to respect me but don't disrespect me because there would be consequences. In those moments, you can walk away from someone who doesn't respect you.

The conference opened with welcome remarks from Professor Cliff McKnight, the Master of Ceremony and Academic Advisor Counselor, and Co-sponsors: Basileus David A. Hill, Esq., a Harvard Law classmate of President Barrack Obama; Montgomery College Vice President, Dr. Beverly Walker-Griffea, former Montgomery College Senior Vice President. Police Officer Lt. Eric Burnett and police officers shared valuable survival tips. Dr. Shawn Joseph, MCPS senior staff member, provided an inspirational message about the importance of becoming a success story.

David A. Hill, Esq. Welcome Remarks at Inaugural 2012 Conference

As part of a panel discussion with the young males, Thabiti Boone, a member of our fraternity, delivered a valuable pointed message addressing the tragic murder of Trayvon Martin. Boone, at the time, served as President Obama's White House champion and messenger for the importance of fatherhood and mentoring.

The initial co-sponsors in the first ten years of the Game Changer Conference were:
- Montgomery College (in partnership with Inter-faith and Community Service), under the leadership of Dr. Clemmie Solomon, Collegewide Dean of Student Engagement, provided financial support for meals and college students as supporters to greet students arriving by buses. Dr. DeRionne Pollard, the

College's President who took the helm in 2010, was a tremendous supporter, as the conference aligned with her commitment to student access and success in higher education.

- Mu Nu Chapter of Omega Psi Phi Fraternity in partnership with former President Obama's White House Fatherhood and Mentoring Initiative Program. Mu Nu Chapter has provided outstanding leadership, facilitated workshops, and outstanding financial support from the conference's inception to the present. The initiative that started under Basileus David A. Hill provided the green light for the chapter to become a key conference supporter.
- National Pan-Hellenic Council (NPHC) of Montgomery County, MD an affiliate charter member of The National Pan-Hellenic Council, a collaborative organization of the 9 major Black Greek-Lettered Fraternities & Sororities. Their mission is to promote programs and initiatives to improve the African- American conditions from an academic, economic, health, social, and civic perspective. The NPHC, from the 2012 inaugural conference, purchased bottled water for 300 participants and has provided annual support under former Presidents Carol Croons, Henry Williams, and Tony Proctor.

The purpose of the annual conference was to empower and prepare our young males for a "game-changing" experience by helping them to build the confidence, competencies, and values they need to get to the next level and become a success story. We wanted to encourage our young males to reach their full potential, boosting high school and college graduation. We want to encourage students to take their education seriously! We also want to show young males they are valued and that we, as a community, care about them doing the work required to succeed.

Community Conference Growth: Divine Connection

DR. SHAWN JOSEPH DELIVERING INSPIRATION /MCPD LT ERIC BURNETT SHARING WISDOM & KNOWLEDGE

During the inaugural 2012 conference, the young males learned essential manhood thinking, life skills, and strategies, and equally as important, gained emotional support. The key message is that it takes work to get better. It is a personal choice to apply yourself to do better, and education is needed to change the world.

The above picture was taken on April 20, 2013, at the Montgomery College Theatre Art facility, where approximately 300 male students were encouraged to strive for excellence. After the opening prayer and welcome remarks by event co-sponsors, the students were treated to a video message from someone they saw on television every football season. Mr. James Brown, CBS host of The NFL Today as well as his show (The James Brown Show) delivered an inspirational message to the students and congratulatory remarks to the community leaders for attending the conference.

Brown, known as "JB," is a local star born in Bethesda and attended DeMatha Catholic High School. He could not attend the conference in person but sent a video with a key message on the "3Cs: Character, Courage, Commitment!" JB graduated from Harvard University with a degree in American Government. A standout on the basketball court, he received All-Ivy League honors in his last three seasons at Harvard and captained the team in his senior season. Police Officer Eric Burnett secured the video clip that impacted all in attendance through his community connections.

THE 3RD ANNUAL 2014 GAME CHANGER MENTORING CONFERENCE FOR YOUNG MALES WAS REMARKABLE, WITH A CAPITAL "A"!

On a chilly, snowy Saturday March 29, 2014, after two years at Montgomery College-Rockville, I moved the conference because of explosive growth to the Montgomery College-Germantown's Globe Hall High Tech building. The conference experienced explosive attendance in its third year with approximately 610 participants and volunteers. This became a "must-attend" event on the community calendars through marketing and promotion efforts to local churches, sororities and fraternities, and other mentoring organizations.

We were very grateful for support from Montgomery County Public School System, (MCPS) who provided transportation for the conference that continues today. In 2014 MCPS step-up, Community Engagement and Partnership Office, under the leadership of Timothy B. Warner, Chief Engagement and Partnership Office and Dr. Joshua Starr, Superintendent of School, approved the support for transportation buses to every part of the county. Also, in later years the Chief of Staff, Dr. Henry Johnson, and the Superintendent of School, Dr. Jack Smith, provided additional marketing support to get the word out to the school district.

The conference yielded positive results through relevant workshops such as Fatherhood Responsibility, using a game from The Price is Right, Man School-What it Means to Man Up, Crucial Conversation Tools for Young Males, Critical Thinking in Global Challenges, Bullying: Change the Game; The Choice is Yours, Study Skills – Become an A Student, and You Want to Be a CSI Expert. The male forums for High school students received such topics from Project Alpha on Positive Relationships, How to Be A #1 Draft Pick, Resume and Interview Strategies, and Dress for Success for employment. The highlight of the conference was the conversations with Montgomery County Police Officer Lt. Eric Burnett and his team of officers. They conducted the discussion early on along with current Chief of Police Marcus Jones.

The conference featured three new innovative initiatives: 1) An introductory workshop for elementary school students, which included a robotic exercise; 2) The Parent Academy Workshop geared toward parents and mentors, which provided ways to better advocate for their students. 3) the first Essay Writing Competition for Students. MCPS Educator Sarah Brower recommended the Essay Contest for students. The students pictured above received a rousing ovation during the awards presentation. The Essay Writing Competition allows students to express themselves by addressing current topics of the day. We need our future leaders to improve overall writing skills to help better prepare them for school and college essay writing. The first essay topic in 2014 was "How Do You Become a Game Changer."

All students who submitted an essay on "How Do You Become a Game Changer" received a medal and certificate. First and second-place winners in each category were recognized as finalists and the winners received Nike signature shoes from NBA stars Kobe Bryant, Lebron James, and Kyrie Irving. Mr. Donnell King, Pride Youth Organization, secured the high-end sneakers for the winners. This "Wow" moment brought an eruption of cheers for the participants. In the words of Mrs. Sarah Browner, MCPS Educator, "we want to do everything possible to encourage our young people, especially our young boys, to master the written language." The inaugural essay winner was a junior, Leonard Grant, Magruder High School, on March 29, 2014.

It can be hard to go against the flow, be your own person, and not take the easy way out. It is easy to be lazy and another statistic; however, this is not true for those game changers in our society. Game changers are things or people who bring something to the table, shake up the status quo and set themselves apart from the average. They are people who are looked up to and who are willing to sacrifice the easy way for the right way. They strive for excellence and maximize their opportunities to better themselves.

To be a game-changer, it requires sacrifice, determination, and dedication. It requires getting in the zone for demonstrating excellence, such as turning in course assignments on time or staying up an extra hour to finish a project rather than settling for a late grade and focusing on learning, paying attention, and getting good grades rather than joking around with your friends and disrupting classroom instructions. I use these examples because achieving and maintaining academic excellence is critical to being a game changer. In saying this, however, you can still be a game-changer in other ways. Game changers are role models for their peers, family members, and community. Being seen as a good influence and a positive person that inspires others to do the same, you could soon have a whole community of game changers looking to be great. This chain reaction can all start with one person going against the crowd and doing what they know is right!

MCPD LT Eric Burnett - Sharing Wisdom and Knowledge

The young males also heard from four Montgomery County Police Officers who shared the community engagement and law enforcement perspective from officers who grew up in the community and serve on the street in your neighborhood. The officers led a frank discussion with the young males about the need to be respectful when stopped by a police officer. They explained that their primary role is safety first, to protect citizens, and for the young males to make good choices that keep them from the consequences of making poor choices. In the words of Lt. Burnett, as a young person, "either you are working to improve yourself or you are working to stay the same."

Key messages from the Co-Sponsors delivered were:

A. Dr. Pollard encouraged the young males to win their future - You need to be "shot callers" and "game changers" by performing well in the classroom and achieving good grades in school.

B. Dr. Clemmie Solomon emphasized the pursuit of excellence. You are not only needed to survive but you are needed to thrive to make a difference in your family's life.

C. Donald Williams message was a challenge to all participants to help flip the script—changing YOUR mind map and getting in the ZONE to get better every day—pursue excellence as a person, student, and athlete. Return to your home, school, and community to be the next "success story" and "game changer."

D. Dr. Starr emphasized reading as a critical study action to improve academic success. He further emphasized that African American students must be more proactively involved in student government activities in Montgomery County.

I was so proud of the men from my home chapter Mu Nu Chapter of Omega Psi Phi Fraternity, that provided leadership for other men in the community to be in the presence of "Black Excellence" on display! There is a scripture that reflects, "Iron Sharpens Iron." What a beautiful sight it was to see Omega men and community men working together to make a difference in the lives of students.

Collaboration Model: Divine Connection

(From Left to Right) 2014 Game Changer Conference, Montgomery College, Dr. Joshua Starr (Superintendent of Montgomery County Public Schools), Captain Clarence Thomas, Jr. (Basileus Mu Nu Chapter of Omega Psi Phi Fraternity), Dr. Beverly Walker-Griffea, former MC Senior Vice President, Dr. DeRionne P. Pollard (Former President of Montgomery College), Mona Williams, former President MCAC/UCF Founder Rev. Timothy Warner (Montgomery County Public School's Director of Community Engagement and Partnerships), Dr. Clemmie Solomon, former Vice President Collegewide Student Affairs, and Donald Williams II, Founder, Game Changer Conference.

The picture above represents executive level teamwork, setting aside personal agendas to accomplish something greater than ourselves. Alone we can do so little; together we can do so much." – Helen Keller

Dr. Gregory Bell, Director of the Office of Diversity Initiatives for the Montgomery County Public Schools, provided closing remarks. Dr. Bell's closing remarks focused on determination and overcoming life's barriers. Dr. Bell was diagnosed with blindness at an early age. He did not let his condition handicap or deter him from pursuing his education. His closing message emphasized dedication, perseverance, and determination. His message was that students must dedicate themselves to their educational pursuits and not settle for anything less, as education is the key to success.

MARCH 29, 2014 MOTIVATIONAL SPEAKER: DR. GREGORY BELL

As the conference ended, Mona and I were pleasantly surprised to be called to the stage to join The Honorable Isiah "Ike" Leggett, County Executive of Montgomery County, Maryland. He presented Mona and me with a "Montgomery County Citation" on behalf of the Unity Christian Fellowship Youth Development Organization. In his remarks, highlighted that the visionaries behind the mentoring conference, (the Williams) saw a critical need to mobilize the community and the community is better for their leadership. We must work together around the vital challenge of finding solutions to reverse the alarming trend and unfavorable disparities of African Americans and minority males of color in education.

Anyone who knows Mona and I know that we operate from a position of LOVE for the youth and to serve others in the community. We believe that LOVE unites, binds, and unifies us to fulfill a greater purpose beyond ourselves. Although we welcome recognition, we don't do this for awards and plaques. It is our love for humanity! When you love your people, you don't tire of serving them. You get tired when you can't help them anymore. UCF Youth Development Organization is on the front lines every day doing the heavy lifting to strengthen our community by working together to increase success stories.

IKE LEGGETT, COUNTY EXECUTIVE, MARCH 29, 2014

The Game Changer Conference has emerged as a conference that provides uplift and student success to the community. We are grateful to everyone who has supported and attended the conference. We are thankful for the many "helping hands" that sponsors, coaches, and mentors bring their young males every year. We will always be grateful to mentors and chaperones from near and far who collectively work together to make a difference.

As the Game Changer Conference grows, corporate sponsors, businesses, and organizations will be needed to join the team to sow financial seeds. The momentum must continue to make our families and community stronger by equipping, uplifting, inspiring, motivating, and encouraging our young males to strive for excellence in all areas of their lives.

(FROM LEFT TO RIGHT) MARCH 28, 2015 GAME CHANGER CONFERENCE AT USG, REVEREND TIMOTHY WARNER'S (MONTGOMERY COUNTY PUBLIC SCHOOL'S DIRECTOR OF COMMUNITY ENGAGEMENT AND PARTNERSHIPS), COUNCILMAN CRAIG RICE, CAPTAIN CLARENCE THOMAS, JR. (BASILEUS MU NU CHAPTER OF OMEGA PSI PHI FRATERNITY), MONA WILLIAMS, FORMER PRESIDENT MCAC/UCF FOUNDER, MR. WILLIAM MORRIS SCHLOSSENBERG, USG DIRECTOR FOR COMMUNITY OUTREACH, DR. CLEMMIE SOLOMON, FORMER VICE PRESIDENT COLLEGEWIDE STUDENT AFFAIRS, AND DONALD WILLIAMS II, FOUNDER GAME CHANGER CONFERENCE AND DR. SHAWN JOSEPH, MCPS SENIOR EXECUTIVE.

There is no better community in which to engage in this type of positive youth development work that focuses on male student success. The signature picture above represented a dynamic community leadership team that operated from a genuine place to help marginalized and disadvantaged students transition from high school to college. They were champions of educational equity and access for the least of these with a desire for academic advancement from MCPS, Montgomery College, and then to the Universities at Shady Grove. Their commitment to work together for a more significant cause showed everyone that "you cannot be great by yourself because you dimmish your impact." Together, they changed the trajectory of operating under a teaming and collaboration model.

As the conference experienced increased support and explosive growth with record-breaking attendance, it was time to seek a new venue to host the 2015 Game Changer Conference in its fourth year. Mr. Sol Graham encouraged me to schedule a meeting with an executive at The Universities at Shady Grove. He stated it was imperative to have the Game Changer Conference on a college campus because our young males needed to be able to see themselves attending college in the future. For some families, this may have been the only time their male student would visit a college campus.

The meeting with Mr. William Morris Schlossenberg, USG Director for Community Outreach, was memorable for its uncertainty and brevity. The UCF team wasn't sure how we would be received because USG was new to our community with its unique partnership concept of nine University System of Maryland universities on one campus located in Rockville, Maryland. Twenty minutes later, after a short introduction and seven slides of the PowerPoint presentation, Mr. Scholssenberg expressed that he didn't need to hear anymore. His statement surprised us, stating that the Game Changer Conference is what our community needs to address diversity. He said that they would provide the facilities, and USG would help finance the endeavor. Divine Intervention and Connection!

As this partnership approaches, a decade between UCF and the Universities at Shady Grove, (USG) continues to work together to make a difference in promoting racial harmony county. The first conference at The Universities at Shady Grove occurred on Saturday, March 28, 2015. As the word got out community wide, mentors and supporters buzzed with excitement. On game day we were thrilled to witness the continued growth with increased volunteer support and the outstanding workshop messaging from presenters.

TIMOTHY WARNER (MONTGOMERY COUNTY PUBLIC SCHOOL'S DIRECTOR OF COMMUNITY ENGAGEMENT AND PARTNERSHIPS), COUNTY COUNCIL PRESIDENT CRAIG RICE AND MR. WILLIAM MORRIS SCHLOSSENBERG, USG DIRECTOR FOR COMMUNITY OUTREACH

Each conference is unique, with different presenters, themes, and relevant topics every year. This was indeed a "game changer" for the young males and adult men to connect and interact, with the adults sharing wisdom nuggets with the young males to inspire and help improve their confidence, expand their competencies, and build the moral values needed to become a success story.

Every conference begins with registration and life skills stations to engage the young males upon arrival. Together men from the community operated the "Life Skills Stations" that offered valuable tools to equip all young males. They engaged, interacted, encouraged, and instruct the young males on how to handle themselves. The life skills stations over the years included the following: how to tie a tie, proper handshake, dental and personal hygiene tips, gentlemen's rules for treating young girls like ladies, auto safety and care, and 30-second interview skills.

The day of enriching presentations consisted of fun, motivational, and interactive workshops that focused on study skills, fitness, and nutrition, a forum that discussed male issues; social media do's and don'ts, and images and stereotypes in the media that affect youth today. The bullying workshop conducted by Dr. Joey Jones and Darryl Johnson emphasized that students have important roles to play in responding to and preventing bullying. The Alpha Phi Alpha Fraternity, Inc. annually presents the Game-Changing Plays for Positive Relationships Workshop, designed for high school adolescent males, advised on maintaining healthy, positive relationships. The Man-Up workshop conducted by author and personality Stacey Jordan shared principles to teach young males how to practice behaviors that would allow them to succeed in classroom and family settings. The men from Mu Nu Chapter of Omega Psi Phi Fraternity, Inc., led by Walter Neighbors, imparted the wisdom of fatherhood principles using the Omega Feud game (modeled after the Family Feud game show). The college-aged students received hands-on resume-building and interview tips and were given and featured at the 2015 Conference.

We will always be grateful to Mrs. Annie Foster Ahmed, Director of Center for Academic Success as our USG campus sponsor for the annual conference for a decade. Mrs. Ahmed is a member Delta Sigma Theta Sorority.

I cannot say enough about the professional and sincere support from the Conference and Events planning team consisting of Mrs. Melissa Marquez and Taishan Gary. It was a joy to work together to plan a fun-filled, exciting, life changing day for young males annually. For a decade, they have been highly supportive of the conference vision, campus experience, expansion, and assistance with marketing.

(LEFT TO RIGHT) MRS. ANNIE FOSTER AHMED, 2018 GAME CHANGER CONFERENCE HOST, DIRECTOR, MACKLIN CENTER FOR ACADEMIC SUCCESS, THE UNIVERSITIES AT SHADY GROVE, DR. JACK SMITH (SUPERINTENDENT OF MONTGOMERY COUNTY PUBLIC SCHOOLS), DR. CLEMMIE SOLOMON, FORMER MONTGOMERY COLLEGE VICE PRESIDENT COLLEGEWIDE STUDENT AFFAIRS, AND DONALD WILLIAMS II, FOUNDER GAME CHANGER CONFERENCE AND MRS. BRENDA SHELTON WOLFF, MONTGOMERY COUNTY BOARD OF EDUCATION.

We conducted the conference at a first-class facility, allowed for a wonderful event for all participants. It improved management control, as we separated elementary and middle school students and placed high school students in separate buildings. Young male hearts and minds were touched by the encouragement to do the work to reach their full potential.

The conference addressed a critical need to find solutions to reverse the alarming trend and unfavorable disparities of African Americans and minorities of color males in education. The enrichment programs held during the day-long conference were formatted to enlighten young males with the increasing demands of this century. The young males acquired life skills to help them build the confidence, competencies, and values they need to graduate and become "game changers" in society. Over the many years since the initial conference, several visitors have been attracted to the conference. Such as elected officials and dignitaries from the Montgomery County government, community leaders, Divine 9 members, sponsorship philanthropists, and educators. They all witness the inspirational and motivational content for the young males and parents in attendance.

MCPD Officer P.J. Gregory and MCPD Chief of Police Marcus Jones

The 2015 Keynote addresses and greetings from Montgomery County Councilman President Craig Rice focused on education. Montgomery County, 3rd District Commander Marcus Jones and his police officers provide encouragement and knowledge for demonstrating excellence, respect, and responsibility while understanding the practical effects of peer pressure by making better decisions.

The conference maintained several breakout sessions on life skills with topics such as How to Tie A Tie, How to Interact and Conduct Yourself during a 30-Second Interview, Auto Care Safety Tips, Dental Hygiene, Positive Relationships, What it Means to Man-Up, Bullying, Forensic Science, Social Media Discretion, Images and Stereotypes

in the Media, Employment Strategies, Team Building, Crucial Conversation Tools, Dress for Success, Fatherhood Initiative, Police and Community
Relationships, and more.

In elementary, middle, and high school, students who participated in a related essay contest with the question "Image is a Game Changer: What can <u>you</u> do to change the negative perception of African American males in the media?" were recognized during a brief ceremony. Finalists from the essay contest was awarded with the latest fashionable sneakers and computer games that excited the entire conference of participants.

Every year, the community conference aims to highlight the benefits of being youth leaders, pursuing excellence in all areas, and making smarter choices with positive consequences. We were blessed to have some of the finest MCPS Educators working side by side to support and conduct workshops annually at the conference.

2019 GAME CHANGER CONFERENCE

The annual Game Changer Conference aims to become the "Community" conference. We invited all stakeholders to view this as a "must-attend" conference. Annually we encourage the community to support MCPS, mentoring organizations, churches, youth ministry groups, Rites of Passage mentoring groups, and coaches of athletic programs. The conference will always strive to be a "life-changing" experience for youth and parents. Students living in Montgomery County and nearby communities will be challenged, uplifted, inspired, and encouraged to be better, do better because they know that we care.

Who would have thought three years ago a global pandemic brought the entire world to a standstill? The devastating COVID-19 pandemic triggered once unthinkable lockdowns, upended economics worldwide, and killed at least 7 million people worldwide, according to The World Health Organization. The CDC recent report reflects 1.2 million deaths because of the COVID-19 pandemic and there still 1,000 deaths weekly.

The 2020 Game Changer Conference at The Universities at Shady Grove Conference, scheduled for March 21, 2020, was forced to send cancellation communication out to supporters. We were within eight days of the annual conference. The Governor made the difficult decision to exercise an abundance of caution in hosting large gatherings. All Maryland colleges and universities were closed, and students were sent home indefinitely.

2019 Game Changer Conference

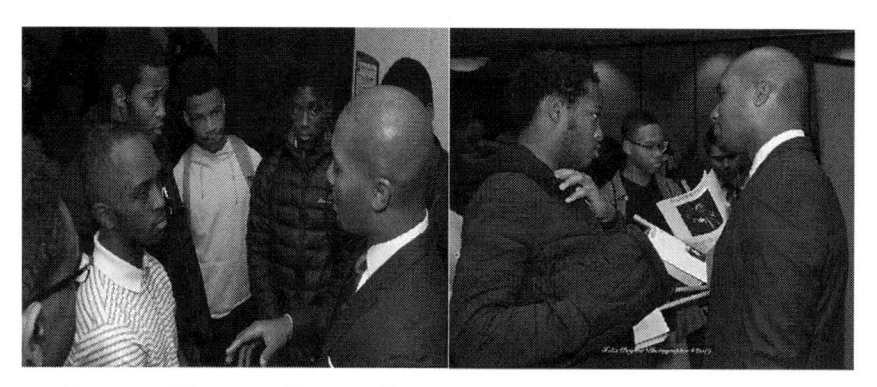

Darren Haynes, Sports Director and Anchor at WUSA Channel 9 in Washington D.C.

The 2019 conference will be remembered as the last in-person conference before the global pandemic disrupted our lives. At the previous in-person conference in 2019, the theme of the mentoring conference was "The Urgency is Now!" As a community leader, my key message to stakeholders was twofold: there is no better investment than our young people.

Those who work directly with our youth must be intentional in touching the hearts and minds to save, shape, and change any negativity in our young males. Secondly, all of us must do better to work together to raise awareness that our young people, especially our males of color, lives matter and count!

The 2019 was excited to feature keynote speaker Darren Haynes, Sports Director, and Anchor at WUSA Channel 9 in Washington D.C. He shared his impactful experience of being victimized by playing a recording of a police officer stop. You could hear a pin drop from the audience of 500

attendees. Mr. Haynes challenged young people to be mindful of their responsibility to pursue excellence and be extraordinary continuously – 24/7 in all areas of their lives!

Several workshops at this conference included: STEM, bullying, student learning styles; college and career preparation; domestic violence; social media literacy; strategic thinking and planning; applying for college scholarships and other financial aid resources; and navigating the middle school and high school experience for maximum academic achievement. A workshop for parents and guardians provided proven strategies and practical solutions for developing the next generation of game-changers.

This essay contest topic was "Responsibility is a Game Changer" and several students received awards for their writing skills. Mu Nu Chapter, Omega Psi Phi Fraternity, provided leadership, workshop facilitators, and significant financial support.

2020 Virtual Game Changer Conference

U.S. Senator Chris Van Hollen delivered Congratulatory Messages to 2020 Game Changer Participants.

During the COVID pandemic UCF leadership team pivoted to use a virtual platform to stay connected and deliver youth engagement content. Four conferences were conducted in the global pandemic. The first-ever virtual Back#2#School Game Changer Conference on October 24, 2020, and second October 23, 2021, and February 27, 2021, February 26, 2022, both during Black History Month.

On Saturday, October 24, 2020, history was made when UCF teamed with Mu Nu Chapter to host the first-ever virtual Back#2#-School Game Changer Conference. Together we planned and organized the Game Changer Conference for families that reached beyond Montgomery County to New York, New Jersey, Delaware, Pennsylvania, and other parts of Maryland.

The virtual platform conference was a tremendous success under the leadership of Dr. Lorenzo Prillman, Vice Basileus and MCPS Assistant Principal. He was the master of ceremonies that engaged students and families. Mu Nu Chapter has been a Co-Sponsor of the youth initiative that started under Brother David A. Hill, 22nd Basileus, in March 2012.

The conference theme was "Mentoring In The Midst Of A Crisis – Make Your Life Matter and Count." We engaged with approximately 200 participants using Zoom. Participants enjoyed youth student DJ LaVon Thomas Jr., (also known as "Young Fresh Prince") and presenters uplifted, educated, equipped, empowered, and encouraged young people to do the necessary work to "Win Their Future" after the pandemic.

Brian Heat, a dynamic motivational speaker, delivered a powerful message that uplifted all participants and was referenced throughout the conference by other presenters. His presentation reached our young males and provided practical applications that encouraged participation. Students shared their thoughts and feelings on their experiences on how COVID was affecting their journey.

2020 Back#2#School Game Change Conference For Families

Omega Men at Work Impacting Lives - October 24, 2020

The Game Changer Conference was significant as school communities were re-opening and students were adjusting after being isolated in the pandemic. The conference provided a platform to assist parents with helping their children to process information during the pandemic experience. It provided a framework for mentors and educators to talk, hold conversations and assist with social-emotional growth. It also helped develop support as students returned to school buildings and parents returned to an uncertainty of the future in a new normal for families.

The annual essay competition took on a new meaning and provided a place for students to share their thoughts on several topics. The first, "Adaptability is a Game Changer," allowed students to express some pros and cons of transitioning to this "new normal" virtual learning experience. The second topic was "Leadership is a Game Changer." We allowed students to unmute and share thoughts and ideas about the overall issue of racial inequity in this country. We provided recommendations to bring about social justice to unlock doors of change at school and in the community.

Thanks to the history makers who participated in the conference, said yes to the invitation, and clicked on the link to provide congratulatory messages. We heard from several dignitaries, and remarks were given by U.S. Senator Chris Van Hollen, Lieutenant General R. Scott Dingle (U.S. Army's Surgeon General and the Commanding General Support) U.S. Army Medical Command; Montgomery County Executive Marc Elrich; Sidney A. Katz, County Council President, Game Changer Conference Co-Sponsor, Mrs. Annie Foster Ahmed (Director, Macklin Center for Academic Success, The Universities at Shady Grove) and Mu Nu Chapter Basileus Gabe Brown, who brought greetings and words of encouragement.

Conference Presenters:

We were grateful to the workshop presenters who sacrificed their time and talent to share wisdom and knowledge. Mr. Don Milner, Montgomery Village Middle School, presented the youth with Strategies for Virtual Learning Excellence; Dr. Darryl A. Hill (MD, FACP) spoke on healthy living during the COVID-19 pandemic, Ms. Carla Dickerson, known as "The Scholarship Lady U.S.," shared the importance of SAT/ACT preparation. Also, the Parent Academy Forum facilitated by Mr. Donald E. Wharton Jr. and Ms. Joyce Walker featured four breakout panel sessions: The Vote: Your Civil Duty: ESQ David A. Hill, Esq. and Walter Neighbors – Attorney at Law, Salute to the Military with Lieutenant General R. Scott Dingle, Surgeon General, Captain Clarence Thomas Jr. (Navy Retired), Glenn Grayer, U.S. Coast Guard, U.S. Army LTC. French D. Pope III, Joint, Staff J-36 Homeland Defense Division.

The third breakout session was led by Police Officer P.J. Gregory MCPD, who spoke on "What should I Do When Stopped by the Police?" There was also a session entitled, "Social Justice Convenience vs. Commitment" by MCPS educators Ed Reed and Darryl Johnson. The teaming partners were encouraged to stay committed, connected, and engaged with young people in the pandemic.

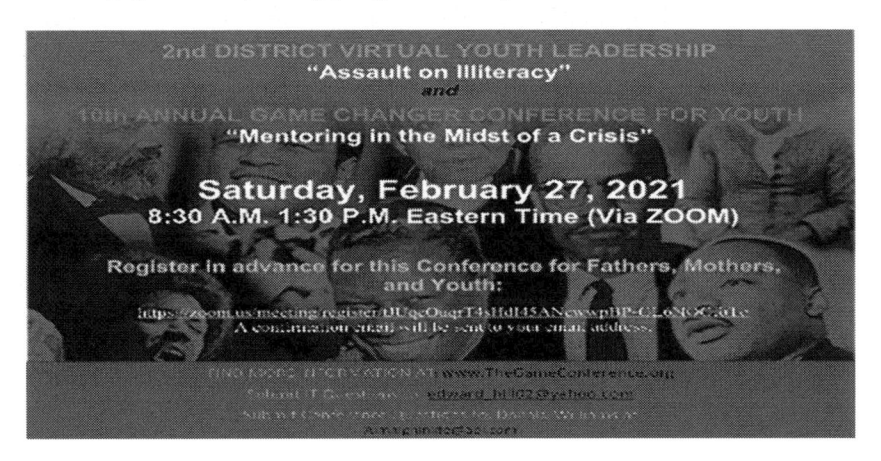

2nd DISTRICT VIRTUAL YOUTH LEADERSHIP
"Assault on Illiteracy"
and
10th ANNUAL GAME CHANGER CONFERENCE FOR YOUTH
"Mentoring in the Midst of a Crisis"
Saturday, February 27, 2021
8:30 A.M. 1:30 P.M. Eastern Time (Via ZOOM)

On Saturday, February 27th, the Game Changer Conference for Families was expanded to include other states. I was excited to receive support from the 2nd District, Omega Psi Phi Fraternity, Inc. The 37th District Representative, Brother Kelvin Ampofo, opened the conference with remarks. The conference brought together stakeholders that work directly with young people and parents to navigate COVID-19, social and political unrest.

The conference impacted approximately 235 participant lives from ten states, including Mothers, Dads, Boys, and Girls. Seeing our community operate effectively using a virtual platform to connect with youth and families was special. Everyone displayed "excellence" from

student DJ LaVon Thomas Jr. (also known as "Young Fresh Prince"), who delivered music interludes to the presenter after presenter. To hear our young people and parents express and share their thoughts at this moment was phenomenal.

The Annual Game Changer Conference, founded by UCF Youth Development Organization, uses a "Collaboration Model" that connects various organizations that work directly with young people and parents, such as The Assault on Illiteracy Committee (AOIC), Churches Youth Ministries, Sororities and other Fraternities, along with the Game Changer Conference Co-Sponsors in Montgomery County, Maryland: Mu Nu Chapter, Montgomery College, Montgomery County Public Schools System (MCPS) District, The Universities at Shady Grove, and the National Pan-Hellenic Council of Montgomery County.

The Collaboration Model demonstrates that we are stronger together in strengthening families in Black and Brown communities. Mentoring our youth is more important now than ever before; during the time society was fighting two pandemics – the ever-evolving COVID-19 pandemic and social injustice unrested, a hurricane season causing flood devastation in the southeast, wildfires in the west, an unseasonal snowstorm in Colorado, and an election season that requires our active engagement today to continue and advance the successes of the next generation! A shift appears to be occurring, and we must transform.

On Saturday, October 23, 2021, the Game Changer Conference for entire families was conducted virtually. The objective was to raise awareness of the challenges faced by black and brown students of color struggling to excel in this global COVID-19 pandemic.

A GAME CHANGER'S PURSUIT

2021 Back#2#School Game Change Conference For Entire Families

Image: Conference promotional banner featuring Mr. Shawn Prez, Motivational Speaker, Entertainment TrailBlazer — Former Bad Boy Entertainment VP, Founder/CEO of the Award-Winning Marketing Agency Power Moves Inc, and Motivational Speaker.

The conference impacted approximately 135 participants, including Mothers, Dads, Boys, and Girls. We were excited to connect with our first celebrity in the pandemic by the name of Shawn Prez. Mr. Shawn Perez was the Motivational Speaker from the entertainment career field that helped Sean Combs, known Puff Daddy, P. Ditty become a famous American rapper. Mr. Shawn Prez also known as "The Coach... The Mentor...The Guy Who Makes It Happen," currently serves as the head of his own company, Power Moves Inc., a trailblazing marketing agency whose clients include McDonalds, HBO, ESPN, EA Sports, And 1, MGM Studios and others. Our young people were grateful for the intimate, sincere connection with the youth and message delivery.

Conference Presenters:

We were grateful to the workshop presenters who were anxious to lend their gifts and talents to encourage our community. Albert Thompson, entrepreneur, and founder of Transient Identiti Company, specializing in branding and market strategy. He shared wisdom and knowledge about social media use, "Deep Fake" your social Identity, and how teens feed themselves the big lie through social media. Dr.

Joey Jones, Principal, Robert Frost Middle Scholl provided helpful strategies on "How to Succeed and Proceed in a Pandemic." Dr. Darryl Hill addressed best practices on how to stay safe and survive the pandemic for the family. Stacey Herring presented How to Be a friend during the pandemic. DJ Fresh Prince provides musical interludes between presenters.

Also, Mr. Donald E. Wharton Jr. and Ms. Joyce Walker facilitated the Parent Academy Forum breakout session. Another breakout session was conducted entitled, Salute to the Military: Joint Service Panel Discussion in an open forum with facilitator Sol Graham connecting MCPS students to service academies. Captain (P) Chelsea Young, U.S. Army; Lieutenant LaMarcus Walker, U.S. Coast Guard, COL Nicci Rucker, U.S. Air Force; Commander Michael Blackman, U.S. Navy; and Master Segreant, (Dr.) J C Chandler.

2022 Virtual Game Changer Conference

On Saturday, February 26, 2022, the third virtual Game Changer Conference for the entire Family included states nationwide. Although the conference was virtual, there was increased excitement and buzz about the special guest, Brother Anthony Anderson, the star from Black-ish. We are grateful for the wonderful delivery that kicked-off the conference that provided inspiration and information to participants in Zoom.

The 37th District Representative, Brother Kelvin Ampofo, was responsible for securing the motivational speaker and conducted an excellent interview with thoughtful questions from the youth. Brother Anderson was a motivational speaker who kept it real when interacting with young people. In the words of the District Chaplain, Reverend Dr. Ronald Williams, "Lives will be better because of the meaningful information provided to families." Together we impacted and uplifted the world. Teamwork makes the Dream work!

Conference Presenters:

We are grateful to all presenters and participants who sacrifice their time to uplift, equip, encourage, and empower our community with important, meaningful messages. Shoutout to Dr. Lorenzo Prillman who was our Master of Ceremony, extraordinaire. So appreciative of the teamwork and workshop presenters that shared wisdom and knowledge.

1. D.J. Mr. Young Fresh Prince, a sophomore at Richard Montgomery High School
2. Ms. Carla Dickerson, known as the Scholarship Lady US
3. Student Open Mic (How to be a Friend in this Moment)
4. Student Poem Competition
5. Dr. Keith Boykin (Safe Practices Surviving COVID-19)
6. Two Panels: Military Career Pathway and Focus to Increase Applicants to Service Academies and Nu Upsilon Chapter Fatherhood Barbershop Conversation (What does Fatherhood mean to you?)
7. Author Mat Stevens – Summer Employment Tips
8. Parent Advocacy Roundtable (School Safety, How to Be Advocate, and Middle School Preparation)

In attendance, were several dignitaries from Education and Military: Brother, Lieutenant General R. Scott Dingle, the U.S. Army's Surgeon General and the Commanding General (Support) U.S. Army Medical Command, COL Nicci Rucker (USAFR), Captain (Retired) Clarence Thomas Jr. (U.S. Navy), LTC French Pope III (U.S. Army), Amir Shareef (U.S. Navy Academy Graduate) and Baltimore County Superintendent, Dr. Darryl Hill.

A STORY WITH A KEY MESSAGE:

I am reminded of a story a friend shared about "warning signs," and the example used centered on how a rattlesnake gives a "warning sign" by using the rattle on the tip of its tail. Rattlesnakes are venomous reptiles with large bodies and heart-shaped heads with a "rattle" found at the tip of the tail. Rattlesnakes don't have ears and can't hear most sounds. They detect movement by sensing vibrations in the ground. The "rattle" is a defense mechanism to warn others and scare predators away. To the person hearing the rattle noise, it alerts one to the immediate danger.

I share this story because a lot is happening worldwide and our communities that affect a vulnerable, underserved population. There are warning signs in our community that should cause us to be morally outraged. There's much going on today with social injustice issues, under-performing schools in underserved communities, voter suppression, equal access in high-performance schools, and safe spaces in neighborhoods due to increased violence --underlying issues all occurring during a global COVID-19 pandemic. In the last decade, other examples of moral outrage increasing, neighborhood drive-by killings of young people, and certainly.

There has been a long history of "warning signs" based on racially motivated violence against black and brown people dating back to 14-year-old Emmett Louis Till, who was abducted, tortured, lynched in Mississippi in 1955. In 2012, the death of 17-year-old Trayvon Martin, who was fatally shot in Florida by a neighborhood watch captain who, was acquitted in the case. There were the deaths of Philando Castile and Alton Sterling in 2016. The murders of George Floyd and Ahmaud Arbery have kept things at a fever pitch.

On Saturday, October 22, 2022, the conference returned to its in-person format and accommodated approximately 125 parents and students. This was the first step for focusing forward to "Make Hope Happen" for students and families as we press through the other side of the pandemic. This one-day mentoring conference was for elementary (4th and 5th grades), middle, high school, and college age students.

Our community has been experiencing warning signs for a very long time. This should cause each one to be emotionally moved and called to action. In a recent webinar co-sponsored by the Community College Equity Assessment Lab (CCEAL) and the Association of Community College Trustees (ACCT) with presenters Dr. Frank Harris III and Dr. Marissa Vasquez, and Dr. Luke Wood. The webinar focused on Increasing Enrollment and Success for College Men of Color. Community colleges across the U.S. have experienced significant enrollment declines during the COVID-19 pandemic. These declines were particularly concerning for men of color. For instance, community college enrollments for Black and Native American men dropped by 26% and 24%, respectively. However, all colleges still need help to return enrollments and retention to their pre-pandemic levels. And future enrollment appears uncertain in the post-pandemic era.

2022 Back#2#School Game Change
Conference For Young Males

In addition, we are seeing significantly high rates of black-on-black crime in our community and an overall increase in violence in society for many reasons. However, we fail to make the connection and understand that crime results from socioeconomic status, connecting to the highest poverty rate based on a report reflecting Native American and Black Americans. As the world rapidly shifts, this is why we must work together in a concerted effort to show young males of color different pathways forward for being successful that start from an early age and the

Research today shows that school districts where most students enrolled are students of color receive $23 billion less in education funding than predominantly white school districts. If you live in a low-income neighborhood and go to an underfunded school with unqualified and underpaid teachers, you'll be less inclined to pay attention in school and more inclined to drop out. You'll be less likely to get a good job without an education. A person without a job, living below the poverty line, may resort to crimes such as selling drugs to earn money. The research is from an article written by Zariah Taylor, age 15, who attends Carver Early College and writes this article as part of her work as a student at VOX ATL's After school program—published on VOX ATL on July 24, 2020.

2023 Spring Game Change Conference For Young Males

The 2023 Spring Game Changer Conference for Young Males was phenomenal, incredible, and amazingly successful, with approximately 500+ males impacted. The second in-person conference on Saturday, March 25, 2023, was tremendous. The theme was the "World Is

Shifting! Being Focus Forward is a Game Changer: How Will YOU Pursue Excellence?"

The all-male conference was electric and just what Montgomery County community in Maryland needed! The explosive record attendance and presence of Black men from fraternities, local Churches, and mentors witness a caring community in action. Sharing knowledge and wisdom made a huge difference in uplifting and inspiring young males to do their very best. Together we changed the trajectory of families and students.

The participant's spirit and high energy were evident from start to finish where young males were paired with men in the life skills portion. The young males rotated from station to station to learned how tie tying, 30-second interviews, a proper handshake, and fitness station. The students were excited to keep and take home the tie that they learned how to tie.

Teamwork makes the dream work when committed stakeholders are intentional about working together. Welcome remarks received from Mu Nu Chapter Basileus Walter Neighbor, the Universities at Shady Grove, Dr. Jeffrey Ash, the first Chief Diversity, Equity, and Inclusion Officer, (Omega Man). Montgomery County Public School District Deputy Superintendent, Dr. Patrick Murphy. Stacey Herring was dynamic as Master of Ceremony introduced the keynote speaker, Dr. Joey Jones. Taking center stage, he asked students how many want to go "PRO?" He commanded and kept the attention of everyone, fellow educators, mentors, and students, giving away money for correct responses to questions throughout his presentation. Its pay to listen and follow instructions was the underline take away for attendees.

Family and Friends, our community can no longer afford to sit on our Blessings; we must build on our Blessings to stay connected and engaged with today's young people!

Again, I am so grateful to past, present, and future volunteers and strategic partners; you have played a crucial role in "making hope happen" for young people, especially young male students. Your support of the Game Changer Mentoring Conference is more important now than ever. We must continue to invest in the community and work together to make a difference in a child's life. Let's continue the collaboration of meaningful, impactful, and important work to help students navigate this ever-changing society.

QUOTE:

"It's important for us to also understand that the phrase 'Black Lives Matter' simply refers to the notion that there's a specific vulnerability for African Americans that need to be addressed. It's not meant to suggest that other lives don't matter. It's to suggest that other folks aren't experiencing this vulnerability."

—Barack Obama

SCRIPTURE:

Do nothing out of selfish ambition or vain conceit. Rather, in humility value others above yourselves, not looking to your own interests but each of you to the interest of the others.

Philippians 2:3-4

Part 4 – Impact

Quintessential Servant Leadership

- Chapter 17: Leadership Philosophy

- Chapter 18: How to Start a Mentoring Program

- Chapter 19: Community Partnership Collaborations Model & Divine Connection

CHAPTER 17

Leadership Philosophy:

What is the meaning of quintessential leaders? When you google the definition, it states that quintessential leaders have character traits that distinguish them from people in leadership positions. These are leaders who have unwavering pursuit of excellence that turn ideas into actions for a greater impact in the community. While quintessential leaders have imperfections, make mistakes, and sometimes fail spectacularly, these character traits define how they handle themselves in both the worst and best times.

Leadership is the ability to ignite, inspire, influence others to achieve greatness. They lead by example, share all they have with others, find creative solutions while empowering people to strive for excellence in service; this is the highest form of leadership. You can inspire and influence others in what you say and the actions you model. The consistency of character traits from my life journey that I have learned, experienced, witnessed, and incorporated into my servant leadership style are demonstrated integrity, confidence, accountability, caring for others, and effectively communicating expectations with other community leaders.

I am grateful to serve and work with dynamic leaders in my professional career in the public, private, and armed forces sectors. In all professional assignments including community service, it is essential to surround yourself with compassionate people that can execute and deliver outcomes for a greater good. I learned to practice and display humility, be grateful for what you currently have and mindful of your imperfections, so on, and admit when you are wrong, it's o.k. to ask for forgiveness.

I have served on the staff of Dr. Earl S. Richardson, who served as the 9th President at Morgan State University, Earl Jenkins, 8A Firm CEO in Washington D.C., and in the military with excellent exposure to outstanding leadership over a twenty-year career. I learned about leadership accountability, accessibility, taking care of soldiers and civilians. I was blessed to serve under Brigadier Collin Powell in the army and when he was Secretary of State. I learned about the importance of "Optics Leadership." Managing the optics of your image means being aware you are constantly on stage, especially in the age of social media branding. Also, being aware of how others see you when ascending to senior level positions is essential. Even during downtime, you must look, act and be a leader 24/7. All Eyes are already on you anyway!

However, the most critical lesson I adopted was to have a strategic vision, with an entrance and exit plan, to keep everyone engaged and focused on "priority outcomes." Managing outcomes is a challenge in the world or sphere of excellence! As a public servant in the federal government, I always learned to express optimism because it is contagious. Surround yourself with people that are comfortable with their own uniqueness, creativity, meaningful skill sets, who are critical thinkers, and problem solvers, and empower them to achieve team greatness together.

Leaders must have visions! I believe God speaks to us through our dreams, thoughts, ideas, and situations as He helps us ignite and inspire others. To be an effective leader, you must know how to follow. If followship is beneath you, then leadership is beyond you. To be an effective leader, you must learn to actively listen and welcome feedback from others. Leadership effectiveness doesn't translate well when your mindset is to demonstrate how smart you are at the table. In other words, believing you are the most intelligent person in the room doesn't allow the team and staff to grow, and hinders the growth of an organization's effectiveness. In our world today, different perspectives-based experience base can strengthen organizations and communities. Your leadership ought to be contagious when you pour into people's lives who are empty and void of vision, dreams, goals, or direction.

Some people can't see for themselves, so God allows you to see for others about their lives. In mentoring young people, you often see something in them that they don't see in themselves. Mentors encourage our young people to pursue higher heights such as acquiring a good education while in high school. We encourage them to go to college and pursue a degree in a meaningful career profession or earn certifications to improve your quality of life and make life better for your family and others. I ask you what visions you have written down for yourself, your family and household. This is a starting point for engaging and connecting with today's young people. Consider the following:

1. The power of the tongue, language, and word usage shape people's lives and culture. The power of your tongue influences thoughts of others positively or negatively. We have seen with mentoring those that broaden their vocabulary broaden their ability to think. What you say can uplift a person or harm a person. I have heard that the tongue is like a boat's rudder. Although the tongue is a small body part, it steers your

thoughts. What you say determines which direction you go. You have control over your tongue, words have power, and they can change the pattern of a person's thoughts and actions! Are you sending your words out in the direction you want your life to go?

2. As stated earlier, mentors and mentees what visions have you written down for yourself and your family? I challenge you to close your eyes to dream and imagine the highest vision possible for your life. Our youth annually participate in creating a vision board by cutting out pictures from magazines for them to take home to hang and review daily. This new generation has digital vision boards to create a vision for tomorrow. We tell our youth that everything good or bad starts with a thought! If you can see how your best life would be in six months to two years, then you can believe it and achieve it. You become what you believe in by putting forth a winning effort and establishing winning habits.

3. The people you are close to influence your thoughts and actions; who is in your corner, friend group, or crew to hold you accountable for creating winning habits? Who is in your corner to instill positive encouragement, this is important because we are living in a time where people want to see you fail. I like to pass on what I learned in my youth; don't be the smartest person in your group. Surround yourself with friends who want to see you be successful. Surround yourself with dreamers, doers, believers, and thinkers. Your group or crew should want the best for you; they should encourage, equip, and empower you to pursue excellence and help you achieve your dreams and goals.

4. Who are you following and why do you choose to follow them? Mentors, this is where you come in by pouring into struggling youth. We are losing too many to foolishness and poor choices

– young people, your choices have serious consequences. Everything in your life reflects the choices you made. If you want a different result, make a different choice. Future leaders stand up and speak up and please don't go along to get along. Someone in your corner, friend group or crew should speak up and say, "Wait a minute" or "let's think this out or consider another way." Future leaders surround yourself with those who see greatness within you even when they don't see it yourself. Lastly, stop living your life based on other people's opinions. Stop living your life up to their standards; stop seeking their approval.

Quintessential leadership is about being great at caring when you serve others. The greatness of a servant leader is when you inspire others and help them improve so they can succeed and shine. It is fulfilling to live a life of service to others and help as many people as possible along life's journey. We encourage stakeholders to celebrate one another's successes and push others toward their destinies. Together we can change our community. Together we can help people improve to become the best they can become. We can win the future with new strategies, thinking, and pathways. Our destiny is on the line as the world continues to transform.

Focus Forward Leadership:

As we still grapple with the aftermath of the pandemic and its profound impact on the mentoring and education arena, what can we accomplish better? How can we ignite today's generation of young people in a world that is constantly changing with the evolution of artificial intelligence?

I believe the emergence of artificial intelligence technology will be the biggest shift that we will experience in our lives.

UCF is on the front lines with those working directly with young people and parents. It is imperative for Mentors to help young people understand that we are counting on them not to settle, but to stand up, to shine by pressing and pursuing excellence to win their future!

Mentoring organizations like UCF have an opportunity to engage, equip, and encourage students who have been significantly marginalized before the pandemic and are now markedly impacted by the COVID-19 pandemic. The ultimate education goal is to prepare young people for college, career, and work force readiness. In the post-pandemic era, students deserve first-class learning experiences that relate to the reality of a rapidly changing world.

As society rebounds from the aftermath of the pandemic, in my opinion was a missed opportunity to reimagine and rethink our public education system. How do we educate the post COVID generation of young people?

The pandemic produced students who were behind in math, reading and social skills. However, they have become consumers of more information via technology than any previous generation. Yet, they lack the intellectual bandwidth to process it all. As a result, we have children who lack the ability to connect with others or demonstrate empathy, compassion, collaboration, or skills necessary to resolve conflicts and self-regulate. Our students must be properly prepared for career readiness for a rapidly changing workforce that demands new skill sets, (both hard and soft) workforce.

How many remember the movie Charlie and the Chocolate Factory where Mr. Bucket loses his job due to modernization by introducing robotics? The toothpaste factory decided to eliminate jobs screwing on toothpaste tap on the toothpaste. In the 21st century, how will integrating artificial intelligence technology impact our daily living in education? How can we educate future generations in this paradigm shift affecting all areas of our daily lives? What does it look like to "reimagine and rethink" education delivery in the 21st century? There must be accountability for preparing students to meet future demands with college readiness or workforce-readiness education. A teaming partner, Cyber Group Green, Inc. says it this way, "the difference between school and life is in school, students are taught a lesson and then given a test from the last century. In todays' life you are given a test that teaches you a lesson.

For many parents educated in the public school system 25-years ago, it appears no change to the learning experience. It looks like leaders, teachers, and those working in the field of education, intentionally co-creating with students' spaces where they simply learn how to learn. In the post-pandemic era we must first figure out how to keep students engage with learning while preparing them for the transforming world.

In a recent publication highlighting, Teachers College-Columbia University professor, Yolanda Sealey-Ruiz said, "I believe in inviting the lives of my students into the classroom. If students see themselves in a book, they engage very differently." I believe students must see themselves in everyday learning experiences and the materials in which they encounter.

Dr. Shawn Joseph, another highly respected educator and the former urban superintendent, and current Co-Director of the Howard University Urban Superintendent Academy recently published an article about "Engaging Black and Brown Students in STEM. Dr. Shawn discusses the causes of underrepresentation in the K-12 STEM Field. He addresses the framework that can be used in the post-pandemic period regarding new thinking that requires rethinking the structure and function of our educational system and its approach to teaching students not only for STEM but for education pathways. He states the best way to reimagine and rethink how to educate today's generation of young people is to look at the way we think about the problems and how students engage with their environments. Although the article centered on STEM, "it is essential for school districts to begin helping parents to feel comfortable with science, technology, engineering, and mathematics. It is important for children to be exposed to STEM as early as pre-school and it must be as important as reading initiatives.

I believe we must reimagine and rethink curriculum in that increases student's engagement where they see themselves in everyday learning encounters experiences. Students are disconnected from the learning process in the post pandemic era. The long-term goal is to provide students with important life skills necessary to succeed in fields beyond science, technology, engineering, and mathematics. Today's curriculum doesn't adequately prepare students for the current workforce with the emergence of artificial intelligence, robotics, etc. In my opinion, the curriculum framework must connect the new reality that intractable real-world issues, student's environment, family, school, and work settings. accounts where students live, to inspire, and motivate them in learning at a higher level.

To illuminate the need to create a new pathway that engages today's students in the new world reality, I believe the author Dr. Joy Degruy spells out in her book entitled the Post Traumatic Slave Syndrome begins to address a pathway of reshaping the education process. She emphasizes the importance of learning through symbolic imagery.

Dr. Degruy shares that in schools across the country, our children are presented with subject matter that is of little interest to students. Today's student disinterest is primarily because our students view their schoolwork assignments as seemingly unconnected to their lives, having little significance in their ultimate success or survival. You have heard it said many times, I have listened to it from my children, "Why are we learning this?" Translations, what does this have to do with my world or reality today?

Dr. Degruy states that when our students do not see the connection between the subject and their lives, they become bored and unmotivated. Conversely, they will become highly motivated and excited about learning when they see the connections. It is through symbolic imagery that these connections can be made apparent, (Pages 25 and

26). Stakeholders must make a concerted effort to enhance students' learning recovery and loss by working collectively together to reduce the windows of vulnerabilities in underserved communities.

We can't go back and apply old thinking, ineffective, outdated learning practices, and strategies from a 130-year educational model for today's realities. What methods will be employed to address students who experience learning loss, have lost confidence, and are walking around in the school building with COVID-fogged? As educators and students proceed in the new reality in the post-pandemic era, we must figure out how to mitigate distractions, competing with students on cell phones and ear pods in students' ears. Because of lack of parental involvement, the social media impacts of students walking into a classroom with ear pods plugged into cell phones is a significant distraction to educating students to standard. Our teachers are fighting for the attention of students allowed to use their handheld devices, smartphones, and ear pods in school that compete with classroom instructions. What are we going to do to address disengaged students?

In this post-pandemic transformation season, greatness comes from the desire to do extraordinary things, to reach beyond the status quo, and relentlessly chase your dreams. It starts with a vision, goal setting, and achieving those goals you set for yourself. And then you aim higher than where you place your mark. You persist in getting better, one step at a time. To be great, you must strive to be great at the little things; this implies tasks you must consistently do with greatness in mind. When I was coaching basketball, I would tell the team that to achieve team goals, each player needs to be excellent in their roles and assignments to create winning habits. I challenged them to be great at rebounding, stealing the ball, on-ball defense, and consistently making free throws. In short, being excellent in your roles leads to champions! Like basketball, it is with life as we press through the pandemic. Today's educators, administrators, parents, and mentors must focus on helping students achieve the greatness harnessed inside them.

What type of Leader are you?

My life's purpose has been to serve others, pouring wisdom and knowledge into others to motivate, inspire, equip, and encourage people to be their best on their life journeys. I cannot talk about mentoring without speaking about leadership. God blesses each person with gifts and talents locked inside. You were born to make a difference and for a purpose, and you must operate with spiritual confidence to move differently at this moment.

Ask yourself, what if God chose you, He loved you so much that he chose you to be his hands, feet, and mouthpiece to love others. To love the other person as much as you love yourself. It's not about where you came from; it's about something greater than yourself. It is about the dedication to putting service above the self to ensure you lift as you climb and leave no one behind. I am grateful that God chose me to use as a living testimony in a world that can't hear God speaking to them and doesn't recognize his Blessings!

Authentic leadership must not be about you; it is not about you being the best. Leadership is about making others better because of your presence and ensuring that impact lasts in your absence. It's called legacy building. Specifically, mentoring leadership is about helping young people be better, helping them believe in themselves to see their potential and realize their dreams. It's about providing opportunities for the least of these. Those that are marginalized, left behind, and below the socioeconomic poverty line. As a mentor, you can be a bridge builder who helps connect young people to their destinies.

In this season of transformation, it is about doing your very best to become the best version of yourself as a leader, mentor, or mentee. I would be remiss if I didn't share some golden nuggets about leadership, specifically positive youth development mentoring required in the 21st Century. When you Google, you will find four types of leadership:

autocratic, democratic, laissez-faire, and transformational. There are many definitions of leadership and descriptions of leadership styles.

Quintessential leadership is truly about striving to become a servant leader with integrity. When you focus on service, you always give your best to serve others. It is gratifying to help nurture others in their growth and development as a person, students, and young adults. I believe teamwork is a force multiplier no matter your occupation. To be an effective leader there is value in building trusted relationships as a military person, community leader, church leader, coach, fraternity or sorority member, or mentor.

Many people wonder if a person is born with leadership gifts or can you learn to be a leader. I have seen people who seem to come out of their mother's womb being a leader on day one. I have also seen those who tirelessly work at developing their skill sets and putting into practice what they have learned to become an effective leader. In my life, I became a student of leadership. As a leader, you can learn much more by attending virtual or in-person seminars, workshops, webinars, and online courses in team building and by seeking mentors who serve in executive positions. You should recognize learning is continuously ongoing, and you can learn so much from best practices and experiences from good and bad leaders. And when you get your opportunity to lead you can incorporate best practices that fit your leadership style. Hit the ground running realizing your assignment may not be long-term.

When inheriting a leadership assignment and responsibility, receive what you inherited, focus, and build upon it to advance and make it more effective in accomplishing the organization's objectives and mission. And then make it better than you found it before departing for your next leadership assignment.

Although there are many aspects of what makes an effective leader, people respond favorably to people with integrity. The group receives a leader who tries to do the right thing favorably. A leader who can communicate a clear vision and promote shared responsibilities and personal growth from people on the team is highly effective.

Focus your energy on leading by example through your actions and encouraging everyone on your team to fulfill their potential! As a leader, you must learn to use your gift of discernment and listen intently to allow God to speak to the heart of those assigned to be a part of your life.

As a leader, you must know why you want to become a leader of an organization, district, team, or staff. I have witnessed people seeking to become leaders for the wrong reasons, such as "this leadership position will round out my resume." The title will look good and catapult you to a higher position." Seeking positions on any level simply for a title while knowingly not being equipped or prepared for the higher-level leadership position is not a winning strategy.

As a leader or supervisor, it is not your job to look good! It is your job to help others on the team be better, help them look good, and celebrate their accomplishments and performance. It is vital to assemble a team of trusted, skilled sets, problem solvers, and innovative thinkers.

Leadership done for the right reasons is best when value is added to an organization. There must be some past demonstrated performance and some indicators that you can perform at a higher level. Don't become a leader if your primary intent is to gain applause. It isn't easy to let others shine when it is about you! It isn't very likely for you to become a successful leader if you are only in it to receive applause from others.

In my experiences serving in senior-level positions, primarily, there were three types of leadership styles. First, you can be a successful leader in a position of authority where you "preside." **Presiding Leadership** is where you occupy the authority positions, establish goals, and create the organization's pathway. The person holds the line, not making any changes and not causing any waves. You can be a successful leader just by staying within the organization's culture. The presiding leadership approach focuses on the organization's compliance. Everything complies with governing regulations.

The second type of leadership is **People Pleaser Leadership** or the Yo-Yo leader. This type of leader makes short-term decisions for one group and then turns around to make another short-term decision to please the other group. This person reacts to the perceived pressure from the loudest noisemakers. This leader appears to be pulled in every direction, going back and forth, waffling, changing the condition and criteria, delaying decisions, and making no progress.

The Servant Leader is the third type of leader who intentionally affects change and will introduce innovativeness and creative business solutions, processes, and practices. This leader is comfortable with who they are and whose they are with keeping their eye on putting people first. This leader's mindset centers on serving people to achieve organizational goals. This leader sincerely cares about the impact of their value-added decisions and the outcomes.

Everyone possesses leadership attributes and must learn to grow into becoming a leader through various God given experiences. Influential leaders in the 21st century must create new pathways and methods, use new tools to inspire, and help people grow and develop to connect with today's young people. Today's leader must be the catalyst for ushering in new possibilities and ways of thinking and staying relevant with transformation times. Influential leaders see new pathways; they listen to others on the team, rethinking what we do daily, and speak about endless possibilities!

Here are a few characteristics I adhere to that have allowed me to provide authentic leadership:
1. Accountability (who is doing what tasks)
2. Belief (everyone can make a difference)
3. C ("sees" the endless possibilities be a visionary)
4. Drive toward excellence by displaying a positive attitude (leaders possesses a "can do" attitude)
5. Enthusiasm is contagious
6. Forward thinking (what are the priorities and what will be the best practices in the future)
7. Inspiration (create a "Wow Moment")
8. Life is a story that you are the author of
9. Leading "up" (know what is important to your bosses)
10. Problem solving (solve the most challenging problems)
11. Relax (don't take yourself so seriously)
12. Strategic risk (Encourage Risk Taking)
13. Uplift (radiate the possibility in every way, the way you live, speak, and act)
14. When you want to contribute, and someone stops you, you'll learn the next time.

What are effective leaders genuinely committed to? Of course, leaders take many actions, every day. I believe three things' leaders must be committed to, the first centers on "making others better." The best leaders of impact have a four-word description, "to make others better."

The second thing I learned from my military experience, is to always take care of your soldiers, team, company, and staff members. They will take care of you when no one is watching. It is all right to say, "I care about you." It is okay to be concerned, and compassionate. Team leaders and team members take care of one another!

Thirdly, as a civilian leader, the simple acronym R.B.I. (Relationship Before Issues) used throughout my professional career reflects another element of caring for each other. It would help if you were interested in developing authentic relationships with co-workers and supervisors two levels up. As a leader or first-line supervisor, you must ensure things are all right with everyone you oversee. Conducting wellness check-ins with your team is essential in the post-COVID era. Finding out how well things are with your team members is alright.

Lastly, leadership starts at the top in shaping attitudes and creating a culture of excellence. The leader at the top understands that all eyes are on them every day. The most effective and impactful leader leads with integrity and by example in every decision, action, and communication. The most effective leaders are the ones that promote and display teamwork. They bring people together for a higher purpose; respect, uplift, love, trust are core values. Conversely, a self-centered leader will end up unfulfilled and empty if it is all about me. Selfish pursuits lead to unfulfillment!

My message to community leaders who manage the "purse string budget," local cities, municipals, counties, etc. Many organizations in the community are committed to positive youth development with mentoring, coaching, and creating new pathways for youth in these challenging times. If decision-makers at the county, township, state level are truly serious about addressing the state of youth in vulnerable communities, then earmark resources to youth organizations that are making the difference in your community.

It would be a welcome change to see resources flow to nonprofit organizations that are spending the time, effort, and energy with mentoring. These nonprofits are not adequately funded equally or equitably while filling the gap that communities and schools cannot. UCF like other non-profit provide meaningful engagement, direction, and guidance for young people that the government cannot perform. Although there are barriers, I'd like to see resources go to local youth organizations on the front lines working with vulnerable populations.

I'd like to see funders transparency with sharing their performance metrics to ease non-profit challenges with securing funds. What we learned for securing funds is that there are strategies that prevent success due to the many policies adversely rooted in structural screening inherent racial inequities.

Therefore, I would like to see equal resources earmarked to community-based organizations that tirelessly spend their time, effort, and energy with mentoring. Sometimes successes are hard to measure (e.g. how do you measure the joy of young people who get to experience a trip out of their neighborhood for the first time (e.g. and opportunity to visit NY). Organizations can't quantify that for the funder, but it makes a difference. I'd like to see resources go to local mentoring organizations on the front lines with proven performance records that positively impact students.

I'd like to see implementation that addresses mentoring challenges verse another "contractual study" that tells stakeholders what we already know. Let's stop kicking the can down the road and start using the existing data to implement new strategies that lead to new pathways that engage and encourage all students to become their best version of themselves.

What our Youth Needs?

I want to tell our young future leaders a story about when I was driving on the Washington Beltway and turned off on the Georgia Avenue Exit.

I saw a man holding a sign, and I assumed the man was holding a sign asking for money. As I waited for several cars back, the sign came into view as the traffic moved forward. I am now two cars from the light and can see the sign. The sign had the following three words: We have PURPOSE! And that is the critical message for anyone who works directly with youth, to remember, on this journey as a mentor or mentee, educator, or funder you have PURPOSE!

Today's young people want the same thing you and I experienced growing up. They want a chance to succeed and have guidance to avoid pitfalls and barriers that hinder success. They want an adult in their life to offer advice and wisdom, to inspire and propel them in the right direction to achieve personal goals. We encourage students to look beyond their current environment, outlive their circumstances, and not become paralyzed by their current situation. In other words, we want them to rise beyond their circumstances to accomplish their personal goals. To live a life that incorporates moral values of preparation, integrity, team building, responsibility, giving back, and respect. These are the soft skills needed for responsible citizenship.

We tell our young people that they can certainly feel sorry for themselves and wallow in despair, to blame the pandemic as a reason to derail their academic dreams that result in underperformance. They certainly have the right to say what they didn't have, what your parents and grandparents didn't do, and make excuses about where they live and go to school – none of this mattered before the pandemic and certainly not now.

We encourage students that this state of mind will only keep them paralyzed in the same position. They also cannot let go of their past, free themselves, or pivot and apply the necessary effort to reach higher and change their circumstances. Mentors can help young people see greater things in store and not let negative influences ruin their future.

We have learned that developing meaningful, trusted relationships with our young people has produced positive results and is the key to future success and development, both tangible and intangible. UCF has experienced positive outcomes by providing social, emotional, academic, spiritual renewal and uplift that supports young people's growth and development as they navigate from adolescence into young adulthood.

As communities nationwide put COVID-19 pandemic in the rearview mirror and pivot to the new reality preparing for the 21st century with new ideas and new pathways, mentors can give the most precious gift-- Love! I encourage mentors and those who work directly with young people to operate from a place of love. I believe love is nothing without action; relationships are nothing without trust and the willingness to change one's perspective with the desire to improve or change directions.

We need community stakeholders to work together, and as we encourage students to aim higher, decision-makers must seek higher. To persist at improving, one policy enhancement, one "this is the way it aways been" process and practice change, and one positive step at a time. An example, in October 2022, Back#2#School Game Changer Conference, MCPS provided bus transportation to transport students to the conference at the Universities at Shady Grove based on school participation.

MCPS has been outstanding in providing buses to schools. In this all-out effort to reengage students with social and emotional support and interaction with sterling Black men, MCPS educator Jason Miller and Ed Reed, designed a new efficient approach that identified seven pick-up points to serve seven school clusters. This is fresh thinking to what has become a routine planning practice. Several people from the county transportation department were upset about the limited number of students who took advantage of the transportation. A newly appointed principal Darryl Johnson, of Rocky Hill Middle School, looked at the practices and came up with a new solution to help with the new reality of the impact COVID has on the community. He appreciated the bus support, and the next time he will have an Assistant Principal on the bus to go into his community. In the Spring Conference assigning Assistant Principal to bus became standard practice. It's about teamwork, trusted relationships, and going beyond to help our children and their families.

To be great, you must persist in the little things to help with pandemic recovery, where our young people have been traumatized. We all see what goes on inside the school building with aggressive behaviors, students cursing, disengagement, lack of conflict resolution, problem-solving, and ineffective communication skills. It's about humanity helping students and families with social and emotional challenges. We need today's students to provide solutions for the next generation. We need young people to be problem solvers, think in a new way, and create new pathways for themselves. We need them to have the courage to be extraordinary: first, learn to listen; second, make required changes in their lives that align with a rapidly changing world. The new reality is that our community and world have transformed right before our eyes in plain sight! We count on young people to renew their commitment to pursue education, develop new ideas, create new businesses, and innovate new pathways. As the world transforms it is imperative for young people to understand that they cannot settle and be satisfied. You are put on this earth to shine, ignite, make a difference while pursuing excellence!

My message to young people, and specifically, to mentors: you aren't called to fit in. Mentors and leaders are standouts. To live their life with a meaningful purpose and be part of the solution for a better community. It takes courage to be extraordinary!

Leadership Philosophy: You Should Have More Than One Mentor

I am genuinely excited to share how God uses ordinary people like you and me to impact and create a better-beloved community of non-believers and believers alike. It is now on us, the latest generation, to be "Game Changers" for future generations. The "ask" is to be responsible for mentoring just "one" person; "each one reaches one" on your life journey.

The Bible in the New Testament offers a spiritual mentoring model for all to follow. Paul and Timothy's relationship is an excellent example of an intergenerational mentoring model in the post-pandemic era. This relationship is a clear example for all who work directly with young people to help them focus forward to reach their full potential in all areas of their lives.

See an elder Paul mentored Timothy, a junior, by equipping him for the ministry tasks. Paul had more experience, wisdom, and knowledge that helped to impact, influence, and positively inspire a young Timothy. Paul aims to add value and lovingly ignite a young Timothy to become the best leader and pursue excellence. I recommend each one be a mentor as an older person to provide direction to a junior person your age. And the junior mentor should be a Paul to someone younger than them. In essence, you will serve as a Paul and, simultaneously, be a mentor as Timothy on your life journey. For example, Brother John Tucker was my Paul, and I was his Timothy. He poured wisdom, wise counsel, and business savvy as I navigated my professional career after the military. He mentored me with a Christian spirit to reinforce my servant leadership style and showed me how to interact with people with a different moral compass.

I was Paul to a young Kareem Johnson, and he was my Timothy. Kareem served as Paul to a young David Hayes in middle school. Kareem, an overcomer, became the first success story in UCF's proud history of shaping and saving young people's lives. He was a 2002 graduate from Magruder High School with the dream of becoming an Educator and Coach. We are so proud of his perseverance in overcoming several obstacles to complete his Education Degree from Fayetteville State University, North Carolina, in 2011 and a master's degree in 2017 from Liberty University. He is living his dream as an educator with Montgomery County Public School District. His success had a far-reaching impact on other young males in the program who looked up to Kareem as a role model. His success significantly impacted other males buying into the UCF program to promote student success, compete, and do the necessary academic work to achieve their goals of becoming the next success story.

In middle school, David Hayes was one young male who paid attention and corrected his approach in high school. I helped him press through a challenging adolescent journey where he found his identity in a house full of sisters where he was the only boy. A maturing David, Timothy to Kareem, changed his mental mind map and shifted his behavior to reach his full potential. David, my 'mini-me," now serves as Paul, an example to other young males as an Educator in the Virginia public school system.

What if each person is responsible for mentoring «one person» to nurture, affirm, change trajectory, and be accountable for connecting a young person to their destiny? What a better world if you step up your mentoring engagement efforts! Who is the one that you add your value to, the one you inspire to pursue excellence in reaching their potential? – Who is your one?

What is mentorship and what is it about?

Overall, it's defined as: "a relationship in which a more experienced or more knowledgeable person helps to guide, influence, or give direction to a less experienced or less knowledgeable person. As I Googled "mentorship," as most will no doubt know, the more "bookish" components of mentorship have four stages: preparation, negotiating, enabling growth, and closure; and four key roles: Consultant, Counselor, Coach, and Cheerleader. Mentoring is about establishing roles and responsibilities, connecting to a new perspective, and creating consistent winning habits as a mentee.

I learned over my life from years of field experience in working, especially with the youth; the basic train of thought that I begin with is <u>that everyone is</u> unique—everyone has wisdom and information to share with others. The mentoring approach and application to mentoring <u>each</u> person must also be unique to *their* needs. With some youths — this may be accomplished merely through "words/listening," while with others, it may be through specific leading by example (s); and, yet, with some others, it may be "tough love." Or it may require a combination of all three plus much more. But the bottom line is that this approach and process must begin with a committed, caring, and loving spirit—especially where our youth is concerned.

In addition to you being responsible for "one" person, "each one reaches one," I believe a person should be intentional about expanding their thinking to have more than one mentor. You cannot do it alone to live a higher quality of life in the 21st century, especially into adulthood. I highly encourage you to develop "trusted relationships" by selecting four mentors on your life journey. To aid in your life growth and development, you should have a spiritual mentor, accountability mentor, financial mentor, and emotional mentor (who keeps it real and tells it straight).

In life, there are difficulties. There are many benefits to having a spiritual mentor. A <u>spiritual mentor</u> can be someone who believes in you despite your shortcomings. When the road gets rough, and the hills are hard to climb, when you feel lost or stuck, and your life appears confusing, there are many benefits to having someone to encourage you from a spiritual perspective. Each arrives at a significant defining point of our lives where you need someone on your team to serve as your <u>accountability partner</u>. This person can help you keep your eye, focus on God, remind you of your value in Christ, and encourage you to continue your journey. You must surround yourself with people who will help you grow, develop to be productive, and walk in victory.

You will need a <u>financial mentor</u> who cares about you and wants the best for you. This person can help you reach your financial goals sooner by providing advice and strategies to create wealth. Before the road gets tough, you need someone on your team to plan for your short-term and long-term financial goals before you feel lost or stuck. They might advise on investments, tax, and insurance and how to leverage credit, including buying a home, paying for your children's education, and retirement.

On this mentoring journey, as a soldier, coach, and mentor, I have learned everyone always needs a cheerleader, <u>an emotional mentor</u> who provides uplift. As humans, we innately desire to receive affirmation, to be encouraged, and to encourage someone else.

You will need an accountability person on your team who "keeps it real" and a mentor who tells it straight. Having a person who you feel can be candid with you no matter what. Someone who doesn't sugarcoat or skirt the challenges and issues can keep you on track to achieve your goals.

In the age of technology, we stay in communication by texting each other daily and weekly. You can use a weekly 30-minute check-in via Zoom, phone, or FaceTime if you can't meet in person.

A mentor's role is unselfish! Mentors look beyond your shortcomings and have your best interest at heart. Mentors are committed to connecting others to their destiny, which is truly important. Mentors see something in you that you possibly don't see in yourself.

To mentor is about dreams, passion, giving back, <u>and</u> reaching back. And to commit to all of this to strengthen your community — where you live and work!

<u>Why Mentorship Is Important?</u>

First, you need to know what mentorship is about. The definition centers on trusted relationships: "a relationship in which a more experienced or knowledgeable person helps to guide, influence, counsel or give direction to a less experienced or less knowledgeable person." The most valuable aspect of being a mentor is consistency. Your presence in young people's lives is significant to help them build trusted relationships and achieve personal goals.

Mentoring relationships, especially youth mentoring, tends to be voluntary. You can't save or connect with everyone without a reciprocal intent and expect successful outcomes. A mentor helps someone to learn and develop faster than they would otherwise. The mentoring relationship focuses on future aspirations and provides guidance and advisement to help a person achieve goals, good or bad. Creating an atmosphere based on "trusted relationships" is extremely important for a young person's growth where validation occurs.

A friend of mine shared that in his youth, he had good and bad mentors. He describes a cousin that got him in all kinds of trouble. He was exposed to street trouble, where he earned "street cred." He found himself doing various things, from selling drugs, stealing, getting arrested, and spending time in and out of jail. It dawned on him that hanging out with his cousin, flunking out of school, not being responsible, and getting into trouble was not fun. He learned the experience from his cousin of what not to do!

Equally important, those actions in his youth didn't improve nor move his life forward positively. His cousin, whom he loved, taught him what not to do. He decided to discontinue the destructive pattern of getting in trouble year after year and to go a different way.

He gave an example of a good mentor who was in and out of his life. His dad was in the military to provide for his family. His father's lengthy tours in the Navy caused him to be out of his life from time to time. However, when he was able to stay with his dad, he stated the most important thing he learned from him was that "a man handles his responsibility for free," meaning you don't get paid to do what you are supposed to do. Being responsible and accountable is what a young person becoming a young adult is supposed to be. For example, he was going to school, turning in his homework assignments on time, being prepared, getting good grades, hygiene wellness, keeping his room clean, doing chores, and making his bed every day. You do all of this for free because being responsible and accountable for your actions is what you should do!

Many students who cross our path get good grades, but if they have a mentor, their grade point average increase is even more noticeable. Many students wander the school hallways, needing to be more responsible, having no dreams, goals, or future aspirations. However, if they have a mentor, their present makes sense, and their pursuit of accomplishing goals secures their future for living a higher quality of life. I have found that countless students get good grades; however, they have a low aim, little confidence, and low self-esteem, resulting in low living without guidance to achieve future goals.

Mentor's Leadership Guidepost (Know Your Alphabets)

1. 5As: Accountability, Availability, Approachable, Academic Improvement, Accessibility opportunities to make a difference on your life journey
2. 3Bs: Be, Better, Best, (Mantra that my mom instilled) "Good, Better, Best - Never let it rest until your good is better and your better is best"
3. 5Cs: Commitment, Competence, Critical Thinking, Communication, and Collaboration
4. 5Ds: Dream, Discipline, Determination, Direction, and Dedication
5. 5Es: Engaging, Embracing, Encouraging, Equipping, and Empowering others to be the best version of themselves and live up to the highest possibilities
6. 5Ps: Preparation is essential for living an impactful and meaningful life. The acronym I learned during my time in the military was the 5Ps—Proper Planning Prevents Poor Performance
7. 5Ws: Who, Why, What, Where and When in planning youth activities

Again, mentoring matters; mentoring works, and mentoring saves lives. Mentorship plays a critical role in young people's lives and helps them create a pathway to learn and develop faster than they would otherwise.

What A Mentor Isn't?

I believe parents are the first role models and teachers who impact and influence children's lives positively or negatively. Your children learn how to act and behave by what they see and learn from their mothers and father's behavior, modeling their examples. I tell parents and mentors alike to be mindful that one day, your sons and daughters will follow your example and not your advice.

I want to be clear on what a mentor is not. A mentor is not a substitute or replacement for a parent. A mentor is a team member who works with mothers, dads, grandparents, guardians, etc., in the growth and development of children. In this new environment of co-parenting and blended families from previous marriages, the top priority must be for a child's wellness, self-esteem, confidence, building, growth, and development. As a parent, you shouldn't harbor any ill feelings of resentment, intimidation, or the wrong thinking that a mentor is a replacement threat. It's truly about the child or children receiving the village's best. If only one young person benefits from being mentored by the village or mentoring program, it's worth it!

Mentors working collaboratively with parents and guardians must focus on creating winning habits to make hope happen and win in life! As society attempts to move beyond the COVID pandemic, you must actively participate in your children's early healthy development. First, you need to work with your child in early pre-kindergarten development to master the basics, such as sign words and sounding out letters, which leads to word recognition and reading. Parents are their children's first teachers and role models; all eyes are on you! It would help significantly if you worked with your child to establish a foundation during early childhood development to prepare them to be ready to learn. I trace mentoring challenges to early childhood development that puts children at a disadvantage and risk due to unpreparedness to learn in kindergarten and first grade. Specifically, academic readiness begins with you working with your child's literacy, colors, and numbers recognition, and writing fundamentals. My message for parents is that they must be diligent, involved, and committed to the healthy development of their children early on.

I also want to be clear to those wanting to be mentors: You cannot be a part-time mentor of convenience. Young people's lives are at stake every day, and their destiny is on the line! It is a disservice to a young person to only show up when you are ready to mentor. A mentor listens, cares about young people, and works with them on self-improvement. A mentor helps work through a child's anxiety and sickness and difficult situations such as COVID-19, bullying, unfair treatment, and peer pressure.

Whatever the challenges that are distracting and throwing our youth off track, a good mentor can be that person who can help our youth succeed. The mentor might be the person whose message reaches and significantly changes the student's attitude. Yes, a mentor might deliver the same message as parents, but the mentee receives the message positively. Parents must learn to embrace the mentors as team member that adds value for reinforcing the parent's message.

Young people still have options, even now in the season of uncertainty. Some of the significant mentoring challenges or achievement barriers consist of abandonment, rejections, and disappointments. All these barriers hinder growth and development regarding low self-esteem, lack of motivation, argumentative attitudes, a lack of respect for authority, defiance, and disobedient behavior. If these issues are not addressed, any one of these can have a negative and far-reaching impact on children's lives as they navigate adolescence. The outcome causes them to be fearful, lose hope, and develop a defeatist or victim mentality. Therefore, if you are not "all in" as a mentor, take the "L" and move on!

Don't become a mentor if you can't be there for a child as they navigate through adolescence. I'd rather you fail at the beginning of becoming a mentor than show up to develop a "trusted relationship" only to quit and abandon a young person." All children must be protected from the experiences of abandonment, rejection, and disappointments, for these have a lasting impact on life.

Here is a story about two young boys who grew up together as next-door neighbors. One house was a family of four with a mother, father, sister, and brother. The next-door neighbor was a single parent with a son. The mother abided by a court order that required the father to spend time with his son. The son looked forward to spending time with his father every other weekend, but his father needed to be more consistent with showing up to spend time with him. This little boy had experienced this kind of disappointment on many occasions. He shared the feeling of his father's chronic lateness, not showing up, and showing up with excuses, i.e., "I had to work, something came up," etc.

One summer day, the family of four was scheduled for vacation, planning to leave at noon. On the same day, the next-door neighbor's son would be picked up by his father early in the morning. The time came and went, 8 a.m., 9 a.m., 10 a.m. through 12 noon, and once again, the young boy looked out the window waiting patiently for his father to pick him up. He had spent the whole week excited, talking about what they would do, and he looked forward to this weekend with his father. You know the rest of the story!

His next-door neighbor sympathized and invited the young boy to vacation with their family. They had a wonderful time together on the family vacation. However, the single mother recognized the need to seek a mentor to help build her son's confidence and self-esteem. You cannot discount the long-term collateral damage children experience from abandonment, rejection, betrayal, unfair treatment, and disappointment caused by parenting.

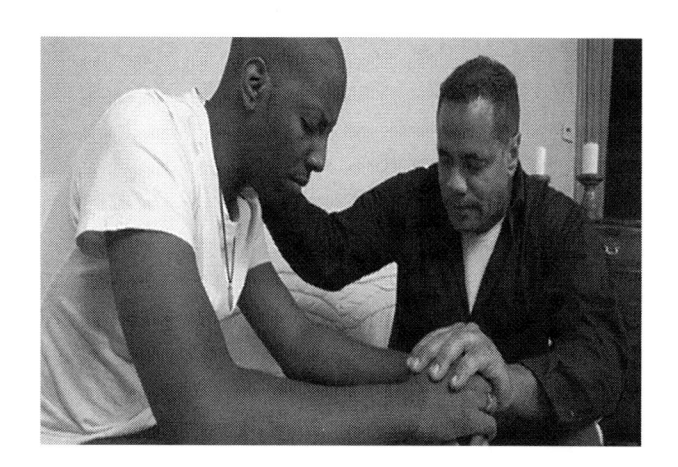

Mentoring is Serious Business!

Mentoring is serious business; your impact is crucial to young people's social and emotional growth, building trusted relationships, and teaching life skills. I implore you only to become a mentor if you are committed fully.

How will you use your influence with the individuals you are mentoring? How will you develop "authentic relationships" to lead young people through these difficult times? Yes, things sometimes look worse before they get better; there are situations that young people are pressing through that look crazy – don't give up on them or give in. One of my mentors always said things always look better in the morning.

Parents, grandparents, and all those responsible for our youth, I encourage you to diligently plan your child's educational success from Pre-K, elementary school, middle school and high school, college, and beyond. Parents, especially Dads, must be presence and involved with their children's developmental activities. The goal should be creating special memories such as classroom visits, reading opportunities, and taking photos with your children at sporting events and extracurricular activities. To the young men who are fathers and first-time Dads, you don't have to be perfect; just be present and love your children unconditionally. Fatherhood is one of the greatest gifts in life!

As I digress, stay in your children's lives no matter what; your legacy is on the line. Be an effective parent that is approachable, available, affectionate, and accessible. Be there for your children and focus forward regarding family planning.

Family Planning Hand-off: Track & Field Analogy

I suggest that the focus for your family is to teach winning habits early on so that your children run their race with meaningful purpose. Parents, Grandparents, and guardians focus on positioning your children for the first three steps coming out of the track starting block.

I use the track analogy coming out of the block before pre-kindergarten, preparing for middle and high school, and preparing to enter the workforce, military, or college.

As the world rapidly shifts, family planning must intentionally prepare members to succeed through proper preparation (5Ps).

For each generation, creating winning habits will always be that education is the passport to improve a person's quality of life. Your education and ability to learn new skills is a small investment for a significant return! Young people must elevate their thinking, make good choices daily, pursue resources early on to secure their footing, and set their pace to do their best.

Life is like a relay race; as you enter the next Chapter of your life after high school, your family or support group has set you up to receive the hand, and we are counting on you to focus forward and run the race that is set before you. Run your leg of the relay race to the best of your abilities.

We encourage young people to pursue excellence in education, whether working toward a certificate or degree or succeeding during the employment probation in their next station of life. We count on you to run your race, not looking at the person to the left or right. We encourage families and mentors to help young people run the race with intellectual skills, historical perspectives, talents, and gifts. When running your race, do your very best, do what is necessary to close the gap, or increase the distance to finish the race. You are in it to Win it!

Leadership and Mentorship Philosophy Is Important

STACEY JORDAN (A GIFT GIVER OF LOVE -TEAMWORK).

I desire to make sure you think about mentoring in a new and effective way. I tell our young people and adults that I don't want you to think what I think. You can establish a mentorship program by sharing your life experiences as a leader. Mentoring is about helping young people think differently by changing their mindset and consistently establishing winning habits. I don't want to teach you what to think; it's about thinking purposefully and strategically that will yield positive outcomes for the next generation.

I heard a sermon by Bishop T.D. Jakes used Psalm 23 to emphasize living your life with purpose. I shared in an earlier chapter about my life-changing heart attack. Psalm 23 is the scripture that I repeated while being rescued at Harpers Ferry Mountain. My talk with my God on the mountain floor bed at Harpers Ferry awakened a sense of purpose where I knew God was directing me. I have learned that life is not a straight line. There will be twists and turns, setbacks, and disappointments. Those occurrences are mountains to climb and valleys to cross to reach your purpose. When you trust Him, God will push you forward, give direction, put you in a position, and elevate you for His purpose.

Bishop Jakes stated, "God will give you divine favor and launch you forward beyond human comprehension." I believe every young person has a destiny with greatness locked inside them. There is greatness inside of you, and at a young age, sometimes the attack comes at an early age. Things like destructive behavior and trying to fit in with those who lack the motivation to do the necessary work to achieve and pursue excellence. Don't give up, don't throw in the towel, stop dumbing down, and don't rely on the small-mindedness of your friends to deter you from your destiny.

If you had to fight and struggle all your life, this might be a sign of greatness locked inside you. Do not limit your vision to your situation. You must go through a process; your current situation may not indicate what God will do in your life. The least likely person to accomplish amazing things could be you in your normal state. God sets it up so that when you win, there isn't any question about how you got to do what you did. He uses ordinary people to do extraordinary things. I encourage you to confidently walk through the doors of faith to live in your purpose! Do you know what time it is? Young people, "It's time to level up, set up, and stand up!"

Bishop Jakes states there are primarily two categories of people. Most people get out of bed to see what is going to happen. Others get out of bed to make something happen. In life, you must decide which category you will be in. Do you sit on the side of the bed saying, "Lord What am I going to do today?" Or are you going to wake up with a positive agenda? Are you going to sit on the side of the bed excited to get at it with a determined mindset, a clear focus, and direction? When you have a clear direction, you resist distractions. You know what or what isn't on your agenda.

Successful mentoring programs must be anchored in a vision and connected to a mentoring philosophy. I believe vision is defined as sight beyond what one can see. Mentors are able to see things in a young person's life that they cannot see themselves. I always say that I am not looking at where you are now; I am looking at where you can be and the endless possibilities of what you can become if you put in the work! Mentors help people see the endless possibilities and then guide them to use youthful energy to accomplish their goals.

VISION-- We agreed that our first action is to look up to God and pray. The second action is to look forward to developing a strategic action plan and trust God for specific directions and next steps. Working together, we learned that when God gives you a vision, He will provide the provision and the pathway forward.

At the center of my leadership philosophy and guiding principles is teamwork. I have learned that no one person can accomplish anything significant alone. Building trusted relationships by showing up and being consistent, committed, and fully engaged is essential.

As a leader, you must be able to pull like-minded individuals together to pursue a common goal. I have learned that no one follows the ordinary, only the extraordinary. I share with mentors and youth alike to be extraordinary, stop trying to fit in, and stand out! If you want to fit in, understand you have the gifts, skills, and talents needed as you pursue your destiny. It takes courage to be extraordinary and to do the hard work, apply yourself, and work to be the best version of yourself right now in elementary school, middle school, and high school. Here is a road map that offers strategies to establish a successful mentoring program.

Mentors help students develop critical thinking and social skills in problem-solving, encourage ongoing learning and academic achievement, and provide positive, life-enriching experiences for students who cross their paths. Everyone needs mentoring at some point in their life. Also, your continued personal growth will be predicated on multiple mentors to help you live your best life purposefully.

I will share some basic leadership thoughts about building a successful mentoring program. I will share some traits, ideas, values, and beliefs on how a leader should establish a mentoring program. Do you recall your first mentor? Who was the first person who affirmed and believed in you? Do you remember the name of your first two mentors and the age at which you received your first affirmation, inspiration, and confirmation? Who was the last person who affirmed you in your growth and development season? What traits do you remember about the mentor(s) in your life?

Observation and Assessment:

As a mentor and program leader, you must assess each person being mentored individually. It would help if you recognized that no two people are alike; each young person is uniquely and wonderfully made differently, with unique gifts and talents hidden inside them. A mentor must be understanding, committed, take a personal interest, and listen actively in developing a welcoming environment that creates a trusted sense of belonging for all mentees.

As a mentor, it is advantageous to assess, conduct an environmental scan, observe situations, refrain from prejudging, and be sensitive and aware of the mentee's situation, culture, the language used to communicate, etc. Share your experiences from 12 to 22 to establish a baseline encouraging students to open up. Help them realize that they can accomplish anything they put their minds to do. There is a quote I grew up with in my youth that served as a guidepost, "If my mind can conceive it, and my heart can believe it, I know I can achieve it." —Reverend Jesse L. Jackson, Sr., politician and civil rights activist.

A Mentor's Traits for a Successful Program:

My leadership experiences in building a successful mentoring program include these traits: mutual accountability, honesty, authenticity/sincerity, openness, and life skill competence. You must be firm to help students first believe in themselves and help them reach their personal goal achievement. Please use what you can to enhance your mentoring program. People in leadership positions who go through the motions without caring are barriers to success. Anyone who works directly with young people understands that children recognize "fake" versus a person sincerely caring about them! Young people want adults who add value and truly care about them. A good friend who professes to be a rapper says, "No books, no brains, no love, no learning! The more you learn, the more you earn! Love makes the difference!"

Mutual Accountability: Be honest, authentic, open, and firm:

Since UCF's inception, a cornerstone trait has been respect and honesty in all undertakings and interactions. UCF impressed young people with the same values we instilled in raising my family.

Nothing but the truth, and we will sort out the pathway forward together when you get in troubled waters. I recall Coach Brown and my mentor shared that coaching, like mentoring, is like a two-edged sword, as 98% of students will listen and embrace your mentoring with positive outcomes. However, there will always be 2% of young people who will only buy in some of the ways and eventually get in trouble.

As a mentor, you must be prepared for those moments of truth and consequences when your youth gets themselves in trouble. The established relationship will be on display at that moment. The trait that rises to the top will be based on mutual trust and accountability, and students must be held accountable for telling the truth, no matter what. Your mentee must be honest with you in all dealings so you can be a change agent who can prayerfully make a difference that yields positive outcomes when young people find themselves in a pinch.

In our early days of UCF meetings, as a communication exercise, we would go around the room and ask students to share one good thing and one bad thing that occurred during the week. We wanted to teach young people that they had control of the good experiences and the bad encounters. More importantly, we desired to teach students how to communicate respectfully and what to say in an honest tone, such as, "My intent is," "I intend to be open and forthright about this situation," or "These are the hard facts."

Successful mentors must operate on the premise of "trust what you see" and "past performance is an indicator as well as an opportunity for a mentor to intervene to proceed accordingly." The great poet Maya Angelo said it this way. "When people show you who they are, believe them."

I cannot emphasize enough the importance of mentors to impress young people and to tell the truth in a verifiable way. We encourage our young people to refrain from telling only half the story, leaving out pertinent facts to hide/withhold information covering the truth, or creating illusions for distractions! Young people, once you lie, misrepresent the truth, and intentionally mislead by not providing all the information or giving alternative facts, you make it extremely difficult to regain trust. Being deceitful is flat-out wrong and leads to yielding adverse outcomes and results!

Whoever said it is worth repeating: "Life is 10% what happens to you and 90% your response." The same thing happens to all of us in one way, shape, or form. Our response to what happens to or around us differentiates us.

I have experienced many situations advocating for young people who got themselves in trouble in the military, on basketball teams, and on this mentoring journey. My key message to mentors is to continuously operate from a place of modeling excellence so young people won't be confused by what they see in you as a leader. Mentors at the moment can be sympathetic to the mentee; however, you must be straight, authentic, and talk truth to establish what occurred.

It is not a question of if your student gets in trouble; it's when they get in trouble. My mentor always stated, "Show me your five friends, and I will tell you your future." As a mentor, I want my mentees to be smart and display sound judgment to help them navigate difficult situations when they get into trouble. We want our students to be the leader instead of the follower so that they can be the voice of reason before something goes awry! Speaking up and saying that's not a good idea that will derail our future or land us in jail!

I recently had a student captured on the school's camera, violating the school's code of conduct. The student was asked to share his account of what occurred, and instead of telling the truth, he chose to lie and misrepresent his actions that were displayed on the school camera. There is a song with the lyrics, "It's hard to keep up with all of them lies." The actions captured on the school camera are like my experience serving on a jury. The jury members saw the criminal activities on the recorded video camera. The game was essentially over despite the person never having a record of causing any trouble.

Every time you lie, you mortgage your future, and while it is not impossible, it is tough to earn back your creditability. The view others have will now be different in future dealings. You must realize that your actions, good or bad, define you. In the school setting, folks will tell others who you are, how you treat others, and how you act in the classroom. They will ask if you are a good or bad student regarding completing your school assignments. In a sporting environment, folks will tell others whether you are a good or bad team member or leader.

As much as you want to help your mentee get out of the troubled situation, Mentors must operate on the premise of "believing what you see." A mentor's added value is when a youth in trouble and a mutually trusted relationship intersect. Your mentee must know that your relationship established from the very beginning is a "safe space." A best practice for building a mentoring program is to incorporate a community service project to help young people understand that they are a part of something larger than themselves. UCF works to connect young people to existing community resources operated by local churches, food distribution sites, other mentoring organizations, and church ministries that work with homeless shelters. Consider teaming with like-minded organizations to be helping hands at an adult living center. Seek volunteer experiences for your students in organizations such as A Wider Circle and Habitat for America. What a joy it is to see student's faces light up when you have them meet on a Saturday to go and help provide services for others.

What I like about exposing students to community service activities is the opportunity for leadership development, planning, organizing, etc. Young people, including parents, teachers, and friends, must be encouraged to participate in the planning process. UCF has found that community service engagement produces positive outcomes, such as youth confidence, teamwork, and humility, that promote caring for each one to help their fellow man or woman. Youth development makes a difference!

Life Skills Matter:

Since UCF's inception, life skills have been at the center of promoting student success with year-around enrichment youth development programs. The ability of young people to communicate effectively and respectfully will always be critical to students' future success. We conducted a communication exercise in UCF's early years emphasizing interactive listening. An interactive session on listening to our young males as they shared their one success and one challenge during a specific period. The exercise taught mentors to put their "listening ears" on to absorb the youth's words with their eyes and heart. While listening, we learned to better understand without assuming we knew what mattered to them and, most of all, not to presume we had all the answers or knew all the questions! This was an effective exercise for the mentor and mentee to learn to repeat what they heard. "What I hear you saying is…" or "let me make sure I understand what you're trying to say." As you reflect on your relationships, many of us listen without understanding. We tend to instead "listen" only to formulate a reply and pretend to listen to push our agendas.

Be human, sincere, relatable and, most of all, respectful:

In addition to LOVE, the world needs humanity more than anything. We impress upon our young people to be confident, thoughtful, genuinely care for others, and demonstrate that they care with acts of kindness and spreading love by doing good deeds. We do this through our community engagement projects that are lovely exposure experiences for our young people. As mentioned above, some projects included the March of Dimes for Babies, the annual MLK Memorial Breakfast, MLK Day of Service, and recently, the Flags for Heroes sponsored by the Rotary Clubs during Memorial Day tributes.

The teachable message is to treat everyone with respect, civility, and dignity, especially those who can't do anything for you. Show kindness in the little things. Don't fake caring, respect, and concern for other people. Planting seeds is the desired outcome of these experiences. We want our young people to walk away thinking, "I am glad for the chance to work with you," or "I respect and appreciate you." Let's work on showing respect in all situations!

Be alert and aware, use straight talk, and think:

Our young people must be around the right people who have their best interests at heart. Young people have the responsibility to choose their friends carefully. This can be challenging when navigating adolescence and the peer pressure of wanting everyone to like you.

Mentors play a serious role in educating future leaders and giving insight into significant historical turning points. We need mentors to connect mentees to their history. UCF intentionally challenges youth to learn and connect their family history to American history. We ensure students and families understand that Black History is American History. Someone down their ancestry line survived being chained to other human beings for several months during the Middle Passage to become enslaved and free labor in building a prosperous America. UCF encourages young people to chart a pathway to become history makers themselves.

Mentors must stay connected, alert, and aware throughout the mentoring journey to prepare and equip young people for future challenges tied to deeply rooted racial policies, practices, and unfair laws from a painful history. As a mentor, I encourage you to acknowledge the unsaid, address the challenging issues directly, and confront them before they become significant problems in your mentoring efforts. UCF addresses those issues to teach young people acceptable and unacceptable behavior and consequences. Young people cannot bury their heads in the sand, ignore facts, and skirt real problems and social media stories.

For example, flash mobs have gained polarity among young people, where a group of students rushes into a store in a large group for disruption and stealing. Another example was the verbal and physical assault by Will Smith, slapping Chris Rock in front of a national television audience at the 2022 Oscar Awards. The moment was seen by 12 million people, including our youth. How many mentors addressed the incident with their mentees about the violence one black man inflicted on another over something he didn't like hearing?

As mentors, stay alert, stay aware, conduct straight talk and rap sessions, and encourage our youth to be intentional about learning to think. Our thinking affects everything we do. How we think determines our character, attitudes, and actions. Learning how to THINK is extremely important. It is not like going to the dentist – thinking isn't painful! Someone once said, "there is nothing you do that you don't think about." It starts with a thought. Our future leaders require a generation to THINK about improving your family, this community, and the world.

Be consistent, flexible, keep commitments, and be there:

As mentors, parents, and leaders, we must encourage young people to move from listening to leading with positive actions to improve our community. This is accomplished by keeping your commitments and being a consistent presence in youth activities that children are involved in. We must learn to mitigate the feeling of abandonment and disappointment of being let down.

We want our young people to learn to say what they will do and then execute what they say they will do. Make commitments carefully, including implicit obligations, and keep them at all costs. Create a performance track record for keeping promises, being consistent, and being present as a symbol of your character and honor. I want to ask ten years from now, "will I be glad I keep this commitment instead of that one? We ask our young people to think about committing in such a way that "is this a commitment I want to make? Can I follow through on this, and can I deliver?"

Your role as a mentor must ensure that young people are not alone in dealing with today's many challenges and pitfalls as they navigate adolescence. You must be able to talk the language, know the culture, and empathize with your young people. That means researching and understanding the problems, challenges, and concerns. Know what is happening in the general environment of your block, borough, township, county, and community. Speak with other mentors who have mentoring programs to witness how their meetings are conducted and how students respond and note the mentoring style/approach used to help young people.

One of the most valuable resources is our young people. They want the same things. Many of us grew up with an adult in their lives who listens to their thoughts and ideas, someone to be honest with, and a space to share and receive straight talk. Today's most important aspect of mentoring this generation is spending quality time and providing social and emotional assurance and support so that young people will know that they matter and their life counts! Today›s youth need mentors who will be «dream inspirers, « not «dream breakers.»

A STORY WITH A KEY MESSAGE: Eagle Story

Here is an inspirational story to encourage you to live up to the highest possibility of your potential and to give your best every day. What charactcristics do you know about an eagle? Yes, some say it is a symbol of strength, power, freedom, courage, and honor. Did you know that juvenile eagles are dark-colored brown with dark heads and bear no resemblance to adult bald eagles with white heads? Second, the eagle is fearless and will never surrender to the size or strength of its prey. It will always give a fight to win. Thirdly, the eagle is tenacious. Watch an eagle when a storm comes. When other birds fly away from the storm with fear, an eagle spreads its mighty wings and uses the current to soar to greater heights. Challenges in the life of a leader are many: new promotions, new levels, etc. Know that there will be new challenges! As a leader, you must rise to greater heights if you take up the challenges head-on without running away.

A story is told about a man on vacation on an island who was interested in buying a chicken. He asked around and was told about the chicken man. He had a chicken farm on the outskirts of the island. The visitor located the chicken man's farm and knocked on the door. The chicken man came to the door and walked with him to the chicken coop. The visitor looked around the crowded chickens in the cage and spotted a bird in the crowd that didn't look much like a chicken. The visitor told the chicken man, "That there is not a chicken." The visitor asked to pick up the bird and exclaimed, "That is not a chicken; it is an eagle." The chicken man emphatically exclaimed, "Oh no, that there is a chicken." The other man replied, "I will show you he's an eagle." So, the man picked up the bird; the bird looked at him. The visitor held it up near his shoulder level, then let it go, and the bird dropped to the ground and went back among the crowd. Again, the visitor asked to pick up the bird, held it above his head, and then let go. Once again, the bird dropped and went back among the crowd.

The visitor then picked up the bird, climbed the ladder to the barn's roof, and whispered a message in the bird's ear. He threw the bird up high in the air, and it began to flap its wings and took flight into the air. The chicken man was amazed and couldn't believe his eyes. He asked, "What did you whisper in the bird's ear?" The other man said, "I whispered to the bird to stop acting like a chicken and be what God created you to be!"

The message is that there are gifts inside of each of you. You have greatness inside of you. I encourage you to commit to excellence and improve yourself every day. I tell students, "You are responsible for getting better every day and improving yourself by learning a new skill." Commit to pursuing excellence to reach your full potential. Stop faking, and stop being afraid to take a risk and fail. We need this generation with the most potential not to be underachievers and be extraordinary!

- The message is that there are gifts inside of each of you. You have greatness inside of you. I encourage you to commit to excellence and improve yourself every day. I tell students, "You are responsible for getting better every day and improving yourself by learning a new skill." Commit to pursuing excellence to reach your full potential. Stop faking, and stop being afraid to take a risk and fail. We need this generation with the most potential not to be underachievers and be extraordinary!
- Your parents are not supposed to be your friends. Your parents are supposed to say "no" and yes to your requests only sometimes. My three-year-old grandson doesn't like to hear the word "no," so he folds his arms and stands in place with a frown. Saying "no" is good; it means a new opportunity to make a better decision and teaches discipline! Students live up to the highest possibility of their potential.

What makes the eagle so important and symbolic to humanity is its characteristics.

Eagles symbolize beauty, bravery, courage, grace, pride, determination, and honor. We want students, parents, and leaders to fight to win, live up to the highest possibility of their potential, and become the best version of themselves. What are you doing today, right now, to change the direction of your life and family? You are responsible for improving every day by learning new skills and giving a winning effort in everything you do. We need our young people to be tenacious, fearless, leaders, problem solvers, attentive, and caring for others.

Mentors must help our young people become eagles and not complain like chickens. You can be a helping hand for this generation who have been affected with so much more at a young age than you and I at the same age. Like the eagle, we must show them how to give a winning effort. As mentors, we must guide and show them the way forward when our young people face challenges, problems, setbacks, and failure. We must uplift and encourage them to face issues head-on and hear God's voice whispering in their ear, "You ought to be what God created you to be!"

To the leaders, stakeholders, and decision-makers, challenges in one's life are many, and indeed, as a leader, the challenges are abundant. I want our mentors and young people to understand that either you are getting ready to go into a storm or coming out of a storm. When troubles and storms come your way, rise to greater heights like an eagle.

Like an eagle, a leader can only rise to greater heights if he takes up the challenges head-on without running away from them. See it through when confronted; don't let your nerves desert you! Please don't give up whatever you do; see it through!

Lastly, did you know the crow is the only bird that will peck at an eagle? The crow will sit on the eagle's back and bite his neck. The eagle does not respond or fight with the crow; it doesn't waste time or energy on the crow. It simply opens its wings and begins to rise higher in the sky. The higher the flight, the harder it is for the crow to breathe, and then the crow falls off due to the lack of oxygen. Stop wasting your time with crow-like people. Just take them to your height, and they'll fade.

QUOTE:

Children have never been very good at listening to their elders, but they have never failed to imitate them.

— James Baldwin

SCRIPTURE:

When a man's ways are pleasing to the Lord, he makes even his enemies live at peace with him.

Proverbs 16:7

CHAPTER 18

HOW TO START A MENTORING PROGRAM?

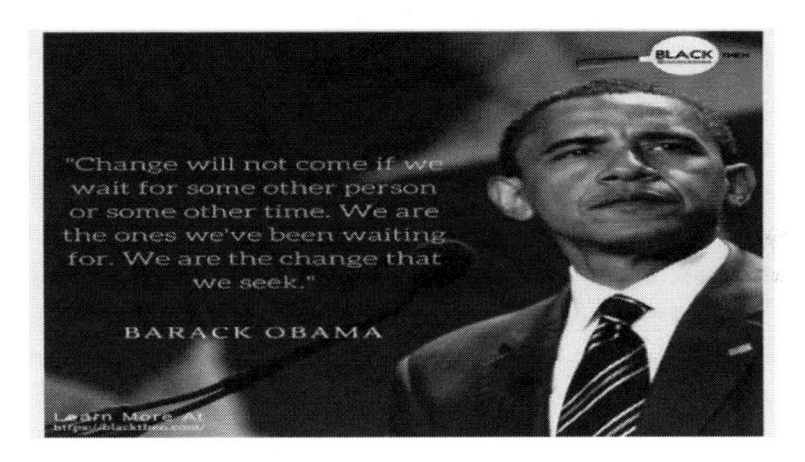

> "Change will not come if we wait for some other person or some other time. We are the ones we've been waiting for. We are the change that we seek."
>
> BARACK OBAMA

The most important thing we can do is to invest in our children, all of them, model decency, display integrity and walk in love. The foundation of every state is the education of its youth!

— UNKNOWN

So you want to be a Mentor?

Wake up, everybody! Take this golden opportunity to establish a youth mentoring program in your community. What does it look like if you increase your engagement with this critical, meaningful, and purposeful mentoring work? If ever there was a time to step up to become a mentor and contribute to the success of our young people – it is now.

No matter how daunting it is to start a mentoring program, the task and challenges are not bigger than God.

Secondly, I wrote this book to inspire others to become mentors. For those who want to be "helping hands," how about joining others in your community who work directly with youth in mentoring organizations? This chapter aims to provide some battle-tested strategies for starting a mentoring program. I have learned to give not because I have much but because I know how having no direction or guidance feels. I am no stranger to adversity, and learning to overcome life circumstances from humble upbringings is used as motivational fuel to transcend circumstances. It is imperative in the post-pandemic era to encourage a new cadre of "mentors" to make hope happen by working with the next generation of young people. Mentoring is a contact sport; it will be essential for mentors and mentoring organizations to build trusted relationships that ignite, inspire, and encourage youth success. Mentoring creates a safe space that allows young people to dream big dreams, bloom, and blossom into success stories.

I encourage you to increase your mentoring commitment, engagement, and investment in the post-pandemic era. I always say that many hands make light work if you put your hand on the plow and pitch in. We are stronger, working together meaningfully to make a difference in children's lives. This chapter will be a guide to start a mentoring program or be an effective mentor.

Your heart will be touched to start your mentoring organization in your neighborhood or team up or work with established reputable youth organizations. Why? Because our communities are in crisis, and young people are crying out for help. If we don't do it now, then who will?

During the pandemic, two friends and advisors in high places shared their thoughts on the looming crisis in education. They warned that educational disparities before the COVID-19 pandemic surfaced, and senior executive administrators would focus on addressing recovery strategy plans. They warned students would be significantly impacted, especially with learning loss, the complexities of math, reading, and other social-emotional challenges.

Dr. Shawn Joseph predicted a colossal problem with literacy proficiency, currently at Howard University, Assistant Professor of Educational Leadership, Administration, and Policy, and former Superintendent of the Metro Nashville Public Schools in Tennessee and author of the first book, The Principal's Guide to the First 100 Days of the School Year: Creating Instructional Momentum, and the second book, Finding the Joseph Within.

With all that went on in the year 2020, we attempted to implement a reading program with a learning matrix across the 2nd District of our fraternity. We wanted to accomplish the following: 1) raise awareness and 2) build capacity and a standard way to measure performance.

Dr. Joseph, who started as a reading specialist, warned that students weren't reading on grade levels before the pandemic, even with special support programs designed to improve reading comprehension.

During the pandemic, our children were learning online at home but less than they had been when they were physically in the school building. All children, especially our males, were at the bottom end of academic performance in the virtual environment. Many studies show when our young people fall behind in reading, they never catch up, and the academic performance gap widens. I love the quote by Henry Adams, a 19th-century American historian, "teachers affect eternity; you can never tell where your influence stops." I go further; teachers, mentors, and anyone working directly with young people affect change and influence learning. The world in the post-pandemic reality and its difficult times need teachers who genuinely care, inspire, and impart valuable life-long lessons and experiences. Students will continue to struggle in recovery from learning loss unless a commitment to not look back but focus forward is made. Leaders must consider innovative approaches, new ideas, thinking, and methods to meet students where they are so they can be more competitive upon graduation.

Reading, literacy, and education are the passports to the future. Mentors and educators must work together to prepare young people for a new and different world that's changing rapidly. Students must embrace each course, experience, and interaction because it shapes them into the person they will become. All of us must be concerned with working with students and must play a role in closing the literacy gap! Are today's youth reading enough and reading at length in one setting? Are students reading in one setting for 2 or 3 hours and comprehending what they read?

UCF Class 2020

In April 2020, Dr. Leonard Haynes, former HBCU President, and White House executive, warned at the beginning of the pandemic that there would be a crisis in education with student's capacity to learn. He emphasized that students would need help to learn, and there would be significant challenges with learning using virtual platforms.

Dr. Haynes also warned about the emerging crisis nationwide with the critical shortages of educators, primarily Black and minority teachers of color. His why was based on the decline in bachelor's degrees conferred by higher education institutions. In addition to the growing attrition among current retirement educators in the next two to five years.

The National Education Association recently reported nationwide that 55% of educators said they were ready to retire earlier than expected. The silent crisis in education, the well-trained, senior, and qualified educators with experience who are critical for our country's future success are retiring. The report reflects that some common themes revolve around inadequate compensation and the teacher's curriculum requires increased workload demands.

Furthermore, today's young people are reluctant to pursue a degree to become a teacher and then work so long to pay off a student loan. Those who become teachers state family balance and mounting workload demands, psychological and mental concerns, and behavioral problems are challenges in classroom management. Another theme to sustaining the workforce is issues dealing with today's generation that are void of respect for authority, let alone teachers and school property. Educators have reported that the "risk factor" exists when breaking up assaults, not a fight! A kid punching another kid in the head four or five times is an assault. Kids stealing and destroying classroom equipment, rudeness, cursing and bullying teachers. Young educators state that the corrective measures you and I grew up with, such as keeping your hands to yourself, warning that I am going to call your mother or dad, communicating respectfully with adults, and conducting yourself to honor your family, don't work anymore. Many young teachers and senior teachers alike are not equipped to handle situations in which they are not trained to operate in the classroom. Why are schools across the country witnessing an increase in our youth disrespectfulness, aggressive behavior, property destruction, and disinterested students committed to pursue a quality education?

I believe the teaming arrangement between educators and mentor's relationships is like a pair of gloves, they go hand in hand with impacting and influence young people in the post-pandemic era. It is imperative to encourage a new cadre of mentors to work with community mentoring organizations. It will be essential for mentors and mentoring organizations to build trusted relationships, tutor floundering students, and teach critical thinking skills, both organizational and conflict resolution skills. Equally crucial in the mentoring arena will be providing social and emotional support for the last three years of the pandemic, where many uncommon and unusual events have impacted us all. Our students have been affected significantly, including a few challenges that lie ahead with reading, literacy, and math deficiencies, as well as gaps in organization skills from two years of isolation.

I want to inspire others to become mentors and join mentoring organizations to help students get back on track and reach their full potential. Mentors can help young people write a new reality and identify pathways forward. Our students must unmute themselves, reimagine themselves, and persevere to view and connect with a new world.

Our students must do their part in planning to move forward. Instead of tracking the number of likes on social media or placing their responses in the "chat," our students must stand up, speak up, speak out, use their voices, and use communication skills in this new reality. The reality of the new challenge for mentoring on the other side of the COVID-19 pandemic must be bold for those who work directly with young people. We must embrace new pathways and new ideas to be innovative. You must build trusted relationships, share your knowledge, and have students exchange their expertise and current life experiences at this very moment.

Mentoring diagram showing: One-on-One Mentoring, Group Mentoring, Peer Mentoring, Distance or E-Mentoring, Reverse Mentoring, Speed Mentoring.

Mentors have an excellent opportunity to help students reach their full potential in this season of transformation! Mentors must help young people understand that they can't stay stuck where they are and challenge them to do the necessary work to grow, improve and prepare for this new world that has emerged.

Our education system and students in the 21st century deserve a first-class middle and high school experience that prepares them to succeed in life such as college readiness or workforce-readiness education. Many of us grew up with the NAACP quote: A Mind is a Terrible Thing to Waste and, for the recent generations – A Great Thing to Invest In! Let's get started with the discussion of how to start a mentoring program or be an effective mentor.

Team Development and Mentoring Model:

When you Google the topic of mentoring, you will find different types of mentoring relationships, as shown above. The mentoring model used by UCF to mentor youth is the "group mentoring" model. This is the primary model used by many athletic teams and youth organizations that work with young people. I perfected my mentoring leadership style while coaching basketball for 25 years, instilling championship principles.

Mentoring Models or Techniques (Reference: What is Mentoring? (td.org))

One-on-One Mentoring: This type of mentoring is the most traditional. Only the mentor and mentee are involved, and it is usually a more-experienced individual paired with a less experienced or much younger mentee. An example is the community-based mentoring program Big Brothers Big Sisters› one-on-one model that matches children with an adult mentor. An example of this type of mentoring is tutoring services. UCF uses this mentoring when parents request additional help for their student to hone their English, math, or science skills to achieve higher scores on SAT/ACT Examination.

Group Mentoring: In this model, one or several mentors work with a group of mentees. Schools and youth programs often apply this model because there may need more time or resources to have one mentor for each participant. UCF uses this type of mentoring at our monthly meetings and the summer reading club, where one mentor works with several mentees individually to share wisdom, knowledge, or specific new skills.

Summer Reading Club with Jason Miller and Chuck Harris

Peer Mentoring: Participants in this model are from the same role or department or have shared or similar experiences in their professional or personal lives. These peers pair up to offer support to each other. This can be a group or a one-on-one mentoring relationship. This model is used by major companies such as Caterpillar, where a younger employee is paired up with more senior members for two to three years. As we press forward out of the pandemic, UCF has begun to use this model to encourage our older students to mentor those assigned to them, as we are our brother's keeper.

Distance or E-Mentoring: With advanced technology, the mentorship relationship no longer must be face-to-face. Using virtual applications, group texting, online software, or even email, participants in this type of mentoring can connect virtually without losing the personal touch. An example of this model was used during the pandemic when we all pivoted to virtual platforms to stay connected with students and each other. The pandemic created new pathways where students can be mentored from various locations.

Reverse Mentoring: This mentoring relationship is flipped from the traditional model. Instead of a senior professional mentoring a more junior employee, the junior employee mentors a more senior experienced. This relationship is usually for the younger or more junior professional to teach the skills or a new application or technology to the more senior one. UCF used this model before COVID during the MLK Day of Service when our students provided reverse mentoring, instructing the elders from an Adult Living Facility on using cell phone features and laptop computers.

Speed Mentoring: This type of mentoring is a play on speed dating and usually occurs as part of a corporate event or conference. The mentee has a series of one-on-one conversations with different mentors and usually moves from one mentor to the next after a brief meeting. The mentee should come prepared with questions for senior-level professionals' advice. UCF used this model at our Professional Career

Day for students to meet with professionals and ask career path-related questions. The objective was to expose students to exciting career fields, teach them networking skills, and how to conduct a 30-second interview. The first question is, "tell me about yourself." We wanted to encourage students to make good grades in school, allowing them to get a good job and earn a higher standard of living.

2017 MLK Service Day

1ST PROFESSIONAL CAREER DAY 2013

EXECUTIVE BOARD MAKING A DIFFERENCE

Step 1: Define Mission Statement & Goals:

You need to know your "why" and think through the main reasons for establishing a mentoring program. Write down your vision, mission statement, overall goals, and objectives, identify implied tasks, and map out the desired program structure. From an organizational point of view, will your mentoring program be all males? Or co-ed? What will be the mentor-to-mentee ratio?

Knowing your "why and reasons" is essential to developing an effective and impactful mentoring program. At all UCF retreats, we reviewed the mission statement, purpose, goals, objectives, and organizational structure. We are intentional about keeping organizational effectiveness in the forefront with the team members to focus on new strategic initiatives.

Secondly, how will you launch your program? Research, read, and visit other youth organizations to see how they operate. This is the same approach mentioned in Chapter 8, my basketball story, where I suggested you must be willing to put in the required work to increase

your knowledge base. I pursued knowledge by reading books, attending mentoring conferences, visiting other mentoring organizations, and seeking knowledge from leaders with successful programs.

Step 2: Team Development:

Many people with good intentions have tried establishing mentoring programs, only to fail because one needs help to do this heavy lifting. As a mentoring leader, you need responsible, reliable, and relatable teammates to help develop an effective mentoring program. Mentoring is a contact sport, meaning you and your mentors will be touching the hearts and minds of young people in their most vulnerable and emotional state of development. And for that reason, screening prospective mentors is critical in establishing a mentoring team. You must recruit, vet, and select persons matching the program's goals and mission. A top priority will be to choose a team that operates as one unit by identifying trusted persons for your team who will be an excellent fit to interact, connect, lead by example, and care about your mentees. A standard practice to screen for mentors is to ask interested members their "why" for wanting to be a mentor with your program. In addition, it is recommended that you document criteria requirements for both mentors and mentees to mitigate risk.

Step 3: Mentoring Program Design and Evaluation:

The trick here is to try and be as detailed as possible and "map out" your whole mentoring program from start to finish. What type of mentoring model will you use? Develop a schedule for the first three to six months that outlines the youth engagement plan. Design an application

for students and parents to complete, outlines roles and responsibilities, including a parent waiver form, ground rules for behavior conduct, and expectations.

What will your first session look like? Discuss it, see it, and rehearse it. You only get one opportunity to make a great first impression. I suggest you include ice-breaker activities designed to get students to feel comfortable with you and each other. As a planning tool, establish a schedule or timeline for each activity to ensure you keep the meeting moving and students engaged.

Your program plan for each meeting should include, as a minimum, basic information such as "Five Ws," **who** the meeting is targeted, **why** the meeting is conducted, **what** the purpose will be, **where** the sessions will be conducted, **when** the meeting is, frequency, and time. What are you looking to achieve from the mentoring program? How will you measure success? What will be your target audience, all males or co-ed? Will your program target early childhood development, middle school, high school, or a combination? What will be the commitment and expectation from participants?

Who will you partner with to reach, connect, and meet the needs of youth in your community? Are you going to reach out to a recreational department, Housing Opportunities Commission (HOC), Department of Health and Human Services (HHS), Department of Juvenile Service (DJS) or the public school district in your community?

What will be the topics and subject matters? What will be the objectives and outcomes achieved in the first three mentoring sessions? How will you get the message out for participants to sign up? How do you attract and recruit young people to your mentoring program? It would help if you also outlined what success could be for the mentees and mentors. How will you track, monitor, and measure performance?

There are a host of other questions to help design your mentoring program. You want to ensure you have an ongoing "mentor training and discussion" after each mentoring session. What went well? What didn't go well, and what needs improvement for the following sessions?

Step 4: Communication Marketing and Advertisement:

Your mentoring advertisement message must align with your goals to achieve the best results and attract participants. How you communicate with each generation of young people will be different. Your messaging must be meaningful and connect to the audience you want to attract.

For example, in UCF's first three years, before the social media explosion, our initial poster campaign reflected the title "You Got Skills" mentoring program for young males.

Although our advertising and promotional campaigns were before the proliferation of social media, word of mouth by participants was the most effective way to stay connected. From the beginning, it was clear that the content of topics had to be meaningful to the youth. UCF centered on creating an excellent meeting experience for students. A staple of UCF meetings is developing an exciting learning environment that results in students sharing their experiences with friends and family members after the meeting.

UCF uses both advertising strategies to connect to the community. For example, the annual Game Changer Conference advertisement is on social media platforms used by today's youth. Also, we select high-traffic areas to hang fliers and posters at barber shops and laundry facilities in town. We provide incentives for students who bring the most friends and acquaintances. As an incentive to increase enrollment, the students who bring a friend receive gifts.

As we enter a new decade in the 21st century, your mentoring advertising message to connect with today's generation must align with your mentoring program goals. We must also understand that we live in the most unique times in American history. For the first time, six generations are alive, living side by side today. Social scientists and researchers have stated that this phenomenon has never occurred in the history of our country.

As you consider establishing a mentoring program in your community, please recognize the intergenerational impact and role social media plays with getting your message out to the public and staying connected.

In starting your mentoring program or developing your skills to become an effective mentor with today's generation of youth, social media advertising must be incorporated into your planning to stay connected and engaged with young people to achieve the best results. Today's mentors, please remember that 90% of listeners use social media digital platforms to stay connected with six generations. Your advertising at this time must reach out to various ages.

I cannot over-emphasize that the best form of messaging will always be personal contact with parents, guardians, and students to support your mentoring program. I encourage you to pick up your phone to speak to sow into another person's life today! Let's be game changers, seed planters, and helping hands to uplift young people into the failed clutches of life! I encourage you to be innovative and discover new ways to use social media to expand your mentoring messaging! You can develop video clips to deliver your message to be used on each platform. As I inspire others to step up and be post-pandemic mentors, be the messenger you want to send to your audience!

Here is a synthesized checklist for your mentoring program:
- How many times a week/month do you meet officially? Where are the meetings going to be held?
- Don't let the mentor meetings become a bore!
- Create a fun environment where people want to return to sports, games, and activities beyond homework and rap sessions; plain talking is always a plus.
- Food can also be a great way to bring people together. Mentors

can take turns bringing in snacks or baking brownies, (the team moms concept is a great way to involve the parents).
- Plan your work and work your plan regarding policies, procedures, financial plan, and budget and identify teaming partners throughout the year to sustain the mentoring program.

SOCIAL MEDIA PLATFORMS	SIX (6) GENERATION
FACEBOOK	THE BABY BOOMER GENERATION – BORN 1946 – 1964 GREW UP DURING CIVIL RIGHTS MOVEMENT, VIETNAM WAR, COLD WAR, SPACE TRAVEL
INSTAGRAM	GENERATION X – BORN BETWEEN 1965 – 1980 GREW UP DURING WATERGATE, ENERGY CRISIS, END OF COLD WAR, AND WERE THE 1ST GENERATION OF LATCHKEY KIDS AND Y2K INTERNET.
TIK TOK	THE GENERATION Y (KNOWN AS THE MILLENNIAL) BORN BETWEEN 1981 – 1995 GREW UP DURING TIME OF FEAR OF TERRORISM, 9/11, OKLAHOMA CITY BOMBING, SNIPPER, ANTHRAX, AND SCHOOL VIOLENCE
SNAPCHAT – YOUTH	THE GENERATION Z – BORN AFTER 1995 -2015 GREW UP DURING THE IRAQ WAR, 1ST AFRICAN AMERICAN PRESIDENT BARRACK OBAMA, INCREASE IN SCHOOL VIOLENCE KILLINGS, MARRIAGE EQUALITY, LGBTQ COMMUNITY, SOCIAL MEDIA IMPACT AND SOCIAL JUSTICE MOVEMENT
UNKNOWN - TBD -WHAT'S NEXT	THE GENERATION ALPHA – THESE ARE THE KIDS BORN **2016** TO THE PRESENT

A STORY WITH A KEY MESSAGE: Readers are Leaders,

The quote by Dr. Seuss reflects the "more that you read, the more things you know. The more that you learn, the more places you'll go."

Gary Robinson, my co-worker at the Nuclear Regulatory Commission (NRC) and friend shared his personal story as a Co-op student at seventeen. He was excited to join the Co-op program at a federal government job. He recalls processing, meeting his supervisor, showing his workplace with a computer on the desk, and receiving his first assignment. His first assignment was to use the office's first data processing system (early computer). He had never seen or used one before. He was not given any guidance, just instruction to put it to use. The task was not given to more experienced co-workers. You see, he represented the emerging computer-literate workforce. The job was for the new guy, the new kid on the staff to teach the other staff members. Gary shared that he was perplexed about completing his first assignment in two days. He looked over this computer and pushed some buttons. He wanted to do well in his first real job. Finally, Gary didn't know what else to do, so he asked someone for help. This person pointed to something that he didn't think of before. He said, "Step one is to open this book to the first page, start reading and follow the instructions." Gary thought about what a revelation this statement was. Why didn't he think of that? That's all it took. Open the book and follow the instructions. This is a great lesson even for today's future leaders!

Reading is essential for those seeking to rise above the ordinary and is extremely important to success. The thing about books is they let you travel without moving your feet. I want to impress upon you to be a reader, increase your vocabulary, and be curious about understanding and learning more. Increase your reading time in one setting to two to three hours sitting, which will be required in college.

GIRLS SUMMER READING CLUB WITH JOYCE WALKER
AND JASMINE ADKINS

It would help if you focused on making good choices, getting good grades, learning new skills, and pursuing your education like the "passion" of your ancestors (the warriors and kings and queens).

A PARENT MESSAGE: What UCF Means to My Family

Hello, my name is Angela Mattox, and my sons have been participating with UCF since 2017. When my older sons were 6 and 9, their father died from colon cancer. My late husband and I were both MCPS teachers, and it was a very devastating blow to our family. We moved to Florida for five years; then, we moved back to Montgomery County. I knew that I could not take my sons into manhood by myself. I needed my sons to have a mentor and an organization that would equip them with the tools they needed on their life journey. I learned about UCF from my oldest son's school counselor, and it changed the trajectory of all our lives.

The first time I spoke to Brother Williams, it was very encouraging. My sons immediately started participating in activities. The first activity was a Georgetown basketball game; my sons enjoyed it. After that, they participated in several activities that would leave a lasting impact on their lives. Monthly meetings before COVID-19, we would meet up at Forest Oak Middle School one Saturday per month. Several impactful guest speakers shared their life experiences. My sons could learn about career paths they would not have typically had access to. Learning from others, mistakes really helped shape their perspective on life. The Game Changers Conference was one of the most important and impactful activities my sons participated in. Young males were taught how to tie ties, shake hands, give a 30-second interview, and other hands-on opportunities. While the young males were participating in the activities, parents attended workshops that helped give us strategies for our sons' achievement. Several African American men dedicated their time to impart knowledge to the young males who participated.

My sons benefited from extra activities. Although Brother Williams is an Omega man, he reaches across to other fraternities and organizations to provide unique opportunities to UCF students. Ryan participated in Kamp Kappa. It was a week camping trip led by a group of dedicated men from Kappa Alpha Psi Fraternity, Inc. The boys learned about leadership and team building and took trips to the courthouse. It had a lasting impact on Ryan.

Ronald had an opportunity to attend the Alpha Phi Alpha Fraternity's Leadership Development Institute (LDI). Ronald went to 2018, Towson University, and he learned about etiquette, leadership, professional dress, and other priceless skill sets specific to becoming a man. Ryan participated in the first virtual LDI camp due to COVID pandemic in 2021 and 2022.

Through UCF, my boys have had several opportunities to speak at events, go to the Congressional Black Caucus, The 100 Ques in Annapolis at the State House, Living Legend celebration, visit the Montgomery County Fire and Rescue Training Facility, SAT/ACT Boot Camps, STEM outings, MLK Day of Service, attending a Redskins game, and so many numerous activities I can't even name them all. Through UCF, they participated in a robotics/coding program and had the chance to visit a couple of engineering firms. They even attended the National Society of Black Engineers conference in Pittsburgh, PA and competed.

This was an amazing experience because there were thousands of African American engineers and college students in attendance.

Through the many opportunities my sons were provided, they could see themselves in a positive light. There is so much negativity in the world; seeing black men in leadership positions who give back is very encouraging to me as a single mother. My sons understand that there will be hardships and challenges, and listening to various experiences helped them understand that they can make it.

UCF support has had an amazing impact on our family. They provided the support system I needed to help me raise my sons. The positivity, support, mentoring, and guidance have helped shape my sons into the young men, they are today. Mrs. Mona and Brother Williams have helped improve my parenting style tremendously. There has never been a time I needed guidance from either him or Mrs. Mona that they were not there in time of need. Not only do they give you excellent advice, but they also provide you with people who can help you get through your situations. We have the utmost respect for UCF and appreciate all the opportunities my family has received.

QUOTE:

My mission in life is not merely to survive, but to thrive; and to do so with some passion, compassion, some humor, and some style.

— Maya Angelou

SCRIPTURE

*If you fully obey the L*ORD *your God and carefully follow all his commands I give you today, the L*ORD *your God will set you high above all the nations on earth.* ² *All these blessings will come on you and accompany you if you obey the L*ORD *your God:* ³ *You will be blessed in the city and blessed in the country.*

— Deuteronomy 28:1-3

CHAPTER 19

Community Partnership Collaborations Model & Divine Connection

I learned the best things in life are the people we love, the places we have been, and the memories we've made along the way!

— Unknown

UCF believes we are stronger working together Why? Our communities are in crisis, and young people cry for help. If we don't do it now, then who will? Just think about each one, reach one, and mentor one person. What will it look like if you step up your mentoring engagement efforts?

The work we do today is so much bigger than any one person. Our young people must understand that what they learn today is essential; knowledge is the new currency for the future. UCF has worked with organizations to increase the success of African Americans and minority students of color over many years. As I reflect on the footprints in the sand, I know God directed several vital relationships over the many years for successful sustainment. This journey has been about collaboration and building trusted relationships with local churches, Divine 9, sororities, fraternities, public school district administrators, and like-minded organizations.

I am still in awe of how God provided a vision, turned an idea into action, and then the provision of connecting UCF to the right persons and resources at the right time. This vision manifested resulted in

UCF is becoming a premier youth organization that promotes student success. As it approaches two decades, UCF addresses the critical need to mobilize our community around the vital challenge of finding solutions to reverse the alarming trend and unfavorable disparities of young people, especially our male African Americans and students of color in education.

I remember attending a gathering with a funder who used an African proverb in her opening remarks that showed how much stronger we are working together. The proverb says, "if you want to go fast, go alone; if you want to go far, go together." I encourage you to think about your priorities and plan your journey the right way with defined outcomes and impact in mind. I learned from my professional career you should never build yourself up by tearing someone else down. This applies to youth organizations; tearing down another organization to build your organization up is a non-starter. There is enough sunshine for every youth organization to conduct the critical work of helping young people reach their potential. I've learned that blowing out someone else's candle won't make yours shine brighter. Mentors must be protective, keep an open mind, and use their intuition with others who may have ulterior motives for working with your mentoring program.

This chapter highlights what I recognize as divine relationships that propelled UCF to become a premier youth development organization in Montgomery County and nearby communities. Some of the most memorable experiences occurred from witnessing young people change their thinking, attitude, and mental outlook. Positive change starts with a thought. Positive thinking comes from looking in the mirror; the person looking back must be willing to do the necessary work for improvement.

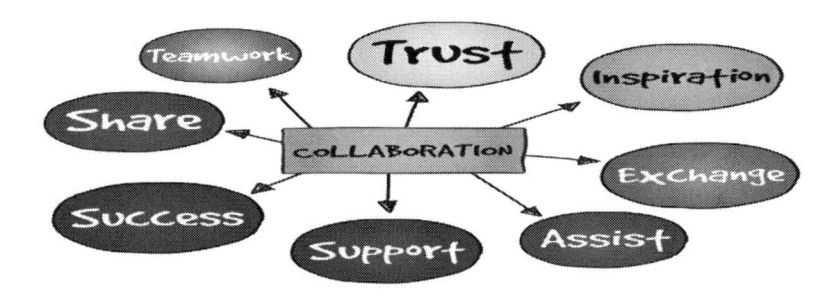

[Diagram: COLLABORATION at center, connected to Teamwork, Trust, Inspiration, Share, Exchange, Success, Support, Assist]

I constantly tell young people they can't stay in their current state to improve their lives. Young people must be willing every day to work to change their attitude toward members in their homes. It is a conscious decision a person must commit to improving where they are, improving their academic performance as a student and staying the course enroute to college, joining the military, or pursuing a vocational certificate that will allow them to earn a respectable living. Watching the maturation process of students we have mentored and cared for thrive as young adults is gratifying.

The definition of collaboration is the process of two or more people or organizations working together to complete a task or achieve a mutual goal. The word collaboration is like operating as one team and one goal. Collaboration might mean something different for each party at the table. It is essential to ask team members what collaboration means to them before proceeding forward. Also, it is crucial to set expectations and identify roles and responsibilities to produce desired outcomes. The most rewarding and fulfilling experiences included partnering with organizations.

Don't underestimate the power of working together for a greater outcome. Remarkable things happen when people care and set aside personal agendas to work as one team. Many of UCF's teaming arrangements involved several stakeholders with a common purpose, each performing their responsibility. Teams that work collaboratively often access more significant resources, recognition, and rewards when facing competition for finite resources.

September 20, 2006

"If you want to go fast, go alone.
If you want to go far, go together."
—African Proverb

UCF's first monthly meeting occurred at the Upper County Community Center, 8201 Emory Grove Road, Gaithersburg, Maryland. Our first community partner was the Upper County's Director, Thelma Nolan, who provided a free meeting room to support the mentoring mission.

A GAME CHANGER'S PURSUIT

I remember the first meeting with the Director, where I shared the mentoring vision, and without hesitation, she provided a meeting room to conduct youth meetings at no charge to support the mentoring mission. UCF kicked off our Aim High Educational and Life Skills Program, entitled initially "You Got Skills Workshop," on September 20, 2006. We met monthly with approximately 15 young male students actively participating in the program. Their grades ranged from 7th through 12th grade, and first-year college students. Youth attendance grew rapidly from hosting youth meetings in a small classroom and then moving to the larger banquet room with the big screen. Reverend Thelma Nolan was vital in launching the Aim High In Life Educational Life Skill Program. She has always had a heart for young people and the community. In the five years we partnered with the Community Center, UCF supported the Club Friday initiative, where our students operated a Snack Shack, providing refreshments to students in attendance.

Dr. Leroy Evans and Councilman Craig Rice

The other three Community Partners whose support was instrumental in the explosive impact on UCF's journey throughout the years were Councilmember Craig L. Rice, Dr. Leroy C. Evans, and Sol Graham.

Councilmember Craig L. Rice—since his first election to the Montgomery County Council in November 2010 through 2022, he was UCF champion. He was the youngest African American ever to serve on the County Council and the second African American man to serve in that role. We are so proud of his public service serving the citizens of Montgomery County with integrity, county knowledge, dignity, and professionalism.

Dr. Leroy C. Evans, Principal Col. Zadok Magruder High School, was the second Community Partner who has played an instrumental role in the strategic direction of UCF's engagement with MCPS. He provided our first grant opportunity by sharing information on how to apply for the grant. The "Under 21 Substance Abuse Prevention Grant" award opened our eyes to the realities of food disparities. The $1,000 award was like mana from heaven because it allowed UCF to feed students at the youth engagement meetings. We were so excited to receive the grant, for this was confirmation from God. It encouraged UCF members to stay the course with the challenging work with our young males and work to increase connection with local stakeholders.

We learned that many of the community's children who crossed our path went hungry over the weekend. The meal provided at the youth meeting perhaps was the only meal received over the weekend until the students returned to school on Monday mornings. This experience raised awareness that there were "food deserts" long before COVID-19, and many families didn't have the resources to feed their children. The young males enjoyed having pizza at each meeting, which led us to provide meals at all planned activities. Our attendance grew once students found out a light meal was provided.

We will forever be grateful to Dr. Evans for sharing the information on local grants. This experience cemented a life-long relationship that continues even today. In 2005 MCPS got it right by assigning Dr. Evans as Magruder's Principal to lead one of the best academic schools with the most diverse population in Montgomery County.

He is an extraordinary leader who genuinely cares about student success and all that is necessary to help provide success. Most of our enrolled students in the early years were from Magruder High, including Melissa Simpson, Ray Simpson, Dinah Simpson, Kareem Johnson, David Diaz,

Katherine Ortega, Leonard Grant, Evan Peace, and Alex Diaz, among many others.

We shared a spiritual connection with the Simpson family as Dr. Evans, and I were summoned to the bedside of Mrs. Simpson when she was called home to be with the Lord. Her message was simple as she slid the oxygen mask down to speak – take care of my children! This was a memory that remains etched in my mind for life.

We are proud of Dr. Evans's steadfast commitment to quality education for all students. Although we experienced some heartbreaks, including MCPS's first in-school shooting of a student, we have shared some wonderful "success stories" working together that resulted in more excellent outcomes throughout the years.

SOL GRAHAM PROVIDES A TEACHABLE MOMENT. GRAHAM STARTED HIS COMPANY QUALITY BIOLOGICAL IN 1983.

Sol Graham, a minority business pioneer in Montgomery County, philanthropist, and mentor to many, was the first business owner to meet with me. The founder and former President of Quality Biological, Inc., located in Gaithersburg, Maryland, grew a bioscience/tech business into an enterprise that grosses about $10 million annually. He was the first African American business owner to sow financial seeds based on the promise to bring community organizations together. Mr. Graham's pioneering success has earned him several accolades.

In 2011, I recalled meeting with Sol at his country club after he had just finished winning a tennis match. I showed up with my "famous" Power Point presentation for an information-sharing session about UCF Youth Development Organization. I shared that we would emerge as a student advocacy champion for African Americans and minority students of color in the county for promoting student success and "change lives in the community one student at a time amongst at-promise youth." He was so impressed that he invited me to his office at Airpark in Gaithersburg.

That was when I shared the vision for the Game Changer Conference for young males. Sol was the first community leader to financially sow significantly in the first three years of the Game Changer Conference.

As I broke through the exterior persona, the conversation became passionate and informative as Sol shared insight and advisement about Montgomery County growing to an estimated 1.3 million residents. He stated that the population grows more diversified every year. He also shared that many organizations are doing good work in the community.

However, each organization was operating in a silo and working independently. He had one "ask," to develop a "collaboration model" that brings organizations together for optimal collective results. Sol believed our community would be strengthened if we worked together! In every conversation with Sol, he provided inspiration, information about the community, and "golden nuggets" for becoming an influential community leader. Sol grew up on a farm in Georgia. At age 17, he joined the U.S. Navy to escape an impoverished community.

I asked him what he attributed his success to, and his immediate response was, "the grace of God!" In an interview with the AFRO newspaper, he added, "lucky was a word he took out of his vocabulary some time ago and replaced with blessed." In another conversation, I asked Sol about his perspective on mentoring; he shared: "to give more than you think is possible, and then give beyond that with more of your time, talent, and treasure." The blessing is that we have formed a wonderful friendship over many years. Sol and I have created a support team of military officers to help increase African American and minority "applicants" attendance at the Service Academies with the outcome of students receiving nominations for the Class of 2023.

Montgomery County Public School District (MCPS) has supported UCF under four Superintendents that started under Superintendent of School, Dr. Joshua Starr and now continue today under Dr. Monifa B. McKnight. The most notable "Collaboration Model" to engage families and students was the unprecedented Game Changer Conference for Young Males founded by UCF, SAT/ACT Boot Camps, Community STEM Expo, Homework Club, and Dream Chaser College Tour.

Montgomery County Public Schools

Reflecting on where God has brought Mona and me from, it's only Him! He has ordered our steps, shielded, and shaped our lives for his purpose. We are grateful to God for surrounding Mona and me with the many Christian friends on our journey. A memorable experience was an invitation to present at the 18th Quadrennial Convention in Indianapolis, Indiana, on July 17-21, 2015. I was selected to participate in the Transition Day Workshop Series centered on the SOS call to Save Our Sons, (SOS) through intergenerational mentoring, based on Proverbs 27:17 – "As iron sharpens iron, so one person sharpens another."

MONTGOMERY COUNTY YOUTH LEADERSHIP AWARD
(MARCH 12, 2013)
SISTER D. FAYE CONLEY (SECOND FROM THE RIGHT), SERVED AS EPISCOPAL PRESIDENT FOR NINE WONDERFUL YEARS (SECOND EPISCOPAL DISTRICT, WOMEN'S MISSIONARY SOCIETY) WHICH CONTINUES TO MEET THE NEEDS OF GOD'S PEOPLE.

As we close this chapter on collaboration, I must recognize Montgomery County, which has provided financial support since 2013 to allow UCF to reach and impact countless families. From an organizational perspective, I learned that an organization like UCF means the world to a community because it inspires other organizations to establish mentoring programs in their school, neighborhood, and community.

Seeing other young organizations willing to step out of their comfort zone to help establish mentoring programs in their community is gratifying. As UCF grew and offered innovative programs, other mentoring organizations emerged to provide many of the same programs. I learned there's enough sunshine for those with a heart to work with our young people and the community.

Community Partners – Dr. Shawn Joseph and Dr. Gregory Bell, Tim Warner, MCPS Executives

The following people are recognized as the ultimate game changers for the Game Changer Conference, playing a significant role from the beginning. Some undergirded UCF with prayers, while others encouraged us by volunteering their time, talents, support, and financial contributions. I want you to know that if you stay faithful, stand firm, and do what He called you to do, you begin to see His hand on your life and purpose for your life. He can do exceedingly and abundantly; you can think or imagine. He will make a way when you don't see a way. He does the miraculous. I feel the presence of God in my life leading the way daily.

The divine connection occurred in 2011 at a meeting with Dr. Joseph in his 850 Hungerford Drive office in Rockville, Maryland. The significance of the meeting with Dr. Joseph was twofold: He believed the conference was important enough to connect MCPS with the Game Changer's Conference and became an advocate. Secondly, he provided the history of Carver Hall by sharing the past found in a time capsule on site near the entrance to the building.

The historical significance of the Carver Educational Services Center, home of MCPS' central administrative office, was only for Black students. The facility opened in 1951 for approximately a decade as George Washington Carver High School and Junior College. It was the only high school in the county for African American students until it closed in 1960 following integration.

Secondly, Dr. Joseph was highly supportive and instrumental in launching the Game Changer Conference 2012. As I shared the conference vision, it was easy to see his joy. Again, this was a faith walk and journey, meeting key leaders one after the other, wondering how the message was received. And with each meeting, my conversation with God while I had a heart attack at Harpers Ferry was confirmed.

I developed an excellent relationship with Dr. Joseph, who helped develop MCPS support. I was unaware he was another esteemed Omega Psi Phi Fraternity, Inc. member. I recall inviting him to the Call for Action meeting in January 2012; however, he was unavailable. I remember him saying he would send his mentor - Dr. Gregory Bell, the Superintendent for Diversity and Equity. What a blessing it was to have Dr. Bell, who is sight impaired, in attendance to deliver a key message to the community leaders gathered. In his address, he noted, "I might be sight impaired, but I am not vision impaired, and this is a vision for us to get on board with." This was the right time for the assembled leaders in the room to work together for the conference to reach its maximum effectiveness. Dr. Bell was the keynote speaker at the record-breaking male conference at the Montgomery County Germantown Campus in the event's third year.

Reverend Timothy B. Warner and I connected at a dinner engagement at the former Red Hot & Blue Restaurant, breaking bread over an information-sharing session with my trustee PowerPoint presentation. The divine connection occurred at First AME Church, where he attended the worship service. He presented Brother Jim Madison, who was one hundred years old then, with a proclamation on behalf of the former dynamic County Executive, Isiah "Ike" Leggett.

Reverend Warner was on the staff of the Montgomery County Executive in his Office of Community Partnerships as the Community Liaison for the African American and Faith Communities. He was then the Chief Engagement and Partnership Officer for Montgomery County Public Schools under Dr. Joshua Starr, Superintendent of Schools.

As he digested his meal, he asked me how to help sustain the conference. I stated that if we were down South, the school district would provide bus support to every part of the county, and that would be a "game changer." He looked at me and asked, "Is that all?" Another confirmation and divine connection!

I would be remiss not to mention increased support under the former Chief of Staff, Dr. Henry Johnson, and former Superintendent of Schools, Dr. Jack Smith, who provided additional resources such as printing and marketing support to get the word out to the principals in the district. MCPS provided bus transportation in support of the conference.

The National Pan-Hellenic Council of Montgomery, Presidents Carolyn Croons, Henry Williams, and Tony Proctor were original supporters who provided resources. The Divine 9 Greek organizations have been fantastic with promoting unity in the community by connecting with their circle of influence for many youth initiatives.

UCF continues to be grateful to receive support from all local churches with distributing UCF youth initiatives to their congregation members for SAT/ACT Boot Camps, Dream Chasers College Tours, Community STEM Day, and monthly youth meetings, including the annual Game Changer Conference.

ONE TEAM, ONE GOAL – EXCELLENCE IS THE STANDARD!

"53 YEARS OF EXCELLENCE AND SERVICE"
COMMUNITY PARTNER –
Mu Nu Chapter of Omega Psi Phi Fraternity, Inc.

David A. Hill, the 22nd (2011-2013) Basileus/President of Mu Nu Chapter of Omega Psi Phi Fraternity, Inc., was instrumental in aiding UCF's programs. At the time of his administration, he shared that he was searching for an innovative mentoring program that impacted the community. I took a trip to Virginia Beach, where the 2011 Shirtsleeve Planning Conference was held at Virginia Beach near Old Dominion University. I had the opportunity as a new member to introduce myself to the brotherhood and share the conference vision given to me with the chapter brothers. Shortly afterward, I was asked to serve as the

Chairman of Social Action under Brother Hill's presidency when he approved the Game Changer Conference teaming arrangement, which Mu Nu continues to co-sponsor.

Since Brother Hill's presidency, Mu Nu Chapter has provided leadership and resources and conducted workshops for the Game Changer Conference that expanded beyond Maryland.

Community Partner - Ms. Michelle Taylor, President/CEO of BETAH Associates Ms. Taylor is the President and CEO of BETAH Associates, Inc., located in Silver Spring, Maryland. Their mission is to transform the lives of vulnerable and underserved individuals in communities. I have had the privilege to work with Ms. Taylor on various outreach and community events and saw firsthand the impact she is making on the young people in our communities. Her motto: "You can do well and do good," a philosophy that she lives by.

Ms. Taylor is a champion of the underserved students of color in the county. She gives her time, talent, and finances to several nonprofit organizations that provide services to Montgomery County youth and adults. She provides financial contributions to community-based organizations and nonprofits in the county dedicated to positive youth development, such as Lead for Life, Pride Youth Services, and the George B. Thomas Learning Academy, which collectively have a tremendous reach in the DMV. UCF has been a recipient of such a significant monetary award.

Ms. Taylor continues to be a vital supporter of the Game Changer Conference for Young Males. She financially supports the Game Changer Conference, which annually averaged 500 attendees before the COVID pandemic. When Ms. Taylor recognized the conference's impact, she immediately extended a helping hand with ideas and personal resources. When it became apparent that one of the conferences was well along in the planning efforts but needed more funding, she reached out to another philanthropist and secured additional funding. Ms. Taylor's generosity has allowed organizations like UCF to increase their reach by exposing young people to new experiences they otherwise would not have and teaching life skills that enable them to make wise decisions throughout their middle and high school years. In January 2018, she "paid it forward" for more than 100 students to participate in a 2-Day SAT/ACT Boot Camp.

2023 Spring Game Changer Conference for Young Males

Team Community Working Together in 2023
to Make Hope Happen!

The UCF "Aim High-In-Life" Youth Development Organization, which celebrates 18 years of promoting student success, proudly celebrated our Game Changer Conference teaming partners. We are incredibly indebted to:
- Montgomery County Public Schools System, under the leadership of Superintendent of Schools Dr. Monifa B. McKnight, Deputy Superintendent Dr. Patrick Murphy, Mr. Everett M. Davis, Director, Student, Family & School Services, Office of School Support & Well-Being.
- National Pan-Hellenic Council (NPHC) of Montgomery

County, MD, an affiliate charter member of The National Pan-Hellenic Council, a collaborative organization of the nine major Black Greek Lettered Fraternities & Sororities. The mission is to promote programs and initiatives to improve African American conditions from an academic, economic, health, social, and civic perspective.

- The Universities at Shady Grove offer career-oriented higher education courses to Montgomery County, Maryland, and the surrounding region residents. We look forward to working with Dr. Anne Khademian, the third USG Executive Director, and Dr. Jeffrey Ash, the first Chief Diversity, Equity, and Inclusion Officer.
- Mu Nu Chapter of Omega Psi Phi Fraternity, Inc.
  * Montgomery College
  * 2nd Episcopal District Women Missionary Society of AME Church
  * GBTLA SATURDAY SCHOOL
  * Delta Sigma Theta Sorority, Inc. Montgomery County
  * Alpha Kappa Alpha Sorority, Inc., Xi Sigma Omega Chapter
  * ICOG Church, West Montgomery United Methodist Women (UMW) and Pythagoras Lodge #74, Historic Emory Grove Rotary and Victims Rights Foundation

UCF is grateful to partner with AAU for the Game Changer Conference where they provided auto safety teaching students basic auto care. Also support the Silent Auction for UCF Scholarship Fund Rasier Dinner for many years with free oil change and safety kits. AAA Gaithersburg Car Care and AAA Auto Care on 355 Rockville Pike where Parnell Singleton was manager.

The Anthony L. Cheatham Leadership Development Institute - Eastern Region South (LDI)

UCF is grateful to "team together" for the last 14 years with the men from Alpha Phi Alpha Fraternity, Inc., to assist in the growth and development of our young males to prepare them for manhood and acquire leadership skills. Shoutout to Dr. Joseph A. McMillan, LDI Coordinator, French Pope and Anthony Cheatham, (RIP) for their friendship. Throughout this partnership, our students have been exposed to different college campuses such as UMBC, Towson, Temple, Howard, and

American Universities to name a few. This is one of the capstone camps for our students to attend before graduating high school.

2013 Kamp Kappa

Alexandria-Fairfax Alumni Chapter - Kappa Alpha Psi Fraternity

UCF is also grateful to work with the men of Kappa Alpha Psi Fraternity, Inc. for the last 12 years. This is a tremendous team-building camp for young males. Every year, UCF selects middle school students based on the merits of scholarship, attendance, and active engagement in UCF youth activities. This outdoor experience focuses on teaching manhood principles, exposure to courtroom experiences, and other fun activities such as swimming.

UCF is grateful to partner with Ms. Carla M. Dickerson (the-scholarshipladydc.com), known as the "Scholarship Lady US," and her team of certified instructors to offer SAT/ACT Boot Camps for students for the last 13 years. Every year countless students increase their confidence level, test-taking skills and understanding to succeed in taking standardized examinations. So many positive outcomes resulting in 80% percentile score or higher on the SAT or ACT Exam that translate into merit scholarships.

A GAME CHANGER'S PURSUIT

BLACK MINISTERS CONFERENCE OF MONTGOMERY COUNTY MARYLAND UNDER THE CURRENT LEADERSHIP OF REVEREND JAMES E. BONEY, FAITH COMMUNITY BAPTIST CHURCH

UCF has been grateful for the support from local churches since inception. They have undergirded UCF with prayers and support for many youth initiatives such as the SAT/ACT Boot Camps and, noteworthy, the Basketball ministry. Sometimes things are set in motion in advance, which was valid with the Christian Youth Basketball Ministry (CYBM). At a community event, two pastors sought a basketball ministry for their church to participate in, the Rev. Dr. Hayward A. Robinson, III, The People's Community Baptist Church, and The Reverend Eldridge Spearman, Mount Jezreel Baptist Church.

As a result of the Christian Youth Basketball Ministry, several churches supported the Game Changer Conference. A small church named West Montgomery United Methodist Church, under the leadership of Pastor Reverend Bernadette Armwood stood out after they learned about the all-male conference. A member and supporter was Mrs. Sarah Browner, an educator specializing in English who was extremely excited to receive a flier about the Game Changer Conference from her church member and my fraternity Brother Preston Phillips. This small church raised an offering to support the conference. My heart was touched, and my emotions moved after learning that they set aside an offering to sponsor students to the conference for ten weeks.

Mrs. Browner was the Educational Coordinator for the West Montgomery United Methodist Women (UMW). In the meeting, they desired to partner with UCF to support and promote students' success, helping them reach their potential.

When we met with Mrs. Sarah Browner, she was ecstatic about the conference she recommended UCF's signature Essay Contest. The UCF Essay Writing Competition allowed students to express themselves by addressing current topics of the day.

Amazingly, she inspired other teachers to identify students to participate in the Game Changer Conference every year. In addition, as a permanent substitute teacher at Roberto Clemente Middle School established an in-school mentoring program for young males at Roberto Clemente and named it after the All-Male Conference. She worked tirelessly to reward male students for good conduct and behavior throughout the academic year with attendance at the Game Changer Conference. She recruited students, connected with parents, and each young male had to submit an essay to attend the Game Changer Conference.

As a result of this beautiful relationship, the small church in Boyds, Maryland, established a scholarship reception to assist students enrolling in college. I asked Mrs. Browner her "why," and she stated, "Although our church's women's group is very small, we wanted to do something to help students." In 2014, the UMW was truly blessed due to generous fundraising contributions throughout the year to give three $500 scholarship awards. She noted, "We only started with one $500 award--which was all we could afford because our group is still very small (seven members). But we're always so excited to be able to assist new African American graduates to attend college to make a difference in their lives."

Mrs. Browner added, "I've just got an education in my bones, and I love to help those who want to learn. I will continue striving to move this initiative to a higher level, where we can increase our scholarships' number and monetary value."

Shaping the Future!

Girl Dads in Actions

The 2012 GIRLS ROCK Conference

The following are photos of established trusted relationships that have supported UCF Mentoring Journey for the past sixteen years.

Collaboration Teaming Partners: (Left to right) Mr. and Mrs. Steve Ruffin, Senator Van Hollen, center and Mr. and Mrs. Donald Williams II

Former Montgomery County Executive Isiah Leggett

CONGRESSMAN DAVID TRONE PICTURED IN 2018 ON HIS WAY TO BEING ELECTED TO SERVE MARYLAND 'SIXTH CONGRESSIONAL DISTRICT THAT INCLUDES ALL OR PART OF MONTGOMERY, FREDERICK, GARRETT, ALLEGANY, AND WASHINGTON COUNTIES. I HAD THE HONOR TO SERVE AS A PANEL MEMBER ON SERVICE ACADEMY NOMINATIONS TEAM.

Historic Emory Grove Rotary Club (HEGRC)

Charter Members: (Left to the right), Donald Williams II, Yvette Gause, Michael Hall (RIP), Carolyn Taylor, Michael Johnson, (Inaugural 2017 President), Greg Wims, (District Governor), Reggie Johnson, William Fields, Warren Fleming, and Gary Bailey.

The above picture shows charter members assembled in September 2017 at the Emory Grove United Methodist Church. Greg Wims, the Governor of District 7620, presided, gave the oath and presented the Rotary International Certificates. District 7620 includes 62 clubs and over 2,100 members in central Maryland and Washington D.C. I first learned about Rotary International when I served in Germany in the 80s. This international organization, founded by Paul Harris, has a global network of more than 1.2 million neighbors. Organization members worldwide work together as problem solvers who see a world where people unite and work collaboratively to create positive change globally and in our communities. Greg Wims, the first Black Rotary District Governor of Maryland Rotary, established a satellite club in the name of Historic Emory Grove Rotary Club (HEGRC) through the Montgomery Village Rotary Club agreement to be the parent organization.

I was honored to be asked by the inaugural President, Michael Johnson, who was born and raised in the Emory Grove community. He allowed me to mentor his son Kareem Johnson, UCF's first college graduate from Fayetteville State University, North Carolina. As a Historic Emory Grove Rotary Club (HEGRC) charter member, the last seven years have been incredible regarding community service impact. I am proud of this team's selfless work, the consistent embodiment of service, and uplifting families from 2017, during COVID, and to the present day. In June 2023, I was surprised by the Montgomery Village Rotary Club under the leadership of Stuart Rutchik and Jim Hamerski, a surprise honor as a Paul Harris Fellow. This award is given in appreciation to individuals who have made a significant impact in their community and furtherance of better understanding and friendly relations among peoples of the world. A $1,000 contribution to the Rotary Foundation of Rotary International in their name is to be spent on humanitarian efforts worldwide. It has been an honor to be recognized along with inaugural HEGRC President Michael Johnson and two-term President Carolyn Taylor for our leadership in the growth of the satellite club.

UCF will always be grateful for the collaboration, immediate charitable support, and volunteer opportunities for our young people, such as COVID Keep-up Youth Initiative grant support for youth who created an educational campaign to connect with young people about safe and healthy lifestyles and site set up for the annual Flags for our Heroes on Memorial Day weekend.

HEGRC Mission: To give our time and resources to uplift Black communities in Upper Montgomery County, Maryland. Our work prioritizes health, education, social justice, and a stable communal foundation. Together, we apply our professional experience and personal commitment to tackle our communities' most persistent problems, finding new, effective ways to enhance health, stability, and prosperity across the community and the globe. I love the Rotary Motto, Service Above Self!

Black History Moment is a son of the Emory Grove community is my fraternity brother, Mr. Greg Wims, the first Black Rotary District Governor who established the satellite club. And founder of the Victims Rights Foundation. He was recently appointed to serve as State Delegate for District 39, his community, where he has made significant contributions to improving the lives of others throughout his life as a public servant. http://historicemorygroverotary.org/

MCPS COLLABORATION TEAMING PARTNERS: (LEFT TO RIGHT SEATED) DR. JACK SMITH, FORMER SUPERINTENDENT, DR. DERIONNE P. POLLARD, FORMER 9TH PRESIDENT, MONTGOMERY COLLEGE, REGINALD "REGGIE" FELTON, FORMER PRESIDENT, MONTGOMERY COUNTY PUBLIC SCHOOLS BOARD OF EDUCATION.
BACK ROW: MU NU CHAPTER MEMBERS SHAUN RATLIFF, WALTER NEIGHBORS, HULA EDMONDS, DONALD WILLIAMS, PRESTON PHILLIPS, KHADIJA F. BARKLEY, GBTLA, EXECUTIVE DIRECTOR, COUNCILMAN CRAIG L. RICE.

STACEY JORDAN, MORGAN STATE UNIVERSITY GRADUATE, GAME CHANGER CONFERENCE FEATURED SPEAKER FOR A DECADE AND FOUNDER OF PODCAST REAL HUSBANDS OF LARGO. (CENTER IN SUIT & TIE).

NATIONAL PAN-HELLENIC COUNCIL OF MONTGOMERY COUNTY

NATIONALLY RECOGNIZED CIVIL RIGHTS ATTORNEY, BEN CRUMP, PICTURED AT CONCLAVE IN NEW ORLEANS. ATTORNEY BEN CRUMP REPRESENTS SOME OF THE MOST HIGH-PROFILE CASES OF OUR TIME. THE REV. AL SHARPTON SAYS CRUMP IS "BLACK AMERICA'S ATTORNEY GENERAL." HE HAS BECOME THE VOICE FOR MANY BLACK AMERICANS FAMILIES BEYOND POLICE BRUTALITY CASES. OMEGA EXCELLENCE!

U.S. CONGRESSMAN JAMES E. CLYBURN, PICTURED AT THE CONGRESSIONAL BLACK CAUCUS! PROUDLY SERVING THE AMERICAN PEOPLE. OMEGA EXCELLENCE!

QUES ON THE MOVE PODCAST ORIGINAL TEAM THAT SHARED THE INCREDIBLE MENTORING AND COMMUNITY ENGAGEMENT STORIES ACROSS FIVE STATES.

We encourage our young people to pursue acquiring a good education while in high school, go to college and pursue a degree in a meaningful career profession, or get certifications, gain experience and try to use your education to improve your quality of life and make life better for your family and others by giving back.

Mentoring Leadership Matters & Mentoring Works & Mentoring Save Lives!

Awards

President Barack Obama's Community Leader Volunteer Service Award

2013 Youth Leadership Excellence Award Xi Sigma Omega Chapter, AKA Sorority, Inc.

2016 Reverend Dr. Martin Luther King, Jr. Community Service Award

Top 30 Nominee of the 2016 John C. Maxwell Leadership Award

2017 & 2013 Montgomery County Dr. Nancy Dworkin Award for Outstanding Service to Youth

Selected for the first-ever (2017) Collaboration Council Mentoring Fellowship Program

Nominator for the Posse Scholar Program

2018 Award Excellence Service to the Faith Community, Church of The Messiah,

2018 National Council for Negro Women Award

2019 No Greater Love Service Award, Friends of Bowie State University

2023 Paul Harris Fellow, Rotary International

2023 and 2017 Committee Chairman of the Year, 2nd District of Omega Psi Phi Fraternity, Inc.

CLOSING MESSAGE

The 36th United States President, Lyndon B. Johnson, once stated, "We must open the doors of opportunity. But we must also equip our people to walk through those doors." As the leader of a not-for-profit youth organization for nearly two decades, I have conducted presentations, attended conferences, and knocked on and walked through hundreds of doors to promote student success on behalf of our youth and their families. Our education system and students deserve a first-class secondary experience that prepares them to succeed in the 21st Century, and it starts with modernizing the current education delivery system.

Unity Christian Fellowship, Inc. (UCF), a nonprofit organization known in the community as Aim High In Life Youth Development Organization, stepped out on faith to provide student advocacy leadership for African-Americans and students of color in Montgomery County, Maryland. UCF encouraged every student who had a desire to improve their quality of life. With access to various opportunities, assistance with academic work, and social and emotional support, students were able to reach their full potential, which in turn propelled them to higher heights.

In the post-COVID pandemic era, we have witnessed the transformation of a new world order and have recognized some of the emerging demands that are ever-present, affecting the lives of our youth daily. There is violence in our neighborhoods and schools, social media targeting youth, social and economic disparities, underlying racial division, row back of affirmative actions, and cultural insensitivity. These things are rising in our Black and Brown communities, putting our students' learning experience at risk. The order of the day must include "new thinking, new pathways, innovations, and creativity," along with collaborative partnerships to prepare our next generation of scholars and leaders.

A lot is at stake as we put the COVID pandemic in the rear-view mirror, and this is not the time to conduct business as usual, go along with an out-of-date educational model, and remain silent for the societal times we are experiencing. Many equity disparity studies have been conducted over the years. The information gathered and recommendations reviewed are helpful only if we implement new models and practices that focus on connecting with students' ability to learn and prepare for today's reality. We must concentrate on preparing our youth for a new world requiring new skills.

There is no better investment than our young people. And we are stronger working collaboratively to address their needs. Mentorship is critical in a young person's life. It helps them create pathways to learn and develop the skills needed to succeed. All stakeholders (i.e., educators, churches, elected officials, communities, social and mentoring organizations) are responsible for developing ways to mentor our young people. The sense of urgency is now! It is our time to be courageous, fearless, and bold. We must collaborate, pool our resources, and be deliberate in making hope happen for our young people.

UCF's vision from the beginning centered on igniting the community and bringing together like-minded people to focus on helping children reach their full potential after high school. The journey continues to be amazing while intentionally using a collaborative model to positively impact vulnerable communities with African Americans and other minority students of color. I have experienced that we can accomplish much when the community works together to yield positive outcomes!

A caring community must have a sincere vested interest and a shared responsibility to ensure that the underserved, marginalized, and least likely youth succeed and have an opportunity to become a success story. The real story is that no organization operating alone can successfully impact a community. It takes teamwork and equal resources in your community to make a difference.

UCF's goal to empower youth was initially viewed as a daunting challenge but has proven to be a blessing in disguise, which led to implementing a "collaboration model" that has united our community. Equally important, lives have been positively impacted, and a new generation of *Game Changers* believe that there is hope, invest in themselves, and operate with spiritual confidence to improve the quality of their lives, the lives of their families, and their community.

QUOTE:

If you give a man a fish, you feed him for a day; if you teach a man to fish, you feed him for a lifetime.

SCRIPTURE:

Philippians 2:12 declares, being united with Christ, in agreement with one another, having the same love, being one in spirit and serving alongside each other, working together, side by side to achieve positive outcomes that impact our young people and their families.

A message from David Hayes, a charter member of UCF, sent Donald Williams, UCF Executive Director, the following message on August 18, 2023. David was a student who overcame home, education, and community challenges. David graduated from Virginia Union University in 2017. After graduation, he began teaching special education in Richmond, Virginia, public school system. Mentoring changes the trajectory of a young person and in this case it improved the trajectory of his entire family.

"First off happy birthday brother Don. It has been a blessing having in my life. I am grateful and appreciative of our journey over the years. You really open my eyes to something I didn't even really believe in and now I am thriving as a man in this world. I love you and I hope you enjoy every second of your birthday." David

I want to give a Birthday shoutout to my mentor and father figure, Donald Williams. This man has been in my corner since the day that I met him. Pushing me to be better than what I believed I could be, never losing faith in myself even when I lost it within myself, encouraging me to be more than just a statistic, opening my eyes and allowing me to see that there is more to life than just existing. He exposed me to the community, and throughout it all he has been there to help celebrate all of my accomplishments.

I will always be grateful for our relationship and everything you have done for me, and I hope you enjoy your birthday.

DAVID HAYES AND PROUD MOTHER ON VIRGINIA UNION UNIVERSITY 2017 GRADUATION

A GAME CHANGER'S PURSUIT

WHAT IF EACH PERSON IS RESPONSIBLE FOR MENTORING "ONE PERSON" TO NURTURE, AFFIRM, CHANGE TRAJECTORY, AND BE ACCOUNTABLE FOR CONNECTING TO THEIR DESTINY?
WHAT A BETTER WORLD THIS WILL BE IF YOU STEP UP YOUR MENTORING ENGAGEMENT EFFORTS!
THIS IS MY ONE – WHO IS YOUR ONE?

ADDITIONAL REFERENCE SOURCES

Useful Web Sites In this fast-paced world of technology, many resources are available to us at the touch of a button and the click of a mouse. The following should be helpful in providing additional information about Mentoring Programs.

1. AABE MENTORING PROGRAM – HANDBOOK (2013)
   https://www.yumpu.com/.../2013-mentoring-handbook/3
2. The Wisdom of Age: A Handbook for Mentors
   https://www.mentoring.org/wp-content/uploads/2020/
3. Effective Practice for Mentoring (MetLife Foundation)
   https://www.mentoring.org/resource/elements-of-effective-practice-for-mentoring/
4. Mentoring Now: Matthew Stevens
   https://makeadecision.me
5. Mentoring To Manhood: Joseph Somerville
   https://Communityyouthadvance.org/Mentoringtomanhood/
6. Manhood 101
   https://www.pgcps.org/schools/charles-herbert-flowers-high
7. Purple Boot Mentoring Program (PBMP): Bernard Jackson
   http://www.jlwcscharityfoundation.org/charity/
8. ANANIZACH is an official technical assistance provider.
   http://www.ananizach.com/

- Intergenerational Mentoring Across Ages: www.acrossages.org
- Intergenerational Practice and Research Center for Intergenerational Learning: www.templecil.org
- Intergenerational Policy and Programs Generations United: www.gu.org
- Cyber-Bullying Committee for Children: www.cfchildren.org

- Substance Abuse Prevention Substance Abuse and Mental Health Services Administration: www.samhsa.gov
- Delinquency Prevention Office of Juvenile Justice and Delinquency Prevention: www.ojjdp.gov
- Suicide Prevention Suicide Prevention Resource Center: www.sprc.org

Made in the USA
Columbia, SC
24 January 2025

e79c7328-73a1-475e-bc42-e227ecd8466dR01